Of the DOMINION, *Or,* Ownerſhip of the SEA

TWO BOOKS.

In the FIRST *is ſhew'd, that the* SEA, *by the* LAVV OF NATURE, *or* NATIONS, *is not common to all men, but capable of* PRIVATE DOMINION *or Proprietie, as well as the* LAND.

In the SECOND *is proved, that the Dominion of the* BRITISH SEA, *or that which incompaſſeth the Iſle of* GREAT BRITAIN, *is, and ever hath been, a Part or Appendant of the Empire of that Iſland.*

Writen at firſt in Latin, and Entituled,

MARE CLAUSUM

SEU,

De Dominio Maris,

By *JOHN SELDEN*, Eſquire.

Tranſlated into *Engliſh*; and ſet forth with ſom *Additional Evidences* and Diſcourſes,

By *MARCHAMONT NEDHAM.*

Publiſhed by ſpecial Command.

THE LAWBOOK EXCHANGE, LTD.

Clark, New Jersey

ISBN 978-1-58477-272-9

Lawbook Exchange edition 2004, 2014

The quality of this reprint is equivalent to the quality of the original work.
The irregular pagination is reproduced as it was found in the original work.

Printed in the United States of America on acid-free paper

THE LAWBOOK EXCHANGE, LTD.
33 Terminal Avenue
Clark, New Jersey 07066-1321

Please see our website for a selection of our other publications and fine facsimile reprints of classic works of legal history:
www.lawbookexchange.com

Library of Congress Cataloging-in-Publication Data

Selden, John, 1584-1654.
[Mare clausum. English]
Of the dominion, or, Ownership of the sea / by John Selden; translated into English and set forth with som [sic] additional evidences and discourses by Marchamont Nedham.
p. cm.
"Two books: in the first, is shew'd that the sea, by the law of nature, or nations, is not common to all men but capable of private dominion or proprietie [sic] as well as the land in the second, is proved that the dominion of the British sea, or that which incompasseth the isle of Great Britain, is, and ever hath been, a part or appendant of the empire of that island : written at first in Latin and entituled [sic] Mare clausum, seu, De dominio maris."
Originally published: London: W. Du-Gard, 1652.
ISBN 1-58477-272-7 (cloth: alk. paper)
1. Law of the sea. 2. Freedom of the seas. 3. Law of the sea—Great Britain. 4. Freedom of the seas—Great Britain. I. Nedham, Marchamont, 1620-1678. II. Title: Ownership of the sea. III. Title.

KZA134O .S4513 2002
343 .4209'6—dc21 2002025939

raigntie of the Seas flowing about
ſland, hath, in all times, whereof th
main's any written Teſtimonie, bo
fore the old *Roman* Invaſion and ſince
der every Revolution, down to the p
Age, been held and acknowledged
the world, as an inſeparable append
the Britiſh Empire; And that by
thereof the Kings of *England* ſucce
have had the Soveraign Guard of the
That they have impoſed Taxes an
butes upon all ſhips paſsing and
therein; That they have obſtructe
open'd the paſſage thereof to ſtrange
their own pleaſure, and don all
things that may teſtifie an abſolut
Dominion; VVhat *Engliſh* heart (
can conſider theſe things, togethe
the late Actings of the *Netherlande*
forth in your *publick Declaration*, ar
bee inflamed with an indignation an
ble to their Inſolence; That theſe l
raiſed out of the duſt at firſt into a ſ
Libertie, and at length to an high deg
Power and Felicitie, by the Arms ar
nevolence of *England*; or that they
in times paſt durſt never enter our Se

the preſent Generation, was the firſt occaſion of elevating them to this height of Confidence, in preſsing upon the Seas of *England*: For, who know's not with what tenderneſs, and upon what terms, they were firſt taken into the boſom of Queen *Eliſabeth*? yet they were no ſooner warm, but they ſhew'd their ſting, and proved the onely great vexation (becauſ deceitful friends) to that excellent Ladie, who, in thoſe Infant-daies, was both Mother and Nurſ of their ungrateful Republick. Too much of the ſame tenderneſs was expreſſed afterward by King *James*, becauſ (as in the former Reign, ſo in his) it was counted Reaſon of State to permit them to thrive; but they turning that favorable Permiſsion into a Licentious Encroaching beyond due Limits, put the King to a world of Trouble and Charge, by Ambaſsies and otherwiſe, to aſſert his own intereſt, and diſpute them into a reaſonable ſubmiſsion to thoſe Rights which had been received before as indiſputable by all the world. For the truth whereof, I am bold to refer your Honors to the Memorials of ſeveral Tranſactions in thoſe daies, which I have added at the

ſouls of men by Reaſon, that o
bodies by force. The *Pen* it is w
nifeſt's the Right of Things;
that is once cleared, it give's ſpurs
tion, becauſ men are never raiſed
a pitch of action, as when they
ſwaded, that they engage in a
cauſ; according to that old Verſi

Frangit, & attollit vires in
cauſa.

Wherefore ſeeing you (*Righ*
ble!) have had ſo frequent experie
truth of this in our late Wars, w
Pen Militant hath had as many
counters as the *Sword*, and born aw
ny Trophies from home-bred E
proſecution of your moſt right
by Land, certainly you will yiel
neceſſarie for the Inſtruction of
rous and ingenious people, in w
your juſt Rights by Sea, againſ
Pretences and Projects of en
Neighbors. For, what true *En*
will not ſwell, when it ſhall bee
and evident (as in this Book) that

Panegyriſt alſo to Conſtantius, *ſaith of the* Franks *that robbed heretofore in a Piratick manner, as well in the Mediterranean as the open Sea,* eventu temeritatis oſtenderant nihil eſſe Clauſum piraticæ diſperationi quo navigiis pateret acceſſus, **they made it appear by the event of their raſhneſs, that nothing could bee ſhut againſt the deſperation of Pirates, where there might bee an acceſs for Shipping.** *That is to ſay, the* Sea *was not ſo ſhut againſt Pirates by the* Roman *Emperor, but that they freely uſed depredation therein. In a word, that which is ſaid by* [q] *Ambroſe,* poſsidere fretum, & ſpatia Maris ſibi vendicare Jure Mancipii, **to poſſeſs a Narrow Sea and challenge ſpaces of the Sea by right of ſubjection,** *is the very ſame with that of* [r] Columella; Maria ipſa Neptunúmque claudere, **to ſhut the Seas themſelvs and** Neptune; *and ſo* Mare Clauſum *is the Sea poſſeſſed in a private manner, or ſo ſecluded both by Right and Occupation, that it ceaſeth to bee common; that is, being claimed by Right of ſubjection. Upon this ground it was, that thoſe Angles were called* Anguli Clauſares, *whereby the* * *Centuries in the Aſſignations of the*

[q] Hexaëmer. lib. 5. ca. 10.

[r] De Re Ruſticâ, lib. 8. cap. 16.

* A Centurie 200 Acres.

the antient Romans *did ſo touch one another, that it might bee known thereby, how far the right of the poſſeſsion of particular perſons did extend, as you may ſee in* [f] Hygenus. *Neither is it neceſſarie, that what may bee rightly ſaid in this ſenſ to bee ſhut, ſhould bee ſhut or encloſed by ſom continued Fence, or by a continued Tract of ſom eminent Limit like a Mound: But any kinde of imaginarie Line, by ſtreight Lines, crooked windings and Turnings and Angles, hath taken place in the deſignation of private Dominions, or in the ſhutting or incloſing of a thing poſſeſſed in a civil acception (as it was uſual among the Antients in thoſe Fields which were termed* Agri Occupatorii *and* Arcifinii) *as well as any eminent and continued Limit or Mound whatſoëver. From whence it came to paſs, that in the Aſsignations of Colonies, they called thoſe places* Clauſa *and* Extracluſa *whoſe Limits were divided onely by ſuch kinde of Lines.* [t] Julius Frontinus *ſaith;* That Field my bee called Ager *extracluſus* which lie's within the bordering Line and the Centuries, and therefore *extracluſus*, becauſ it is cloſed with the bordering line beyond the limits. *So the Territories, aſsigned*

[f] Lib. de Limitibus Conſtituendis.

[t] Lib. de Limitibus Agrorum.

assigned as well in the Colonies at this day carried into America, *as in that prodigious gift of Pope* Alexander VI *in the former Age, which is bounded by an imaginarie Line from the* [u] *Artic to the Antarctic Pole, are closed by Lines of Longitude and Latitude drawn through the degrees of Heaven, that they may bee possessed in a private manner. So the Greek Sea, which is within the* Cyanean *and* Chelidonian *Islands, was by* [x] *Agreement shut and prohibited by the* Athenians *to the* Persian *Emperor. So the Sea flowing about is shut or closed within the compass of the Royal Patrimonie of the* British *Empire. Other passages there are every where of the same kinde. But I enlarge my self too much in a thing so manifest. Therefore I forbear to light a Candle to the Sun. Farewel Reader. From the* Inner Temple, IV *November* MDCXXXV.

u Laërtius Cherubinus, Bullar. tom. 1. pag. 393. Hieronym. de Monte Brixiano, lib. de finibus regundis, cap. 7. § 8.

x Plutarch. vitâ Cimonis.

The

The Contents of the first Book, according to the several Chapters.

The Contents of the ſecond BOOK.

CHAP.

The Contents of the second Book.

The Contents of the second Book.

The Contents of the second Book.

The Contents of the second Book.

Amend the Errors thus.

PAg.2. lin.31. *read* Question. *p.15.l.25. r.*Hostages, blot out *Right.* *p.29.l.2.* also over all other. *p.33.l.7. r.* Thus it is. *p.38.l.27. r.* within the Creeks. *p.49. l.31. r.* that of *Neptune.* *p.53.l.29. r.* in any wise. *p.56.l.6.r.* or which. ibid. *l.14. r.*translation. *p.61. l.2. r.* hereto. *p.64.l.22. r.*in the first. *p.70.31. r.*they required. *p.71.l.9. r. Antigonus* wittily replied, that hee himself: *p.74. l.6.r.* Counsel. *p.75.l.21.r.* first. ibid. *l.28. r.* League that was. *p.79.l.28.r. Misenum.* *p.82.l.5. r.* account. ibid. *l.26.r. Theodosius.* *p.87.l.13.r.* that it cannot. *p.94. l.30. r.* that servitude. *p.95.l.14. r.* that servitude was imposed. *p.95.l.19. r.*this servitude. *p.98.l.2. r.* Ells. *p.105.l.12.r.* of. *p.106. l.10.r.*or. *p.122.l.25. r.*places according. *p.119.l.11.r.* I run. *p.142.l.32. r.*might bee. *p.144.l.11. r. Alciatus.* *p.156.l.1. r.* contemporarie. *p.161.l.19.r.* were it (saith. *p.163.l.9. r.* cotton. *p.184. l.12. r.* Barangi. *p.189. l.4.r.* too much. *p.190. l.23. r.* Their. *p.192.l.27. r.* trimming. *p.203.l.22. r.* I am. *p.216.l.4.r.* thrive. *p.218. l.30. r.* throughout Britain. *p.221. l.6. r.* throughout Britain. *p.232.l.17.r.*at that time. *p.243.l.31. r.*or strand. *p.250. l.28.r.* Danemarc. *p.255.* in the margine. *r.*Cottonianâ. *p.281.l.12.r.* Achilles Tatius. *p.303.l.29.r.* entend. *p.306.l.8.r.* Office of our. *p.315.l.25. r.Guisnes.* *p.316.l.20.r.Guisnes* and *Amiens.* *p.317.l.6.r.* the opposite. *p.322.l.31. r.*piece-meale. *p.328. l.24.r.* Account. *p.333.l.14.r. Cæsarea.* *p.336.l.2.r.* so that it. ibid. *l.5.r.* knew. ibid. *l.13.r.* English by Norman. *p.339.l.16.r.* the Islanders. *p.384.l.31.r.* of a publick. *p.413.l.1.r.* was his Fiduciarie. *p.448.l.11.r.* Feroe.

OF

OF THE DOMINION, OR, Ownership of the Sea.

BOOK I.

The Division *of the Work, and the* Method *of the first Book.*

CHAP. I.

THE Design beeing to treat of the *Dominion* or *Ownership* of the *Sea*, incompassing the Isle of *Great Britain*, as belonging to the Empire of the same; two main particulars are chiefly to bee consider'd. The one concern's matter of *Law*, the other matter of *Fact*; both of them beeing denominated (as is usual) from the major part: For, as the point of *Law* hath many things mingled with it, which manifestly arise from matter of *Fact*; so this of *Fact* comprehend's not a few which relate unto that of *Law*. As to what concern's the point of *Law*, this Question fall's chiefly under debate, to wit, *Whether by Law the Sea bee capable of private Dominion, or Proprietie?* And by matter of *Fact* is meant only such a collection of Testimonies, or clear shewing forth of Evidences by which may bee proved and mainteined, *The long and continual conjunction with the British Empire, of enjoiment and possession, or lawful prescription; whereupon as on a most strong Title, the Dominion or Ownership of the same Empire herein may bee founded*; it beeing first made manifest, that the Sea it self is not only not repugnant by any Law to Dominion or Ownership, but every way capable thereof. To each of these Particulars a several Book is allotted. In the first, is discussed matter of *Law*: In the second, that which concern's matter of *Fact*: For, except manifest proof bee made of the first point, it will bee utterly in vain to discours about the second. But for those things which are to bee handled in the first Book, it seemed meet to observ such a Method, as in the first place to lay open the Rise or Original ground of those Disputes that have occasioned this enquirie into the point of Law, together with the Opinions of those men, who denie that the Sea is capable of private Dominion or Ownership, or that it may pass into the Proprietie of any one particular, so as in the mean time to exclude it from beeing common to the rest of mankinde. Next are premised som things, for explaining the terms of the Questions, that it may bee clearly thence understood, as well what kinde of *Mediums* are to bee used, as what the Thing is, whereof wee intend to Treat; lest by neglect of such a Cours, wee

bee

bee perplex't with Doubts about the notion and acceptation, either of the Terms themselvs, or of the Subject in Controversie. After this preparation thus duly made, it is then demonstrated, that not onely no kinde of Law whatsoëver, rightly understood, doth deny a Dominion over the Sea, but that all kinds of Law, even the most known and approved, whereof there may bee any use in Disputes of this nature, do acknowledg and allow a proprietie and private Dominion over the Sea, as well as the Land. Lastly, the Objections usually brought against such Dominion or Ownership of the Sea, are cleared and answered; And with these wee shall now begin; for the Method of the second Book is more conveniently put there before it.

What Occurrences seem to oppose the Dominion of Sea, *and what Arguments are wont to bee made against it.*

CHAP. II.

THe Arguments usually brought against the Dominion of the Sea, are of three sorts. *Som* are drawn from freedom of Commerce, Passage, and Travel; *Others* from the nature of the Sea; and a *third* sort from the Writings and Testimonies of learned men. And as to what concern's the freedom of Commerce or Traffick, and Travel, this som men affirm to bee so natural, that they say it can no where bee abolished by any Law or Custom; yea, and that by the Law of Nations it is unjust to denie Merchants or Strangers the benefit of Port, Provisions, Commerce, and Navigation; Adding moreover, that wars have been justly commenced upon denial of Port, Trade, and Commerce; And for proof, they produce the example of the *Megarans* [a] against the *Athenians*, the *Bononians* [b] against the *Venetians*, and of the *Spaniard* against those of the *West-Indies*; for that, the expedition of *Spain* against the *Americans* is pretended, by very learned men to bee upon a [c] just Ground, becaus they denied them a freedom of Commerce within their Shores and Ports. And in justification hereof, They use that of *Virgil*, as spoken out of the Law of Nations;

> *Quod genus* [d] *hoc hominum, quæve hunc tam barbara morem*
> *Permittit patria? hospitio prohibemur Arenæ.*

> **What barb'rous Land this custom own's? What sort**
> **Of men are these? Wee are forbid their Port.**

Now, if such a Proprietie or Dominion of the Sea were admitted, that men might bee forbidden the libertie of Navigation and Ports, at the will of any Proprietor, then, say they, it would bee an infringement of that Law of Commerce and Travel (by them styled the Law of Nature) which they would not have to bee indured.

Touching the *second* sort of Objections drawn from the nature of the Sea it self, it is commonly alleged; That the Sea is alter'd and shifted every moment, and the state of it, through a continued Succession of new waters, alway so uncertain, and remain's so little the same in all things (the Channel onely excepted) that it is impossible it should ever bee retained in the possession of any one Particular. Moreover, they say the nature of Possession consist's chiefly in a separation or distinction of Limits and Bounds, but

no

a *Thucidid. lib* 1. & *Diodor. Sic. lib.* 12.

b *Sigon. de Regno Italiæ, lib.*20.

c *Franciscus Victoria de Indis, tract.*2. §.2.3. & 4. *Joannes Solorzanos de Indiar. Jure lib.*2. *cap.*20. §.34. & *seqq. Gregor. Lopez in Partid.*2. *tit* 23. *l.*2.

d *Æneid.*1.

no ſuch Materials or Inſtruments can poſsibly bee found in the Sea, as that the Law for regulation of Bounds, which hath a principal place in all Controverſies about Dominion or Ownerſhip may bee grounded thereupon. They produce alſo a ſaying out of [e] St *Ambroſe*, ſpeaking about the lurking-holes or holds of Fiſhes; *Geometram audivimus, Thalaſſometram nunquam audivimus; & tamen Piſces menſuras ſuas nôrunt.* **I have heard of a** Geometrician, **or one that could meaſure Land; but never of a** Thalaſſometrician, **one that could meaſure or lay out Bounds in the Sea; and yet the Fiſhes know their own Bounds.** They are pleaſed likewiſe to inſinuate, what a world of Sea room there is, that all Nations may have ſufficient for watering, fiſhing, and Navigation: And therefore that the peculiar Dominion thereof is by no means to bee appropriated unto any.

[e] *Hexaëmer. lib. cap.* 10.

A *third* ſort of Arguments lie's in thoſe Teſtimonies that are drawn out of antient Writers; partly out of old Poëts, Divines, and others writing of other ſubjects; partly from ſuch Lawyers as handle the matter purpoſely. Of the firſt kinde is that of *Gripus* the Fiſherman, and *Trachalio* the Slave, as they are brought upon the Stage by *Plautus*, quarrelling about a Bag that was found in the Sea.

[a] Gr. *Mare quidem commune certò 'ſt omnibus.* Tr. *Aſſentio.*
Quî minùs hunc communem quæſo mihi oportet eſſe vidulum?
In Mari inventum eſt. Commune eſt.——

[a] *In Rudente, Act.* 4.

Gr. **The Sea is common certainly to all.**
Tr. **True.**
Why not this Bag to mee then too, thou brawl?
It was found within the Sea.
Therefore common it muſt bee.

They produce likewiſe a piece of a ſupplicatorie

ſpeech of *Latona*, to a ruſtick Rout in *Lycia*, as it in *Ovid*[b],

[b] *Metamor.* 6.

Quid prohibetis Aquas? uſus communis Aquarum eſt.
Nec Solem proprium Natura, nec Aëra fecit,
Nec tenues Undas. In publica munera veni.

——— **Why hinder you,** ſaid ſhee,
The uſe of Water, that to all is free:
The Sun, Aër, Water, Nature did not frame
Peculiar; a publick Gift I claim.

And that of *Virgil* too[c]

[c] *Æneid.* 7.

——— *Littúſque rogamus*
Innocuum, & cunctis undámque, Aurámque patentem.
Nothing but what is common wee implore,
Free Aër, and Water, and a harmleſs ſhore.

Phænicides ſaith alſo in *Athenæus*[d], τὴν μὲν θάλασσαν κοινὴν ἔτι, *that the Sea is common.* To which may bee added that memorable ſaying of certain *Jewiſh Rabbins*, who, when they acknowledged *Alexander* to bee Lord of the whole world, did it nevertheleſs with this Caution, that they conceived hee had by his Conqueſts gained a Soveraigntie onely over the Earth or drie Land, but none at all over the Sea; it beeing ſubject onely to God himſelf, as its ſole Commander. The words are theſe out of the Ebrew, [e] *Non Dominabatur in Mari, ſed Deus O. M. Dominatur, tàm in Mari quàm in Tellure.* **Hee ruled not over the Sea, but God Almightie is hee onely that rule's by Sea as well as by Land.**

[d] *Dipnoſoph.* 8.

[e] *Gemara Hieroſolymit. tit. Abada Zara, ſeu de* cultu extraneo. *fol.* 42. *col.* 3. *cap.* 3.

The ſecond kinde of Arguments here, found among the Lawyers, are of two ſorts. *Naturali jure, omnium communia ſunt illa, Aër, Aqua profluens, & Mare, & per hoc littora Maris.* Item, *Nemo ad littus Maris accedere prohibetur bibetur piscandi caussâ, dum tamen villis & ædificiis & Monimentis abstineatur; quia non Juris Gentium, sicut & Mare. Idque Divus Pius piscatoribus Formianis & Capenatis rescripsit.* **By the Law of Nature, the Aër, Rivers, the Sea, and it's Shores, are common to all. Also, None are prohibited to use fishing upon the Shores, as long as they meddle not with Towns, Buildings and Monuments, in regard these are not common by the Law of Nations, as is the Sea; And this was prescribed by the Emperor** Antonius Pius, **to the Fisher men of Formiæ and Capena;** which are the very words used by [f] *Marcianus* the Lawyer, and by [g] *Justinian* in his Institutions. And *Ulpian*, [h] *Mari, quod Naturâ omnibus patet, servitus imponi privatâ lege non potest.* **The Sea, beeing by Nature free for all, cannot bee vassalised by any particular Law.** And in another place, saith hee; [i] *Mare commune omnium est & litora, sicut Aër. Et est sæpissime rescriptum, non posse quem piscari prohiberi.* **The Sea and Shores are common to all, as the Aër. And wee finde it very often prescribed or commanded by the Emperors, that none bee prohibited from Fishing:** With which agree's also that saying of [k] *Celsus. Maris esse usum communem omnibus hominibus ut Aëris.* **A freedom of the Sea, as well as of the Aër, is common to all men.** In like manner, som would have it that the *Romane Emperor* himself was Lord onely of the Land, and not of the Sea; for proof whereof, they mention an Answer given by the Emperor *Antoninus*; [l] *Se quidem mundi Dominum esse; legem autem Maris*; **That himself was Lord of the World, but the Law of the Sea;** pretending this Answer of his to bee commonly understood, as if hee refused to arrogate

f *L. 2. & l. 4. ff. de Rerum Divisione.*

g *Tit. eodem, § & quidem.*

h *L. 13. ff. tit. communia prædiorum.*

i *L. 13. § 7. ff. tit. Injuriis, & vide eam l. 24. ff. de damno infecto.*

k *L. 3. ff. Ne quid in publico § 1.*

l *D. D. ad lib. 9. ff. ad legem Rhodiam.*

rogate the Dominion of the Sea unto himſelf. And in the [m] *Baſilica* or Laws of the Eaſtern Empire, wee finde it thus written, Οἱ αἰγιαλοὶ ἐν τῇ πάντων ἐξουσίᾳ εἰσί· *The Shores are within the power of all men.* So alſo ſaith *Michaël Attaliates*, a man learned in the Laws of that Empire, [n] Τινὰ δὲ πάντων εἰσίν· οἷον ὁ Ἀὴρ, τὸ ῥέον Ὕδωρ, ἡ Θάλασσα, ὁ αἰγιαλὸς τῆς θαλάσσης, καὶ οἱ Ποταμοί· *Som things are common to all, as Aër, Fountains, the Sea, Shores, and Rivers.* And the ſumme is, that ſom antient Lawyers of both Empires write, that the Sea is common to all men, by the Law of Nature and Nations; which if it were truly proved, either from the nature of the Sea it ſelf, or from either of thoſe Laws, then it could not poſsibly bee admitted, that the Sea might becom the peculiar poſſeſsion of any one, unleſs a change were made of the Law of nature, which is commonly ſaid to bee altogether unchangeable; or that the conſent of Nations, that have intereſt herein, were obteined to admit of ſuch a Dominion or Ownerſhip. And therefore from thence they ſeem to hold, that a Dominion over the Sea cannot bee atteined by any antient uſage, cuſtom or preſcription, nor under any other pretence or title whatſoëver, for (ſaie they) no Plea or Barr is to bee allowed againſt nature, *Nor* (as [o] *Papinian* ſaith) *is a Preſcription of long poſſeſsion wont to bee admitted for the holding of ſuch places as are publick and common by the Law of Nations.* And theſe antient Lawyers here mentioned are followed by no ſmall Train of Interpreters; though nevertheleſs there are not a few even of them, who reſtrain and qualifie that antient opinion more waies then one, touching the neceſsitie of a common Intercourſ and freedom at Sea, as wee ſhall ſhew hereafter.

[m] *Eclog. Baſilic. lib.* 50. *tit.* 1. *cap.* 13.

[n] *Pragmat. tit.* 2.

[o] *Neque præſcriptio longæ poſſeſſionis ad obtinenda loca jure Gentium publica ſolet concedi. li.* 45. *tit. de uſucapionibus & uſurpationibus.*

But of our modern Lawyers, thoſe that have appeared

ed most forward in opposing a Right of Dominion over the Sea, are onely two, both indeed very eminent men, but of unequal learning and elegancie of wit; by name *Fernandus Vasquius* the Spaniard, and *Hugo Grotius* the Hollander: the former an honorable Counsellor to King *Philip* the 3. of *Spain* in his high Court of Exchequer. The later was heretofore Advocate Fiscal of *Holland, Zeland*, and *West-Friesland*, and most deservedly adorned with divers other honors in his own Countrie; a man of an acute judgment, and for his excellencie in all kinds of learning incomparable. But *Vasquius*, in his discours both of the Law of Nature and Nations, as also concerning the Rights of Dominion, Prescription, and other things of that nature, speak's to this effect. [p] *From hence* (saith hee) *it appear's how little esteem is to bee had of their opinion, who suppose that the* Genoëses *or* Venetians *may without injurie, forbid others to sail through the Gulph in their respective Seas, as if they could have laid claim to those Seas by Prescription; which is not onely contrarie to the Imperial Laws* (above mentioned) *but also against the Primitive Law of nature and nations, which cannot bee alter'd. And that it is against this Law, is evident; becaus by the same Law not onely the Seas, but all other immovable things whatsoëver, were common. And although in after-time that Law came to bee abolish't in part, so far as concern's the Dominion and Proprietie of Lands, which beeing enjoied in common, according to the Law of nature, were afterwards distinguish't, divided, and so separated from that common use; yet it hath been otherwise, and is still, as to the Dominion of the Sea, which from the beginning of the world to this present daie, is, and ever hath been in common, without the least alteration, as 'tis generally known. And though I hear many of the* Portugals *are of this opinion, that their King hath had such an antient Title by Prescription in that vast Ocean*

[p] *Fernandus Vasq. Controvers. illustr: lib.* 2. *c.* 89. § 30. *Ex his apparet quàm suspecta sit &c.*

of the West-Indies, *so that other Nations have no right to sail through those Seas; and also that the ordinarie sort of our own Nation of* Spain *seem to bee of the same opinion, that no people whatsoëver, but Spaniards, have any right to sail through that immens and most spatious Sea, to those Indian Countries that have been subdued by the most mightie Kings of* Spain *(as if they onely had a right by Prescription thereto;) yet all these men's opinions are no less vain and foolish, then theirs, who use to dream the same things of the* Genoeses *and* Venetians. *The follie of which opinions appear's the more clearly even in this respect; becaus neither of those Nations singly consider'd can prescribe ought against themselvs; that is to saie, neither the Republick of* Venice *against it self; nor that of* Genoa *against it self, nor the Kingdom of* Spain *against it self, nor that of* Portugal *against it self; for there ought ever to bee a difference between the* Agent *and* Patient: *Much less can they prescribe ought to the prejudice of other Nations, becaus the Law of Prescriptions is purely Civil. Therefore such a Law can bee of no force, in deciding Controversies that happen betwixt Princes or people that acknowledg no Superior: For the peculiar Civil Laws of every Countrie are of no more value, as to Forrain Countries and Nations, or their people, then if such a Law were not in Beeing, or never had been; and therefore in Controversies of that nature recours must bee had unto the common Law of Nations Original or Secondarie; which Law certainly did never admit of such a Prescription or usurpation of Title over the Sea.* Other matters hee hath of the same kinde, beeing a very confident opposer of any peculiar Dominion over the Sea.

But in the year *MDCIX* (it beeing the year after that large Treatie held at the *Hage* betwixt the Spaniard and the Hollander, about freedom of Trade

Trade and Navigation to the *East-Indies*) there was published that Book of *Hugo Grotius*, entituled MARE LIBERUM, *or a discours concerning that Right which the Hollanders have to Trade in the* Indies. Wherein hee endeavor's first to prove, that, by the Law of Nations, there ought to bee such a freedom of Navigation for all men whatsoëver, which waie they pleas, so that they cannot, without injurie, bee molested at Sea. Next, that the Atlantick and Southern Ocean, or the Right of Navigation to the *Indies*, is not, nor indeed can bee, any peculiar of the *Portugalls*: *forasmuch as the Sea* (saith hee, according to the [q] Laws and reasons already mentioned) *can in no wise becom the Proprietie of any one; becaus nature not onely permit's, but require's it should bee common.* Several other passages hee hath about this matter, in his excellent Book *De Jure Belli & pacis*; of which more hereafter. Thus much in brief, concerning those arguments that are usually brought against the Dominion or Ownership of the Sea. The next thing therefore is to explain the sens of the Question, and its terms.

[q] *Mari Libero cap. 5. Mare proprium omnino alicujus fieri non potest; Quia natura commune hoc esse non permittit, sed jubet.*

What is meant by the word SEA, *in the Question. Also a division of the* LAVV, *in order to the discours.*

CHAP. III.

AS to what concern's the present Question, *Whether the Sea bee capable of private Dominion*, wee take the word CAPABLE in the same sens, as it was used by the Emperor *Traian* in an Epistle of his, to his beloved *Plinie*; [a] *Solum peregrinæ civitatis capax non esse dedicationis quæ fit jure nostro*; **The soil of a strange Citie is not capable of such a dedication as is made by our Law** Moreover, wee shall explain what is meant by the SEA, as also by those Terms of LAW and DOMINION. By the SEA wee understand the whole Sea, as well the main Ocean or Out-land Seas, as those which are within-land, such as the *Mediterranean*, *Adriatick*, *Ægean* or *Levant*, *British*, *and Baltick* Seas, or any other of that kinde, which differ no otherwise from the main, then as Homogeneous or Similary parts of ihe same bodie do from the whole. But the *Law* (as it is the rule, measure, and pointing out of things lawful or unlawful) fall's under a twofold consideration. Either as it is *Obligatorie*, which is called also *Preceptive*; or as it is *Permissive*, which is also by writers commonly termed *Concessive*. As *Obligatorie*, it is known by such things as are commanded or forbidden, as *to give every man his due*, *not to forswear*, and the like. As *Permissive*, it is set forth by things whose use is neither commanded nor forbidden, but permitted; as in the very Act of buying, selling, infranchisement, framing conditions of contract according to the will of the contractors, and many more of the same nature. But both these kinds of LAW concern either mankinde in general, that is, all Nations, or not all. That which relate's to the generalitie of mankinde, or *all Nations*, is either *Natural* or *Divine*. That is, either manifested by the light of nature or the use of right reason, beeing elegantly described by *Tertullian* to bee the [b] *Common Law written throughout the whole world, in the very Books of nature*

[a] *Plin.lib.*10. *Epist.*59.

[b] *Lex communis in publico mundi, & Tabulis naturalibus scripta. Lib. de Corona militis.*

ture; and by the Grecians called [c] *the Law of mankinde*, and by the Civilians the *Primitive Law of Nations*; or elſ it isſ declared and ſet down in thoſe Divine Oracles that have been committed to writing: Both which may properly bee termed the *univerſal Law of Nations*, or the *Common Law of mankinde.* And whatever is *Obligatorie* in either of theſe, either out of the nature of the thing it ſelf, or rather from the autoritie of the father of nature, is reputed by men to bee unchangable; according to that ſaying ſo often uſed by [d] Philoſophers, [e] Divines, and [f] Lawyers, *That the rights and Laws of nature are immutable,* Which cannot bee ſaid of the *Permiſsive* Law, whether Natural or Divine, relateing to mankinde in general: for it is obvious to every man, that as *Permiſsive*, it muſt needs bee various and changable, according to the judgment and pleaſure of perſons in power; and therefore ſubject to Repealings, Qualifications, and daily Alterations; whereas in the mean time that kinde which is *Obligatorie* may admit *Additions* or *Inlargements* (ſuch as may ſerv for more certaintie and convenience of obſervation,) but no *Alterations*, in any wiſe to diminiſh it's autoritie. Out of ſuch *Additions* as are made to that which is *Obligatorie*, and *Alterations* of that which is *Permiſsive*, another kinde of *Law* takes it's riſe, which is of a more narrow Senſ and Acceptation, and relate's, not to all Nations or the Univerſalitie of mankinde, but onely to ſom particulars thereof, and it is ordinarily well termed *Poſitive* (as beeing poſitively ordained either by God or men;) Somtimes alſo it is termed [g] *Civil*, and an Addition of right Reaſon. This *Poſitive Law* may bee divided into that which is ſingular and peculiar

c Κοινὰ τῶν Ἀνθρώπων δίκαια. *Thucyd. l.* 4. *Polyb. l.* 2. *& alij.*

d *Andronic. Rhodius, Michaël Epheſius, Euſtratius, alii, ad Ariſt. Nicomach.* 5. *cap.* 10. *Cicero, apud Lactantium lib.* 6. *cap.* 8.

e *D. Thom. Aquin.* 1. 2æ. *q.* 94. *art.* 5. *&c.*

f *Inſtit. de Jure Nat.* § *ſed Naturalia.*

g *Philo Judæus, lib. de Joſeph ſeu de Viro Civili.*

culiar to any one particular Nation or Societie of mankinde (as was the [h] Law concerning Paternal power among the *Romans*, and the custom of the [i] *Athenians* touching the same;) or into that *which is received by divers Nations*. Again this last is divided into two parts; either into that which *bind's divers Nations jointly, equally, and indifferently, by som common obligation*; or ell into that which *bind's divers Nations or people, not jointly, and equally, or by any common obligation, but singly and by Accident.* And of this threefold kinde of *Positive Law*, wee may call the first the *Law purely Civil*, as it relate's to any one particular civil societie. The second the *Common Law of divers Nations*, so named from som common tie or obligation betwixt them. The third the *Law of som or divers Nations, Civil* or *Domestick*, by reason of that Domestick and Civil tie onely, whereby they are bound singly among themselvs, without any obligation to each other in common. As for example, the Laws of the XII Tables that were brought from *Athens* to *Rome*, remained in force in both Nations, as well in the *Romane*, as in the *Athenian*; but not by any common or mutual obligation between them: And therefore that Law of the XII Tables ought much more properly to bee called the Civil Law of those Nations, then simply of both Nations (in any such sens as import's a Joint-Interest or Communion.) But as to that which jointly concern's divers Nations by mutual obligation, that is, *the Common Law of divers Nations*, it is divisible likewise into two parts, to wit, into that which is *Imperative* over divers Nations or people; or that which is *Intervenient*. By the *Imperative Law of Nations*, is meant that which is observed or receiv's Autoritie among several Nations or people, who are subject to supreme

[h] *Instit. tit. de patriâ potestate. §. Jus autem.*
[i] *Demosthen. Orat. contra Aristocratem.*

supreme Powers that otherwise are distinct, and this by reason of an Obligation equally common to them all, but derived from som other, and enjoined by som special Command, either from God or man. Of this kinde was that Law of the *Dolopes*, the *Magnesians*, *Phthiotæ*, *Thessalians*, and other people of Greece, who beeing equally obliged by the command of [k] *Acrisius* King of the *Argives*, submitted to the jurisdiction of the grand Parlament or Assembly of *Amphictyones*. Of the same kinde likewise was that * Militarie Law enjoined by God, not onely to the People of *Israël*, but also to the *Canaanites* with whom they were to wage war: For, they were both obliged by the Autoritie of him that commanded, though after a divers manner. And when any Nations, in obedience to the *Pope's* Autoritie and command, do alike submit to one and the same Law, it may bee rightly called the *Imperative* Law of Nations. But that is to bee called the *Intervenient* Law of Nations, which take's it's rise, not from any command imposed upon several Nations in common, but through the intervention either of som Compact, or Custom; and it is commonly styled the *Secondarie Law of Nations*: The principal heads whereof are conteined in the Laws about *proclaiming War*, *Ambassie*, *Prisoners of War*, *Hostages*, *Right*, *Remitter upon return from Captivitie*, *Leagues and Covenants*, *Commerce*, and other matters of that Nature which usually intervene betwixt divers Nations. For, as much as in these Laws here spoken of, it is in several Nations wholly composed of such *Additions* as have been made to the *universal Obligatorie Law of Nations*, and of such *Alterations* as have accrued to the *Universal Permissive*, and no more may challenge the name of *Imperative* or *Intervenient*. And it is most plain, that the

rest

[k] *Pausanias in Phocicis*, *Strabo lib.* 9. *Æschines in Orat.* περὶ παραπρεσβείας.

* *Deut.* 20. 10.

rest retain's still the name of the *Universal or Primitive Law of Nations.* Moreover also, the *Imperial Law*, which usually take's place in all Controversies about the aforesaid Particulars of the *Intervenient Law*, so far as it agree's with the Universal Law of Nations, Natural or Divine, is to bee comprised under the same Notion; But as by the consent of some certain Nations, with whom it is in use, divers principal heads and determinations of it (beeing no part of the *Universal Law*) are so made use of, it most clearly fall's under the name of the *Intervenient Law of som Nations.* Lastly, as it is received and used at home by som particular People in their Courts of Judicature, it is to bee called the Law *Civil or Domestick of divers Nations*. And thus having given you a plain Scheme of the *Law*, in all those various Notions and Acceptions that are to bee used in the Controversie; it remain's that in the next place that of *Dominion* or *Ownership* bee taken into consideration.

Of *Dominion*, both *Common* to all, and *Private*. Also its Original, either by *Distribution*, or *Primarie Occupation*.

Chap. IV.

Dominion, which is a Right of Using, Enjoying, Alienating, and free Disposing, is either Common to all men as Possessors without Distinction, or *Private* and peculiar onely to som; that is to say, distributed and set apart by any particular States, Princes, or persons whatsoëver, in such a manner that others are excluded, or at least in som sort barred from a Libertie of Use and Enjoiment. As to the first kinde of *Dominion*, or that which is Common to All,

fre-

frequent mention is made of it, in relation to that State of Communitie, which was in antient times. And of which *Virgil* speak's in his Georgicks [a]

[a] *Georgic.*

Nec signare quidem, aut partiri limite Campum
Fas erat; in medio quærebant ——

Nor was it lawful then their Lands to bound;
They liv'd in common All upon the Ground.

And *Seneca* [b],

[b] *In Octaviâ, Act.* 2.

——— —— *perVium cunctis iter;*
Communis usus omnium rerum fuit.

All men might pass what way they pleas'd to chuse,
And all things were expos'd for common use.

And *Tibullus* [c],

[c] *Ad Messalam. Eleg. lib.* 1.3.

Non domus ulla fores habuit; non fixus in agris,
Qui regeret certis finibus arVa, lapis.

Men did not then with dores their Houses build,
Nor were they wont with stones to bound the Field.

Many more there are of the like nature. But yet [d] *Lactantius* would have them to bee so understood, *not that wee should conceiv that nothing at all was priVate or peculiar in those daies; but in a figuratiVe sens after the manner of the Poëts, to let us know that men were then so free and generous, that they did not hoord up the fruits of the Earth for themselVs, nor dwel in an obscure solitarie manner, but admitted the poor to partake of the benefit of their labors.* And truly, wee finde divers passages plainly pointing out this state of Communitie, in that Divine Act of Donation,

[d] *Divin. Institut. lib.* 5. *seu de Iustitiâ. cap.* 5.

whereby *Noah* and his three sons *Shem*, *Cham* and *Japhet* (who represented as it were the person of *Adam*, for the restoring of mankinde after the flood) became Joint-Lords of the whole world. The form of Donation, is expressed in these words, [e] *Bee fruitful, and multiply and replenish the Earth. And the fear of you, and the dread of you shall bee upon every Beast of the Earth, and every Foul of the Aër, upon all that moveth upon the Earth, and upon all the Fishes of the Sea, into your hands are they delivered.* Also, *Justin* the Historian speak's aptly and to the purpose, [f] *In the Age of Saturn* (saith hee) *all things were without distinction common to all, as if all men had lived upon one stock or Patrimonie.* From whence it came to pass, that in the Festivals of *Saturn* all things were enjoyed in common. To which likewise accord's that of *Cicero* [g], *No thing is private or peculiar to any by Nature; but either by occupation of old, as in the case of those who first inhabited Vacancies; or who became possess't by right of War and Conquest; or by virtue of som Law; or by Compact, Covenant, or by Lot*: Yet 'tis not probable, that this kinde of Communitie was of any long continuance. But as for *Private Dominion*, or that distribution of Possessions and Bounds which depriveth or in any sort barreth all others, besides the known possessor, from a libertie of use and enjoiment, they say it was not in beeing till those golden daies were over. And so, as the Poët sings [h],

Communémque priùs, ceu lumina solis & Auræ,
Cautus humum longo signavit limite Mensor;

The Earth, as common once as Light or Aër,
They then by Art did measure, bound and share.

It appear's also by holy Writ, that the Earth was divided by the Posteritie of *Noah*, som Ages after the Flood.

[i] By

[e] *Gen. cap.* 9. *v.* 1. 2.

[f] *Erant Saturni ævo omnia communia & indivisa omnibus, veluti unum cunctis Patrimonium esset. lib.* 43.

[g] *Privata nulli naturâ; sed aut veteri occupatione, ut qui quondam in vacua venerunt; aut bello, &c. Offic. lib.* 1.

[h] *Ovid, Metamorph.* 1.

[i] By *Japhet* and his sons *were the Isles of the Gentiles divided in their Lands, everie one after his Tongue, after their Families, in their Nations*; as it is recorded by *Moses*: That is to say, they settled themselvs as private Lords, and appointed Bounds accordings to the number of their Families, from the River *Tanais* even as far as the Atlantick Sea, or through a great part of the Western *Asia*, as it bend's towards the North, and throughout all Europe. In like manner, *Cham* and his Posteritie possessed themselvs of that Part which lie's open to the South and South-west; as *Shem* did the Eastern Countries as far as *India*: As you may see it in *Josephus*, *Eusebius*, the Autor of the Chronicle of *Alexandria*, *Zonaras*, *Cedrenus*, *Eustathius* of *Antioch*, *Freculphus*, and others. It hath been received also by Tradition, that *Noah* himself, as if hee had been absolute Lord or Arbiter of the whole world, was the first man after the Flood that revived this kinde of distribution or private Dominion; which they say also hee did *by Command from God*, and that in the nine hundred and thirtieth year of his Age (which was three hundred and thirtie years after the Floud, and twentie before his death) hee confirmed it by Will, and deliver'd it a little before his death into the hands of *Shem* his eldest son, admonishing them altogether, *that no man should invade the Bounds of his Brother, nor should they wrong one another; becaus it would of necessitie occasion Discords and deadly Wars among them*: As it is expresly mentioned, both in *Eusebius* and *Cedredrenus*. But howsoëver the matter hath been; this is very certain, that private Dominions or Possessions were revived again after the Flood, in the same accustomed manner as they had been before from the daies of *Adam*. For, hee also received such a [k] Donation from God, as wee have told you *Noah* and his Sons did

[i] *Gen.* 10. 5. 5. & 25.

[k] *Gen. cap.* 1. 2, 28.

afterward, and ſo became Lord of the whole World, not without ſuch a peculiar poſſeſsion or proprietie to himſelf, which (ſo far as wee are are able to judg of Affairs of that Age, according to the waies and means received by Poſteritie) did exclude his children from all Right, but by his voluntarie Grant or Reſignation : But yet, whether it were by Donation, Aſsignment, or any other Grant whatſoëver, it appear's (before hee died or left any Heir to ſucceed him) his children did enjoy their ſeveral Bounds and Territories, in a way of peculiar Dominion or Poſſeſsion. Thus *Abel* had Cattel and Paſtures of his own; as *Cain* had Lands and Plantations that were his own. Hee poſſeſſed himſelf alſo of the Land of *Nod* or *Naida*, where hee built the Citie of *Enoch*, and ſettled his abode. After this, [l] Exchanges, Buying, and ſelling came in faſhion; and beſides Weights and Meaſures, they appointed Judges of Covenants and Contracts, and added Bounds or Limits to Fields and Paſtures. And of *Cain*, it is ſaid, that [m] *hee firſt ſet Bounds unto Fields*. So at length came in private Dominions or Poſſeſsions; which (whether by virtue onely of a preceding univerſal dominion of a ſingle perſon, as in *Adam*; or of ſom univerſal and common intereſt in Things, as betwixt *Noah* and his Sons) hapned firſt by the Donation, Aſsignment, or ſom other Grant of thoſe whom it concerned, either to Princes, or Communities repreſenting a ſingle perſon, or to any others whomſoëver, as particular Lords. So that neither the Law Natural nor Divine which was univerſal (except you pleaſ to credit that Divine Oracle ſaid to bee given unto *Noah*) hath expreſly commanded or forbidden, but permitted both; that is to ſay, a common enjoiment, as well as a private dominion or poſſeſsion of the Things of this life.

[l] *Joſeph Orig. Judaïc. lib.* 1. *c.* 3. *Euſtath. Antioch. Hexaëm. pag.* 46.

[m] Ὅρυς γῆς πρῶτος ἔθετο.

But

But in this division of Bounds and Territories, there intervened, as it were, a consent of the whole bodie or universalitie of mankinde (by the mediation of somthing like a compact, which might binde their posteritie) for quitting of the common interest or antient right in those things that were made over thus by distribution to particular Proprietors; in the same manner as when Partners or Co-heirs do share between themselvs any portions of those things which they hold in common. But as for the rest, which neither are possessed in several, nor expresly held in common, that is, which have continued vacant or desert, what shall wee saie? It hath been truly a custom of old, and which hold's to this daie in the more eminent Nations, that Vacancies are his who apprehend's them first by occupation; as wee use to saie of those wee call, *no man's Goods.* This appear's plain in the Imperial Law; nor do wee know of any Nation where it is not received, save in those where by the * *Civil Law of som Nations*, any things of this nature are appropriated to their Princes, that their Subjects gain not an interest by occupation: For there others have sufficiently disclaimed the acquiring of any title by occupation; and in the present case wee must ever have respect unto this Qualification. But as concerning such a right by occupation, there is an antient and very famous decision made in a Controversie that happened betwixt the people of *Andria* and *Chalcidia.* Both of them beeing upon an expedition against *Thrace*, for the finding out of [n] new habitations, news was brought that the Barbarous people had quitted the Town of *Acanthus*, hereupon, two men were chosen, and sent out as Spies, the one beeing of *Andria*, the other of *Chalcidia*, who beeing informed of the enemies flight, began both to run, and strive

* *Municipal.*

[n] *Plutarch in Quæst. Græc.*

which of them should first reach and take possession of the Citie thus forsaken. It happened that hee of *Chalcidia* out-ran, but the man of *Andria* darting a Javelin stuck it in the Gates: This cried out hee got thither first with his Javelin, but the other, that hee was first with his bodie. A controversie hapning hereupon, the *Erythræans*, *Samians*, and *Parians*, are called to decide it. The *Andrians* had most voices; for the *Samians* and *Erythræans* gave judgment for them. But the *Parians* were for the men of *Chalcidia*. The Reasons alleged on both sides are very well described by [o] *Petrus Ærodius*, not fit here to bee repeated: But in the mean time it is manifest, that all those men, even the persons contending, as well as the Nations to whose determination the matter was committed, were of opinion, that places abandoned and forsaken becom theirs who first acquire them by occupation; nor is there any other ground in reason for that Law or Custom, whereby wilde-Beasts, Fishes, Birds and the like, whether yet unpossess't or relinquisht, becom theirs who catch them: which is usual likewise, according to the Laws and Customs of the [p] *Hebrews* and [q] *Mahometans*, as well as the *Christians*. But now, if so bee that all men were indifferently and without distinction Lords of the whole, before a division was made of som parts, then of necessitie wee must conceiv, they all ought to remain, equally and without distinction, Lords of those parts which never came under a division, even as they were before; unless som Compact or Covenant intervene, whereby all kinde of antient Right or Title of common Interest shall bee so renounced, that any persons whatsoever might afterwards becom particular masters of those places which should remain vacant or undisposed, who should first corporally seiz them, with

[o] *Rerum judicatarum, lib. 5. tit. 21.*

[p] *Misna & Gemara utraque tit. Baba metzia cap. 1. & Maimonides tit. Zachia Wemithna cap. 1.*

[q] *Alcoran. Azoar. 12. de venatu; & Azoari 34.*

with an intent of possessing, holding, using, and injoying. Nor can it otherwise bee conceived in the case of Partners or Co-heirs (such as all men seem to have been in the State of Communitie) how those things which com not under division, should not continue common, as before. Therefore (I suppose) it must bee yielded, that som such Compact or Covenant was passed in the very first beginnings of private Dominion or possession, and that it was in full force and virtue transmitted to posteritie by the Fathers, who had the power of distributing possessions after the flood. So that wee may conclude no less concerning distribution by Assignment, then touching Seisure by occupation of things relinquish't at pleasure, that a general compact or Agreement was made or ratified, either expresly in words, or implicitly by custom. And truly, the self same thing seem's to bee the opinion of the most excellent *Hugo Grotius* [r], who speaking of the original of Proprietie saith, *Things became appropriate, not by the bare Act or Intent of the minde (for som could not know what others desired to possess, so as to abstein from the same; and perhaps many might desire one and the same thing) but by som Compact and Agreement either express, as in the case of Division; or Tacit, as in that of Seisure or Primarie occupation. For as soon as men grew out of love with Communitie, and no Division was yet appointed, wee must conceiv they agreed all together, that what every man held, hee should possess as his own.* And truly there is a paritie of Reason also for this; that any man might afterwards make Seizure of that which was left.

[r] *De Jure Belli ac pacis lib. 2. cap. 2. §. 2.*

The

The effects of private Dominion. *And what regard hath been had of the* SEA, *in the more antient Distributions and Divisions of things.*

Chap. V.

BY the introducing of *private Dominion*, in the aforesaid manner, it came to pass, that the same Territorie or Field, whose use before was free for all men alike in Tillage, Building, Pasturage cutting of wood, gathering of Fruits, egress and regress, was either by distribution or occupation so peculiarly appropriated unto the possessor, that hee might lawfully hinder such a Communitie of use and injoyment, nor might any other man use it lawfully without his permission. And from this Original sprang every Dominion or Proprietie of things, which either by Alienation, or any other kinde of Cession, is transferr'd upon others, or held by a continued possession; respect beeing alwaies had to those particular Forms and Qualifications, which usually relate unto Dominion, either by Law, Custom, or compact, according to the various Institutions of several people: For by these, the free and absolute power of the Proprietor, in what hee enjoie's, is lesned and restrained; but when this Reason wholy ceaseth, then what the Proprietor possesseth is so his own, that it cannot lawfully in any wise, without his consent, becom another man's. And all these things are derived from the alteration of that *Universal* or *Natural Law of nations* which is *Permissive*: For thence came in private Dominion or Possession, to wit from the *Positive Law*.

But

But in the mean while it is established by the *Universal Obligatorie Law*, which provide's for the due observation of Compacts and Covenants.

These things beeing thus premised, wee shall next see what respect hath been had unto the Sea, either in the very first or any more antient Distribution or Division of things. For if it appear that the Sea also hath been assigned over with Lands, it must certainly bee confessed, that from the same original there spring's a private Dominion of the Sea, as well as the Land, and so that it is equally capable of the same, with this. And truly, in the distribution of Land which was renewed after the flood (so far as wee are able to collect by Tradition from the Antients) wee finde no express mention made of any Sea, as a part assigned: But yet somtimes the Sea is added as a Bound to a part assigned. As where the part first assigned unto the Sons of *Cham*, is extended from the Borders of *Egypt* through *Africa* as far as *Hercules's* Pillars, or [a] *unto the Western and African Sea.* And the Portion of the *Canaanits* (situate within the Territorie of the Sons of *Cham*) is twice so described in the *Samaritan Pentateuch*, that it is expresly said to reach from the River of *Egypt* or *Nilus*, to the great River, that is, the River *Euphrates*, *and* [b] *unto the utmost Sea*, or the *remotest*, which is the great or Western Sea. Which last words are used in the laying out of that Portion which the Sacred Scripture mention's in *Deuteronomie.* Somtimes also, som Seas may seem to bee so comprehended in the part assigned, that they appear to bee no less assigned then the Land. For unto the Sons of *Japhet* were assigned [c] *those Countries which extend from* Media *towards the North and the West, as far as* Cadiz *and the Islands of Britain.*

[a] *African. apud Euseb. in Chronic. pag.* 10. *Cedrenus pag.* 10.

[b] *Pentateuch. Samar. Ms. Genes.* 10. 19. *& Deuter.* 34. 2.

[c] *Euseb. & Cedrenus locis citatis.*

Wee ſee alſo, that certain Seas are included within the compaſs of Aſsignment as the * *Ægean, Mediterranean, Adriatick*, and *Britiſh* Seas: whether by Donation, or not, wee cannot ſay. But in that antient apportioning of the holy Land (whereof God himſelf was Autor) the Sea ſeem's rather to have been accounted a boundarie, then any part of the Territorie allotted. Concerning the South-Quarter, the words are theſe; [d] *The Bounds of it ſhall bee the outmoſt Coaſt of the ſalt Sea Eaſtward*. And a little after; *The Border ſhall fetch a Compaſs from Azmon unto the River of Egypt, and the goings out of it ſhall bee at the Sea.* Alſo concerning the Weſt-Quarter, *its Border ſhall begin at Sea, & ipſo fine claudetur,* **and by it it ſhall bee bounded**, as it is in the vulgar Tranſlation; to which ſenſ agreeth alſo the modern: But concerning this place, and the reſt here quoted, wee ſhall ſpeak more in the next Chapter. Then it follow's, according to the true ſenſ of the Hebrew, *And this ſhall bee your North-border: From the great Sea you ſhall point out for you Mount Hor.* And a little farther, ſpeaking of the Eaſt-Quarter; *Its Border ſhall deſcend, and ſhall reach unto the ſide of the Sea of Chinnereth Eaſtward; And the Border ſhall go down again to Jordan, and the goings out of it ſhall bee at the ſalt Sea: This ſhall bee your Land with the Coaſts thereof round about.* Which is repeated almoſt word for word, in the diſtribution that was made by [e] *Joſhua*: And in another place of holy Scripture, the bounds of the Dominion is ſaid to bee [f] *from Sea to Sea*. But, ſuppoſe at laſt it were granted, that the Seas came not into thoſe more antient diſtributions of Territories, then it remain's next to bee conſider'd, whether they might not lawfully bee acquired afterwards by Title of occupation, as things vacant and derelict; that is, either by the *Natural* or *Divine univerſal Law* which is *Permiſsive*, or by the *Law*

of

* *Now called the* Levant.

[d] *Num.* 34. 3, 5, 6, 7, 12.

[e] *Joſh. c.* 15. *&c.*

[f] *Pſal.* 72. 8. *Syracid. c.* 44.

of divers Nations, Common or *Civil,* which, in judging matters of this nature, is the best Interpreter of the *natural Law* which is *Permissive.* For, if in the *Permissive* which is *Universal,* nothing bee repugnant thereto; or (which is in a manner all one) if by the *Positive Law of Nations,* such a Dominion of the Sea, as wee intend, hath been introduced and admitted by the consent of the more famous Ages and Nations; then (I suppose) it will not bee doubted, but that the Seas are, by all manner of Law, every way capable of private Dominion, as is the Land.

That the Law of God, *or the* Divine Oracles *of holy Scripture, do allow a private Dominion of the Sea. And that the wide Ocean also, which washeth the Western Coast of the holy Land, or at least a considerable part of it, was, according to the Opinion of such as were learned in the Jewish Law, annexed to the Land of Israël, by the Assignation or appointment of God himself.*

Chap. VI.

As to what concern's here the Law of God, wee finde very plain passages therein, which do not a little favor a Dominion of the Sea. In that first and most antient Donation of things after the Flood, whereby God invested *Noah* and his Posteritie, in the Dominion of the whole Earth (of which Globe the Seas themselvs are a part) and of the conterminous Aër, seem's to bee no otherwise granted, then as mention is made of the living Creatures, the Earth, and the Fowls of the Aër. That is, by an express grant of the free use and benefit of the thing, the thing it self was granted or conferred. Nor is the Dominion of the Sea otherwise granted there, where it is said, [a] *The fear of you, and the dread of you* (which are Tearms signifying Dominion) *shall bee also all the Fishes of the Sea. Little different from this is that which was spoken to our first Parents,* [b] *Replenish the Earth and subdue it, and have Dominion over the Fish of the Sea, and over the Fowl of the Aër, and over everie living thing that moveth upon the Earth:* So here also, the grant of the thing it self is signified by its use and enjoiment. 'Tis confess't, that these words were not meant of private Dominion, or that which was not common to all men: But yet it appear's thereby, the Earth and Sea did so pass together at first, and after the same manner, into the common enjoiment of mankinde, that from this Donation or Grant of God, wee may well conclude; that their condition, as beeing both but one Globe, must needs bee alike, at the pleasure of men, in the future distribution of Things, or the introducing of private Dominion therein. Neither is the Proprietie, nor the Communitie of either appointed but both seem equally permitted by the very form of Donation. And therefore that is very vain which is objected by som [c], *That the Earth is given to the children of men, but that* [d] *the Sea belong's onely to God himself*; as if Dominion not common indeed, but onely a common use of the Sea, were permitted by the words of holy Scripture: And as if it were not said in like manner, [e] *The Earth is the Lord's, and fulness thereof: The tops of the Hills are his also.* Who know's not, that such sayings as these cannot in any wise weaken the Dominion of Mankinde? For, whatsoever is acquired by men, still God

[a] Gen. 9. 2.

[b] Gen. 1. 28.

[c] Psal. 115. 16.

[d] Psal. 95. 5.

[e] Psal. 24. 1. 50. 12. 89, 11. 95, 4.

God Almightie, as Father of the Univers, retein's his supreme Dominion both over men, as also all other Things; which never was denied yet by any sober man. But the Controversie is about the Dominion of man, to wit, that which comprehend's any enjoiment or proprietie whatsoëver, saving still that right of the Dominion of God, which cannot bee diminished. And the distinction about this matter is very ordinarie in the Schools: According to the first sort of Dominion, nothing whatsoëver, much less may the Sea belong unto men: According to the second, all things indeed are or may bee theirs, which can bee apprehended, seized, and possessed. Add moreover, that in the old Testament express mention is made more then once of such a Seisure, possession, or private Dominion as this whereof wee Treat; and that as of a Thing lawfully brought in use. There wee finde that the men of *Tyre* were Lords and Masters of the *Phœnician*, and the *Egyptians* of the *Alexandrian* Sea. Concerning the *Phœnician*, saith the Prophet unto *Tyrus*; [f] *All the Princes of the Sea shall com down from their Thrones, &c. And they shall take up a lamentation for thee, and say to thee, how art thou destroyed that wast inhabited of Seafaring men! the renowned Citie, which wast strong in the Sea!* Here the Dominion of the *Tyrians* at Sea is plainly set forth. And in the following Chapter [g], *Thy Borders are in the midst or heart of the Sea*; as wee read it in the Hebrew, and also in an [h] *Arabian Manuscript*, which render's it to the same purpose: For, both the *Greek* and *vulgar Translation* differ there from the Original. It follow's also thus; [i] *All the Ships of the Sea with their Mariners were thine to occupie thy Merchandize.* In stead of which last words, these are put in the *Greek* Copies, ἐπὶ δυσμὰς δυσμῶν, *even Westward of the West*, or through a great part of the main or Western Sea; that

[f] *Ezech. c.* 26. *v.* 16.

[g] *Cap.* 27. 4.

[h] *In Bibliocâ Arundelianâ.*

[i] *Vers.* 9.

is, the *Phœnician* or *Syrian.* Again, [k] *Becaus thine heart is lifted up, and thou hast said, I am a God, I sit in the seat of God, in the mid'st of the Sea.* Hee threaten's not the *Tyrian*, becaus hee had gotten him a Dominion over the neighboring Sea, but becaus beeing lifted up with pride, hee had taken unto himself the name of God. The *Tyrian* is called likewise in another Scripture the [l] *Sea it self, and the strength of the Sea.* But concerning the *Egyptian* Sea, another Prophet speak's thus unto *Ninive*; *Art thou better then populous Alexandria* (in the Original the Citie is called *No*, taken here for *Alexandria*) *which is situate among the Rivers, that hath the waters round about it, whose Riches and strength* (as it is in the *Hebrew*) or (as the *Greek* render's it) Ἀρχὴ, that is, *whose Empire* or *Dominion is the Sea.* Moreover, it seem's to make mention of Kings of the Sea, as well as of Islands; [m] *The Kings of Tarshish and of the Isles shall bring presents.* For, *Tarshish* or *Tharsis* in Hebrew signifieth the Sea, [n] as it is often confessed both by the Greek and Chaldee Interpreters. Although *Munster*, a man otherwise very learned, speak's unadvisedly upon the fore-mention'd place, and will not have *Tharsis* there to signifie the Sea, *becaus* (saith hee) *Kings have nothing to do at Sea, but rule onely upon Land*; forgetting (what wee have alreadie told you) that express mention is made by *Ezechiel* concerning *Princes of the Sea.* With which agree's also that saying, [o] *I will set his hand in the Sea, and his right hand in the Flouds*; upon which place *Aben-Ezra* note's, that God Almightie assigned the Dominion of the Sea there unto King *David*, *That hee might rule over those that sailed either through the Sea or the Rivers.* It is written thus likewise in the Apocrypha; [p] *O yee men, do not men excel in strength that bear rule over Sea and Land, and all things in them? But yet the King is more mightie; for, hee is Lord of all these things* and

[k] *Cap.* 28. *vers.* 2.

[l] *Isai.* 23.4.

[m] *Ps.* 72.10.

[n] *Hieronym. ad Isaiæ c.* 2.

[o] *Ps.* 89.25.

[p] *Esdras, l.* 1. *chap.* 4.

and hath Dominion over them. And in another place, saith the Angel to Esdras, [q] *The Sea is set in a wide place, that it might bee deep and great. But put case the entrance were narrow, and like a River, who then could enter the Sea, to look upon it, and have Dominion over it, if hee went not through the narrow?* The Dominion of the Sea and of the Land is granted alike in both these places. It is said also of King *Ahasuerus*; [r] *That hee made not onely the Land, but all the Isles of the Sea to becom tributarie,* which words truly do clearly shew a Dominion of the Sea; for, so they are expressed in the vulgar Edition, out of the Hebrew Original, which is lost. But the Greek Copies are more plain there; [s] *The King wrote to his Kingdom of the Land and Sea.* Nor must wee omit that of *Moses* when hee blessed the people; [t] *And of Naphtali hee said, Naphtali shall enjoy abundance, and bee full with the blessings of the Lord; hee shall possess* or *inherit the Sea and the South*; as the vulgar and the *Greek* do render that place. But by many others, the Sea is taken there for the West-Quarter, as it is often in the Scriptures. Yet truly, it is clear those words are meant of the Sea of *Galilee*, or of the Lake of *Tiberias*, not of the great or *Phœnician* Sea, which lie's Westward, becaus the Land of *Naphtali* was situate near that Lake, which also is often called the Sea. As it appear's likewise out of *Onkelus* his Paraphrase, where express mention is made of the Sea of *Genesareth*, called also the Lake of *Tiberias*, or the Sea of Chinnereth, and by this name it passeth with the salt Sea, or the Lake of *Asphaltites*, in the [u] sacred description of the Eastern part of the holy Land. But the former place of *Deuteronomie* is erroneously rendred by *Rupert* the Abbot of *Tuitium*; [x] *Mane & Meridiem possidebit*, for *Mare & Meridiem*, **hee shall possess the Morning and the South,** for **the Sea and the South.** However, it is clear (I suppose) out of the

[q] *Esdras, l.* 2 *cap.* 7.

[r] *Esther.* 10. 1.

[s] Ἔγραψε δ' ὁ Βασιλεὺς ἐπὶ τὴν βασιλείαν τῆς τε γῆς καὶ τῆς θαλάσσης.

[t] *Deuteronom. cap.* 33. 23.

[u] *Numb.* 34. 11. & 3.

[x] *Ad Deut. lib.* 2. *c.* 1

the places alléged, ſuch plain Teſtimonies are found in holy Writ touching ſuch a Dominion of the Sea, that in the mean time it muſt bee granted, that according to the *Univerſal Permiſsive Law*, any man may acquire it as well as the Land. And truly, as for thoſe places quoted in the foregoing Chapter, concerning the South, Weſt or Sea and Northen Bounds of the holy Land, they are ſo underſtood both by the Jewiſh Lawyers and Divines, that they would have either the great or *Phœnician* Sea it ſelf, or at leaſt ſom adjoyning part of it to bee aſsigned alſo by God unto the *Iſraëlites*, as Lords of it for ever; of which point wee ſhall diſcourſ a little more fully. As for that which is rendred there out of the vulgar Edition, touching the South Border, [y] *As far as the river of Egypt; and it ſhall bee bounded by the ſhore of the great Sea*, the Hebrew ſaith, *ad Torrentem Ægypti* **unto the River of Egypt** (or the North entrance of *Nilus*, which divided the Land of *Iſraël* from *Egypt*, at the Sea) *& erunt exitus eius in Mare*, **and the goings out thereof ſhall bee into the Sea.** So that concerning that Borders beeing bounded by the ſhore (as it is in the vulgar) wee finde it no otherwiſe expreſſed there in the Original. Then, it is added next, concerning the Weſt-border or that which is at the great Sea, word for word out of the Hebrew. *As for your Sea border, you may have the great Sea, And let this bee your border, or let it bee your* Sea *border, or border of the* Sea. And there the Greek Interpreter's render it thus, *you ſhall have the bounds of the* Sea, or *they ſhall bee your bounds. The great* Sea *ſhall bound you*: wherein (after their uſual manner) they plainly follow the Text of the *Samaritan* Copie: For, there wee read it thus, *And you ſhall have a* Sea*-border. The great* Sea *ſhall bound you. Let this bee your* Sea or *Weſtern-border*. And thus the word SEA beeing uſed as well for the Weſtern Quarter as for

[y] *Uſque ad Torrentem Ægypti; & magni Maris littore finietur.*

for the Sea it self, that place is for the most part so rendred, that in so short a period the Sea is taken for both. *As for the West-Border, you shall have the great Sea. And this Border shall bee your West-Border.* As it is expressed by the Jews of *Spain*; *y Termino de ponente; y sera à vos el mar el grande: y Termino este sera à vos Termino de ponente.* Thus is also in *Onkelus* and *Erpenius* his Arabick; save that *Onkelus* render's it thus, *But your West-border shall bee the great Sea and the Border thereof; the same shall bee your West-border.* But an Arabian Translation in manuscript, for which wee are beholden to the Earl of *Arundel's* Librarie, after these words, *unto the River of Egypt*, add's also, *And the going out thereof shall bee at the Coasts* or *parts of the Sea. And the Border of the Sea shall bee your Border. Also the great Sea in their Borders. This shall bee your Border from the Sea Coast.* But the North part, as appear's by the particulars alleged in the former Chapter, is bounded by mount *Hor*: so that it appear's hence, that the more Northerly enterance of *Nilus*, that is the *Pelusiock* (as it seem's; for they are not well agreed about the very particular place) served instead of Bounds to the South part of the Land of Israël, which border'd upon the Sea, as also to that part of the Promontorie or foot of mount *Hor*, which was situated North-East by the Sea. But this mount is that which in the vulgar edition is called *an exceeding high mountain.* In the Jewish Commentaries it is known also by the name of *Amana*, and *Amanon*, and *Amanus*, and by som it is taken for that mountain in the *Canticles*, called [x] *Amana.* And in the Jewish *Targum*, [z] *Manus* is put for mount *Hor.* It is taken also for *Libanus*, by such as in their [a] Descriptions of the Holie Land, are wont to make mount *Libanus* its Northern Border. But as touching this mount *Hor* or *Amanus* (of

[x] *In glossâ Jarchii ad cap. 4. Cant.*

[z] *In Num. 34 & vide gloss. talmud ad tit. Gittin. cap. 1. fol. 8.*

[a] *Lyran. ad Numer. 34. Andr. Masius ad Josuam. Adricomius, Jacob Bar Abraham in Tab. Chorographica Terræ sanctæ &c. Et vide Abulens. ad Num. 34. q. 2.*

(of the ſame name with that mountain, which but's out into the Gulph now called *Golfo dell' Aiazza* by ſom alſo taken for the ſame [b] or rather mount *Taurus*) it is deſcribed after this manner by *Solomon Jarchius*, *it is ſeated in a north weſt corner. It's head bending downward ſtret-cheth out into the very ſea. And it is waſh't in divers places by the main.* Betwixt theſe Bounds, to wit, the Southern part or the *Peluſiack* entrance of *Nilus*, and the North-Eaſt Bound or Promontorie of the aforeſaid mount, the great ſea, which is reckoned the Weſtern Bound or Border, haivng divers windings and turnings along the ſhore, is ſtretcht out in ſuch a manner above 200 miles, that if a ſtreight line ſhould bee drawn from the North-Eaſt Border to the Southern, a great part of the Sea that extend's it ſelf within the line for ſo many miles, muſt needs bee intercepted. which alſo is very eaſily to bee underſtood without the help of a Map.

[b] *Gloſſ. ordinar. ad numee.* 34.

Theſe things beeing thus premiſed, briefly, but ſo far as the matter in hand require's, to diſcover the weſtern part of the Holie Land, bordering wholy upon the Sea, and that according to the judgment of the antient Hebrews, not by modern Deſcriptions; it is to bee conſider'd, that the Jewiſh Divines and Lawyers, when they diſcourſ *about the precepts and Laws belonging to the Land of Iſraël*, that is, of thoſe to which they conceiv themſelvs not bound by the Holy Law, without the Limits of that Land, uſe to treat very preciſely, even to an hair, touching the Borders of their Dominion, as it was appointed by the Command of God. To wit, touching the Bounds of their Territorie, as the name Territorie ſignifie's the whole, not onely Lands and Fields, but Rivers alſo and all other waters within the circuit of each Citie, as it is rightly taken alſo by the

[c] Civil Lawyers. The Precepts spoken of, are those which are received by the Jews, touching the observation of the *Sabbaticall year, oblations of Fruits,* the *Levitical custom of Tithing*, and others of that kinde. For by the Law of God, they will not yield that those things should bee observed out of the Israëlitish Dominions, although, [d] by Tradition of their Ancestors, they were usually observed in *Egypt, Idumæa*, the Land of *Moab*, and *Shinar*, both by reason of their neighborhood, and the frequent convers of the Israëlits among them. But now so far as concern's the western or Sea-bordering of the Land of Israël, as it was assigned at first by God, in observing Precepts of this kinde, according to the holie Law, wee meet with two opinions in their Commentaries, from both which indeed it will appear, that the Sea was assigned by God Himself unto the Israëlites, as Lords thereof, in the same manner as the Land, though one opinion assign's larger Bounds, the other much more narrow: So that they all agree about the thing, differing onely about the latitude. The first opinion is of those who affirm, that the whole western Sea (as it lie's before the western Coast of the Land of Israël or as it is bounded inward by streight lines drawn on both sides, from the North-east and South border before mentioned, through that Ocean into the west) together with the Continent was given unto them by God; and therefore that those Precepts are to bee observed in that vast Ocean, as in the Territorie of Israël. The chief Autor of this opinion was an antient and very famous Interpreter of the Law, by name *Rabbi Jehuda*, who also from the express words of the Holie Law above-mentioned, conclud's

[c] *Cæpola de Servitutibus Rustic. Præd. cap. 26. § 26. Hieronym. de monte, l. de finibus regundis cap. 6. § 8. Alberic. Gentilis de jure Belli lib. 3. cap. 17. Dd. in l. 9. ff. de judiciis.*

[d] *Moses Maimonides halach. Therumoth cap. 1. & Mikotzi, Præcep. Affirm. 133.*

conclud's that the western Ocean, thus bounded on both sides, was asigned. His Doctrine is deliver'd after this manner, as wee finde it in the most antient Digests of the Jewish Law. [e] *Whatsoëver lie's directly opposite to the Land of Israël, it is of the same account with the Land of Israël, according as it is written;* [f] *As for your West-Border, let your Border bee, or you shall have, the great Sea. Also let this bee a Border to you, or your Border. To wit, the Border of the Sea, or of the West. Also the Collateral Islands situate on both sides in the same direct line, fall under the same accompt with the sides themselvs. So that if a line were drawn from Cephaloria through the Isles to the main Ocean, and from the River of Egypt to the Ocean, then that which is within the line, is to bee taken for the Territorie of Israël, and that which lie's without the line to bee out of the Dominion of Israël.* The line drawn from *Cephaloria*, was directed by the Promontorie of mount *Hor* or *Amanus*, as is said before: For that Citie was seated on the top of that mountain, which is here the North-east Border; as it is observed in the Gloss upon the place alleged, and in many other. There also this opinion is thus explained. *According to this opinion of* Rabbi Jehuda, *all that* Sea *which lie's opposite to the length of the Land of Israël, even to the main Ocean, West-ward, where the World it's self is bounded, is to bee reckon'd within the Territorie or Dominion of Israël; even as it is written, the great Sea, and your Border* (the whole place wee gave you a little before out of *Numbers*) *where [and your Border] is added the more fully and plainly, to intimate that the great and wide Sea is contained also within it's Border.* And it follow's there thus; *Between those little Cords or Lines* (directed, as wee said, on both sides to the main Sea) *there*

[e] *Gemara Babylonia ad tit. Gittin, seu de libellis Divortii & manumissionis cap. 1. fol. 8. a. Idem, sed depravatè legitur in Gemara Hierosolymitanâ, ad tit. Shebiith seu de Anno Sabbatico, cap 6. fol. 36. col. 4.*

[f] *Numer. 34. 6.*

there are Islands belonging to the Territorie of Israël; the Islands and waters have both the same Law &c. Hence also the ordinarie Jewish Gloss upon those words in *Numbers*, *And you shall have the great Sea*, saith, *The Isles that are in the midd'st of the Sea, even they also are part of the Bound* or *Border.* But the Jewish Paraphrase is more plain there, *And let your Border bee the great Sea, that is, the main Ocean, and it's Isles, and Cities, and Ships, with the principal waters that are in it.* Nor was it upon any other ground, that [g] Rabbi *Aben-Ezra*, [h] Rabbi *Becbai*, and others, conceived so great a part of the Sea, did belong to the Israëlites by this assignation, that they interpret the great Sea also to reach through the Sea הספרדי that is, the Spanish Sea, distant so many miles Westward from the Continent of Israël. In both the forenamed places, the words are, *The great Sea, to wit, the Spanish. And your Border; as if it had been said, The great Sea shall bee your possession, which of it self also is your Border.* But in the mean while it is to bee consider'd, that the whole western Ocean as far as the narrow channel of *Cadiz*, is by the Arabians and so by the modern Jews, who were their Disciples, indifferently called the *Romane Sea*, mare *Al-shem*, or the Sea of *Damascus* (that is the Syrian Sea) mare *Al-Andalús* (or the Spanish) and lastly, the *mediterranean Sea*; the whole beeing denominated from the Coasts of som particular Countries: As it may bee clearly collected both out of the Nubian Geographie, as also out of the Geographical Abridgment of [h] *Abu Elchasen Hali* an Arabian. But this is most certain, that the name of the Spanish Sea hath been used here by the Rabbins, not from such a promiscuous or common denomination of the Sea; but according to the explanation of such an antient Assignation of the Dominion of Israël as wee have

[g] *Ad Numer.* 34.

[h] *Ad Numer. pag.* 199. *col.* 3.

[h] *Ms. in Bibliothecâ Oxoniensi.*

have mentioned. And so this first opinion would have the whole Western Ocean, as far as the streights of *Cadiz*, which the Antients thought the utmost Bound of the world, to bee reckoned for that part of the Territorie of Israël, which is included within the lines drawn from the Promontorie of mount *Hor* or *Amanus* and the entrance of *Pelusium*, into the West. But by the other opinion, which seem's much more agreeable to reason, it is determined, that the Divine Assignation of the Territorie of Israël is comprehended indeed within more narrow Bounds of this Sea, but yet Sea-room large enough: so that according to this opinion, the North and South-Borders do end at the very shore, or at the utmost point of the said Promontorie, North-East, and at the entrance of *Pelusium*, towards the South; not stretching any farther, into the West. But indeed the Autors of this opinion would have a streight line drawn from that Promontorie to the entrance of *Pelusium*, to wit from the North-East into the South, thereby to limit and bound the Western part of the Dominion of Israël; so that what portion soëver either of the Sea or the Isles should bee comprehended within such a line, or lie on the East-side of it, the whole were to bee reckoned a part of the Territorie of Israël, as well as any Coast upon the Continent or main Land. And so after this manner, the aforesaid line, included within the nooks and windings of the shore of that Territorie (possessed by the Tribes of *Asher*, *Ephraim*, *Dan*, *Zabulon*, and *Simeon*) was situate before very large spaces of of the Sea, for above two hundred miles; and supposed to bee of the same accompt with the shore it self. In the Digests of the Jewish Law, this opinion is explained thus; [i] *That it may bee known what com's under the name of*

[i] *In Gemara Babylonica ad tit. Gittin seu de libellis Divortii & Manumissionis. cap.* I. *fol.* 8.

of the Territorie of Israël, and what is to bee reckoned out of that Territorie (as to the North-East and Western bounds;) *whatsoëver is stretcht forth on this side and within Mount Amanus, is the Territorie of Israël. And that which is placed beyond that Mountain, is without this Territorie. And so by the same reason it is to bee determined touching the Isles of the Sea that are seated over against that Mountain. Let a small Cord or Line bee drawn over those Islands, from Mount Amanus to the river of Egypt; that is conteined within the Line, is the Territorie of Israël; but that which lie's without the Line, is no part of that Territorie.* With this agree's that of *Ezekiel*, concerning the Sea-Coast of the holy Land, after hee had described the South part which is near the Sea; [k] *The West-side also [shall bee] the great Sea from the border till a man com over against Hamath. This is the West, or Sea-side* (or Coast.) The vulgar read's it thus, *The great Sea also shall bee its Sea border, strait along from the border till you com to Emath. This is the Sea-side:* Which the Greeks render thus; τȣ̃το τὸ μέρος νότος ϗ λίψ. *This part is South and South-west*, according to the translation of the fore-going words. Then, according to what hath been alleged out of the Hebrew, it follow's in the Greek, *This is part, or this divide's part of the great Sea, untill a man com over against the entrance which lead's to Hemath, even to the entrance thereof. These are they which lie near the Sea of Hemath.* So that every Translation speak's to the same purpose. But that which wee have added to the Hebrew, agree's both with the Chaldee Paraphrase, and the Exposition of the Spanish Jews. Moreover, *Solomon Jarchius* expound's it there after this manner, according to the doctrine of the Antients; *From the South-Corner* (for, so hee interpret's this word, from the Border) *which is the river of*

k Ezek. cap. 47.20.

of Egypt, till a man com over against the entrance which lead's to Hamath; that is, to the Corner situated under the North-West, which is the very Mount Hor over against the entrance unto Hamath. For, Hamath was seated on the North-west side near Mount Hor. And so that which is cut off here by the Border in a strait line (as the *vulgar* hath it) drawn from the entrance of *Nilus* to the Promontorie of Mount *Hor*, contein's no small portion of the Sea as assigned unto *Israël*. And this later Opinion is the better received, whereby onely the nearer Parts of the Sea are, by God's appointment, conceived to bee in the very same condition with the continent; as appear's not onely out of the more antient *Digests*, or both Volums of the *Talmud*, but also by the Testimonie of those most learned Rabbins, [l] *Moses Maimonides* and [m] *Moses Cotzensis*, besides others of a less account, who in express terms imbrace it. Also, according to both these Opinions, that is in the mean time of sufficient Autoritie, which is deliver'd in general terms touching the beyond-Sea Provinces, by [n] *Solomon Jarchius*, [o] *Rabbenu Nissim*, [p] *Obadiah Bartenorius*, and others; *to wit, That whatsoëver lie's without the Territorie of Israël, that whole Province or Citie is often comprised under the Notion of the Sea, except Babylon.* After the example of the Sea-Provinces, situated afar off in the West, without the Lines drawn according to this or the other Opinion, the Mediterranean Provinces and Cities also, which were seated in other remote Parts, without the Borders of *Israël*, have in stead of beeing called a strange Land, been termed the Provinces or Cities of the Sea. Which point is very well handled by *Rabbenu Nissim* in the former place. But as these, which were seated without their Territorie in the continent, were onely by the said Custom of speech called Cities of the Sea, so also it

[l] *Halach* Therumoth, *seu de Oblationibus*, c. 1.
[m] *Præcept. Affirmat.* 133.
[n] *Ad Tit. Gittin. cap.* 1. *fol.* 1.
[o] *Ad Alphesium, part.* 2. *pag.* 554.
[p] *Ad Misnaioth, tit. Gittin, cap.* 1. ubi & vide *Rabbi Jom Tob.*

it is clear by what wee have shewn you, that according to the same way of speaking it is granted, that other Cities also within their Territorie were seated in the verie Sea. And so at length, from both the Opinions, here recited, wee have sufficiently proved, that such an Exposition of the divine Asignation was received by the antient Interpreters of the Jewish Law, to whom that Asignation was made, that they made no doubt but the Sea was every jot as capable of private Dominion, as the Land; and so reckoned those Ilands placed in the neighboring Sea, as belonging to the Territorie of *Israël*, becaus of their Dominion over the Sea that did flow between them. Nor doth it hinder at all, that in their Asignations or Distributions wee so often finde this Particle *usque ad Mare*, **unto the Sea**, as appear's in the former Chapter; or that the Sea was their Border. For, the word *usque*, **until** or **unto**, is not onely often [q] inclusive, but also the Borders or Limits themselves are [r] many times all one with the thing limited; after the same manner as all Bounds that are bounded. Touching which Particular, both the Canonists and Civilians are very Copious; as also the Jews in those other Particulars alreadie mention'd. And therefore wee conclude out of the Premisses, that neither the *Divine Law* which is *universal*; nor the *Positive*, as it appear's, in Scripture, to bee *Imperative* or to have a command over som certain Nations (for, there is a true picture of the *Imperative Law* in the aforesaid distribution of Bounds) doth oppose a private Dominion of the Sea; but that both of them do sufficiently allow it; and afford also very clear examples of such a Dominion (if wee may believ the Jews themselvs.) In the next place then, let us consider (what is yet behinde) of the *Law natural* and of *Nations*.

[q] *Bartol. ad lib. 35. Patronus ff. tit. de legat. 3. & l. Nuptæ ff. de Senatoribus.*

[r] *Archidiac. in c. Ecclesias 13. q. 1. Hieronymus de Monte, lib. de Finibus Regundis,* 23.

That

That the natural-Permissive *Law (whereof any use may bee in this place) is to bee derived out of the* Customs and Constitutions *of the more civilized and more noble* Nations, *both antient and modern.*

Chap. VII.

As to what concern's here the *Law Natural*, as one head of the *universal* or *Primitive Law of Nations*, in our former Division of the Law, commonly derived from a right and discreet use of Reason; that it doth in no wise gainsay a private Dominion of the Sea, but plainly permit it, wee shall prove hereby; becaus by the *positive Law of Nations of every kind*, which is humane, (for wee have alreadie spoken of the Divine) to wit, as well by the *Law Civil* or *Domestick of divers Nations*, as the *Common Law of divers Nations*, whether it bee *Intervenient*, or *Imperative*; that is to say, by the Customs of almost all and the more noble Nations that are known to us, such a Dominion of the Sea is every where admitted. It is not indeed to bee denied, that a right use of humane Reason, which usually serv's as an Index of the natural Law, cannot well bee gather'd from the Customs of several Nations, about things Divine or such as relate unto Divine Worship. Nor are the Points either of the *Obligatorie* or *Permissive* kinde of natural Law relating thereunto, to bee thence determined. For, it hath been the common Custom of men, in all Ages and throughout all parts of the known World, to conclude of such maters, either without exact and convenient examination, or els for the serving of their

their own Interests, or elſ to ſuit with the humor and diſpoſition of the people whom they are to rule and keep in order; as do the Pagans, Mahometans, and others of that ſort, as well modern as antient. And therefore *Antiſthenes* of old taught well and boldly at *Athens*,[a] as many other Philoſophers have don, *Populares Deos eſſe multos, ſed naturalem unum eſſe*, **That there are many National Gods, and but one Natural**, contrarie to what the moſt uſual practice of men and Cuſtom had introduced among the ordinarie ſort of People. So that as of old in the *Jewiſh* Church, ſo alſo in the *Chriſtian*, the uſe of humane Reaſon among the vulgar, though free in other things, yet when it dived into the contemplation or debate of Religious matters, it hath often been moſt deſervedly reſtrained, by certain ſet-Maxims, Principles, and Rules of holy Writ, as Religious Bolts and Bars upon the Soul; leſt it ſhould wantonize and wander, either into the old Errors of moſt Ages and Nations, or after the new devices of a rambling phanſie. And truly, ſuch a courſ as this hath ever been obſerved in Religious Government. But in ſuch things as are meerly humane, and ſo humane that they reflect only upon matters of dutie betwixt man and man, and are not forbidden by any command of God (of which kinde you cannot ſo much as imagine any thing more plainly to bee, then a diſtinction of the Dominion of Territories, and the manner thereof which is wholly grounded upon the conſent of men) that which ſhall bee permitted by the *Law Natural*, is no leſs rightly determined by the Laws, Placarts, and received Cuſtoms of divers Ages and Nations, both antient and modern, then it may bee collected what every Clime will or will not bear, by the diligent obſervation of Countries, Shrubs, Trees, Plants, and other things

a *Cicero de Naturâ Deorum, lib.* 1.

which belong unto the bodie of Husbandrie. For, as many Nations as have admitted such a private Dominion as wee inquire after, whether by a Law Civil or Domestick of their own, or by any Law common to themselvs and their neighbor-Nations, are either to bee allowed competent Witnesses of the *natural permissive Law* (so far as there is any use of it here;) or els it must bee said (which I believ no man dream's) that so many and those the more famous Nations, have for so many Ages erred against Nature. Concerning the *Law Natural, Justinian* saith, [b] *Quod Naturalis ratio inter omnes homines constituit, id apud omnes populos peræquè custoditur, vocatúrque Jus Gentium, quasi quo Jure omnes Gentes utuntur* **What Natural reason establisheth among all men, that is observed by all people alike, and is called the Law of Nations, as it were by a Law which all Nations use.** And *Caius*; [c] *Jus Gentium ratione naturali inter omnes homines peræquè servatur*; **The Law of Nations is by natural reason observed alike among all men.** But where are all Nations? It is not yet discover'd how many there are, much less upon what Customs they have agreed. Nor is that in any wise found in the Customs of all those Nations that are discover'd, which som notwithstanding imbrace as a part of the *Law Permissive*. What have the midland Nations to do with that Law concerning the Confiscation of wrecks at Sea, which hath been used by the *English*, *Britains*, *Sicilians*, and som other Nations bordering upon the Sea. The inslaving of Prisoners of War is grown out of date, as a thing not permitted among Christian Nations, which nevertheless is in use still among the *Mahometans*. In vain therefore is a Rule and Direction sought here out of the

Customs

[b] *Instit. de Jure Nat. §. Jus Naturale.*

[c] *L. 1. ff. de Adquir. rerum Domino.*

Customs of all Nations; but especially seeing som are not wanting who

——non fœdera Legum
Ulla colunt, placidas aut Jura tenentia mentes;

Whom neither League nor lawful compact bindes;
Nor Laws that rule and pacifie men's mindes.

as hee saith [d] of the *Bebrycians*. That there have been som such Nations, is expresly recorded also by [e] *Aristotle*. And *Salust*, out of the mouth of [f] *Hiempsal*, saith concerning the *Getuli* and *Libyans*, the antient Inhabitants of *Africa*, *Neque moribus, neque Lege, neque Imperio cujusquam regebantur*, **They were ruled neither by Custom, nor by Law, nor by the command of any.** And in another place concerning the [g] *Aborigines*; *Genus hominum agreste, sine Legibus, sine Imperio, liberum atque solutum*; **A rude sort of men, without Laws, without Government, free and dissolute.** Therefore wee must have recours here unto the more civilized and more eminent Nations of the past and present Age, and of such whose Customs wee are best acquainted with. And among them truly, not onely such as those very Nations, whom it may chiefly concern here, have ever highly esteemed; but also those Nations, who are concerned at present, shall bee proved competent Witnesses.

[d] *Val. Flacc. Argonautic.* 4.
[e] *Nicomach. lib.7.cap.6.*
[f] *In bello Jugurthino.*
[g] *In conjurat.Catilinar.*

But of the Testimonies, that wee intend to use there is a twofold kinde. Som are those which shew, that a Soveraigntie and private Dominion of the Sea hath been by Historians and other Writers, almost in all Ages, acknowledged and granted to Princes, people

People, and others. Other Testimonies there are which demonstrate out of Lawyers, also by Leagues and Treaties, and other particulars of that nature, that such a Dominion of the Sea, is in like manner agreeable unto Law. Both which wee interweav, as the order of Things direct's us. But yet so, that what matters, either of Fact or Law, do appertain unto the *British* Sea, are wholly pretermitted in this collection of Testimonies, with an Intent to dispose them apart in the *second Book*. And so at length it will bee very clearly manifested together, both what the *Civil Law of Nations*, as also what the *Common Law of divers Nations*; and lastly, what the *natural permissive Law* (which in this case is to bee drawn out of the Customs of Nations) hath determined touching private Dominion of the Sea.

The manner, whereby the Law Permissive *touching private Dominion of the Sea, may bee drawn out of the Customs of many* Ages and Nations. *That there were Testimonies hereof manifest enough in the* Fabulous Age. *Also, a word by the way, touching the* Mediterranean Sea *in possession of the Romanes, when the* Command *thereof was committed to* Cneius Pompeius.

Chap. VIII.

THe Ages, out of whose Monuments and Actions the aforesaid Customs, determinations, and Decree's of People and Nations, are to bee derived, I divide into two parts. Into the *Fabulous Age*, and the *Historical*.

Historical. But wee do not, according to *Varro,* call that *Fabulous* which wholly preceded the beginning of the *Olympiads;* but that which is obscured onely by the most antient Fables, at least under a fabulous Representation; The *Historical* beeing in the mean time divided into that which is more antient and comprehend's the Customs of such Empires and Commonwealths as expired som Ages past; And into that which is modern, and shew's the practice of those Nations, in the present case, which are now in Beeing. But in applying our selvs unto the *fabulous Age*, wee do not ground Arguments upon Fables, as they are meer Fables; but wee manifest Historical Truth out of the most antient Historians, though wrap't up in the mysteries of Heathen Priests and Poëts. For, (as [a] *Lactantius* saith well) even *Those things which the Poëts speak are true, but cover'd under a certain veil or Figure. And yet they have so veiled the Truth with Fiction, that the Truth it self might not take off from the common belief of the People.* They write, that in the fabulous time afore-mentioned, the *Titans* beeing subdued, the Brother-Deities, *Jupiter, Pluto,* and *Neptune*, divided the world by Lot; And that Heaven was allotted unto *Jupiter*, Hell to *Pluto,* the Sea to *Neptune.* But omitting those Trifles, whereby the vulgar suffered themselvs with patience to bee cozen'd, touching the Heaven or Skie, the kingdom of Hell or of the dead, and of the whole Earth's beeing common, after this division, to all the [b] Brothers, som of the Antients have taught, that the Truth it self which lay couched in this Fable, was quite another Thing. They say these were not gods, but men. Also that *Jupiter* was not King of Heaven, but of the Eastern part from whence the Light

[a] *De falsâ Religione, lib.* 1. *cap.* 11.

[b] *Homer. Iliad.* 15. *seu* o.

Light first dawn's upon mortal men; by which means also it seemed the higher part, and therefore was called Heaven: And that *Pluto* was King of the West, which point's at the Sun's setting and Night, from whence it was said to bee lower and Hell. Lastly, that *Neptune* was Lord of the Sea and the Isles scatter'd therein. Thus it appear's here, that a private Dominion of the Sea, no otherwise then of the Land, arose from *Humane* distribution. And that the case stood thus, it was affirmed long since by *Euhemerus Messenius*, an old Autor, in his Historie of the Affairs of those men who were supposed gods, recorded and translated by *Ennius*. For, *Lactantius* saith thus; [c] *Concerning the lot or share of Neptune, it is manifest I say, that his Kingdom was such as was that unlimited command of* Cneius Pompeius, *who, by decree of the Senate, had Autoritie given him over all the Sea-Coast for suppressing Pirats, and scouring the whole Sea. Thus all things belonging to the Sea with its Islands fell by lot unto Neptune. But how may it bee proved? To wit, by antient Histories.* Euhemerus *an old Autor, who was of the Citie of* Messina, *hath collected the Affairs and Atchievments of* Jupiter *and others that are reputed gods, and compiled a Historie of those sacred Titles and Inscriptions that were found in the most antient Temples, and especially in the Temple of* Jupiter *of Triphylia, where a golden Pillar was placed by* Jupiter *himself, as appeared by the Inscription: Upon which Pillar hee wrote his own Actions, that it might remain a Monument of his Affairs unto Posteritie. This Historie* Ennius *did both translate and follow, whose words are these;* Jupiter *grant's the Dominion of the Sea unto Neptune, that hee might reign over all the Islands, and all Places near the Sea.* But both the Translation of *Ennius*, and the Commentaries themselvs of *Euhemerus*, are utterly lost; nor

[c] *Loco jam citato.*

is

is it to bee thought, that they were lost without the knowledg and design of the chief Priests of *Jupiter* and other Deities. For, doubtless whatsoëver had been written touching the Originals of the gods, was so much the more odious, by how much the more it did lay them open, and discover, that those great Names which were magnified in their Chappels and Temples, were taken out of the List either of great Kings, or Heroës, and obtruded upon the credulous vulgar. For, from hence it was, that *Euhemerus*, with *Diagoras* and som others, was branded an Atheist, who is used as a singular Autor, not onely by *Lactantius*, but also by *Clemens Alexandrinus*, *Eusebius*, *Augustin*, *Arnobius*, and others; to whom wee know very great credit is given in those Arguments that are pieced together against the vain Theologie of the Heathen. It is (I suppose) the same man that is called by *Plutarch* [d] *Tegeata*, when hee is ranked in the same form with *Diagoras*. But hee is by the same Autor called *Messenius*, when as beeing very obstinate in the [e] superstition of his Ancestors, hee brand's him as a great Patron of Impostures, and beeing induced (it seem's) by hatred against *Euhemerus*, hee conceit's there never were any such Nation, as the *Triphylians* or *Panchæans*, whereas *Panchæa* is an Island situate about *Arabia* in the more Southern Ocean, wherein *Euhemerus* placeth the Temple of *Jupiter Triphylius*, from whence that Storie touching the Dominion of the Sea was taken. Truly [f] *Diodorus* useth him also, as a grave Autor. A late Lawyer also make's use of that *Neptune* in *Homer*,

Ἤτοι ἐγὼν ἔλαχον πολιὴν ἅλα ναιέμεν αἰεὶ
Παλλομένων —————————

[d] *De Placitis Philosophorum, lib. 1. cap. 7.*

[e] *Plutarch. lib. de Iside & Osiride.*

[f] *Bibliothec. lib. 6. atque apud Eusebium de præparat. Evangelic. lib. 2. c. 4. Adde Gerard. Vossium de Græcis Historicis, lib. 1. cap. 11.*

H But

But of those things which were distributed by lot, I have taken the Sea for my share, that I might dwell therein for ever; so hee translate's it, that hee may with the more confidence take the whole matter related concerning the three Deities, as meant of *Noah's* three sons. His words are these; [g] *Id proculdubio ex partitione terrarum inter tres filios Noachi, ex quibus Japheto Insulæ obvenerunt, causam traxit*, **It may without question bee proved from that partition of Lands which was made betwixt** Noah's **three sons whereby the Isles of the Sea fell to** Japhet.

[g] *Jo. Gryphiander, de Insulis, cap.* 31. § 75.

So that in that fable hee would have [h] the Dominion not onely of the Isles, but also of the Sea, to bee assigned unto *Japhet*. But that which *Lactantius* saith touching the unlimited Command of *Pompey*, as parallel to the example of *Neptune's* Dominion, it is so to bee understood, that regard bee had also, as well of those that gave the Command to *Pompey*, as of him to whom the Command was given. As for instance, *the* Cilicians *had infested the Seas* (as Florus *saith*) *and having spoiled commerce, behaving themselvs like enemies of mankinde, they shut up the Sea with warr as it were a tempest.* Therefore the Romans, haveing a special eye to their provision of Corn, did by a decree of the Senate, procured by *Gabinius*, send out *Pompey* to [i] *free the Sea from Pirats.* And there was granted unto him by that decree, *a Command of the Sea which lie's within Hercules's pillars; and also of the continent about* 400 *furlongs from the Sea.* Hereupon, beeing master of a huge Navie, and having dispoſed divers Lievtenants through all parts of his Command, Hee so scoured the whole Sea from the straits of *Cadiz* to the *Cilician* shore

[h] *Genesis* 10.

[i] *Plutarch. in Pompeio, & Appianus Alexandrin. in Mithridaticis.*

ſhore, [k] *that none was able to stand before him either by Sea or Land.* Certainely *Pompey* had a Commiſsion onely as Admiral of the People of Rome, as, *Paterculus* ſaith; *Mark Antony* had the like about two years before. But that people which intruſted him, was Lord of this Sea, as the Romane Territorie, as well as of thoſe 400 furlongs of the Continent, which were joined alike with the Sea in the Grant of that Commiſsion, though no more lyable to Dominion then the Sea it ſelf. *Florus* ſaith alſo; [l] that *Tiberius Nero* (who was one of *Pompey'es* Lievtenants) *blockt up the Streights of Cadiz, at the first entrance of our Sea.* Hee beeing a Romane rightly call's it *our Sea* (as alſo [m] *Saluſt* doth more then once) becauſ it was ſo wholy ſubdued under the Romane power. And *Dio Caſsius*; *Hee ſcoured the whole Sea, which was under the Romane obedience.* And, ſaith *Mela*, of the Mediteranean Sea, *all that Sea, whenceſoëver it flow's, or whitherſoëver it ſpread's it ſelf, is called by one name, Our Sea.* So it is called likewiſe by others. [n] And *Mela* uſeth the name *our Sea* very often afterwards. But more of this hereafter, where wee treat more largely concerning the Dominion of the *Romanes* by Sea. Nor did *Pompey's* commiſſion extend onely againſt thoſe Pirats, as enemies of humane ſociety (after the ſame manner as wee ſee Commiſsions daily granted againſt Pirats, that rob and ſpoil in any Sea not yet poſſeſſed) but that very Sea-Territorie, which the *Cilicians* had invaded, was recover'd by Arms. From whence [o] *Manilius* break's forth in a Poëtical rapture,

[k] *Dio. lib.* 36.

[l] *lib.* 3. *cap.* 6.

[m] *In bello Jugurthino.*

[n] *Oroſius. lib.* 1. *cap.* 2.

[o] *Aſtronomic. lib.* 4.

Quis te Niliaco periturum littore, Magne,
Post victas Mithridatis Opes, pelagúsque receptum,
Crederet? ———

Who would have thought, great Pompey,
when for Rome
Thou Mithridates **forces had'st o'recom,**
And did'st from Pirats hands the Sea restore,
Thou shouldst have perish't on th' Egyptian
shore?

Therefore, *Lactantius* ought not so much to have resembled *Neptune* to *Pompey*, as to the People of Rome, in beeing Lord of the Sea. Other matters there are in the *fabulous time*, which beeing spoken of the Gods, may seem to shew, what opinion the Antients were of touching the right and custom of men in this particular. For, when they cloth their Gods with the persons of men, they commonly speak such things of them as belong unto men. From whence *Hesiod* sayeth, *Jupiter* granted unto *Hecate, that shee should possess part of the Sea, as well as the Land.* Hereunto also belong's that of *Oppianus*, concerning [p] *Amphitrite's* beeing made Queen of the Sea by *Neptune*,

[p] *Halieutic. lib.* 1.

—ἁλὸς βασιλείαν ἔθηκεν,
Hee constituted Her Queen of the Sea.

Also *Nonnus*, [q]

[q] *Dionysiac. lib.* 34.

—Βερόη κράτος ἔσχε θαλάσσης.

Beroë had the Empire or *Dominion of the Sea.*

Instances of this kinde are innumerable. And therefore thus much concerning the *fabulous time*.

The

The first Dominion of the Sea *among the* Greeks *in the* Historical age; *that is, the Dominion of King Minos, or the Cretan.*

CHAP. IX.

THe former part of the *Historical time*, or that which comprehend's Kingdoms and Commonweals, which expired som ages since, wee begin from the Empire of the *Cretans* at Sea. Afterwards wee trace a catalogue not onely of very many People of old Greece, and other nations famous heretofore in the East, of like Command and Dominion in the *Syrian*, *Egyptian*, *Pamphilian*, *Lydian*, and *Ægean* Seas, and the several changes thereof; but also wee shew, that the Dominion both of the *Romans* and *Carthaginians* in their adjoyning Seas, as the upper, the lower, the more Easterly Sea also, and others of that kinde in the West, hath been received into Custom, as a thing very usual, and agreeable to Law.

I.

MInos the son of *Lycastus*, said to bee the son of *Jupiter* King of [a] *Crete*, possessed the *Cretan* Sea on every side and a great part of the [b] *Ægean* as Lord and Sovereign. So sayeth *Thucydides*, [c] Τῆς Ἑλληνικῆς θαλάσσης ἐπὶ πλεῖστον ἐκράτησεν, *Minos held the greatest part of the Greek Sea as Lord thereof.* So truly, the word κρατεῖν is to bee construed both here and in the following instances. Nor is it any

[a] Now called *Candia*.
[b] Now called *the Levant*.
[c] *lib.* 1.

wise to bee imagined, that so to *have Command* (as κρατεῖν commonly signifie's) can bee otherwise meant, than very plainly thus, that any one who is Lord, or at least doth Act as Deputy or by permission of him who is Lord, may prescribe Rules and Laws to the number of other men's ships, and passage, Tolls or Tributes, throughout the several limits of the Sea, after the same manner as when hee withold's or permit's the use of his Land to husbandmen, according to his own will and pleasure. Which in this case is all one. Howsoëver, wee are not ignorant, that Θαλασσοκρατεῖν somtimes signifie's only [d] *to bee strong and powerfull in shipping.* In like manner, [e] *Diodorus Siculus,* [f] *Nicolaus Damascenus,* [g] *Strabo,* [h] *Cedrenus,* [i] *Suidas,* and others speak expresly. And *Phædra* likewise in *Seneca.*

> [k] *O magna vasti Creta Dominatrix freti,*
> *Cujus per omne littus innumeræ rates*
> *Tenuere pontum; quicquid Assyriâ tenus*
> *Tellure, Nereus pervium rostris secat.*

[d] *Is. Casaubon in Comment. ad Polyb. pag.*209.
[e] *Biblioth.* 4.
[f] *Apud Stobæum Eclog. cap.* 42.
[g] *Geograph.* 10.
[h] *Pag.* 11.
[i] *In Minoe.*
[k] *In Hippolyto act.* 1.

> O mighty Creet, thou Mistress of the main,
> Whose many ships have fil'd both Sea and shores;
> As farr as Nereus doth, to Ashur's Land,
> Plow out a passage with his stemm's and oars.

And the first Dominion of the Sea, that is, the first possession of that part of it which was not yet possessed but remained vacant (from whence this kind of Dominion doth arise) they attribute for the most part unto *Minos.* But there is an error touching this matter, in [l] *Jerom's* Traslation of the Chronicle

[l] *Euseb. Hieronym. Num.* 765.

nicle of *Eusebius*; nor is it to bee passed by, unless wee will carelesly neglect that which in plain terms may seem to oppose the most eminent Soveraigntie of the Sea among the Grecians. The Translation run's thus, *Minos Mare obtinuit & Cretensibus Leges dedit, ut Paradius memorat, quod Plato falsum esse convincit*, Minos **possessed the Sea, and gave Laws to the** Cretans, **as** Paradius **recordeth, which** Plato **prove's to bee fals.** What then? Doth *Plato* prove it to bee fals, that *Minos* gave Laws to the *Cretans*, and held the command of the Sea? or that either of Them is fals? The place is plainly fals and very much corrupted, both in the fained name of *Paradius*, an Autor, never heard of in any other place, as also in the very Translation of the Greek words of *Eusebius*. *Paradius*, I know not by what negligence (for I would not believ it of *Jerom* a pious and most learned man; but perhaps of som smatterer in learning, who presumed to enlarge those brief summarie discourses of his in that Chronicle) did arise even from *Para Dios*, that is, *ex Jove, from Jupiter*, which is found in the Greek words of *Eusebius*? For, there *Eusebius* saith, [m] *Minos* ἐθαλασσοκράτει *possessed the Sea, and gave Laws unto the* Cretans, *which hee brought* παρὰ Διὸς *from Jupiter, out of the Cave where hee had retired himself for nine years.* Touching those Laws received from *Minos*, which [n] expired not before *Crete* was subdued by *Cæcilius Metellus*, also concerning his Cave in Mount *Ida*, and the nine years, the matter appear's very plain out of *Homer*, *Plato*, *Porphyrie*, and others. But in the Greek of *Eusebius* it immediately follow's; ὅπερ ὁ Πλάτων ἐν τοῖς Νόμοις ἐλέγχει, which certainly here signifie's, *id quod Plato in Legibus adprobat* seu *confirmat*, **that which** Plato **in his Laws approve's**

[m] *Chronic. Canon.* 110. *in Thesauro Temporum.*

[n] *Eutropius lib.* 6.

prove's or **confirm's.** For, *Minos* his receiving of of such Laws is the very [o] foundation of *Plato's* Books *concerning Laws*. So little reason is there it should have been translated, *Quod Plato falsum esse convincit*, aut *quod Plato refellit*, **Which** Plato **prove's to bee fals, Which** Plato **disprove's:** whereas notwithstanding that eminent man *Joseph Scaliger*, using far less diligence here then was meet, or then hee hath been wont to do, would have the latter to bee added in that place. For, howsoever according to the meaning and more common usage of the word ἐλέγχειν, it may seem rightly translated; yet the matter it self, and the other signification of the word, doth manifestly prove our trans-action to bee true. But wee read the very same too, according to *Jerom's* Translation, as copied out, by *Marianus Scotus* [p], and *Florentius* of *Worcester*, save that in *Florentius* wee read *Plato falsum esse affirmat*, Plato **affirm's to bee fals.**

[o] *Plato de legibus, lib.* 1.

[p] *Anno Mundi*, 2944.

That after Minos of Crete, Seventeen Nations *of Renown in the East, succeeding each other, did for very many years even without Intermission, enjoy a Dominion of the* Syrian, Egyptian, Pamphylian, Lydian, *and* Ægean Sea, *no otherwise than of the Continent or Islands.*

Chap. X.

AFter the times of *Minos* the *Cretian*, wee finde in the Chronicles of *Eusebius* and *Africanus* no less then seventeen Eastern Nations, part of *Europe*, part of *Asia*, who for very many years so held the

the inner neighboring Sea, as Lords one after another, that, according to the *Intervenient Law of Nations*, it is most evident a private Dominion of the Sea took place among them all. For, changing by cours, and by length of time after long possession, through War, Victorie, or som other kinde of Cession, they every one shared their period of Domination, accomplishing among them all above five hundred and sixtie years without Intermission. But from the beginning of the Sea-Dominion of *Minos* or the *Cretan*, to the next which follow's in the aforesaid Chronicles, there fell out one hundred seventie five years. Those beginnings are placed about the time of the Judges of *Israël*. They which succeeded, are ranked after this manner.

II.

IN the second place the *Lydians* were Lords of the Sea. The Greek of *Eusebius* saith, [a] Λυδοὶ, οἱ καὶ Μαίονες, ἐθαλασσοκράτησαν ἔτη ϟϐ, *The Lydians, called also Mæonians, were Lords of the Sea* XCII *years.* The beginnings of this Dominion are reckoned about the time of *Æneas*. But as to what concern's the number of years, although it hath been the same both throughout the whole Historie of *Eusebius*, as also in his Chronicle; yet since the Empire of the *Pelasgi*, which next follow's, is severed by the space of CXX years or thereabout, perhaps it ought to bee amended, and ρκ or CXX to bee put in its place. Which that most excellent man *Isaac Casaubon* observed doubtingly, also in his Commentarie upon *Polybius*, where hee treat's very learnedly concerning those, who have had Dominion of the Sea in the East. Likewise,

[a] *Pag.* 31. & *pag.* 115. *num.* 940.

Marianus Scotus and *Florentius* the Monk do mention the Sea-Dominion of the *Lydians*, as also of the *Pelasgi*, without any number of years.

III.

THe *third* Lords of the Sea in this Catalogue, were the Pelasgi. Yet *Eusebius* saith, [b] Πελασγοὶ δεύτερον ἐθαλασσοκράτησαν ἔτη πε, *The Pelasgi in the second place possessed the Sea* LXXXV years. Which is referr'd to the times of *Solomon*, and those which follow. But the beginnings of the *Thracians*, who immediately succeed, require that they should bee reckoned here rather LV years. And indeed the *Pelasgi* were second Lords of the Sea, if (according to som) you either make the *Lydians* the first, or place them the first after *Minos* or the *Cretans*. For, so the *Pelasgi* are plainly the second, otherwise the third. Which also is to bee observed in the following particulars.

[b] *Chronic. lib.* 1. *p.* 34. & *num.* 960.

IV.

F*Ourthly*, the *Thracians* were Lords of the Sea, οθ, or LXXIX years (as wee finde in the [c] Greek of *Eusebius*;) which neverthelesse are not reckoned above nineteen in *Jerom's* Translation. But *Isaac Casaubon* is of Opinion, beeing induced thereto from the beginnings of the *Rhodians*, who were next Lords, that it ought to bee written πθ or LXXXIX. *Marianus* and *Florentius*, following the translation of *Eusebius*, accompt onely XIX years to the Dominion of the *Thracians*. And it is observed more then once by them, as well as in the aforesaid translation, that the *Thracians* were Lords of the Sea. This was in the time of King *Jeroboam*.

[c] *Ibid.* & *num.* 1014.

V.

V.

FIfthly, the *Rhodians* held the Sea, as Lords[d] XXIII years. And hereupon [e] *Strabo* commend's their industrie in matter of Navigation, who saith, *Rhodes was soveraign Ladie of the Sea a long time, and suppressed Pirates.* In the Latine of *Eusebius*, the *Rhodians* are said to have been the fourth in order that were Lords of the Sea. But in the Greek, that they were the fourth Lords of the Sea, and according to som, the fifth. Whence this difference arose, appears by that which hath been said about the *Pelasgi*. Of all the antient Lords of the Sea the *Rhodians* are most renowned; chiefly in this respect, becaus the Sea-Laws which were used and in full force and virtue in both the Empires, were borrowed from them, and put into the *Digests* by *Justinian*. Saith the Emperor *Antoninus* to *Eudæmon* of *Nicomedia*[f], *Lege Rhodiorum decidantur lites Nauticæ*, **Let Suits about Navigation bee decided according to the Law of the** Rhodians. And by the Testimonie of *Constantinus Harmenopulus* a [g] Judg of *Thessalonica*, they are the most antient of all Sea-Laws, that have not been lost. They were taken into use among the *Romanes* from the time of [h] *Tiberius*. Their beginnings are placed about the Reign of *Jehosaphat*: But the *Rhodians* are wholly omitted both by *Marianus* and *Florentius*.

d *Chron. Canon. pag.* 128. & *num.* 1100.
e *Lib.* 4.
f *Ad Legem Rhodiam ff. l.* 9. ἀξίωσις. *De Legibus hisce vide etiam Basilic. lib.* 53. *tit.* 8.
g *Prochir. Juris lib.* 2. *tit.* 11.
h *Jus Græco-Rom. Tom.* 2. *pag.* 265.

VI.

SIxthly, the *Phrygians* had dominion over the Sea XXV years; but (as it is in the [i] Greek of *Eusebius*) ac-

i *Chro. Canon. p.* 129. *num.* 1127.

according to others $\overline{XXVI}$. In the Latine wee finde onely $\overline{XXV}$, as alſo in *Marianus* and *Florentius*. But yet ſeeing, in the Greek of *Euſebius*, the *Phrygians* are (for the aforeſaid reaſon) counted the fifth Lords of the Sea, *Iſaac Caſaubon* (I think) well obſerve's that that number of ſix doth not denote the years, but the order of Dominion. This Lordſhip is reckoned in the time of *Lycurgus*.

VII.

SEventhly, the *Cyprians* poſſeſſed the Sea, as ſom ſay, $\overline{XXIII}$ years; according to others, $\overline{XXXI}$. For, this is found in ſom [k] Editions of *Jerom's* Tranſlation of *Euſebius*. That in the Chronicles of *Marianus* and *Florentius*, compiled for the moſt part out of *Euſebius* and *Jerom*. But neither in the Greek Copies of *Euſebius*, which are extant, nor in the Tranſlation ſet forth by *Joſeph Scaliger*, is any mention made of the *Cyprians*: nor truly in the accompt of *Iſaac Caſaubon*. This was in the time of *Joas*.

[k] *Edit. Baſil.* 1549.

VIII.

EIghtly, the *Phænicians* poſſeſſed the Sea. So *Euſebius*, *Marianus*, and *Florentius*; ſave that they make them the *ſeventh* by reaſon of that different manner of accompt, which hath been ſhewn you. Touching their Dominion the holy Scriptures themſelvs ſpeak plainly enough; which alſo wee have noted before in our diſcourſ concerning the Divine Law. The memorial of this Dominion is placed about the Reign of *Uzziah* King of *Judah*. Alſo this Nation of the *Phænicians* became renowned for their skill in Navigation,

Navigation, as wee are instructed by *Pliny*, and others And heretofore (perhaps) that ought to bee referr'd, which is delivered by *Antipater Tarsensis* and *Manaseas*, two antient writers, touching *Gatis* Queen of the *Syrians* (who themselvs also were *Phenicians*) whom they will have therefore to bee called *Atergatis*, becaus (*as Antipater* saith) shee set forth an Edict, [1] *that none should eat fish without Gatis*; or, as *Manaseas* saith, *that no man should eat fish without her licence and permission, but that everie one should bring the fish they caught unto her*. That which they hold concerning the Original of the word appear's sufficiently ridiculous, whil'st they derive a *Syrian* or *Phenician* name from the Greek fountain. But the very thing which (I suppose) they would have, is this; That *Atergatis* was Queen or Sovereign Lady, not only of *Syria* or *Phenicia* (which is the Sea-cost of *Syria*) but also of the Sea lying before it, in such a manner that it was not lawful for any one to fish freely therein, at least not to enjoy the benefit of fishing, without her consent. From whence it was a Custom to consecrate fishes of Gold and Silver to her, after shee was placed among rhe Deities.

1 Ἄτερ Γάτιδος μηδένα ἰχθὺν ἐσθίειν, ἀλλὰ πρὸς αὐτὴν ἀναφέρειν. *Apud Athenæum, dipnosoph.* 8.

IX.

N*Inthly*, after the *Phenicians*, the *Ægyptians* [m] possessed the Sea under their Kings *Psamnitis*, and *Bocchoris* who lived immediately before the beginnings of the Olympiads. Mention is made of them also in *Marianus* and *Florentius*.

m *Euseb. Num.* 1230.

X.

IN the *tenth* place, the *Milesians* were Lords of the Sea. The books of *Eusebius* do not shew the number of years. But both in *Marianus* and *Florentius* wee read, that the *Milesians* possessed the Sea XVIII years. *Stephanus*, concerning Cities, saith, *Naucratis, a Citie of Ægypt, was built* [n] *by the* Milesians *then possessing the Sea.* And *Eusebius* also mention's the building of that Citie, together with their Dominion at Sea, about the time of *Romulus*. In like manner they built *Sinope*, seated by the *Euxine* Sea, which (as *Strabo* saith) [o] commanded that Sea which flow's within the *Cyanean* Islands.

[n] ἀπὸ Μιλησίων τότε θαλαττοκρατούντων.

[o] *lib.* 12.

XI.

ELeventhly the [p] *Carians* possessed the Sea. Their Sea-Dominion is remembred by [q] *Diodorus Siculus*. It was about the time of *Hezekiah*.

[p] *Euseb. Num.* 1281.

[q] *Biblioth.* 5.

XII.

TWelfthly, and next to the *Carians*, the *Lesbians* held the Sea in possession. [r] LXIX years. So it is in the Latine of *Eusebius*. But *Marianus* rendreth it LVIII years.

[r] *Euseb. Num.* 1341.

XIII.

THirtenthly, the *Phoceans* possessed the Sea, about the Captivitie of *Babylon*. Their Dominion lasted XLIV years. So saith the Greek of *Eusebius*

Eusebius, [s] Φωκαεῖς ἐθαλασσοκράτησαν ἔτη μδ' *the Phoceans were Lords of the Sea* XLIV *years.* Before which words the number ιβ' or of twelve is prefixed, whereby it is signified, that they were the twelfth after the *Lydians*, and the thirteenth from *Minos*.

[s] *Chron. lib.* 1. *pag.* 42.

XIV.

FOurteenthly, the *Corinthians* were Lords of the Sea. I do not finde, that they were thus ranked. But it appear's clearly out of [t] *Thucydides*, that they were very potent at Sea, and did so repress Piracies by their strength in shipping, that they gained themselvs a very large command by Sea, as well as by land. The same autor also mention's their extraordinary industry in restoring the affairs of Navigation. Nor doth time gainsay, but that wee may well place them here, as also the *Iönians* next. But wee do not as yet finde, that these fourteenth and the fifteenth are received by writers into the Catalogue of those, who have thus held the Sea in possession.

[t] *lib.* 1.

XV.

FIfteenthly the *Iönians* were neighboring Lords of the Sea. Concerning them *Thucydides* saith, [u] *A good while after, (to wit after the power of the Corinthians by Sea) the power and interest of Navigation was in the hand of the Iönians, in the time of* Cyrus *the first King of the* Persians, *and of his son* Cambyses; *And* [x] *contending also with* Cyrus, *they injoyed their own Sea for som time.* where the old Scholiast add's by way of observation, γείτονος, οὐ γὰρ πάσης, *the neighboring Sea; but not all.*

[u] *Lib. citato.*

[x] Κύρῳ πολεμοῦντες ἐκράτησάν τινα χρόνον.

XVI.

XVI.

SIxteenthly, the *Naxians*, were Lords of the Sea. *Eusebius* saith, [w] *In the fifteenth place the* Naxians *possessed the Sea, ten years.* About the time of *Cambyses.* It is spoken of the *Naxians*, named from the Island *Naxos*, which is one of the *Cyclades*, or Isles in the *Archipelago.*

[w] *Chronic. lib.* 1. *pag.* 43.

XVII.

SEventeenthly, the *Eretrians* succeeded into this Sea-Dominion. *Eusebius,* when hee speak's of the *Naxians*, saith, ϰ μετ' αὐτοὺς &c. *And after them the* Eretrians, *in the seventeenth place, held it* VII *years.* *Eretria* was heretofore a famous and wealthy Citie in the Island of *Eubœa.*

XVIII.

And lastly, the last or *eighteenth* Lords of the Sea in this Catalogue were the People of *Ægina.* The Latine of *Eusebius* saith, [y] *the People of Ægina possessed the sea* XX *years, even until Xerxes his passage;* which is noted in the fourth year of the sixtie seventh Olympiad. But *Xerxes* made his passage in the seventy fift Olympiad, aud in first year thereof. Therefore there passed XXVIII years between. But truly *Joseph Scaliger* observe's here, from this carelesness in counting of years, that those are meer triflings which are found in the Latine. *And* hee saith, *they are so discovered by the Greek*, wherein wee read onely Αἰγινῆται ἐθαλασσοκράτησαν ἔτη ι. *The People*

[y] *Num.* 1058.

people of Ægina held possession of the Sea X *years.* Which truly wee finde as well in the former Chronicle of *Eusebius*, as in his Canon : nor is it otherwise placed then in the *Latine*. Also [z] *Strabo* and [a] *Ælianus* make mention of their Sea-Dominion.

[z] *Lib.* 8.
[a] *Var.Histor. lib.* 12.

Touching the Sea-Dominion *of the* Lacedemonians *and* Athenians. *Moreover also, that it was acknowledged not onely by the* Greeks, *but also by the* Persians, *in a Treatie of Peace.*

CHAP. XI.

NOr are those Particulars which are to bee applied hither out of the East, found onely in the Customs and Sea-Dominion of so many famous Nations thus continued one after another (the years of whose Empires have usually been reckoned from their subduing the Sea;) but in the Customs of others also, who truly were more famous, though they bee not registered any where in such a kinde of Catalogue. It is written of *Polycrates*, that renowned King of the *Samians*, who about the beginning of the *Persian* Empire, vanquished the *Lesbians* and *Milesians* in a Sea fight, that hee so earnestly aspired after a Soveraigntie of the Sea, that it was manifestly acknowledged to bee capable of Dominion. *Herodotus* saith, *Polycrates is the first of those that wee have known, who had an intent to acquire the Dominion of the Sea unto himself, except* Minos *of* Crete, *and if there were any other that enjoyed the Sea before him.* Hee speak's,

I suppose, of Kings. For, those *Greeks* in whose hands the Dominion of the Sea was (as wee before have shewn you) so often changed, were commonly govern'd either by a Popular, or an Aristocratical form of Government. Nor could *Herodotus*, I think, bee more ignorant of their Dominion, then of King *Minos*. For, hee lived after the fore-mentioned Dominion of the People of *Ægina* was ended, or about the *eightieth Olympiad*. Therefore, either hee spake onely of Kings, or was extremely mistaken.

About the *eightieth Olympiad*, and the times following unto the *Grecian* Monarchie, those most renowned People of *Greece*, not onely the *Athenians*, but the *Lacedemonians* also, did somtime enjoy a Dominion of the Sea flowing about them. *Demosthenes* saith of the *Lacedemonians*, [a] *They had Dominion over the Sea and the whole Land.* Others also have testified as much. Concerning the *Athenians* either the same man, or *Hegisippus*, in that Oration touching * *Halonesos*, making mention of *Philip* K. of *Macedon's* affecting a Dominion of the Sea, speak's thus, *De Prædonibus æquum esse aït Philippus &c?* **Concerning Pirates,** Philip **saith, it is meet, that both hee and you should by common consent, drive away such as offend upon the Sea, requiring no other thing than this, that hee may bee put in command over the Sea by you, and that you would confess your selvs unable to defend and guard the Sea** (which hitherto hath been yours) **without the help of** Philip. They did also by League impose a certain size and proportion upon all sorts of Bottoms, both for qualitie and quantitie, which their neighbors should have leav to use. It is an Article of the Treatie made with the

[a] *Philippic.3. vide etiam Themistoclem. Epist. 14.*

* An Island in the *Ægean* Sea, now called the *Levant*.

the *Lacedemonians*; [b] *That the* Lacedemonians *and their Confederates might indeed use the Sea, but not sail in a long ship, but any other kinde of vessel; which beeing rowed with Oares should not exceed the freight of five hundred Talents*: That is to say, not in a vessel with one range of Oares, much less in one of two or three ranges, or others that were men of War, but in vessels to bee rowed nevertheless with certain pairs of Oars, beeing vessels onely for carriage, and those small enough. other passages of this kinde there are in *Thucydides*. Hereunto belong's that of *Æmilius Probus*, touching *Timotheus* a famous Captain of the *Athenians*. *Hee brought Corcyra* (saith hee) *under the command of the* Athenians, *and made the people of* Epirus, *the* Athamanians, Chaonians, *and all those Nations which border upon that Sea, to bee their Confederates. Whereupon the* Lacedemonians *desisted from long contentions,* and of their own accord *yielded a pre-eminence of Sea-Dominion to the* Athenians, *and setled Peace upon this condition, that the* Athenians *should bee chief Commanders at Sea. Which Victorie was received with so much joy among the* Athenians, *that Altars were then erected unto* PEACE, *and a Temple appointed for that Goddess.* And *Demosthenes* concerning [c] *Archebius* and *Heraclides*, *who when they had deliver'd* Byzantium *to* Thrasybulus, *they made you* (saith hee, speaking to the men of *Athens*) *Lords of the Sea, so that yee might sell the Tenth*; To wit, the Customs *of the Merchandize of such Merchants as should trade in the Hellespont*; which is noted there by *Ulpianus* the Rhetorician. From hence also, *Cicero* would have that barbarous Decree of this Nation to have had its rise concerning the people of *Ægina* somtimes Lords of the Sea. [d] *The* Athenians, saith hee, *dealt very cruelly, who passed a Decree, that the* Æginetans, *who were powerful*

[b] *Thucydides, lib.* 4.

[c] *Orat. advers. Leptinem.*

[d] *De Officiis lib.* 3. *sic Valerius Maximus, l.* 9. *c.* 2.

ful in Shipping, should have their thumbs cut off; to the end, that they might not grow strong in Shipping hereafter, or by force enter upon that Sea then possessed by the *Athenians*: For, in som Books wee read, *quia classe valebant*, **becaus they grew strong in Shipping**, as it is noted by *Carolus Langius*. Though it bee conceived by [e] *Ælian* the Decree was therefore made, that they might not bee able to use a Spear, and yet to handle Oars. This crueltie is detested by Writers. But it is evident, that by this means they were deprived of a free use of the Sea. Nor was such a Dominion of the Sea approved onely among those people of *Greece*; but allso by the *Persians*, who at that time ruled the East, as appear's in that notable League made after the Victory at *Eurymedon*. For truly, *Cimon* Captain of the *Athenians* having vanquish't the *Naval* Forces of *Artaxerxes Longimanus* King of the *Persians* (which had infested the Sea about the *Chelidonian* Islands) the King's courage was so broken, *That* (as [f] *Plutarch* saith, and [g] *Aristides* almost the same) *hee concluded that notable Peace, upon such terms that hee was to keep the distance of an hors-race from the Greek Sea, and that hee should not have a Ship built long or beaked, within the* Cyanean *and* Chelidonian *Islands*. So that the King was to keep out of every part of the *Ægean*, *Rhodian*, *Carpathian*, and *Lydian* Sea, and that which bend's thence into the West towards *Athens*: Becaus the *Athenians* were clearly Lords thereof. For, the *Greek*, which of old was called the *Carick* * Sea, spread its self to a very great latitude, from *Caria* or the shore of the Western part of *Asia*. Moreover, subjection was imposed upon the Sea of *Pamphylia* and *Lycia*, as also the *Euxin* Sea, that no Ship of the King's which should bee

e *Var. Hist. lib.* 2. *cap.* 9.

f *Ex Cratero in Cimonis vitâ.*

g *In Panathenaïcâ.*

* *Scholiast. lib.* 1. Adde *Dionys. Halicarnass. lib.* 1.

bee long-built or beaked (that is to say, a man of War) could according to the League bee admitted, either in this beyond the *Cyanean*, or in that beyond the *Chelidonian* Islands. This certainly was the very meaning of [h] *Isocrates*, when making mention of the *Athenian* Dominion, hee saith, *it was not lawful to sail in long Ships or Gallies beyond Phaselis.* For, *Phaselis*, a Town either of *Lycia* or *Pamphylia*, is situate in the same direct line with the *Chelidonian* Islands. But *Suidas* tell's us, that *Castor Rhodius*, an antient Writer, had compiled an Historie περὶ τῶν θαλασσοκρατησάντων *of such as have enjoied a Dominion of the Sea* [i] Learned men are upon very good ground of Opinion, that those Lords of the Sea, reckoned up in the former Chapter, were taken by *Julius Africanus* and *Eusebius* out of that Autor. It is almost out of question too, that hee added the Soveraigntie both of the *Athenians* and *Lacedemonians* by Sea. *Castor* lived about the time of *Augustus Cæsar*. That work of his is utterly lost.

[h] *In Panathenaïco.*

[i] *Jos. Scaliger in Eusebianis ad num.* 840. *Gerard. Vossius de Historicis Græcis, lib.* 1. *cap.* 25. *Alii.*

Other Testimonies, which are found scatter'd up and down, touching the Dominion of the Sea, in the Customs *of the* Eastern Nations.

CHAP. XII.

MOreover, very many things are found scatter'd up and down in those Writings that concern the Customs of the Eastern Nations, which clearly prove it to have been a most received opinion touching private Dominion of the Sea. *Antiochus*

Epiphanes, King of *Syria* saith, speaking of the *Syrian* Sea, [a] *Are not both the Sea and the Land mine?* And *Xerxes* that *Persian* King, when in a ridiculous humor hee scourged the *Hellespont*, stigmatized it, and cast a pair of Fetters into the Waters, said, [b] Δεσπότης τοὶ δίκην ἐπιτιθεῖ τήνδε, *Thy Lord inflict's this punishment upon thee.* Also, whereas *Agatharcides*, following the storie of *Boxus* the *Persian*, write's that the red or *Erythrean* Sea was so called from King *Erythras* or *Erythrus* (that is, from *Edom* bordering thereupon who also was [c] *Esau*, and signifieth the same that *Erythrus* or *Rubrus* doth in Ebrew) hee add's also this Exposition doth imply [d] κυριεύσαντα τῆς θαλάττης ἄνδρα, *A man enjoying the Dominion of that Sea.* And truly wee read in [e] *Philostratus*, that there was an old contract touching the Red-Sea, *which King* Erythras *had contracted, when hee had Dominion over that Sea*, that no *Egyptian* ought to enter that Sea in a long Ship, but to imploy there onely one of Burthen. And [f] *Quintus Curtius* saith of the Citie of *Tyre*, that *beeing built by* Agenor, *shee made not onely the neighboring Sea, but what Sea soever her Ships sail into, to bee of her Dominion.* From whence also *Tyria Maria, Tyrian Sea's*, became a [g] Proverb, to signifie a Sea so possessed, that free passage could not bee had, without leav of the Lord or Possessor. There was also a very antient Custom used in the East, that when great Kings having designs to bring any Nations under their power, commanded the pledges of Empire and Dominion to bee deliver'd to them, they were wont to demand *Water and Earth* together. That is to say, there quired them φέρειν γῆν καὶ ὕδωρ, *to bring earth and water*, and ἑτοιμάζειν γῆν καὶ ὕδωρ, *to prepare Earth and Water.* They conceived that their Dominion of the Sea as well as the Land, was signified by such a

kinde

[a] *Joseph Ben. Gorion. lib.* 3. *cap.* 12. Edit. Munster. Ebræo-lat. in fol.

[b] *Herodotus, lib.* 7.

[c] *Jos. Scaliger ad Festum, verb. Ægyptinos, & Nicol. Fuller, Miscellan. lib.* 4. *cap.* 20.

[d] *apud Photium, cod.* 250.

[e] *De vita Apollonii, lib.* 3. *cap.* 11.

[f] *De Rebus Alexandri, lib.* 4.

[g] *Afranius apud Festum, verb.* Tyria Maria.

kinde of pledg or token. Thus [h] *Darius* demanded Earth and Water from *Indathyrsus* King of the *Scythians*; Thus [i] *Xerxes* from the *Lacedemonians*; and thus both of them from the People of *Coos*, which is witnessed by the *Coans* themselvs in a publick Decree or Epistle, in answer to *Artaxerxes* his most imperious demand, that *Hippocrates* should bee rendred up to him; wherein the *Coans* slighting the threats of that great King, decreed that what hazzard soëver they might seem to run, *Hippocrates* should by no means bee rendred. They added also to that Decree [k] Καὶ γὰρ Δαρείου καὶ Ξέρξου ἀπὸ πατέρων &c. *How that when his Predecessors,* Darius *and* Xerxes, *had by their Letters demanded Earth and Water, the people of* Coos *did in no wise yield it; forasmuch as they were satisfied, that those who had sent unto them were mortal, as well as other men.* And in the Greek Copies of the Historie of *Judith*, *Nabuchodonosor* beeing about to denounce War against the neighbor-Nations, saith expresly, the form of submission which hee expected was, [l] *that they should provide for him Earth and Water.* Unless they conceiv themselvs to bee Lords of the Waters as well as the Land, I do not well see wherefore they should demand Earth and Water as tokens of universal Dominion. Moreover also, *Achmes Ben Seirim*, an *Arabian*, writing of the Sea saith, that according to the Doctrine of the *Indians*, *Persians*, and *Egyptians*, in expounding of dreams, [m] *If any one* (in a dream) *seem to himself to bee made Lord of the sea, hee shall bee heir of the whole Kingdom, and shall reign.* Add hereunto that Oracle of *Delos* concerning the Sea-Dominion of the *Athenians*. The men of *Athens* offering sacrifice in *Delos*, a Boy that drew water to wash their hands, poured Fish out of the pot together with the water. Hereupon this Oracle

h *Herodotus lib.* 4.

i *Polybius, lib.* 9.

k *Hippocrates, Epistol.* 9.

l *Judith, cap.* 2. 7. *Græcè.*

m *Cap.* 178.

Oracle was delivered by the Priests, *ὡς κυριεύσουσι τῆς θαλάττης*, *That they should becom Lords of the Sea.* The Autor is one *Semus* an antient Writer in [n] *Athenæus*; where *Phylarchus* also relate's, how that when *Patroclus*, a Captain of *Ptolomie*, the son of *Lagus*, had sent fish and fresh figs together unto King *Antigonus*, and those that stood by were in doubt what was meant by that present, *Antigonus*, said hee, himself very well apprehended what might bee the meaning of *Patroclus*: For, saith hee, either *Patroclus* mean's, [o] *That wee must get the Soveraignty or Dominion of the Sea, or els gnaw figs.* Or that hee must seem slothful and effeminate, or becom Lord of the Sea. Therefore hee made no doubt touching private Dominion of the Sea. And there also the Glutton in *Antiphanes* the Comedian saith, it is neither profitable for life, nor to bee endured, *That som of you should claim the Sea as peculiar to themselvs, and spend much monie upon it, but no victual for Navigation, not so much as a bit.* Add also that of *Theocritus*, touching the Dominion of *Ptolomeus Philadelphus* King of Egypt, over the Sea as well as the Land,

[n] *Dipnosoph. lib.* 8.

[o] ὁ θαλαττοκρατεῖν ἡμᾶς ἢ τῶν σύκων τρώγειν

[p] Πολλᾶς δὲ κρατέει γαίας πολλᾶς δὲ θαλάσσας
Hee is Lord of much Land, and also of much Sea.

[p] *Jellio.* 17.

And a little after, hee speak's of the *Pamphilian, Lycian*, and the inner part of the remaining Sea, *that the whole Sea, and Land, aud Rivers were subject to King* Ptolomie. Also, [q] *Philo Judeus* saith, let not Princes glory in that they have conquer'd many Nations, *or that they have brought all the rivers and Seas so exceeding vast both in Number and magnitude under their power.* Moreover, though *Isocrates* in his Oration con-

[q] *Lib. de plantatione Noë.*

concerning Peace seem's to hint, that the Sea-Dominion and Soveraignty, which the *Athenians* endevored to maintain, brought many mischiefs upon them; and also that it somtimes occasioned them to use Tyrannie against the Neighbor-Cities of Greece; yet hee dispute's it as a thing that may com into examination, under the account of profitable and unprofitable, and by accident, of unjust; but hee doth not in anie wise endeavor to prove it unjust from the nature of the thing it self. Yea, in another place hee sufficiently commend's that Dominion, though not all things in preserving it. And the same [r] Autor saith expresly, of both Cities, the *Lacedemonian and Athenian; It hapned that both Cities did enjoy a Command of the Sea; which when either of them held, they had most of the other Cities obedient thereto.* Wee read also a dispute in *Aristotle*, [s] *concerning a Communion or common enjoyment of the Sea*; to wit whether it may bee convenient or not for a well order'd City? whether it were better it should remain common to all men, so that no man might in any wise bee denied passage, traffick, merchandise, and fishing; Or that the use of it may bee so restrained, that it might bee received into the Dominion of any Citie, so as to exclude forreiners? Hee dispute's this point whether it bee profitable, or unprofitable; but question's it not at all as unjust; having been abundantly instructed out of the Customs of the Nations round about, touching a propriety of the Sea as well as the Land. Also his Scholar *Alexander* the Macedonian, beeing victorious in the East, prepared for an expedition against Europe, *that Hee, might becom Lord of the whole Land and Sea*, as saith the Emperor [t] *Julian.* And truly among the People of *Greece*, especialy such as border'd

[r] *In Panathenaïco.*

[s] περὶ τῆς πρὸς τὴν θάλατταν κοινωνίας.

[t] *In Oratione 3. seu Eusebiæ Encomio.*

upon the Sea, and others of that nature in the East, to hold supreme power and Soveraigntie above others, and to enjoy a Soveraigntie of the Sea, were accounted almost one and the same thing. Nor did they conceiv that could bee obteined without this. From whence arose that Council of *Themistocles*, which *Pompey* the great also followed at *Rome*; [u] *Qui mare teneat, eum necesse esse rerum potiri &c.* **Hee which can possess the Sea, must need's have Command of all.** So also saith *Isaac* [w] *Casaubon* upon *Polybius*; *To have Dominion of the Sea (which is expressed by the Greeks* Θαλασσοκρατεῖν*) is wholly, and ever hath been a great strengthning, and as it were a pledg of extraordinarie power. Therefore, the old writers of Chronicles among the* Grecians*, seeing before the institution of the* Olympiads, *there was no Sovereign power of any People of* Greece *in beeing, upon whose actions a knowledg of times might bee grounded, therefore among the other times that they made use of for the computing of times, they omitted not that particular, but carefully kept an accompt of those* People, *who had once enjoyed a* Dominion *of the* Sea, *and they exactly observed in their Chronologies all such changes as hapned in that matter.* But you have more then enough touching those Customs that have been received in the *East*, about the Dominion of the Sea.

[u] Cicero ad Atticum, lib. 10. Epist. 7. Plutarch. in Themistocle.

[w] Comm. in Polybinm pag. 199.

Of the Spinetans, Tuscans, Carthaginians, *and other Lords of the Sea in the* West.

Chap. XIII.

NOr is such a Dominion of the Sea, as I have mentioned, less clear and evident, in the antient Customs of the Western Nations. The *spinetans*, so called from the City *Spina* situate near the entrance

entrance of the River *Po*, were a long time Lords of the upper or *Adriatick* Sea, beeing wont to send very liberal Tenths out of their profits by Sea, to *Apollo* at *Delphos*. So saith [a] *Strabo* and [b] *Dionysius Halicarnass*. Who write expresly in like manner of the *Tuscans*, that they were Θαλαττοκράτορας, in command of the lower Sea, or that which washes the South-Coast of *Italy*; that is in plain terms that they were *Lords of the Sea*. And [c] *Diodorus Siculus* saith, the *Tyrrheni* (or *Tuscans*) *possessing the Sea a long time as Lords, called it by their own Name*. But afterwards, the [d] *Carthaginians* became Lords of almost the whole *Mediterranean*, which is more westward, to wit of the *Sicilian* and *African* Sea; who beeing overcom in battel, *Agathocles* King of *Sicily* enjoied the same power for som time; from whom the People of *Africa* revolting, that Dominion was soon restored to the *Carthaginians*. These things were don in CXVIII *Olympiad*. Then, for 40. years or thereabout, the *Carthaginians* continued Lords of the Sea, and gave Laws thereto; that is to say, until the fist *Punick* War, whch began in the last year of the CXXVIII *Olympiad*. So also *Polybius*, [e] *The* Carthaginians *enjoying the Dominion of the Sea without controversie* And a little after; *The* Carthaginians *enjoyed the command of the Sea without all controversie, as received from their Ancestors*. But the *Carthaginians* enjoyed the same, even long before the time of *Agathocles*, as it sufficiently appear's by that League of all that was made first of all betwixt them and the *Romanes*, at the beginning of their *Consuls*, or about the sixtie eight *Olympiad*. One Article thereof is in *Polybius*, who onely mention's it to this effect; *That neither the Romanes nor their Confederates were to sail beyond the * fair Promontorie, unless driven by Tempest, or forced by enemies*. That was a Promontory

[a] *Lib.* 5.

[b] *De Orig. Rom. lib.* 1.

[c] *Biblioth. l.* 5. πολλοὺς χρόνους θαλαττοκρατήσαντες.

[d] *Diodorus Sic. lib.* 20.

[e] *Histor. lib.* 1. & 3. Adde *Appian. Alexandrin. sub. Initiis Belli Punici.*

* *A Promontorie of* Africa, *near* Car-

promontorie of *Africa*; and the *Carthaginians* were so far Lords of the Sea, that they would not permit the *Romanes* or their Confederates, to sail beyond that Promontorie: which the *Romanes* themselvs acknowledged to bee just in the *League* that they made. But in the second *League* or Treatie of Peace betwixt these famous Nations in the West, it was farther provided; that no *Romane* should touch either upon *Africa* or *Sardinia*, unless it were either to take in Provision or repair their Ships, as you may see also in *Polybius*: so that the use of the Sea was taken away, or restrained. And hereunto belong's that of [f] *Pompeius Festus*, touching the *Pœni* or *Carthaginians*; *The* Carthaginians *having their original from* Tyre, *were so powerful at Sea, that Navigation was hazardous to all men*; For, the *Carthaginians* were the chief of the *Pœni*. Moreover, [g] *Julius Cæsar* writing of the *Veneti* a people of *Western Gallia* about the entrance of the River *Loire*, and of old very industrious in Sea-affairs above their Neighbors, saith, *That in a great and open current of the Sea, having but a few Ports lying here and there which are in their possession, they make almost all men pay Custom, that were wont to use the same Sea.* Tribute was paid to them as Lords, for the use of the neighboring Sea. Nor must wee pass by that here, which [h] *Paulus Warnfredus* relate's of *Autharis* King of the *Lombards*. There was a Pillar placed within the very waters of the Sea, which wash the City of *Rhegium*. *To that Pillar* (saith Warnfredus) *King* Autharis *came on hors-back, and touched it with the point of his spear, saying, even in this place shall bee the bounds of Lombardie.* But wee must treat next concerning the people of *Rome*, the most noble precedent of all both for Law and Custom.

[f] *In verbo*, Tyria Maria.

[g] *De Bello Gallico, lib. 3. cap. 8.*

[h] *De Gestis Longobardorum lib. 3. cap. 33. quod memorat etiam Sigonius de regno Italiæ, lib. 1.*

The Sea-Dominion of the people of Rome, *and of such as followed their Customs in the* Eastern Empire.

CHAP. XIV.

BEfore the first *Punick* War, the *Carthaginians* and the *Romanes*, both strove with equal Forces and affections for the Empire of the World; save that they of *Carthage* seemed the more potent, by reason of that Dominion of the Sea by them held so many years. But then *C. Duillius* beeing made General of a Navie of CLX Ships, riding at Anchor, and arm'd within sixtie daies after the wood had been cut, almost undid *Carthage* in that Sea, and wholly reduced it under the *Romane* power. And *Florus* saith, [a] *when the Sea and the Isles were taken away, it shamed that noble Nation to pay Tribute, who were wont to command it.* So, the *Carthaginians* beeing deprived of this kinde of Dominion, the *Romanes* got it by the Law of Arms and Victorie; so great and so constant honor beeing, for this caus, paid to so renowed a *General*, that Minstrels were ever sent to make him musick after Supper, and a Torch was carried before him. Moreover, both the *Phœnicians* and *Cilicians* had Dominion over the *Romanes* Sea, as appear's by the League made betwixt them and *Antiochus* King of *Syria*; wherein it was thus provided: *That* Antiochus *should surrender his long ships and their warlike furniture; and not have more than ten nimble Gallies (none of which should bee rowed with above thirty Oares) nor so much as a Galley with one range of Oares when hee shall have any oc-*

[a] *Lib.* 2. *cap.* 6.

casion to make a War.Nor should hee sail on this side the Promontories of Calycadnus *or* Sarpedon; *unless it bee a ship imploied to convey money, pay, or Embassadors, or Hostages.*So saith [b] *Livie.* But wee read in Polybius, *Nullam habeto triginta remis actam navem*, **Let him have no Ship rowed with 30 Oares.** In like manner *Hannibal*, in a speech made unto *Scipio*, saith thus, [c] *Wee deny not, but that all those places are yours for which the War hath been undertaken,* Sicilie, Sardinia, Spain, *and all the Isles contained in the whole Sea, betwixt* Africa *and* Italie. *And may wee* Carthaginians, *that are confined within the shores of* Africa, *see you (when it so pleaseth the Gods) ruling foreign Dominions by Land and* Sea. And a little after, the Peace beeing agreed, five hundred Ships of the *Carthaginians* that were rowed with Oars, were by them seized and burnt. To wit, that they might not use the Sea, which was then to bee in the Dominion of others. Afterwards also, the Senate of *Carthage* was chastised, [d] *becaus they had an Army, and materials for shipping, (contrary to the League: And it was decreed, that War should bee proclaimed against them, becaus they had caused their Armie to march beyond their bounds, &c.* Also, *Plinie* saith expresly concerning *Pompey* the great; [e] *That hee freed the sea-Coast from Pirates, and restored the Dominion to the people of* Rome. Moreover, as touching the vast Sea-dominion of the *Romane* people, *Dionysius Halicarnass* saith; [f] Rome *is Ladie of the whole sea, not onely of that which lie's within* Hercules's *Pillars; but also of the Ocean it self so far as it is navigable.* This is indeed an *Hyperbole*; But in the mean time a clear Testimonie of a very large Sea-dominion. As also that of [g] *Appianus Alexandrinus*; *The* Romanes (saith hee) *hold the Dominion of the whole Mediterranean* Sea. Other instances there are of the same nature. But truly, that expression of a very [h] eminent

[b] *Decad. lib.*8.

[c] *Livie, lib.* 30.

[d] *Epit. Liv. lib* 48.& 49.

[e] *Nat.Histor. lib.*7.*cap.*26.

[f] *Orig.Rom. lib.*1.

[g] *In præfatione.*

eminent man is not to bee admitted, who saith of examples of that kinde, *that they do not prove a possession of the Sea or of a Right of Navigation. For as particular private men, so also people and Nations may by Leagues and Agreements, not onely quit that Right which peculiarly belong's to them, but that also which they hold in common with all men, in favor and for the benefit of any one whom it concern's.* And for this hee referr's himself unto *Ulpian*, who will have that Cessation of fishing for *Tunies* in the Sea (of which more * hereafter) to bee derived from the Autoritie of som stipulation or Covenant, not from any vassalage imposed upon the Sea. Surely by such a kinde of distinction, whereof *Ulpian* is indeed the Autor, the same may bee said either of Dominion or vassalage (as wee call it) of every kinde. If to occupie and enjoy in a private manner, by Right to hinder, and forbid others, bee not Dominion, it is nothing. Moreover *Cassandra* in *Lycophron*, prophesied that the people in *Rome* should have such a Dominion, where shee attribute's to them

[h] *Hugo Grotius, de Jure Belli & pacis lib. 2. cap. 3. §. 15. Possunt enim ut singuli, ita & populi, &c.*

* *In capite proximo.*

Γῆς ϗ θαλάσσης σκῆπτρα ϗ μοναρχίαν.

The Scepter and Monarchie both of Land and Sea.

Hereunto belong those things above mentioned, touching the Command of *Pompey* held by Commission from the people of *Rome*, as also those other which wee meet with now and then among writers, concerning the Sea-Dominion of the *Romans*. *Suetonius* saith of *Augustus Cesar*, [i] *Hee placed one Navie at* Mesinum *and another at* Ravenna, *to guard the upper and lower Sea.* But [k] *Aristides* saith this Dominion was not limited to the *Romans* by certain Bounds (as of old to the *Athenians*) but that it incompassed their Empire round like a girdle. And *Themistius* speaking of the Emperor

[i] *In Augusto, cap. 49.*

[k] *In Romæ encomio.*

Theodosius

Theodosius the elder, saith; [l] *what would you say of him, who is Emperor or Ruler of almost the whole Earth and Sea.* In like manner, *Procopius* making mention of a Statue of a Romane Emperor, holding a Citie in his left hand, saith, that the Statuarie's meaning was, [m] *that the whole Land was subject to him, as well as the Sea.* To the same purpose speak's *Nicephorus Callistus* in the Preface to his Ecclesiastical History. And [n] *Julius Firmicus*, speaking of such persons who have in the Schemes of their Nativities, the *Moon* encreasing in the thirtieth Degree of *Taurus*, fortified with a friendly Aspect of *Jupiter*, saith, *they shall possess the Dominions of Sea and Land, whithersoëver they lead an Armie.* *Oppianus* saith to the Emperor *Antoninus*,

Orat. 5.

[m] *De ædificiis Justiniani, cap. de Augustæo.*

[n] *Matheseos, lib. 6. cap. 1.*

——[o] Σοῖς μὲν γὰρ ὑπὸ σκήπτροισι θάλασσα
Εἰλεῖται καὶ φῦλα Ποσειδάωνος ἐναύλων,

Under thy Laws or Scepter the Sea role's,
And Fishes swim throughout thy Sea in sholes.

[o] *Halieutic. lib. 3.*

And *Venus* to *Jupiter*, concerning the future Empire of the Romanes

[p] *Certè hinc Romanos, olim volventibus annis,*
Hinc fore ductores, renovato sanguine Teucri,
Qui Mare, qui Terras omni ditione tenerent,
Pollicitus: quæ te, genitor, sententia vertit?

[p] *Virgil Æneid. 1.*

Hence Romans **their Original should take**
In after-years, thou once didst promise make,
And Leaders spring, to rule both Land and
Sea,
From Teucer's **bloud: What alter's thy decree?**

From

From whence the same Poët, in another place, speak's of *Augustus Cæsar*,

> [q] *An Deus immensi venias Maris, ac tua Nautæ*
> *Numina sola colant; tibi serviat ultima Thule,*
> *Téque sibi generum Tethys emat omnibus undis.*

[q] *Georgic. lib.* 1.

> ——* Or whether thou the God wilt bee
> Of the vast Sea, and Thule's farthest shore,
> Or thee alone the Sailors shall adore,
> As Thetys Son-in-law with all her Seas
> Given for a dower, &c.

* Translated by my worthy friend *Thomas May*.

And *Claudian* of *Scipio Africanus*,

> [r] *Ergò seu patriis primævus Manibus ultor*
> *Subderet Hispanum legibus Oceanum.*

[r] *Præfat in lib.* 3. *de Laudibus Stiliconis.*

> Then whether in revenge to's Father's ghost,
> Hee quell'd the Sea upon the Spanish Coast.

Or what other business soëver hee did, *Ennius* was still at his elbow. In like manner, *Constantinus Monomachus* is, by *John* Bishop of *Euchaïta*, in his Iambicks, called indeed Emperor of the *East*; but according to the custom of the *Western* Empire,

> Γῆς καὶ θαλάσσης Κύριος καὶ δεσπότης,
> *Lord and absolute Soveraign both of Land and Sea.*

As also the Emperor *Leo* by *Varadatus*, [s] *Terræ Marisque Dominus*, **Lord of the Land and Sea.** So that in the Empire of *Constantinople*, which followed the Customs of the *Western*, the *Ægean* Sea it self was reckoned among the Provinces, no otherwise then *Samos, Cyprus*, or other Islands or Territories of any kinde whatsoëver. This appear's out of [t] *Constantinus Por-*

[s] *Concil. Chalced. part.* 3. *Tom.* 2. *part.* 1. *Edit. Binianæ.* 1618.

[t] *Lib.* 1. *Them.* 17.

Porphyrogennetus his *Themata*, where also the *Hellespont* is expresly assigned to the Commander in chief of the *Ægean* Sea, together with the Territories lying round about. And truly the Customs out of this Sea were very great, onely upon the accompt of Fishing. Somtimes ten, somtime twelv thousand Crowns, were collected out of it yearly. Wee learn this also out of a Decree, whereby *Andronicus Palæologus*, one that kept the State of an Emperor, but lived a chambering idle life within his Palace, had for the victualling of himself and his retinue, the *yeerly profit of the fishing before* Constantinople, *wont to bee valued at that time, at ten thousand Crowns*, as saith,[u] *Nicephorus Gregoras*. The same is by som called *Topiaticum*, [x] *Topicum*, It is named also *Piscinica* and *Topice*. Moreover, in the servey or breviarie of the Dignities of the East, onely three Provinces are reckoned under the *Proconsul of Asia*, after this manner:

u *Lib.* 9.

x *Vide J. Cantacuzenum, hist. lib* 2. *c.* 1. *Et lib.* 4. *cap.* 42. *præter Jo. Meursium in Glossario, verb.* τοπικὸν *Et Jul. Cæs. Bullinger. de Imperio Romano, lib.* 9. *cap.* 72.

These Provinces under-written are under the charge of that eminent person the Proconsul of Asia.

Asia;
The Isles;
Hellespont.

Also, *the Office of the Consular Governor of Hellespont* is mentioned in the Decree of the Emperors [y] *Honorius* and *Thedosius*, where it is transferr'd out of the power of the *Deputie* of *Asia* into that of the *Proconsul* of *Asia* (who at that time was *Simplicius*.) In another place also, in the Novels of *Justinian*, wee finde *Hellespont* joyned with * *Pontus Polemoniacus* by the name of a Province or Lievtenantship. I know indeed

y *L. unic. C. de Officio Comitis sacri Patrimonii.*

* So called from *Polemium* a City of *Cappadocia*.

indeed that *Hellespont* is taken here by learned men, not so much for that narrow Sea which divide's *Europe* from *Asia*, as for the Sea-coast of *Asia*. So [z] *Guidus Pancirollus* upon the *Breviarie*. *In this place* (saith hee) *that Countrey of* Asia *is signified which is situate near the the shore of Hellespont.* Certainly, it is seldom enough I suppose, that wee finde the name of *Hellespont* used elswhere for any Countrie of [a] *Asia*, but rather *Hellespontia*. But if not the narrow Sea it self, but a Countrie of the same name were described in the *Breviarie*, wherefore then is this Countrie onely so remarkably named with *Asia*, whereof it self could bee but a small part? If you take it for that very Sea, the matter is evident, and seem's to agree very well with it self. It is most consonant to reason, that the spatious Province of the *Proconsul* of *Asia* was denoted by *Asia* it self, the neighboring narrow Sea, and the Isles; Not thus, by *Asia* it self and the *Isles*, adding moreover I know not what pettie Countrie, obscure enough, and supposed also to bee a part even of *Asia*. Also the Custom of the following Age seem's to interpret a more antient Government in this place. The very *Ægean* Sea (which comprehend's almost all this neighboring Sea) is expresly number'd by the aforesaid *Constantinus Porphyrogenitus*, among the Jurisdictions, Lievtenantships, or Provinces of the East. His words are, [b] *But the* Ægean *Sea it self also is reckoned among the Provinces.* And a little after also concerning the Isles, he saith, *There belong to the command or Government of the Ægean Sea the Isles called* Cyclades, *and the most eminent of the* Sporades, Mytilene, *and* Chios, *and* Lemnos *it self.* So that the Isles and the Sea it self might bee conteined here, as particular parts of the Government or Province, as well as any other Regions whatsoëver. Moreover, it is to bee observed out of the *Notitia* or *Breviarie* of the

z *In Notitia Orient. cap.* 102.

a *Vide Ortelium in Thesauro Geograph, verb. Hellespont.*

b *Lib.* 1. *Them.* 17.

East, that in the *Badges* or signal *Ornaments* of the *Proconsul* of *Asia*, which were usually painted in that Commission whereby hee was established in his Government, there were contained (besides the *effigies* of the Princes, and the Book of instructions) representations of *three women*, set forth alike with towred Diadems on their heads, according to the patern which wee shall present you with by and by, representing those three Provinces together, to wit, *Asia*, the *Isles*, and *Hellespont* in such a manner, and so remarkbly noted by an addition of their names, that there is not the least shadow of Reason, why wee should grant the last to have been a part or Region of the first. I thought fit also, to add here *Pancirollus* his description of those Pictures or Represensentations, who hath made use not onely of the printed Books of the *Breviarie*, set forth by *Alciatus* (from whom wee have taken the Figure) but also of the Manuscripts of *Fulvius Ursinus* and others. This *Proconsul* (saie's Pancirollus) *underneath the Book of Instructions, hath the pictures of three women which represent the Provinces committed to their charge, to wit,* Asia, *the* Isles, *and* Hellespont, *as the Inscriptions of their names upon them do shew. These bear a kinde of royal Ornament on the head* (the printed Books say, each of them had a towred Diadem) *and vessels full of coin in their hands, which signified that the levying of Tributes in those three Provinces, belong'd to the* Proconsul. *They were apparell'd also in long garments of Gold. The Manuscripts say they have white or skie-colour'd.* Asia *weareth shoos or Sandals and a skie colour'd Mantle; The other are without shoos: Shee which represent's the* Isles *weareth a purple Mantle; Shee which represent's* Hellespont *a green one. But in the Book of* Ursinus, *they are all shod high with red Buskins, not differing in their habit. In* Mandrucianus *they are set forth in long garments, which almost cover their feet.* Thus far hee. And now judg yee, whether it bee likely ly or no, that any pettie Countrie of *Asia* ſhould bee ſet forth in theſe Ornaments in an equal ſtate and majeſtie with *Asia* it ſelf, ſeeing even this had comprehended that alſo, no otherwiſe then the whole doth the ſmalleſt part.

Their towred *Diadems*, equal Stature, majestie and wealth not differing at all, seem to point out such an equalitie, that neither of them, can appear, by this form of description, to bee reckoned a part of another. And so, that *Hellespont* cannot in that place bee any other then the Sea it self, or that Arm of the Sea flowing between; which beeing thus joyned with the *Isles* to the Proconsulship of *Asia*, upon one and the same account of Dominion, the Provinces of *Asia* and *Europe* became in a civil sens, either continual or contiguous. Yea, when there was no such distinction of Provinces, the adjacent Isles and the Sea it self, made one entire Provincial bodie also with the continent. And hence it came to pass that the Isles of *Italy* were [c] part of *Italy*; as also of every Province; and such as were divided from *Italy* by a small arm of the Sea, as *Sicily*, they [d] were to bee reckoned rather among the Provinces of the Continent. The Seas lying between did not hinder, but that one continued Territorie might bee made of the continent and the Isles. And that also by the Autoritie of *Ulpian*, who notwithstanding useth to say, that the Sea is common to all men. But of this hereafter in our Answers to the *Objections*. The same *Ulpian* also in another place saith, [e] *Si quis me prohibet in mari piscari, vel everriculum, &c.* **If any man forbid's mee to fish in the Sea, or to draw a Drag-net** (which the Greeks call σαγήνη) **may I sue him or no at Law upon an action of Trespass?** *som there are of opinion that I may sue him upon a Trespass; So* Pomponius, *and many others say, hee is in the same condition with him that hinder's one to wash in a publick Bath, or to sit in a publick Theatre, or to act, sit, and convers in any other place, or put case, there bee any one that permit's mee not to use that which is my own. But the Antients allowed an Interdict to him that hired*

[c] *L.9.ff. tit. de Judiciis, de quâ vide J.Gryphiand. Tract. de Insulis, cap.15.*

[d] *L.99.ff. de verb.signif.*

[e] *L.13.§. si quis ff. tit. de Injuriis.*

hired the Sea, if so bee hee hired it in a publick manner. For, force by that Interdict is allowed, that hee may enjoy what hee hath hired. Therefore the Sea, becaus it was possessed by the people, was reckoned among publick things; that is, those things which are proper and peculiar to the people of *Rome*, not common to all men, after another manner then publick Baths, Theatres, and other things of that kinde. And what doth to hire in a publick manner signifie in this place, but to becom a hirer or *Conductor* of the Sea, as the people was Lord thereof and Letter or *Locator*? I suppose no man doth affirm, that any thing may bee let for Rent or hired, which may not so belong to one man, that can not bee anothers. But becaus publick Places, by the * *Civil Law* do serv for the uses of [f] private persons, therefore *Pomponius* and others were of opinion, that there might have been here an action of Trespass. Moreover, it was an Edict of the *Prætor*, *That you do nothing in a publick place or cast any thing into it, whereby it may bee endamaged.* Hereupon *Ulpian* saith [g], *against that man who hath cast a Dam or Pile into the Sea, an Interdict is allowed him who perhaps may bee endamaged thereby. But if no man sustain damage, hee is to bee defended who build's upon the shore, or cast's a Pile into the Sea. If any man bee hinder'd from fishing or Navigation by Sea, hee shall not have an Interdict; nor hee likewise, who may bee restrained from playing in the common Field, or from washing in a publick Bath, or from beeing a spectator in a Theatre. But in all these Cases hee must use an Action of Trespass.* Therefore a Prohibitorie Interdict or Decree was to bee used, when dams were cast into the Sea no otherwise then when damage was don to a Theatre, Bath, Court, or any publick place whatsoëver. To these things, which manifestly belonged to the people of *Rome*, and were

* *Roman.*

[f] *L.* 2. *ff. Ne quid in Loco.* § 2.

[g] *Loc. citat.* §. 8. & 9.

were not common to all men, is the Sea everie way compared, even by *Ulpian* himself. There is also the same account made of the shores and Sea [h] by those that speak for a Communitie of the Sea. Nor are they said to bee less common by [i] som, who treat of them apart, as by *Neratius*, and *Ulpianus*. But [k] *Celsus* saith, *I think those shores do belong to the people of* Rome, *over which the people of* Rome *have dominion.* But that which follow's there, *that the use of the Sea is common to all as the Aër, and that the Piles cast into it belong to him that cast them,* is plainly qualified, and manifestly restrained to the manner of the Dominion of the people of *Rome*, in the words immediately following, where *Celsus* saith, *That is not to bee granted, in case the use of the shore or Sea may by that means becom the wors.* Certainly, if the former words were meant of such a Community or enjoyment common to all men, as would not in any wise permit the Dominion or propriety of a particular person, what mean's that then, *that the use may becom the wors?* For, if a place should becom the proprietie of him that doth possess it, in the same manner as that which had before been possessed by no man, and no regard should bee had here of the Dominion or Right of another, then it would bee no less lawful for him that should possess it, to make the use thereof the wors to others for the benefit of himself, then for him that shall settle in a Field that never was seized yet in the possession of any. Therefore, *Celsus* would have the Shores and Sea so to belong to the people of *Rome*, that the condition of them, as serving the uses of all private persons (and that, as hath been said, according to the * Civil Law, and such qualifications as are added out of the Edicts of the *Prætors*, and the like) could not without injury bee made

h *Instit. de Rer. Divis.* § *litorum. Marcianus*, l. 2. *ff. de Divis. Rer.*

i *L.* 14. *ff. de Acquir. Rer. Dom. l.* 13. *ff. de Injuriis.* § 7.

k *L.* 3. *ff. Ne quid in publico loco.*

* *Roman.*

made worſ, to the prejudice of the Commonweal. Of the ſame minde is *Scevola*, [l] *That by the Law of Nations men may build upon the ſhore, if the publick concernment do not hinder.* And *Ariſto*, [m] *quod Mari occupatum eſt fit publicum*, **that which is poſſeſſed in the Sea becom's publick.** It paſſeth into the patrimonie of the people of *Rome*; for ſo the word *Publicum* **Publick** doth ſignifie; which the Greek Lawyers term δημόσιον or *that which belong's to the people*, not equally common to all men; by whom alſo the Sea it ſelf is [n] in that ſenſ called *Publick*. Other Inſtances there are of the ſame nature: Whereby it is made manifeſt, as well out of the determinations of Lawyers, as the Tranſcripts of Leagues and Treaties, and the writings of Hiſtorians, Orators, and Poëts, that a Dominion of the Sea was in uſe among the *Romans*, after the ſame manner as the Land.

[l] *In litore, jure gentium ædificari niſi uſus publicus impediret. L. 4. ff. nè quid in loco publico.*

[m] *L. 10. de rer. diviſione.*

[n] *Gloſſæ vet. juris verb.* Δημόσιον.

The Dominion of the Sea, as it belonged to private perſons *under the* Roman *Empire, together with that* Sanction eſtabliſhed in the Eaſtern Empire; *whereby the perpetual community of the Sea which was pretended to by ſom, beeing utterly aboliſhed as a* thing unjuſt, *the Dominion even of* private perſons *therein is aſſerted.*

CHAP. XV.

WHat hath been delivered in the fore-going Chapter, touching the Dominion of the Sea, hath relation to the Dominion of the whole bodie of the *Romane* people, that is to say, to the publick patrimonie of the State, wherein a private Dominion is proved, no less then in that of particular persons. Moreover, there are to bee found among the *Romane* Customs, very ample testimonies to prove that a proprietie in the Sea hath been instated also on particular men; such, to whom either the people or Emperor of *Rome* according to the Civil Law and Custom of the *Romanes*, demised, rented, or made a grant of any part of their Sea within the Empire. The rich and more magnificent sort of Citizens, for the conveniencie of larger Fish-ponds, bringing the Sea into their grounds, made it their own, and became Masters thereof with as good a Title as they had to their adjacent Land. *There beeing* (saith [a] *Varro*) *two kindes of Fish-ponds, one of Fresh, the other of salt Water; the former sort are ordinarie and little Worth, such as our Countrie Fish-ponds that are supplied With Water by little streames; but those salt-Water-Ponds are to bee found in the possessions of Noblemen, and are supplied by the Sea as Well With Fish as Water; yet they yield more delight then profit, the filling of those Ponds beeing commonly the draining of the Owners purs.* Now what was this, but to becom proprietaries of the Sea, so far forth as it was derived, or inclosed in their possessions?

[a] *De re Rustica, lib.* 3. *cap.* 17.

And [b] *Columella*, who lived in the time of *Claudius*, relate's that the *Romanes* in antient times for the most part used none but in-land Fish-ponds, storing them with Spawners of the larger size; presently adding; *Not long after that good husbandrie Was laid aside, When the Wealth and luxurie of the succeeding age made inclosures of the Ocean and Seas themselvs.* And the yearly

[b] *De re Rusticâ, lib.* 8. *cap.* 16. & 17.

yearly Revenue of such Demains, which bordered upon the Sea, was advanced by those Ponds or Inclosures of the Sea as well as by any Lands, Lakes, or Vineyards appertaining thereunto. The same *Columella* discoursing hereupon, hath this passage, *But seeing the custom of the times hath so far prevailed, that these things are not onely in use, but have gotten the reputation of magnificent and noble contrivances, wee also, least wee should seem morose and importune reprovers of so long and settled a practice, will show what profit may redound from them to the Lord of the Manor; how hee may rais an incom by the Sea, if having made a purchase of Islands or Lands bordering upon the Sea, hee cannot reap the fruits of the Earth, by reason of that barrenness of the soil which usually is near the Shore.* So that wee see the Revenues of a Manor were improved by managing the Sea, as well as Land; and the Possessor was counted Lord of the one no more then of the other.

This usual right of Dominion over the Sea is mentioned also by [c] St *Ambrose*; *For the serving of their prodigious luxurie* (saith hee) *the Earth by digging of chanels is forced to admit the Ocean, for the making of artificial Islands, and bringing litle Seas into their own possessions. They challenge to themselvs large portions of the Sea by right, and boast that the Fishes, like so many bond-slaves, have lost their former libertie, and are subjected to their service. This Creek of the Sea* (saith one) *belong's to mee, that to another; Thus great men divide the Elements among themselvs.*

[c] *Hexaëmer. lib. cap.* 5. 10. *& lib. de Nabuthe cap.* 3.

For Examples, there are the Fish-ponds of *Lucullus*, famous for his expensiveness in this kinde: Hee, having made way through a Mountain near *Naples*, inclosed the Sea and became master of those water-courses which [d] *Plutarch* call's *Sea-Courses and Chases for the* breeding

[d] *In Lucullo.*

breeding of Fish. Whereupon *Pompey the Great, in merriment* (saith [e] *Paterculus*) *was wont to call* Lucullus *the* * *gowned* Xerxes, *in regard that by damming up of Chanels and digging down Mountains, hee took the* Sea *into the Land. The same* Lucullus (saith [f] Plinie) *digging down a Mountain near* Naples *at greater charge then hee built his Villa, took an arm of the Sea into his Manor, which gave occasion to* Pompey *the Great, to call him the gowned Xerxes.* The same conceit in *Plutarch* is attributed to *Tubero* the Stoick. That concerning *Xerxes* is very famous

[e] Histor. lib. 2.
* Xerxem togatum.
[f] Plin Nat. Histor. lib 9. cap. 54.

[g] *Hoc terræ fiat; hâc Mare, dixit, eat:*

Here run the Sea, hee said;
There, let firm Land bee made;

[g] Epigramm. Vet. lib. 2.

When hee commanded the Sea to bee brought round about the Mountain *Athos.* [h] And *Valerius* saith of *Caius Sergius Orata, That hee might not have the serving of his palate depend upon the pleasure of Neptune, hee contrived Seas of his own, intercepting the waves with his trenches, and so inclosing divers sholes of Fishes with dams, that what tempestuous weather soëver happened,* Orata's *Table was never unfurnished with varietie of Dishes.* The same libertie was used upon the *Formian* shore by *Apollinaris*, of whose Fish pond *Martial* [i] speak's,

[h] Lib. 9. cap. 30.
[i] Lib. 10. Epigr. 30.

Si quando Nereus sentit Æoli regnum,
Ridet procellas tuta de suo Mensa,
Piscina Rhombum pascit, & Lupos vernas.

When winds do Lord it o're the Sea, & fright
The Fisher, his Table laugh's at their spight;
By its own private store secur'd from need,
While captiv'd Pikes and Turbot's Fish-ponds breed.

All

All the varietie of Fish which the wider Sea afforded, *Apollinaris* had readie at hand in his Fish-pond; which was nothing els but the Sea let in from the shore into his possession.

> *Contracta pisces Æquora sentiunt,*
> *Jactis in altum molibus.*——

> **Such dams are cast into the main,**
> **The Fish for want of room complain.**

So saith *Horace*: and in another place,

> [k] *Cæmentis licèt occupes*
> *Tyrrhenum omne tuis Mare Ponticum.*

> **—— though thou thy walls do rais**
> **Through all the Tuscan and the Pontick Seas.**

[k] *Lib.3.od.1. & 24.*

And saith *Salust*; [m] *To what purpose, should I relate those things which cannot seem credible to any, but those who have been eie-witnesses; how Mountains have been removed by severall private persons, and Seas brought into their places?* Of this sort, were the Fish ponds of [n] *Philippus, Hortensius*, and others, all made by taking in the Sea. Moreover, wee finde that Soveraigntie and Dominion over the Sea, hath been somtimes conferred by the Patents of Princes. The Emperor *Trajan*, when hee endowed the Citie of *Tharsus* with Immunities and Privileges, besides the Territorie of Land lying about, added also a grant of *Jurisdiction and Dominion over the river Cydnus and the adjacent Sea*, as may bee seen in *Dion* [o] *Chrysostom.* And it is very probable, that the Maritimate rights of *Neocesarea* [p], which *Theodorus Balsamon* saies, were compiled by the *Metropolitan* of that Citie, had respect unto the like Original: as also those privileges in the Sea, which the Emperor *Comnenus*

[m] *In Conjurat.Catilinæ.*

[n] *Varro, de re Rusticâ, lib.3.cap.3.*

[o] *Orat. 34.*

[p] *In Concil. Chalcedon. can.4.& in can.12.Synod.7.*

nenus granted to a great number of Monasteries, according to the same Author.

The ancient Lawyers also are not silent, as touching the Dominion of particular persons in the Sea. [q] *Paulus*, one of greatest note among them, declare's himself expresly thus; *Verily, whensoëver a proprietie in som part of the Sea belong's to any person, that person may sue out an interdict of* uti possidetis, *in case hee bee hindred from the exercise and enjoyment of his right; becaus this matter concern's a private, not a publick caus; seeing the suit is commenced for the enjoying of a right which ariseth not from a publick but private Title. For, interdicts are proper to bee used in private cases, not in publick.* Nothing could have been more plainly spoken, to show, that, beyond all controversie, hee admit's a private Dominion in the Sea, even of single persons. Yea, *Ulpian* himself, who was so fondly inclined to favor the opinion of a perpetual communitie of the Sea, doth sufficiently acknowledg, that common practice and received custom was for the other part. [r] *In case* (saith hee) *I forbid any man to Fish before my Hous or Roialtie, what can bee said? may hee sue mee upon an action of Trespass, or no? The Sea and the shores indeed are common to all, as the Aër. And it hath been declared, that no man can bee prohibited from Fishing, or fowling, any otherwise then as hee may bee debarr'd from entring upon another man's ground. Yet for a man to bee forbidden to Fish before my Hous or Royaltie is the common custom, although grounded upon no Law. Wherefore if any man bee prohibited, hee hath for all that an Action of Trespass.* Hee grant's it was a received use and custom, that subjection should bee thus imposed on the Sea, and so a private Dominion thereof bee admitted; but least hee should bee found unconstant to his espoused opinion of the communitie of the Sea, hee hath presumed to declare it

[q] *Lib.14.ff.de Injuriis.*

[r] *L.13.ff.de Injuriis.§ 7.*

it don without any Law or Justice. Yet hee himself deliver's his judgment in another place thus, *The vender or seller of the* Geronian *Farm imposed such a condition on the* Botrojan *Farm, which hee still kept in his hands, that from that time forward no fishing for Tunies should bee used upon the Coast thereof, although no private contract can lay a restraint upon the Sea which nature set's open to all. Yet in regard honestie and faithful dealing in the agreement require that this Article of the sale bee observed, the persons that are in present possession, and they that succeed into the said Farm, are obliged by the condition of the covenant or bargain.* In this case, the owner of the *Botrojan* Farm renounceth his right of Fishing. And *Ulpian* might as well have said, that restraint or subjection was imposed upon that adjacent Sea (as indeed it was) but that hee was so unwilling to forgo his Opinion of the Seas unalterable communitie. Moreover, the purchaser of the *Geronian* Farm was so fully possessed of the Sea that lay before the *Botrojan*, that by virtue of this subjection really imposed on that Sea-territorie, the Owner of the *Botrojan* Farm could never after justly claim or exercise a privilege of Fishing for Tunies, without his permission. Whereupon, [r] *Stephanus Forcatulus*, once Professor of the Civil Law at *Tholose*, conclude's to the purpose; *That there is nothing to hinder, but that the Sea, though common to all, may by publick decree bee subjected to a Prince by the same right that hee hold's his adjoyning Kingdom; since the same thing may in a manner bee effected by virtue of a private compact*: Where, by private compact, hee mean's that concerning the Purchaser of the *Geronian* Farm, as hee himself saith expresly in the same place. But the opinion of *Ulpianus* for a perpetual communitie of the Sea, was so entertained as authentick by the Lawyers of the *Eastern Empire*, that there was no

[r] *In Cupidine juris perito. cap. 9. §. 3.*

Law

Law in force among them whereby an adjacent Sea might bee made appropriate, or any man bee debarr'd the libertie of Fishing by the Owner of such Lands as border'd thereupon. And if any one were debarr'd, hee might have an Action of Trespass. Which is manifest enough, not onely in the *Basilica* [t] (which before the dismembring of them were a bodie of the Law of the *Grecian* or *Eastern* Empire) but also by the Decrees established by the Emperor *Leo*; by virtue of which that stale opinion of the communitie of the Sea, beeing utterly cashiered, as not agreeing with equitie, that ancient one of the lawfulness of a possession and private Dominion in the neighboring Sea, back't with the Autoritie of other eminent Lawyers, was entertain'd again. Moreover also, it was so firmly ratified by an *Imperial Sanction*, that from that time forward it passed over all the *Ægean* Sea without controul. That Law (saith that *Eastern* [u] Emperor, who reigned about the nine hundreth year of our Lord) which so take's away the right of possessions bordering on the Sea, as to make the Lord thereof liable to an Action of Trespass if hee prohibite others to Fish upon those Coasts, in our judgment * *seem's to determine that which is not equitable or just.* Hee add's the reason, becaus whatsoëver com's into the possession of any man, by good and lawful Title, whether by succession, art and industry, or any other way which the Law approve's, there is no reason that other men should have the use and benefit thereof without the owners leav. Thus the matter beeing duly examined hee judged, that hee who held any part of the Sea in the aforesaid manner, had a Title grounded upon a very clear Right. *Therefore*, saith hee, *wee decree that every man possess his* vestibula *or Seas lying before his Lands and bee master of them by*

[t] *Eclog. lib.* 53. *tit.* 6. περὶ ἁλιέων. *seu de Piscatoribus.*

[u] *Leo Imperator in Novel* 56.

* ἡμῖν οὐ δίκαια ἐπιτρέπουσα ἐφάνη.

an

an unquestionable right, and that hee have power to keep off any persons whatsoëver that go about to enjoy the benefit thereof without his permission. And in that which follow's, hee make's the Proprietie of Sea and Land altogether equal. The Seas which laie thus in the face of Manors, were called πρόθυρα τὰ θαλάττια, *Sea-Courts or Entries*, nor did this sanction of *Leo* serv onely for the ratification of former Titles, founded either upon particular possession, or any other, but ordained in general, that every man for the future should bee Lord of that neighboring part of the Sea which laie before or flowed by his Lands, although hee had never been possessed thereof before. In this very sens it is taken by *Constantinus Harmenopulus*, a Judg of *Thessalonica*; [x] *Touching Sea-Courts or Entries by* Sea (saith hee) *it is decreed in the thirtieth Novel of the Emperor* Leo, *that every one bee master of that which is adjoyning to his Lands, and that power bee given him to prohibit such as at any time go about to make any benefit of these Vestibulas or Entries without his permission. Harmenopulus*, following a different order of the *Novels* call's that the thirtieth, which in the printed Copies is the fiftie-sixth.

[x] *Prochir. Juris*, lib. 2. tit. 1.

But now how much of the Sea directly forward did pass into the possession of the same person that was Lord of the adjoyning Lands either by antient custom, or by virtue of this decree is not yet certainly known, nor is it necessarie to our purpose, but for latitude, even as it were in a field, those *Vestibulas* or Entries of the Sea were bounded by the same limits with the adjacent Lands. And it was the custom for particular owners to have their *Epoches* or Pens for fish (which the [y] later *Greeks* call Τράνας) that is to saie, Nets spread between stakes driven into the Sea; but limited upon this condition that every *Epoche* should

[y] *Michaël Athaliates, Pragmatic.* tit. 95.

bee distant from the other [z] three hundred sixtie-five Cubits if so bee the breadth of Land could conveniently permit. And such an equal distance was observed on both sides, that a direct line from each *Epoche* to the extremitie of the *Vestibulum* or Entrie was extended one hundred eightie two ells and a half; but this rule for limitation became useless after a ten years prescription.

[z] *Leonis Novella* 57. 102. 103. 104. & *Athaliates loco jam citato.*

The Lord of a Manor bordering upon the Sea improved his yearly Revenue by these as by other commodities, which profit arising from those Entries is usually stiled by the *Eastern Lawyers* προθύριον κέρδος, and τοπιατικόν, which may bee translated *locarium*, for the price which was paid for hire of a Stall, Shop or Farme, is called in [a] Latine *locarium*; so that wee see private persons raised their *topiatica* or *locaria*, that is, their Rents, out of the adjacent Sea. And out of those Rents they paied to the Prince a yearly Tribute amounting to no inconsiderable summe (as was shewed before) levyed upon that accompt. So that by the custom of the Eastern Empire, not onely the Soveraigntie of a Prince (which is the point in question) but also the Dominion of private persons in the Sea, beeing ratified by Autoritie of publick decrees, enacting it, and repealing as unjust whatsoëver gainsai'd it, it was in use beyond all dispute above five hundred and fiftie years: for so many are reckoned to the taking of *Constantinople* from the date of the aforesaid decree of *Leo*; which concerned not onely *Bosphorus* in *Thracia*, the *Hellespont*, the *Ægean* and the narrower Seas, but all those that were under the Dominion of the Emperor of *Constantinople*. And this may serv to bee spoken of the more antient *Historical* Age or that which contain's the

[b] *Varro de lingua latina. Et de Topiatico* videsis *Jac. Cujacium Observat. lib.* 14. *cap.* 1.

customs

customs and Laws of Kingdoms and Common-weals that are long since exspired.

Touching the Dominion of the Sea, according to the Customs of such Nations as are now in beeing. First of the Adriatick Sea *belonging to the* Venetians, *the* * Ligustick *to the* Genoëses, *the* Tyrrhen *to the* Tuscans, *and lastly of the Sea belonging to the* Church, *or Pope of* Rome.

* *Mare Ligusticum* is now called *Mar Leone*, and *Mar di Genoua*.

CHAP. XVI.

IF wee take a view of later times or the Rights and Customs of Nations which at this present are in high repute and autoritie, there is nothing that can more clearly illustrate the point in hand then the Dominion of the *Adriatick* Sea, which the most noble Common-weal of *Venice* hath enjoyed for so many Ages. The truth of this is every where attested and acknowledged, not onely by *Historians* and *Chorographers*, but by very many Lawyers [a] *Bartolus*, *Baldus*, *Angelus*, and a companie of above thirtie the most eminent among them; unless they bee mis reckoned by *Franciscus de Ingenuis*, who saith hee counted so many, in that Epistle of his to *Liberius Vincentius*, written som years ago, in defence of the Dominion of the *Venetians* over the *Adriatick* Sea, in answer to *Johannes Baptista Valenzola* a Spaniard, and *Laurentius Motinus* a *Roman*; who (as hee saith) to gratifie the Duke of *Ossuna* Vice-Roy of *Naples* whose creatures they were, wrote against the Right of Dominion which belong's to the *Venetians* by Sea.

[a] *Ad ff. tit. rer. divis.* & *ad l. sanè* 13. *tit. de injuriis.*

Venice is commonly styled the *Mistress of the Sea*; and the *Queen of the Adriatick Sea*, though the Controversie about its Bounds bee not yet decided. And [b] *Sannazarius* write's thus of this Citie,

[b] Epigr. lib. 1.

Viderat Adriacis Venetam Neptunus in undis
Stare urbem, & toto ponere jura Mari.

Neptune saw Venice in the Gulf to stand
Of Adria, and all the Sea Command.

Nor doth this Dominion arise from any jurisdiction or protection over the persons of such as frequent the Sea (as is imagined by som, miserably [c] carried away with the autoritie of *Ulpian*, so often affirming that the Sea by the Law of nature is commnn to all men;) nor is it a qualified Dominion (as saith *Angelus Matthæacius*, professor at *Padua*;) but this Sea doth so properly belong to the *Venetians*, that it is not lawful for any other to use or enjoie the same without their permission; forasmuch as they have right to prohibit any to pass, to impose custom upon those whom they permit, to do any other thing in order to the raising of benefit and advantage out of the water, as any man may do in his proper possessions by Land. As concerning Navigation in that Sea, that it may bee prohibited at their pleasure, and that by approved right, wee have the testimonies of many Lawyers. *It cannot bee denied*; (saith [d] *Angelus de Ubaldis*) *but the* Venetians *and their* Signiory, *for very many Ages, have been and are in possession as it were of the aforesaid Gulf: wherefore the* Venetians *by virtue of that antient possession which they have had so long, and do yet enjoie, may by putting a restriction into the form of their Covenants, binder the* Genoëses *or any other whatsoëver that shall offer*

[c] Vid Jul. Pacium de Dominio Maris Adriatici. Alb. Gentilis, de Jure Belli, lib. 1. cap. 19. Roderic. Suarium, de usu maris. Angelum Matthæacium de viâ & ratione artificiosâ juris universi lib. 1. cap. 36.

[d] Consil. 190. Idem ad l. 13. ff. tit. de Injuriis.

to sail through their Gulf. The same saie others also, quoted by [e] *Benevenutus Straccha*, [f] *Antonius Peregrinus*, [g] *Marta Neopolitanus*, [h] *Julius Pacius*, [i] *Mantua Patavinus*, [k] *Franciscus de Ingenuis*, and *Fulgentius Monachus Venetus*, who all have written more particularly, and made it their business to assert the right of the *Venetians*. And there are examples to bee produc'd which shew, how Princes, as well neighbors as others, have made it their suit to the State of *Venice* to obtain leav to pass through that Sea, which somtimes was granted, and somtimes denied. In the year 1399, *December* 12. *Radulphus* Earl of *Otranto* made a request to that State in the behalf of *Uladislaus* King of *Naples* and *William Archduke* of *Austria*, that leav might bee granted to pass through the *Adriatick* Sea with Galleyes and other Ships, to conveigh the Sister of the King out of *Apulia* to the Territories of the *Archduke* her husband, which the Republick granted, but with this condition, that no person that had been banished from *Venice*, or was guiltie of any capital crime against the State, should bee taken aboard those Ships. Which the *Austrians*, imbarking at *Trieste*, faithfully observed both in their voiage and in their return. There are extant also two Letters, [l] wherein the Emperor *Frederick* the third, in the years 1478, and 1479, desire's of *Giovanni Mocenigo* Duke of *Venice*, and of the State, that leav might bee granted him, to transport corn from *Apulia* through the *Adriatick* Sea. *Franciscus de Ingenuis* make's mention of others to the same purpose, written to the same Duke from the Kings of *Hungarie*. And this they intreat as a matter of great favor, for which they shall acknowledg themselvs obliged. *Matthias* King of *Hungarie* in a Letter to Duke *Mocenigo* dated 1482. write's, That whereas the State hath been wont to give

[e] *Tract. de Navigatione*, §. 8.
[f] *De jure fisci, lib.* 8. §. 14.
[g] *De jurisdictione, lib.* 1. *cap.* 33. §. 25. & 26.
[h] *Lib. de Dominio maris Adriatici.*
[i] *Fragment. de Venetiis subnex. Epitome de juris consultis illustr.*
[k] *Franciscus de Ingenuis, In Epist. de Venet. jure.*
[l] *Anton. Peregrin. de Jure Fisci, lib.* 8. §. 19.

leav to the Earls of *Frangipanis* and *Zenga*, and others whose Territories laie upon the Sea Coasts every year to transport a certain store of corn, from *Apulia* through that Sea, hee desire's that the same libertie might bee vouchsafed to himself, who had now succeeded into the Dominion of the very same Countries.

And as touching the right which the *Venetians* had to impose custom on passengers, as travelling through their peculiar Territorie, there are frequent testimonies among the Lawyers. [m] *Salicetus* mentioneth a Decree of the *Venetians*, that all who passed through the Sea should bring in their merchandise to *Venice*, and there paie custom. And saith [n] *Bartholomeus Cepola*, *The* Venetians *within their Dominion have several Roialties and Rights belonging to their Exchequer: and,* de facto *at least, acknowledg no Superior; so that they have power to impose Gabels, to confiscate goods and commodities in the aforesaid Sea, as well as in the Citie of* Venice; *having as full jurisdiction in the Sea, as in the Citie.* *Antonius Peregrinus* also, who was advocate of the Exchequer at *Padua*, after a large discours upon this subject, [o] *the conclusion,* saith hee, *is this; that the right of Fishing in the Adriatick Sea is one of the Roialties belonging to the Duke of* Venice; *and therefore hee hath power to forbid, permit, and charge Gabels upon it.* *Julius Pacius*, *Marta*, and others both modern and antient treat at large of this particular. And the reasons of som *Neapolitans* that are the most obstinate opposers of this right, are onely drawn either from that [p] opinion for so many Ages since exploded by the custom of Nations, that the Sea is naturally common to all; or from that chimera of the universal Dominion of the *Roman* Emperor. Whereas

[m] *Ad L. 3. De Nautico Fœnore.*

[n] *De servitutibus Rusticorum Prædiorum, cap.* 26. §. 10.

[o] *De Jure Fisci, lib.* 8. §. 43. & *lib.* 1. *cap.* §. 18.

[p] *Franciscus de Ponte, de potestate Proregis, Collateralis Consilii, tit.* 11. §. 19. & *seqq.*

[q] *Marta*

[q] *Marta* himself, who was a Lawyer of *Naples*, write s thus; *The* Venetians *are Lords of the* Adriatick *Sea, the extent whereof is* 80 *miles, reaching from that place heretofore called* Aquæ Graduatæ *unto the Town of* Loreto, *seated now near the River* Po. And *Francisco di capoblanco*, a *Neopolitan*, also [r] confesseth that *now the Rivers and Seas are passed into the hands of Lords and Patrons.* And in a Letter of [s] *Lewis* the 2[d] to *Basilius* Emperor of the East, *Nicetas Patricius* is mentioned under this title, *The Protector of the* Adriatick *Sea.* And *the Gulph*, saith [t] *Cardinalis Tuschus, doth properly belong to the* Venetians, *by virtue of a long prescription of possession, as it hath been declared in an agreement made between the States of* Venice *and Genoa.* For confirmation whereof, hee cite's *Angelus* and *Jason.* But the first time, they saie, wherein custom was charged upon those that passed through the *Adriatick* Sea, was the year 1263. when *Lorenzo Tepulo* was Duke of *Venice.* The Republick of *Genoa* beeing distressed with war and famine, and their neighbors not releiving them with provisions, *this Tepulo* (saith [u] *Flavius Blondus*), *began to impose a new custom, or to speak more plainly, laie a Restraint upon those that sail'd through the* Adriatick *Sea. For, upon that occasion a Law was made, which remain's in force to this very daie; that all who sailed between the Gulf* de Quevera, *and the* * *Promontory of* Sola, *and Coast of* Ravenna, *should com into* Venice, *to paie Custom, and (if the Officers thought fit) to unlade their Merchandise and Goods. And an Officer was ordained for that purpose, to scout daie and night with his Barks, about the Coasts and Harbors of shores to see to the Observation of this Statute.* But above all, wee must not pass by that Controversie which happened about this time, between the people of *Ancona*, and the *Venetians*, in

[q] *De Jurisdictione part.* 1. *cap.* 33. §. 25.

[r] *De Jure Baronum Pragmatic.* 14. §. 27.

[s] *Apud. Goldastum in Constit. Imperialibus, Tom.* 1. *pag.* 198. *& Baronium, Annal. Tom.* 10. *ann.* 871.

[t] *De Jure statuum in Imp. Romano membro* 25.

[u] *Decad.* 2. *Lib.* 8.

* *Capo di Pola.*

in a general Councel at *Lions* the *Anconitans* complained that the *Venetians* had usurped the Sea and Custom, and other things against all right. Pope *Gregorie* the tenth referred the matter to the examination of the Abbot of *Nervosia*. He rejected the allegations of the *Anconitans*, as weak and wanting proof, and by the Autoritie of the *Pope* (saith the aforenamed *Blondus*) commended to the *Venetians*, the care of defending the aforesaid Coast of the *Adriatick* Sea, against the *Saracens*, and Pirats; allowing them withal the rights of their Customs and Impost. Whereat the Ambassadors which were then present, did not interpose a word; but the debate was thus determined with the approbation of all, except the Complainants. But the Dominion of *Venice* over that Sea, is of far greater Antiquitie; to signifie which, they have an annual cerimonie, instituted, they say, by Pope [x] *Alexander* the third, I mean the use of the Ring, which every year, upon *Ascension* daie, the Duke, in a solemn manner, rowed in the *Bucentoro*, accompanied with the *Clarissimos* of the Senate, cast's into the midst of the water, for the perpetuating (saith [y] *Paulus Merula*) of their dominion over the Sea; signifying by that love-token, that hee betroth's the Sea to himself in the manner of a lawful Spous, using such a form of matrimonie, *Wee take thee to our wedded wife, O Sea, in token of a true and perpetual Dominion.* What should hinder then, but that wee may conclude, that the *Venetians* were looked upon, not onely by themselvs, but by their neighbor Princes, as Lords of that Sea, by as unquestionable and full a title, as of their Land and Citie?

[x] *Anton. Peregrin. de Jure Fisci, lib.* 8. §. 18.

[y] *Cosmograph. part.* 2. *lib.* 4. *cap.* 36. de quo more item *Stephanus Forcatulus, de Gallorum imperio & philosophia lib.* 3, *alii,* præter Scriptores de Venetorum Republicâ.

There are other States also in *Italy*, that have Maritim

ritim Rights of the ſame nature. Princes (ſaith [z] *Benedictus Bonius*) *have right to laie impoſitions upon the* Sea-*ſhores, foraſmuch as what nature had left at libertie, is brought by them into ſervitude and proprietie: as the* Tyrrhen Sea, *which is under the command of* Piſa *and* Tuſcanie, *the* Adriatick *of* Venice; *the Liguſtick of* Genoa, which is affirm'd in like manner by [a] *Angelus*, [b] *Baldus*, [c] *Cepola, and others.* The Biſhop of *Rome* alſo hath his Sea, which is called likewiſe the *Churches Sea.* The Bull, intituled *Cœnæ Domini*, which is [d] wont to bee publiſhed every *good Friday*, for the excommunication of Delinquents, run's thus; *Item, wee excommunicate and anathematize all Pirats, Rovers, and Robbers upon the ſea, thoſe that haunt and infeſt our ſea*, eſpeciallie *that part lying between the Mountain* Argentaro, *and* Terracina. And [e] *Bartholomæus Ugolinus*, a famous Lawyer, ſaith, that this Excommunication did involv *Pirats, Rovers,* or *Robbers upon the Sea, ſuch as haunted the Churches ſea, eſpecially that part lying between the Mountain* Argentaro, *and* Terracina. The ſame is called by others *the Pope's Sea.* And although a [f] certain Autor would there by *Our Sea*, have the whole Sea underſtood in all parts of Chriſtendom, yet it is the unanimous conſent of the moſt famous Interpreters of that *Bull*, as [g] *Tolet*, [h] *Suarez*, *Ugolinus*, [i] *Antonius de Souſa*, and others, that by that name is ſignified the Sea which is part of the peculiar patrimonie of the *Pope.* Nay, more then this, ſom of thoſe Autors now mentioned, will have this curſ of Excommunication to bee incurred not onely by committing piracie, but by a harmleſs paſſage of Pirats through this ſea; it being all one as if a profanation or injurie were committed upon Church-land. So that ſuch a dominion over the ſea is plainly avouched by the Canon

[z] *Lib. de Cenſibus artic.* 16. § 40.

[a] *Conſil* 290.

[b] *Ad l.* 1. *& de Sentent. ex Brevic. recitanda.*

[c] *De Servitutibus Ruſtic. præd. cap.* 26.

[d] *Laertius Cherubinus in Bullario, tom.* 3 *p.* 251.

[e] *De Cenſuris Pontificî reſervatis, part.* 2. *cap.* 3. § 1.

[f] *Graffius, lib.* 4. *deciſ. cap.* 18. *n.* 53.

[g] *Summa, li.* 1. *cap.* 20.

[h] *De Cenſuris Diſp.* 21. *ſect.* 2. *num.* 18.

[i] *Relict. de Cenſuris Bullæ Cœnæ, cap.* 4. *diſp.* 25. *& ſeqq.*

non Law. And it is confirmed by what may bee gathered out of the gloss of that body. If Herrings were taken upon an holy day, a convenient part of them, by the Canon Law, are due to the next neighboring Churches. There the [k] *gloss* add's *especially to those in whose Territories the Fish were caught.* By a Decree of a General Councel at *Lions*, if the *Pope* dyed beeing out of the Citie, the *Cardinals* are to meet for the Election of his Successor in that Citie, within whose Territorie of Jurisdiction hee died. If the *Pope* die upon the Sea, the Election is to bee made in that Citie or [l] place which is next to the Sea. This intimation is given by the *gloss*, and acknowledged by others.

[k] *Gl. ad C. licet. 3. tit. de Ferris.*

[l] *Gl. ad C. ubi periculum, §. 3. porrò 6. de Electione, & ibi Jo. Andreas.*

But notwithstanding this, the Citizens of *Rome* were allowed the privilege of Fishing, in the *Sea of the Church* (as they call it) or of the *Pope*; as the Inhabitants of a Village bordering upon a pasture-ground, may by virtue of som compact, usage, or custom, put in their Cattel to grase there, though perhaps it bee in the possession of som particular person. This is a Statute of the Citie of [m] *Rome. Everie Citizen of* Rome *and Inhabitant of the Citie, and within the liberties thereof, shall have libertie to Fish, at any time, and with any instruments whatsoëver, in the stream both of* Tiber, Anien, *and in the Sea, so far as the Banks of the Rivers and the Sea-shore do reach. And no person ought to prohibit or forcibly take any thing away from them, so long as they forbear to trespass upon any Lands, Houses, and Fish-ponds, which belong to private Owners; or to com upon the Banks of the Coast of* Arenula, *namely, of* St Severia *and* Paul, *in which places it is not lawful for any to Fish without warrant from the State's Advocate.* And such a kinde of privilege as this, qualified either by

[m] *Statuta, urbis Romæ, lib. 3. cap. 72.*

by grant, or covenant, or custom, is verie often found in such places as enjoy a Dominion of the Sea.

Concerning the received Customs of the Portugals *and* Spaniards, *about the Dominion of the Sea.*

CHAP. XVII.

THat Dominion over the Sea, is acknowledged in the Customs of the *Portugals*, is apparent to any man that will but observ the usual Title of their Kings; King *Emmanuel* in his preface to the Laws of *Portugal* style's himself; *Dom Manuel, per grace de Deos Rey, &c. Senhor de Guinee, & da conquista & Navagaçam & commercio d' Ethiopia, Arabia, Persia, & da India à todos &c.* which ellwhere is rendred in [a] barbarous Latine thus, *Emanuel Dei gratiâ Rex &c. Dominus Guineæ & conquistæ Navigationis ac commercii Æthiopiæ, Arabiæ, Persiæ &c.* Emmanuel **by the grace of God King &c. Lord of** Guinee, **and by Conquest of the Navigation and Commerce of** Ethiopia, Arabia, Persia &c; where *conquista* in the language of *Spain* and *Portugal*, signifieth that which is acquired by War. The same Title is often found in the Letters Patent and Commissions of the ancient Kings of *Portugal*: whereupon *Jacobus* [b] *Valdesius* write's, *that they are, and are acknowledged to bee Lords and Masters of Commerce, Traffick, and Navigation.* But for any person to bee Lord of Navigation and Traffick by Sea, without Dominion over that Sea, is all one, as to use and enjoy a piece of Land, to have right to prohibit all other from doing the like, and yet not to

[a] *Concil. general. Lateran. sub Leone,* 10. *sess.*9.

[b] *De dignitate Regum Hispan* c. 12.

bee owner thereof. But among the Laws of *Portugal* there are yet clearer evidences for private Dominion over the Sea; even of the *Atlantick* or Ocean it self. For, therein it is forbidden that any person either Forraigner or Native (the words of the Law are [c] *Assi Natural commo estrangeiro*) in any shipping whatsoever to pass, *ditas partees, mares de Guinee & Indias, & qualsquer outras terras & mares & lugares de nossa conquista, tratar, resgatar, nem guerrear, sem nossa licença & autoridade, sob pena que fazendo ho contrario moura por ello morte natural & por esso mesmo feito percapera nos todos seus beens moveis & de rays*; that is to say, *to the said countries, lands and Seas of* Guinee, *and the* Indies, *or any other Lands, Seas, and places under our Dominion, for Commerce, or Traffick, or making of War without our Licence and Autoritie, under pain of death and total confiscation of estate, to bee inflicted upon any that shall presume to do the contrarie.* And for the execution hereof, the Commanders of those Fleets, who had leav from the King to sail thither, had Commission given them, to call to account all whom they found in any kinde transgressing this Law. So that, wee see the Nation of *Portugal* also made no question, but that Dominion might bee justly acquired over the Ocean it self. And this Law, in the extent of it, reached as well to forraigners, as to the King's subjects. Although forraigners do not acknowledg that *Portugal* hath acquired any such right. However, that in the Law of Nature which is obligatorie, there is nothing to hinder, but that such a right may bee acquired, is (I suppose) acknowledg'd by all the Nations in *Europe*, except som perhaps who are not yet in fair and lawful possession of any Sea; if so bee at least a man may rightly gather their acknowledgments from their received customs. And truly, about the beginning of Queen *Elizabeth's* reign, there

[c] *O Quinto libro des Ordennaçones,* tit. 112.

there was a hot dispute between [d] her and *Sebastian* King of *Portugal* touching the Dominion of the *Atlantick* and South-Sea that open's the way to the *East-Indies*, which was claimed by the *Portugals*. But the question in that dispute was not, whether or no *Sebastian* could bee Lord of that Navigation or Sea, but whether hee had made any lawful acquisition of such a Dominion. But in the Common Law of *Spain* or *Castile*, although, it bee true, that the use of the Sea is most free, and that in such a manner almost as if no positive Law had ever laid any restraint upon the natural [e] Communitie thereof; yet the *Spanish Lawyers*, and those not of the meanest account, do in most express terms declare it capable of Dominion, yea, and that it was acquired by the King. *The Prince* (saith *Gregorius* [f] *Lopez*) *may grant any man a priviledg to fish in a certain part of the Sea.* And *the Sea* (saith *Joannes* [g] *Garcias* a Spaniard) *belong's to him, who is Lord of the adjoyning land*: This hee speak's of som particular Sea belonging to *Spain*; for to speak it of the sea in general, were idle. There are other also, as *Didacus Couvaruvias*, [i] *Joannes de Hevia*, who are plainly for the Dominion of the Prince, as well for a controlling the libertie of Navigation, as restraining the common use of Fishing. And how frequent this Opinion is among the Lawyers of *Spain* and *Portugal*, is acknowledged by *Fernandus Vasquius*, (though hee himself do extremely oppose it) as appear's by those words of his alreadie cited in the *second Chapter*.

Moreover, it is sufficiently manifest, out of [k] *Rodericus Suarius*, that such rights & priviledges were exercised by private persons, grounded either upon custom, or som grant of the Prince, which demonstrate a dominion over the Sea among the *Spaniards*; although that Autor taking the measure of Law, rather from the Dictates of the

[d] *In Schedis ejusd. Temp. in Biblioth. Cottoniana.*

[e] *Vide Alphons. ad Azeved. ad Constit. Regias, l.* 7. *tit.* 8. *Partid.* 3. *tit.* 28. *l.* 3. *Recopilat. l.* 7. *tit.* 10. *l.* 9. & *Partid.* 5. *tit.* 9. *l.* 7. & 8.

[f] *Ad Alphonsinas, Partid.* 3. *tit.* 28. *l.* 11.

[g] *Lib. de expensis & Meliorationibus, cap.* 21. *num.* 34.

[h] *In Relect. peccatum, part.* 2. §. 8.

[i] *Laberinto de Commercio, lib.* 3. *cap.* 1. §. 12.

[k] *Consil. de usu Maris* § 13.

Schools, then the received Customs of Nations, is the more earnest for that antient opinion of a perpetual communitie. Yea, the verie title of the King of *Spain* hath that in it which may seem to import, that hee call's himself King of the Ocean; especially, if you consider those words which wee finde somtimes among Germane Writers, in the Title of *Charls* the fifth Emperor, and King of *Spain*. In the Preface to the constitution concerning publick Judicatories, in the Empire, hee is called *King of the Canarie Ilands, also of the Islands of the Indies, and of the Continent, and of the Ocean, Archduke of Austria &c.* And in the Imperial Sanctions published in high Dutch **Konig under Insulen** *Canariæ*, **auch der Insulen** *Indiarum*, **und** *Terræ firmæ*, **des Maers** *Oceani &c.* as you may meet with it at least six hundred times. The word Ocean is added, as if hee entitled himself *King of the Ocean*. But this is a mistake: for, the same in Spanish is *Rey &c. de las Islas, y terra firma del mar Oceano &c.* that is, *King of the Islands and of the* Terra firma *of the Ocean*; namely, the Islands or Continents of, or lying in the Ocean, (which Pope [1] *Alexander* the Sixth, gave to *Ferdinand* the Fifth King of *Spain*, all of them lying Westward from the very first Meridian) of those hee entitle's himself King, not of the Ocean it self.

1 *Laërt. Cherubin. Bullar. tom. 1. pag. 392. de qua donatione fuse Joannes Solorzanus de Jure Indiarum, lib. 2. cap. 22.*

How

How far private Dominion over the Sea is admitted, according to the Customs, or opinion of the French.

CHAP. XVIII.

AS concerning Dominion of the Sea according to the Customs of the *French*, som perhaps may seem to have met with verie ancient evidences thereof, in those *Officers deputed for the guard of the Sea-Coasts*, whom wee read of in the [a] Statute-Books, and in that *Rotlandus, Governor of the British* (that is, the *Aremorican*) *shore*, mentioned in the life of *Charle-maign* by *Eginhartus* a Writer of that time. But those dignities have relation, not so much to the Sea it self, as to the shore and Sea-Coast, or the border of the Land confining with the Sea; notwithstanding that *Rotlandus* is, by the *French-men* of this and the former Age, promiscuously styled [b] Governor both of the Sea and Shore, as if there were no difference. But it cannot bee denied, that Princes heretofore upon the Shore of *Aremorica* or *Bretaign* (as the *Veneti* * of whom wee spake before, did upon the same Shore) impose Custom upon Ships, as for the use of the Road upon their Coasts, and challenge to themselvs other Rights of the like nature, called *Nobilitates super navibus*. So it is to bee read in an ancient Record, made in the time of Duke *Alanus* in the year MLXXXVII, concerning Precedence of Place among the Nobles of *Bretaigne*. In that Record, the second place is assigned to the Viscount of St *Pol de Leon*, who (as the very [c] words of it are) had verie many of those Cu-

[a] *Capitular. Caroli & Ludovici Impp. lib.* 4. *tit.* 5.

[b] *Choppinus de Domanio, lib.* 1. *tit* 15. *Pasquier*, en les recerches de la France, *lib.* 2. *cap.* 14. *Simon Marion*, Plaidoye, 5. *edit. Paris.* 1591. *Tilius, & alii.*

* The *Veneti* were an antient people inhabiting that part of *France* now called *Bretaigne.*

[c] *Apud. Bertrand. Argentræum, in hist. Britan. minoris, lib.* 1. *cap.* 13.

Customs called *Nobilitates super navibus*, imposed on such as passed the Ocean upon the Coasts of *Osismer* or *Leon*; *which* (as it was said) Budicius, *an antient King of* * Bretaign, *did give and grant to one of his predecessors, upon Marriage, in reward of the virtue, fidelitie and valor of that Viscount: but with the consent of the Prelates, Counts, Barons, and Nobles of Bretaign.* What these *Nobilitates* were, and whence they had their original, is partly declared *by Bertrandus Argentræus,* somtime President of the Province of *Renes,* where hee discourseth also of the right of giving Pass-ports (which they call *brefs de conduicte*) at this time in use on that shore. [d] *That* (saith hee) *whereas till then it had been a right peculiar to the Princes, beeing given, by way of Dowrie, to the Barons of* Leon (of which wee have alreadie spoken out of the aforesaid Record) *remained an hereditarie and proper right to that Familie, until* Joannes Ruffus *the Duke redeemed it for a vast sum of monie, of* Guynomarius *Baron of* Leon, *after that* Peter Mauclerc *of* Dreux, *Duke of* Bretaign *had in vain attempted to re-assume it by force of arms. It had its original, they say, upon this occasion: When our Princes and antient Kings considered the daily Shipwracks made upon that shore, where there were many Rocks and but few Havens, they made a Law that none should set to Sea without their leav. Such as did set out, paying a certain rate, had passes, and guides appointed them,* that were well acquainted with the Sea and Shores: *They that refused, forfeited their ships with all their tackling and furniture thereof: and if the Ship were cast away, their goods also were confiscate. They that had leav were in no danger of confiscation, and if they suffered Shipwrack, had libertie to recover as many of their goods as they could. And these guides were paid their* σῶστρα *or Conduct-money, which* wee

* *Aremorica* or *Bretaign* in *France.*

[d] *Ad Consuet. Brit. Art.* 56. § 44.

wee have mentioned elswhere, called by them droit de salvage. *These Tickets or Passes are given out now, as heretofore, at a certain price : And among other Revenues of the Exchequer, they also were rented out to the Farmers of the Custom.* So far *Bertrandus*, from whom *Renatus* [e] *Choppinus* borroweth almost the very words. But [f] *Petrus Berlordæus*, Advocate of the Parlament of *Reines*, tell's us, that the Custom of taking forfeiture in that manner of all shipwrack't goods, was abolished there, by an Edict, in the year MDLXXXIII. But in the mean time, for so much as concern's any part of that Western Sea lying next the Shore, these are manifest evidences, either of Dominion or of subjection in the Sea; which indeed sufficiently prove, by the Customs of that people, that the Sea is capable of Dominion. Moreover, upon occasion of these Passes, there have been controversies raised somtimes between the Dukes of *Bretaign*, and the Kings of *England*; as may bee seen in certain [g] memorials of the affairs of *Bretaign*, which have relation to the times of our *Richard* the second, and *John* the Fourth, Duke of *Bretaign*. But this wee know for certain, that in the agreement made between our *Edward* the Fourth, and *Francis* the second, Duke of *Bretaign*, in the year MCCCCLXVIII, concerning mutual traffick and free passage to and fro for the subjects of each Nation, during a [h] truce of thirtie years, there is an express *proviso* concerning Wrecks; but such a one as left an equal right to both of them; not altogether unlike that which for many ages hath been in use upon the *English* Shore : No mention at all beeing made in the Articles of the Truce, either of the right or use of these aforesaid Passes, as beeing a thing in no wise admitted by the *English*. But som modern Lawyers

[e] *De Domanio, lib.* 1. *tit.* 15. §. 10. & *& Thom. Cormer. Cod. Hen.* 4. *lib.* 7. *tit.* 1. *cap.* 6. §. 106.

[f] *In Consuetud. Brit. Art.* 51.

[g] *In Bibliotheca Cottoniana.*

[h] *Ibid. & Rot. Franciæ* 8 *Ed.* 4. *membran.* 20. & *seqq.*

among the *French* do vainly affirm, that their King is Lord not onely of a part of the Sea neighboring upon the Territorie of *Bretaign*, but of the whole Sea that is adjoyning to any part of *France*, and so of the *British* or *English* Sea also: By which very Assertion of theirs, they sufficiently declare their judgment, that there may bee a soveraign over the Sea. *The King*, saith [i] *Charondas Caronæus, is supreme Lord of the Seas, which flow about his Kingdom: the ground whereof is this, becaus the Universal right of all those things which were common, either by the Law of nature or Nations, is transferred into his Dominion.* And other passages hee hath much to the same purpose; as also [k] *Stephanus Paschasius*, [l] *Ludovicus Servinus*, somtime Sollicitor general for the King, [m] *Popellinerius*, and others. If they speak of the Sea of *Marseille* or *Narbon*, wee shall not oppose them. But as to what concern's the bodie of the Sea which lie's Northward or Westward of the *French*, or that flow's between *France* and the Islands of *great Britain* (for that which lie's Westward from them upon that crooked Shore, or the gulf of *Aquitaine*, doth indeed flow between the more Westerly Coasts of our British Isles, and of *France*, as well as that which lie's Northward from them, flow's between *England* and *Normandie*) they neither produce any Testimonies of Antiquitie, nor indeed can they if they would: Unless you will have that admitted which hath been cited out of *Cæsar* concerning the *Veneti* of * *Aremorica*, and that which wee said before of the Sea bordering upon that shore. Both which indeed do rather import som service, called heretofore *Nobilitates super navibus*, then any kinde of Dominion. But the soveraigntie of this Sea which flow's between them and us, became absolutely

ap-

[i] *In not. ad Codic. Henrici, 3. l. 20. tit. 7. Constit. 28 & constit. 1.*

[k] *Recerches, liv. 2. c. 14.*

[l] *Playdoies tom. 2. playd. 11.*

[m] *L'Amiral de France.*

* Now *Bretaign* in *France.*

appropriate to the Kings of *England*, as wee ſhall make it appear in the next Book. And the truth is, if wee look upon the Cuſtoms moſt in uſe among the *French*, or the Civil Law of that Nation, there is nothing in it that derogate's from the antient communitie of the Sea, but as to them it remaine's as yet not poſſeſſed, but common to all men, and therefore not to bee reckoned among the Revenues or Patrimonie of their Kings; if ſo bee credit may bee given to that Treatiſe lately publiſhed of the Civil *Romane* and *French* Law, by *Thomas Cormerius* Counſellor to *Francis* Duke of *Anjou* in his Parlament of *Alençon*. The matter that it pretend's to treat of, is the *Romane Gallick* Law. There are in it the Cuſtoms of *France*, decrees of Princes, and Privileges often intermingled. But under the [n] Title *of things common to all*, hee make's the Sea and Shores common to all, according to the antient Law of the *Romanes*, as if in this matter it did exactly agree with the Law of *France*: which certainly is an argument, that the *French* have no Dominion over the Sea. Nor muſt wee let it paſs, that ſomwhile ſince, there were two Conſtitutions pretended to in *France*, one of [o] *Henrie* the Second, the other of [p] *Henrie* the Third, wherein they required that the Ships of Forraigners which ſailed through the Sea bordering upon *France*, ſhould ſtrike their top-ſail forſooth, in acknowledgment of that Dominion the *French* had over the Sea. But neither of them were autorized, or (as they ſpeak) ſimply verified by the Eſtates in Parlament, yea, nor ſo much as admitted into Cuſtom. Nay, the later of them was plainly rejected as to any effect in Law. And this the *French* Lawyers themſelvs confeſs

[n] *Cod.Hen.* 4.*lib.*3. *tit.*1. *cap.*2.

[o] *Ann.*1555.

[p] *Ann.*1584.

in a [q] notable case between som Merchants of *Hamburgh*, that were *Plaintiffs*, and *Michaël Butardus* and others *Defendants*, in a Parlament held at *Tours*, in the time of *Henry* the Fourth. But that cerimonie hath by most ancient right and custom been observed and paid to the ships of the Kings of *England*, out of respect, and in acknowledgement of their Dominion, as is shewn in the following Book, where wee treat of this particular more at large. I know very well, [r] it was ordained by an Edict of the French King, that one third part of all goods, recovered out of the Sea, should belong to the King, another to the Admiral, and the remainder to the Sea-men that found them. And that the French do reckon very many Commanders in Chief at Sea, or Admirals in a line somtime continued, and somtime interrupted, which for the most part they begin from the time of *Philip* the son of S^t^. *Lewis*; that is, from the year MCCLXXXIV. as is to be seen in [s] *Joannes Feronius*, [t] *Stephanus Paschasius*, and others. But that division of goods recovered out of the Sea beeing simply considered, doth prove any Dominion over the Sea, no more then the Tenths of any Prizes taken from an Enemie at Sea, which, by the grant of the King also, were allotted to the [u] Admiral of the Navie. Rights of this nature are grounded upon the consent of persons, to wit, subjects; transferr'd unto the King, not upon any title of Dominion, whereby any Pretence may bee made to an acquiring of the Sea it self; and they are paid no otherwise then Imposts or Customs, in the importation or exportation of Merchandise. But no man (I suppose) will imagin that from such Imposts or Customs upon Merchandise any proof may bee

[q] *Lud. Servinus in Placit. vol. 2. Placit. 11, 12. dec. 1592. pag. 262. b. Edit. 1609.*

[r] *Edict. Francisc. 1. promulg. 1543. art. 11. Choppin. de dom. Franc. lib 1. tit. 15. & Edict. Franc. tom. 3. tit. 2.*

[s] *Catalog. Admiral. Franc.*

[t] *Recerches, lib. 2. cap. 14.*

[u] *Edict Fran. Tom. 3. tit. 2. Constit. 4. & 5.*

bee made of a Dominion over thoſe paſſages through which the Merchants ſail before they arrive. Neither indeed was there any ſuch cuſtom as this in uſe among the *French*, before the time of *Francis* the firſt; that is to ſay, plainly, not beeing Lord of the Sea, hee deſired to bee and was made a Sharer of thoſe goods which ſhould bee drawn by his ſubjects, out of any Sea whatſoëver. Whereas the King of *Great Britain* by virtue of his Dominion over the Sea, is wont to take as his own whatſoëver is left or loſt in the ſea, beſides other emoluments of the like nature, and that by ſo ancient a right, as (for ought wee know) bear's a date no leſs ancient then the Kingdom it ſelf. And as for thoſe Admirals of *France*, they were no other then Chief Commanders of Navies and Perſons, and of the Forces by ſea, and Judicatories at home: but not qualified as Preſidents of a Sea-Province or Territorie, as the *Cuſtodes ipſius Maris*, the Guardians of the ſea among the *Engliſh*, and the Admirals of *England*. But more of this in the *Second Book*. Nevertheleſs, from what hath been alleged concerning the Cuſtoms, Opinions, or Conſtitutions, among the *French*, I ſuppoſe it ſufficiently appear's, that they do alſo acknowledg, that private Dominion over the ſea, is not repugnant to the Law either of Nature, or Nations; which ſerve's fully for the clearing of the point in queſtion.

The private Dominion of the Sea, according to the received Customs of the Danes, *the People of* Norway, *the* Swedes, Polanders, *and* Turks.

Chap. XIX.

WEE finde clear Testimonies in the Customs of other Nations, also of *Europe*, touching private Dominion of the sea; as the *Danes*, the people of *Norway*, the *Polanders*, to whom may bee added also the *Turks*. Wee have observed by the Tolls or Customs of *Denmark* and *Norway*, what Revenue the King of *Denmark* raiseth out of the very Navigation of the *Baltick* Sea (as is commonly known) and what is paid out of the Roialtie of the *Norwegian* sea to the King of *Norway*, who at this time is also King of *Denmark*. For, in the year MDLXXXIII. *Frederick*, the second, King of *Denmark* and *Norway*, made a Grant of the use of the Northern or *Norwegian* sea, for a certain time, to our Merchants of the *Muscovie* Companie in such a manner, as if hee had rented out any Land whereof hee stood fully seized and possessed. Hee limited the Grant also with such conditions, as hee thought fit. The publick Instruments or Records about this Particular, are [a] yet extant; whereby the King had an annual Tribute in recompence, other Merchants were excluded, and the Grant it self was to continue no longer then the Peace made between that King and the *Moscovit*. Wee read also in the ancient Histories of *Denmark*, of King *Harald Hildetan*; *that no man did presume to usurp a Domination*

[a] *In Thesauro Cottoniano.*

in

in the Sea without his consent. And that which follow's next, ought especially to bee taken notice of as to this Particular, *becaus the Empire of Land and Sea was once divided in the Republick of Denmark.* And *Olo* (who afterwards was King) succeeding his Father *in the Dominion of the Sea, vanquish't* LXX *Kings of the Sea by Sea-Fight.* Which things are written by [b] *Saxo Grammaticus*, and other also of that kinde. And in the [c] Treatie held at **Koppenhagen** betwixt *Christiern* the fourth of *Denmark*, and *Gustavus Adolphus* of *Swedland*, the *King of* Swedland *renounceth the right,* Soveraigntie, *and Dominion of the Sea,*and the other Roialties by him formerly claimed over the said sea, *in* Norway, Norland, *and in the Jurisdiction of* **Wardhuisen**. But touching the Sea of *Norway*, as it lie's more Northward, wee shall add more at the latter end of the second Book.

[b] *Daniæ Hist. lib.7.*

[c] *20 Jan. 1613. in Rot Tract. Amicit. Temp. Jacobi Regis.*

Mention is made likewise of the Sea belonging to the Realm of *Poland*, and the Dominion thereof, in that Promise which was made by the *French* Ambassadors, in the name of *Henrie* III of *France*, when hee was elected King of *Poland*. *The aforesaid Ambassadors do promise, in the name of the most illustrious King now chosen, that assoon (God willing) as hee shall com to his Kingdom, hee will at his own charge maintain a convenient Navie, sufficient to defend the Ports and the Soveraigntie of the Sea, belonging to the Kingdom and the Provinces adjoyning, even to the utmost bounds of the whole Dominion of Poland*; as it is recorded by *Janus Januszowskius* in his [d] *Syntagma* of the statutes of *Poland*. But the *Turkish* Emperor, (who by Conquest succeeded in the right of the Emperors of *Constantinople*, and so purchased both the *Ægean* and *Euxin* sea, calling this the *black*, the other the *white sea*) is wont solemnly to intitle himself *Lord both of the white and*

[d] *Lib.3.tit.1. fol. 109.*

and black sea; as you may see in the League betwixt *Achmet* the *Ottoman* Emperor, and *Henry* the IV. of *France*, made above thirty years since, and [e] printed both in the *French* and *Turkish* Tongue. Moreover, in the same League, the *Turk* grant's the *French* free leav to Fish, and search for *Coral*, in certain Streits and Creeks of the *African* Sea, within his Kingdoms of *Algier* and *Tunis*. And hee farther confirm's all that had been granted to them by his Predecessors, for freedom of Fishing in those parts. In like manner [f] *Coriolanus Cippicus*, relating the Actions of *Pietro Mocenigo*, General of the *Venetians*, saith; *The Ottoman Emperor built two Castles very well fortified, over against each other, on both sides the Hellespont in its narrowest passage, which hee stored with Ordnance of an extraordinary bigness, and charged the Governors of the Castles to shoot and sink any ship, that should endeavor to pass without leav.* Which is plainly to domineer over the Sea, and agreeable to his Title, of *Lord of the white and black Sea*. Neither is that to bee sleighted here, which wee finde in the Letters of *David*, Emperor of *Ethiopia*, or the *Abassins*, to *Emmanuël* King of *Portugal*. Hee entituleth him [g] *Lord of* Africa *and* Guinee, *and the Mountains and Island of the Moon, and of the Red Sea,* Arabia *and* Persia, *and* Armutia, *great* India, *&c.* Hee useth here an *Hyperbole*, after the manner of the *African* Princes, and attribute's those things to *Emmanuël* which were none of his: But in the mean time, hee admit's that hee might have been Lord of the Red Sea, as well as of any other Territorie, and that that Title doth not intrench upon the Law of Nature or Nations, any more then this.

Now that wee may at length conclude this part touching the Dominion of the Sea, as admitted among

[e] 20 *Martii*, 1604. *Parisiis*, 1615.

[f] *De Asiatico Bello, lib.* 2.

[g] *Apud Franciscum Alvarum de rebus Æthiopicis, & Damianus à Goes, lib. de Æthiopum moribus.*

among those things that are lawful, and received into the Customs of Nations; there are not onely very many Testimonies every where (as hath been shewn you) concerning it; but nothing at all (I suppose) can bee found to impugn it in the Customs of those Nations that have been of any note in later times; unless it bee where som of them, that are Borderers upon the Sea-Dominions of others, do strive to violate or infringe the Rights of their Neighbors, under pretence of that Natural and perpetual communitie, so often insisted on out of *Ulpian* by such Writers, as too much prefer that obsolete Opinion before the Universal and most antient Customs of Nations. Of which kinde truly the first Article of that League seem's to bee, which was made above twentie or about thirtie years past, betwixt the States of the *United Provinces* and som of the *Hans-Towns*, as it was translated out of Low-Dutch by a [h] Dutch-man, to this effect: *That this Conjunction or Union ought not to bee intended for the offence of any, but onely for the preservation and maintenance of the freedom of Navigation, Commerce and Merchants, in the Eastern and Northen Seas, and also in all Rivers and* Streams *running into the Eastern and Northern Seas; nor ought any other thing to bee meant in this place, so that their Citizens and Subjects joyned in this League respectively, may according to the Law of Nations use and enjoy the Liberties acquired and obtained, together with the Rights, Privileges, and Customs received from their Ancestors, throughout the Eastern and Northern Seas aforesaid, and in the aforesaid Rivers, Streams, and waters, without any Let or Impediment.* They promise also to aid each other, in opposing any that should hinder such a freedom of Navigation in that Northern and Eastern Sea; that

[h] *Eman. Meteranus, Histor. Belgic. lib.* 36. *& apud Gasper. Klockum, lib. de Contributionibus, c.* 14.

that is to ſay, the *Baltick,* and that which waſheth the Coaſts of *Denmark*, *Lituania*, *Pomerania*, and the Dominions of the King of *Poland*: where it ſeem's they pretend not onely Rights and Liberties peculiarly granted to them long ſince, but alſo to the very Law of all Nations. It is no hard matter to gueſs what the Intent of that League might bee; For, about that time, the King of *Denmark* had raiſed his Toll in the *Baltick* Sea, and in like manner the King of *Poland* within his Territories by Sea. And that for the maintenance of that Dominion which they enjoyed; which that kinde of League betwixt the States of the *Hanſ-Towns* and *United Provinces* did ſeem to oppoſe. But, to paſs over theſe things, ſeeing a private Dominion of the Sea, which is the point in Queſtion, is founded upon ſuch clear Teſtimonies, out of the Cuſtoms of ſo many famous Nations both antient and modern (whereto wee ſhall add many other alſo, when wee treat of the *Britiſh* Sea in the next Book) nothing now, I ſuppoſe, hinder's why wee may not determine, that the Sea is capable of Dominion as well as the Land, not only by the *Law Natural-Permiſſive,* but alſo by the Law both *Civil* and *Common of divers Nations*, and in many places almoſt according to the *Intervenient Law* (which in caſes of this nature is the ſureſt demonſtration of the *Natural-Permiſſive*) unleſs there remain any impediment in the objections, which are next to bee handled.

An Answer to the Objection, concerning Freedom of Passage *to* Merchants, Strangers, *and* Sea-men.

CHAP. XX.

THe usual Objections (as hath been more fully shewn before in the second Chapter) are derived, som from the Freedom of Commerce, Travel, and Passage, pretended to bee common to all: Som also from the very Nature of the Sea: And others out of the Testimonies of Writers. As to what concern's the first sort; the Offices of humanitie require, that entertainment bee given to Strangers, and that inoffensive passage bee not denied them. So [a] *Gratian* out of [b] *Augustin* saith, *It is to bee observed how the war of the* Israëlites *became just against the* Amorites: *For, they were denied an inoffensive Passage, which ought in all equitie to lie open by the Law of humane Societie.* And [c] Cicero saith, *It is an inhumane thing, to denie Strangers the use of a Citie.* Verie many other Passages there are of that sort, which seem to strengthen the *Objection*; to wit, as it relate's unto the Office of Humanitie, not disturbed by war, fear, jealousie, enmities, or any other of the same kinde. But what is this to the Dominion of that thing, through which both Merchants and Strangers are to pass? Such a freedom of Passage would no more derogate from it, (if so bee it were without question free and open to all upon that accompt) then the allowing of an open waie for the driving of Cattel, or Cart, or passing through upon a journie, or any other Service of that nature, through

[a] *Caus.* 23. *Quest.* 2. c. 3. & *videsis Hug. Grotium de Jure Belli & Pacis, lib.* 2. *cap.* 2. §. 13.

[b] *In Numer q.* 41.

[c] *Offic. lib.* 3.

another man's Field, could prejudice the Ownership thereof. Suppose it bee granted, that, by the Law of all Nations, the *Spaniards* had a free Passage over the *Pyrenean* Mountains into *France*; the *French* over the *Alps* into *Italie*; the *Italians* into *Germanie*: What doth this concern a Dominion of the *Pyrenies* or the *Alps*? And for any man to allege here, what is commonly talked, of the lighting of one Candle by another, of the not denying a common use of Water, and other things of that nature, it is plainly to give over the disquisition of *Law* and *Right*, to insist upon that of *Charitie*. At the request indeed of *Asclepiades* Bishop of the Citie of *Chersonesus*, under the Emperors [c] *Arcadius* and *Honorius*, certain persons, who had taught the barbarous people the Art of building ships, whereof they were ignorant before, were for Charitie's sake freed from the pains of Prison and punishment. And though the Art of those that taught them was no whit the less, becaus of that skill which the Barbarians had gained; yet by the Law, it was death to communicate that Art unto them: And at this day, there are other instances of the same nature: So that it in no wise diminisheth from any man's Right or Power, to permit another to participate of what is his, when hee himself loseth nothing thereof. And that wee may determine this point in brief, it is most evident from the Customs of all times, that free Passage (as they call it) is wont ever to bee so limited by Princes in their Territories, that it is permitted or prohibited, according to the various concernments of the Publick Good, and not otherwise. *Albericus Gentilis*, upon that Passage concerning the *Amorites*, saith, [e] *I am of the same opinion, with* Augustine, *in case there bee no fear of hurt*,

[c] *C. Theodos. lib.* 10. *tit.* 40. *l.* 24. & *C. just. tit. de Pœnis. l.* 25.

[d] *De Jure belli, lib.* 1. *cap.* 19.

hurt, and an assurance that no hurt may bee don. Princes are concerned to bee warie and careful, that they admit no such strangers, or Commerce, where, *pro re natâ*, the Common-weal may receiv any damage thereby. Upon which ground also it is often provided in Leagues;[e] *That it shall not bee lawful for either Partie to sail unto each others Ports, Coasts, or Harbors*, (and this when neither of them hath any right to the waie by which they pass) *with such a number of ships or Men of War, as may give a just occasion of any fear or jealousie that force is intended, except leav bee first had of that Partie under whose Jurisdiction those Places are; or unless they bee driven thither by Tempest or som other necessity, to avoid a greater force, or the danger of Shipwrack.* According to the fear or suspition of the Lord in possession, and at his discretion, all Merchants, Strangers, and Foreigners whatsoëver may bee prohibited, unless som other special right or custom do intervene. And [f] *Aristotle* saith plainly, Provision ought to bee made by Laws, *with whom subjects may, or may not convers.* [g] *Bodin* also saith well, *That the Laws of Commerce are contained in the particular Compacts and Agreements of People and Princes.* And in another place hee add's, *It is lawful to forbid a Foreigner from entring the Borders, and also to force him out if hee have entred the* Borders, *not onely if a War bee on foot, but also in time of Peace, that the manners of the Inhabitants may not bee corrupted by convers with Strangers.* But that Wars have been lawfully undertaken for a denial of Commerce, unless the denial were given contrary to som antient League, or unless that freedom depended upon som special Title to Commerce, wee do as easily deny as any other man can affirm. And though, according to the opinion of [h] *Franciscus Victoria*, who also is followed chiefly by [i] *Joannes Solorzanus*

[e] *Induciæ Hispan. & Ordin. Fœderat. Belg. Anno 1609. & Art. 12. &c.*

[f] *Polit. lib. 7. cap. 6.*

[g] *De Repub. lib. 1. cap. 7. & 6. & vide eum, lib. 4 ca. 1. & lib. 6. cap. 2.* ubi de Aditu ad Moluccas.

[h] *Tit. de Indis.*

[i] *De Jure Indiar. lib. 2. cap. 20. § 55.*

I. V. D. it bee affirmed, that the *Spaniard* had a lawful Right to subdue the *Indians*, becaus they denied Commerce and Entertainment; yet they are in plain tearms opposed by [k] *Ludovicus Molina*, who will have no Nation or Common weal bound, either with or without danger to it self, to admit Commerce or Foreigners, but in case of great and imminent necessitie, or unless any League, Agreement, or som other special privilege do intervene. But there are other pretences not a few which the *Spaniards* allege for the Conquest of the *Indies*: For, they pretend also a Right of Discoverie, primarie occupation, Conversion to the Faith, and other things of that nature, besides the Donation of the *Pope*. Of all which, *Solorzanus* treat's at large. And it is strange, how the *Spaniards* should have a Right to acquire the *Indies*, upon a denial of Commerce, since it is [l] very well known, that both They and the *Portugals* do openly profess, that they may lawfully prohibit Commerce in both the *Indies*. Nor doth it prejudice the point at all, that according to the Imperial Law, no Prince, nor any other holding Royalties by his Grant, can [m] forbid men passage in the common Road without som just caus, which must bee determined in an Imperial Diet; nevertheless, it is wrested by som to prove a freedom of Navigation at Sea. For that happen'd by a particular Law, agree'd upon by the Estates of the Empire, who themselvs also are subject to a *Diet*. But other Nations that are under several and distinct Soveraignties, have not as yet made any such Agreement, that there should alwaies bee a libertie of Passage to and fro; nor have they (like the *Germanes*, and others within their Dominion) referr'd themselvs unto an Umpire to determine the business.

[k] *De Justitiâ & Jure, Tract.* 2. *Disputat.* 105.

[l] *Georgius de Cabedo Decis. Lusitan. part.* 2. *Decis.* 47. *& diploma Regis Hispan* Mari Libero. *Hug. Grot. subnexum.*

[m] *Rothensal. de Jure Feudali, cap* 5. *de Regalibus, conclus.* 21. *Sixtinus de Regalibus, lib.* 2. *cap.* 2. *&c.*

An

An Answer to that Objection concerning the uncertain fluid nature of the Sea, *and its continual Alteration. It is proved, that* Rivers *also, and the* adjoyning Aër *(which are more fluid and uncertain) may becom appropriate.*

CHAP. XXI.

BUT they say, that the very Nature of the Sea render's it unfit for privat Dominion; both becaus it is ever in Motion, and in no wise remain's the same; as also becaus a convenient matter, as well as Instruments, are wanting therein to make a distinction of Bounds; without which private Dominions cannot well consist: yea, and becaus by reason of its vast and spatious Body, it is alwaies sufficient for all. As to what concern's its fluid Nature, are not Rivers and Fountains much more in a perpetual Flux or Motion? Rivers alwaies run forward, wherewith the Sea beeing compared, it seem's to stand immovable, as saith [a] *Strabo.* And [b] *Eustathius* saith, that *Homer* therefore call's the Sea by the name of a standing Pool; *becaus it run's not forward (as Rivers do) but is very stable.* And [c] another saith, *the Sea stands without Motion, as it were som dull heap of matter that Nature could not bring to perfection.* But suppose wee grant it bee so fluid, as is usually said of the most Northernly Seas and Channels; yet certainly the Channels and places out of which the waters flow, remain ever the same, though the waters themselvs do shift and change

[a] *Geograph. lib.* 1.
[b] *Ad Iliad.* &
[c] *Seneca, Suasor.* 1.

change continually. Nor yet can it be supposed that the Right of private Dominion over Rivers, is any whit prejudiced thereby. In the *Romane-Germane* Empire, Rivers, according to the Civil Law, are of publick use; yet they are reckoned in the *Emperor's* [d] private Patrimonie, and among the Rights or Roialties belonging to his Exchequer: so that either the *Emperor* or others by his Grant, have in like manner a yearly Revenue out of the *Fisheries* in them. Upon which accompt it come's to pass, that they of *Lombardy*, and other particular People throughout *Italy*, enjoie all the Rivers of their Territories, as proper and peculiar to themselvs by Prescription, as wee are told by [e] *Cæpola*. Nor is any thing more common, then an asserting of the private Dominion of Rivers as well as their Banks, in the Laws of *Spain*, *France*, *Poland*, and *Venice*; and in a word, of all Nations whose Customs are known to us. Nor, as to what concern's this Objection (fetch't from the fluid Constitution of the sea) is there any difference in nature between a greater and a lesser, a private and a publick River. Even [f] *Ulpian* himself concerning Rivers, saith, *There is no difference between a private River, and other private Places.* And [g] *Martianus*; *If a man hath fish't all alone many years in a Corner of a publick River, hee may hinder any other from using the same Libertie.* Moreover, oftentimes heretofore in the *Romane* Empire, Rivers were made over as well as other Parts, after the manner of Lands assigned. [h] *Siculus Flaccus* saith, *In som Countries, even the Rivers themselvs are assigned out by measure. But in som the subcesive or remanent part onely is left out unassigned; and yet it is excepted out from the parts assigned, as belonging still onely to the river it self.* After the same manner also [i] *Aggenus Urbicus*. For, it was never conceived, that the

[d] *Feud. lib. 5. tit. Quæ sint Regalia. Rothensal. de Jure Feud. cap. 5. Conclus. 23. & 24. Sixtinus de Regalibus, lib. 2. cap. 3. &c.*

[e] *De Servitut. Rustic. Prædiorum, cap. 31.*

[f] *Lib. 1. § 4. ff. de Fluminibus.*

[g] *L. 7. ff. de Divers. Temp. Prescript. Vide l. 45. ff. de Usucapionibus.*

[h] *Lib. de Conditionibus Agrorum.*

[i] *Comm. ad Jul. Frontin. de limitibus Agrorum.*

the Rivers were otherwise acquired by the People or Emperor of *Rome* then the adjoyning Lands; according to that of the river *Danubius*, speaking to the Emperors;

> [k] *Danubius penitùs caput occultatus in oris,*
> *Totus sub vestrâ jam Ditione fluo:*
> *Et quà Dives aquis Scythico solvo ostia Ponto,*
> *Omnia sub vestrum flumina mitto Jugum.*

[k] *Ausonius*, *Epigr.* 4.

> **Danubius, I, whose Fountain few do know,**
> **Now wholly under your Dominion flow:**
> **And when full-charg'd run to the Euxin sea,**
> **I make all Rivers to you Tribute pay.**

Wee know, that an Island newly sprung up in a river, as also a Chanel that is deserted, is even by antient Custom[l] common to such, as upon the Bank of any river do possess Lands that are not limited, that is to say, after the manner of Lands or Possessions; unless there bee som special Law or Custom to the contrary. And touching the Division of such an Island according to the nature of several Lands, situate near one Bank or both, *Bartolus in Tiberiade*, hath written long since; but of later time *Joannes Buteo*, *Baptista Aymus*, *Antonius Maria*, *Joannes Gryphiander*, and others. Therefore, in that case, a Proprietie of the Chanel, and so of the River (even of that which according to the Civil Law, is of publick and common use; as well as of a Field that hath a common Thorowfare) was common before to the Owners that had Lands lying on both sides. By the same reason almost, an Island newly sprung up in any sea, that never was possessed by any, and whatsoever shall bee built upon it, become's his that first enter's it by

[l] *L.*7.29,30 65. *F. de Acquir. Rer. dominis & Instit. de Rerum divis.* § *Insula.*

occupation: For, the Chanel and that Sea, at first belong'd to all men in general. But by virtue of that Universal Compact or Agreement (before mentioned) whereby things not yet possessed, were to becom the Proprietie of him that should first enjoie them by Occupation; hee that shall so possess them by Occupation, receiv's the Island and Building as it were by a Surrender of Right from former Owners. Seeing therefore that a Proprietie and private Dominion of Rivers hath been every where acknowledged, why should it not bee acknowledged in like manner that there may bee Owners of any Sea whatsoëver? Since the fluid nature of water can no more hinder a Dominion in the one, then in the other. Yea, the Rivers themselvs are onely lesser Seas, as also the Fenns and Lakes; even as the Sea it self (as to its fluid Constitution) is no other then a River, Fen, or Lake, differing onely in bigness from the rest: And so it hath been taken by the Antients. In the very storie of the Creation, all the Gatherings together of the waters are called Seas; which hath been observed also by the [m] Fathers to this purpose. There are also very eminent examples in holy Scripture touching the two Lakes of *Asphaltites*, and *Tiberias*, both which are equally called Seas. *Asphaltites*, is by *Pliny*, *Ptolomy*, *Josephus*, *Solinus*, and *Vitruvius*, tearm'd a Lake: But by *Moses* [n] the *salt Sea*; and by most of the late Writers, *the dead Sea*. *Tiberias* is in like manner by the Antients, and also by S^t^ [o] *Luke*, called a Lake; by the other *Evangelists* a Sea, as also in the Syriack and Arabick Translation of St *Luke*. And [p] *Aristotle* saith, that about the Mountain *Caucasus*, there is a Lake or λίμνη, *but the neighbouring People call it a Sea*. Hee speak's of the Lake *Mæotis*, which by reason of that abundance of Waters

[m] *Eucherius ad Genes.* 1. *D. Hieronymus*, & *alii.* Adde *Jo. Philoponum de Mundi Creätione, lib.* 4. *cap.* 6.

[n] *Gen.* 14. 3.

[o] *Luc.* 5. 1.

[p] *Meteorologic. lib.* 1. *cap.* 13.

Waters which it dischargeth through the *Cimmerian Bosphorus* into the *Euxin Sea*, is by the Antients called [q] *Mother of the Sea, or Mother of the* Euxin *Sea.* From whence also it was the opinion of som, that *Mæotis* stood in the same relation unto *Pontus, Propontis*, and the *Ægean* Sea, as the Ocean doth to the *Mediterranean.*

[q] *Herodotus, in Melpomene. Plin. lib. 6. cap. 7. Dionys. Afer, & ad eum Eustathius.*

Oceanúmque negant solas admittere Gades,

They do deny, that Cadiz **Streight**
Alone, admit's the Ocean's Freight;

As [r] *Lucan* saith concerning it. But [s] *Agathia* tell's us, that in *Justinian*'s daies, it was called *The little Sea.* And saith [t] *Festus Avienus* to *Probus*; *Thou did'st question mee (if thou dost remember) about the situation of the* Mæotick *Sea.* By which means it hath happen'd, that even at this day it is called *Mar delle Zabach,* and *Mar della Tana.* So seven Lakes of the River *Po* in *Italy* are usually tearmed [u] *Seven Seas.* And wee read in [x] *Cassiodorus*, that *Addua*, a River of *Cisalpin Gallia*, emptie's it self into the Lake called *Lago di Como*, as into its proper Sea. Hence it is, that in *Hesychius* and *Suidas*, a Lake or λίμνη denote's the Ocean and Sea, and ποταμὸς, or a River, the Ocean it self. Nor is it in this place impossible, that *a River should contend with the Sea*; However, otherwise it hath been used as a Proverb, of such as strive with men mightier then themselvs. Also in *Homer*,

[r] *Pharsal.* 3.
[s] *Histor. lib.* 13.
[t] *In oris Mæotinis.*
[u] *Plin. lib.* 3. *c.* 16. *Herodian. lib.* 8.
[x] *Variar. lib.* 11. *Formul.* 14.

—— [y] βαθείης βένθεσι λίμνης.

[y] *Iliad.* ν.

The depth of a deep Lake is used for the depth of the Sea. And in another place hee put's περικαλλέα λίμνην, *a very fair Lake* in stead of the Sea, as it is observed also by [z] *Olympiodorus.* Yea, som of the Antients have

[z] *Ad Aristot. Meteorolog. lib.* 1. *prax.* 16.

have ſaid, that the Ocean it ſelf is one of thoſe [a] four huge Rivers, which ſpring out of ſuch a Hell, or ſuch a deep Gulf; as [b] ſom feign to bee found towards the North; the other three beeing impriſoned in ſecret Paſſages of the Earth. Moreover, *Lucan* call's the *Britiſh* Ocean,

[a] *Plato in Phædone.*

[b] *Vide Girald. Cambrenſ. Topograph. Hibern. diſt.* 2. *cap.* 14.

——— [c] *Incerti ſtagna profundi*

[c] *Pharſal.* 2.

An unſtable deep ſtanding pool.

And in barbarous Latin, the word *Mariſcus*, as a Diminutive of *Mare* the Sea, is uſed in many Places for a *Marſh* or Lake, under which notion alſo it hath been Tranſlated into ſom other Languages, beeing varied according to their divers forms of Expreſsion. Other obſervations have been made by [e] others to the ſame purpoſe. So then, both in Subſtance, Nature, and Name, the Seas, Rivers, and other Bodies of Waters (ſo far as concern's the Point in queſtion) are all the ſame, that whatſoëver may bee ſaid of theſe, may bee applied in like manner alſo to the other; ſave that there may ſom difference bee alleged onely from the largeneſs of the one and the narrowneſs of the other, which in the Point of Dominion (as it relate's to Poſſeſsion) is of no account. Add moreover, that the uſual Objection touching their fluid Nature, or the continual ſhifting of Waters in the Chanel, doth here no more prejudice the cauſ of Dominion and Poſſeſsion, then the fluid nature of the Aër doth the Dominion and Poſſeſsion of that ſpace which confine's a Houſ from the Foundation upward. That ſpace ſeem's as a Chanel to the whirling Aër; whereof notwithſtanding hee, according to the Civil Law, is the undoubted Owner, who poſſeſſeth the Ground and

[d] *Claudius Salmaſius, in Plin. Exercitat. ad Solinum, pag.* 577.

[e] *J. Druſ. Obſ.* 9. *cap.* 20. *& ad difficil. loca. Numer. cap.* 133. *& Albericus Gentilis in Lectionibus Virgilianis, cap.* 17. *Cæl. Rhodigin. lect. Antiq. lib.* 26. *cap.* 14.

Buil-

Building. Hereupon * Servitudes have been impo-sed, against the rearing of Houses higher then ordinary, also against hindring of Light, or Prospect, and other of that kinde in the very ambient Aër; So that where a * Prohibition of a new Building hath issued, *Pomponius* saith, *the Aër ought to bee measured as well as the Ground.* And it is evident, that the Aër is his who is owner of the plot of ground. So that as to that saying of *Paulus*, that a Tree growing in the very Confine betwixt two Lands is [g] common to the Owners on both sides, for so much as grow's in the ground of either; *Joannes Buteo* discoursing of the Division of the fruit of such a Tree, saith, [h] *Wee must suppose the ground to bee the Aër it self that is spread over the ground,* which hee measureth by direct lines from the outmost boughs. And therefore, surely, wee are owners of the ground, hous, and space, which wee possess in several as owners, that every one, for his best advantage, may freely and fully use and enjoy his own bordering Aër, (which is the element of mankind) how flitting so ever it bee, together with the space thereof in such a manner, and restrain others thence at pleasure, that hee may bee both reputed and settled owner thereof in Particular. Much less then doth the fluid nature of Waters, which is far less then the other, in any wise hinder an ownership or Dominion over them. And even those things which naturally are thus flitting, do notwithstanding in a Civil sens remain ever the same; as the ship of *Theseus,* a Hous, or a Theatre, which hath been so often mended and repaired, that there is not so much as one part or plank left of the first building.

But they which make use of so frivolous a subtil-

tie

* *Servitutes sunt Jura Prædiorum.*

* *In novo Opere Nunciato.*
[f] *L.21. ff. tit. quod vi aut Clam. § 2.*

[g] *L.83. ff. tit. Pro Socio.*

[h] *Tract. de Divisione Fructus arboris in confinio natæ.*

tie as this to oppose a Dominion of the Sea, should bee turned over to the Philosophers; especially [i] *Heraclitus*, and *Epicharmus*, whose Doctrine was, that every thing is so changed, altered, and renewed every moment, that nothing in the world continue's at this instant, the same, that it was in the instant immediatly going before. *No man* (saith [k] *Seneca*, in imitation of *Heraclitus*) *is the same in the Morning, that hee was the day before. Our Bodies are hurried like Rivers. Whatsoëver thou see'st, run's with time. Not one of all those things that are visible, continue's. I, even whil'st I speak of these Changes, am changed my self.*

[i] *Diog. Laert. in Heraclito, &c.*

[k] *Epist.* 58.

It was seriously affirmed also by *Heraclitus*, that not onely the same River could not receiv a man twice, but also that the same man could not enter twice into the same stream. So that *to cast all into* Heraclitus *his River*, became an usual Proverb, to express a continued and perpetual change of every thing from it self. But let such as dream, that the fluid inconstant nature of the Sea disprove's the private Dominion of it; entertain the same opinion (if they pleas) with these men, of things that fall under a Civil consideration, and then they must of necessity grant also, that themselvs are not Owners or Possessors, either of Land, Houses, Clothes, Monie, or any other thing whatsoëver.

An

An Answer to the Objections touching the defect of Bounds *and* Limits *in the Sea; as also concerning its* magnitude *and* inexhaustible abundance.

CHAP. XXII.

THE Objection, touching the defect of *Limits* and and *Bounds*, follow's next. And truly, where Dominions are distinguished, nothing can bee more desirable then known and certain Bounds in every place: Nor was it without caus, that [a] *Terminus*, the God of Bounds, was received heretofore among the *Romanes* for the God of Justice. But the nature of *Bounds* is to bee consider'd either upon the Shores, or in the open Sea. And why Shores should not bee called and reputed lawful Bounds, whereon to ground a distinction of Dominion in the Sea, as well as Ditches, Hedges, Meers, rows of Trees, Mounds, and other things used by Surveyors in the bounding of Lands, I cannot fully understand. Nor is [b] *Sylvanus* any whit more a Guardian of Bounds, then *Neptune*. But yet a very learned man saith, [c] *there is a Reason in nature, why the Sea under the aforesaid consideration cannot bee possessed or made appropriate; becaus possession is of no force, unless it bee in a thing that is bounded; So that* Thucydides *call's a Land unpossessed,* ἀόριστον *unbounded; and* Isocrates *the Land possessed by the* Athenians, *a Land bounded with Limits. But liquid things, becaus of themselvs they are not bounded, cannot bee possessed, save onely as they are conteined in som other thing; after which manner Lakes and Ponds are possessed,* *and*

a *Plutarch. in Numâ.*

b *Sylvanus*, made by Heathens the God of the woods, and *Neptune* of the Sea.

c *Hugo Grot. de Jure Belli ac Pacis, lib.* 2. *cap.* 11. §. 3.

and Rivers also, becaus they are conteined within Banks. But the Sea is not conteined by the Earth, it beeing of equal bigness, or bigger then the Earth; so that the Antients have affirmed the Earth to bee conteined by the Sea. And then hee bring's divers Testimonies of the Antients, whereby it is affirmed more then once, that the Sea is the girdle or Bond of this Globe of Earth, and that fetching a compass, it incloseth all the Parts thereof together; and it is very often said by the Antients, that the Land is conteined and bounded by the water or Sea; as if the whole Earth made as it were one Island, beeing [d] surrounded by the Sea. But admit it were to bee granted (which, I suppose, neither that learned man nor any other will grant;) yet I do not well see, why the thing conteining should not in truth bee bounded by the thing conteined, as well as this by that. May not a lesser bodie that is spherical, or of any other form, beeing conteined by a greater which is every way contiguous to it, bee said to bound and limit the Concave of the greater Bodie, as well as this to limit the Convex of the lesser? But *Julius* [e] *Scaliger* saith very well of the Sea and Land; *That the one is not so conteined by the other, but that it may also contein. Nor are they so disjoyned from each other, but that they may both encroach upon each other and retire by Turns.* The Sea and Land mutually imbrace one another with crooked windings and turnings; this with Peninsula's, and Promontories butting forth, and Creeks bending inward; that working up its waves about all the Passages of its vast Bodie. Thus it is evident that the one indifferently set's Bounds to the other, no otherwise than Banks, and Lakes, or Rivers; which also appear's more evident in the [f] *Caspian* Sea

[d] *Cicero in Somn. Scipionis.* & vide *Jo. Philopon. de Mundi Creatione, lib.4.cap.5.*

[e] *Exercit.* 37.

[f] A Sea near *Hircania,* like a huge Lake, beeing incompassed with Land, and hath no passage into any other Sea.

Sea that is encompassed with Land. And in like manner in the *Mediterranean*; before that *Hercules*, or (as the [g] *Arabians* say) *Alexander* the great did, by cutting the Mountains, let in the *Atlantick* Ocean through the streights of *Cadiz*. And thereby it is made up one single Globe, wherein divers Seas are bounded, as well as the Isles or main Land: as it is more clearly proved out of holy Scripture. There the waters are gathered together, and limited by their Places and [h] Bounds. And saith the Lord himself of the Sea, [i] *I encompassed it with my Bounds, and set Bars and Doors; and said, hitherto shalt thou com, but no farther.* And in another place, [k] *Hee gave unto the Sea his Bounds, his Decree unto the Waters that they should not pass their Bounds*: So that it cannot bee doubted every Sea hath its Bounds on the Shore; as the Land it self. Nor had I made mention of this Particular, had I not found it impugned by so eminent a person. And truly there is but a very little more difficultie, to finde out *Limits* and *Bounds* in the main Sea, for distinguishing of private Dominions. Wee have high Rocks, Shelvs, Promontories opposite to each other, and Islands dispersed up and down, from whence as well direct Lines, as crooked windings and turnings, and angles, may bee made use of, for the bounding of a Territorie in the Sea.

[g] *Geograph. Nubiens. Climat. 4. part. 1.*

[h] *Damascen. de Orthodoxâ fide, lib. 2. cap. 9.*

[i] *Job 38. 10.*

[k] *Pro. 8. 29.*

> *Mille jacent mediæ, diffusa per æquora, terræ;*
> *Innumeri surgunt Scopuli, montésque per altum.*

> **A thousand Lands within the main do lie;**
> **Rocks numberless, and Mountains rise on high**
> **Throughout the deep.**

The antient Cosmographers also reckon up the Seas of the world, no otherwise then Towns, Rivers, Islands, and Mountains, as beeing no less distinguished from each other by their respective Bounds. [l] *Æthicus* saith, *Every Globe of Land* hath XXX *Seas*, CCCLXX *Towns*, LXXII *Islands*, LVII *Rivers*, *and* XL *Mountains*,&c. After this also, hee reckon's the Seas of the Eastern, Western, Northen, and Southern Ocean one after another, after the same manner as hee doth the Provinces and their Isles. How truly, I dispute not; but in the mean time hee made no question, but that the Seas are sufficiently distinguished by their Names and Bounds. Add hereunto that useful invention of the *sea-man's Compass*, and the help of Celestial degrees either of Longitude or Latitude, together with the doctrine of Triangles arising therefrom. Also in those Plantations that in our time have been carried out of *Europe* into *America*, the degrees of Latitude and Longitude do serv the Proprietors in stead of Bounds; which with as little difficultie are found in the Sea. In like manner [m] som would have had the Tropick of *Cancer* and the *Equinoctial Line* to have been the Bounds in the Sea, for the limiting of that Agreement, which was to have been made in the year MDCVIII, between the States of the *United Provinces*, and the Hous of *Austria*. And in the late Agreement betwixt the Kings of Great *Britain* and *Spain*, [n] the *Equinoctial Line* is the Bound appointed in the Sea. Other Instances there are of the same nature: For, *Sarpedon* and *Calycadnus*, two Promontories of *Cilicia*, were designed as Bounds for distinguishing the Dominion of the Sea, in that League made betwixt the [o] *Romanes* and *Antiochus* King of *Syria*. Also, by Decree of the Emperor *Leo*,

[l] *In Cosmographiâ.*

[m] *Apud. Emanuel. Meteran. Rer. Belgic.lib.* 28.

[n] *Anno* 1630. *Art.*2.

[o] *Polyb. in Eclog. de Legationibus,cap.*35. *& Livius, decad.*4.*lib.* 8.

Leo, of which wee have alreadie ſpoken, the [p] *Fiſhing Epoches* or Fiſh-pens that were by men placed in the Sea lying over againſt their Lands, were limited to certain number of Cubits. The caſe was the ſame likewiſe touching the *Cyanean* and *Chelidonian* Iſlands, in the League made by the [q] *Athenians* with the King of *Perſia*; which hath been mentioned alſo before.

Moreover, Pope *Alexander* VI and his Cardinals, or the King of *Spain*'s Agents made no ſcruple touching Bounds of this nature, when the King obteined that famous *Bull*, whereby hee had a Grant of the Weſtern world; but ſo to bee limited, that the thing given ſhould, in the hither part of it, bee bounded by an imaginarie Line drawn from the *Artick* to the *Antarctick Pole*, [r] *which ſhould bee diſtant from each of thoſe Iſlands called* de Los, Azores y cabo verde, *one hundred Leagues towards the Weſt and South* (which are the verie words of the Bull.) Whereupon [s] *Hieronymus de Monte,* ſaith, *Bounds were ſet in Heaven and in the Aër, in the time of Pope* Alexander VI *between the* Portugals *and* Caſtilians, *in dividing the Indian Iſles then newly diſcover'd by the degrees of Heaven; and ſo all that was found Eaſtward, was allotted to the* Portugals, *and that which lay Weſtward to the Caſtilians.* Certainly, in this place, no more regard was had to the portions of Land, whether Iſlands or continent, in the meaſuring of Bounds, then to the ſpaces of the Sea. Moreover, it is ordinarie among the Lawyers, even thoſe who are moſt earneſt for a Communitie of everie Sea, to limit an hundred miles [t] juriſdiction to the Lord of the adjacent Coaſt. Somtimes wee finde ſixtie. *It is in a manner received* (ſaith [u] *Bodin*) *by the common cuſtom of all Princes*

[p] An *Epoche* was a device to keep ſtore of Fiſh, made of Nets that were ſpread between Stakes driven into the Sea.

[q] *Plutarch. in vitâ Cimonis.*

[r] *Laërt. Cherubin. Bullar. Tom.* 1. *pag.* 393.

[s] *Tractat. de finibus regundis, cap.* 7. 8.

[t] *Bartolus Tract. de Tiberiade & D. D. in l. Inſulæ Italiæ ff. tit. de Judiciis.*

[u] *De Repub. lib.* 1. *cap.* 10.

Princes bordering upon the Sea, that for sixtie miles from the shore, any Prince may give Law to those that sail near their Coast; and it was so adjudged in the Case of the Duke of Savoy. Which hee observeth out of *Cacheranus* his decisions of *Piemont*. Yea, and it is mainteined by very [x] eminent Professors of the Civil Law, that an Action at Law may bee allowed for regulating of Bounds in the Borders of the Sea. Therefore they sufficiently acknowledg the Custom of measuring and setting Bounds, even in the Sea.

[x] *Hieronym. de Monte, Tract. de Finibus regundis, cap. 39. Baldus, & alii ibi citati.*

But as to what concern's that saying of *Ambrose*; Geometram *audivimus*, Thalassometram *nunquam audivimus*, Wee have **heard of a** Geometrician, **one that measureth land; but never of a** Thalassometrician, **or one that could measure and lay out Bounds in the Sea**; This truly is rather a quibling of words, then any Argument against the point in hand. And the holy man speak's in that place, of the various lurking-holes, or holds of divers Fishes, which God hath appointed for them in the Sea, not touching a civil distribution of the Sea. Nor was there any reason why hee should speak thus of a *Thalassometrician, as a thing never heard of before*. For, wee know that even *Thalassometricians* were ordinarie among the *Grecians*, who had Dominions by Sea, with very frequent and various distinctions of those Dominions; And that the Sea was measured according to the Rules of Geometrie, no less then the Land. *Proclus* a famous Mathematician, treating about the excellencie of Geometrie, saith, [y] *It hath discover'd the Situations of places, the measures also of Voiages by Sea, as well as journies by Land.* Moreover, they had Instruments to measure the Sea, which the Grecians,

[y] *In Euclidis, lib. 1. lib. 2. cap. 3. in Græcis, pag. 18.*

Grecians, or at least the modern Greeks, called θαλασσοδομέτρας, *measures of Sea-voiages*; and have written that *Hero*, *Anthemius*, and other antient Mathematicians, learn't the Art from *Archimedes*, and transmitted it to Posterity. Yea, it is said by [z] *Joannes Tzetzes*, that those men discover'd both water and winde-instruments out of the Books of *Archimedes*, *and Engines to move things of weight*, *and instruments called* Thalassodometræ, *for measuring of Sea-voiages*: so that as concerning the business of measuring the sea, there is nothing to hinder, but that both matter and instruments may bee had for the distinguishing of its Dominions.

[z] Chiliad. 13. cap. 457.

Lastly, that which is objected, touching the vast magnitude of the Sea, and its inexhaustible abundance, is of very little weight here. Suppose it bee inexhaustible, so that hee which shall appropriate it to himself, can receiv no dammage by other men's using it, what more prejudice is this to the right of Ownership or Dominion, then it is to the Owner of a Fire or Candle, that another man's should bee lighted by his? Is hee therefore less Master of his own Fire or Candle? But truly wee often see, that the Sea it self, by reason of other men's Fishing, Navigation, and Commerce, becom's the worse for him that own's it, and others that enjoie it in his right; So that less profit ariseth, then might otherwise bee received thereby. Which more evidently appear's in the use of those Seas, which produce Pearls, Coral, and other things of that kinde. Yea, the plentie of such seas is lessned every hour, no otherwise then that of Mines of Metal, Quarries of stone, or of Gardens, when their Treasures and Fruits are taken away. And it is a custom of the *Mahometans*

(who

(who are very great and Potent Nations) to estimate their seas no less upon this accompt, then by the Revenue either of Fishing or Navigation; as wee may see in that their *falſ Prophet*, when speaking of the most holy God hee saith, [a] *It is hee that hath prepared the Sea for your use, that thence yee may take fresh Food* (and use Fishing) *and also that out of it yee may draw ornaments to adorn you.* *Mahomet Ben Achmed*, the best Expositor of the *Alcoran*, interpret's those ornaments by *Coral* and *Pearls*; which words also are used in another [b] place of the *Alcoran*, for the chief Commodity of the Sea. From whence also it is, that a special Licence to search for *Coral*, hath somtimes been granted in Leagues made by the grand Seignieur, as is observed before. Yea, and [c] *Pliny* speaking, especially of the more Easternly Seas, saith; *It had been counted a small matter, that men swallowed whole Seas into their throats, if both men and women also did not wear them up and down upon their hands, ears, heads, and all parts of the Body.* But it is well known to us, that precious Stones and Pearls, are very often found also in the Western Seas, and hee tell's us, they were frequently found in antient time. Moreover (saith hee) *It is certain that in* Britain *they are produced, though small and ill colored* (as wee all see at this day) *forasmuch as* Julius Cæsar *would have it understood, that the breast-plate which hee consecrated to* Venus *in her Temple, was made of British Pearl.* Yea, it is written by many, and testified by [d] *Suetonius*, that *Cæsar* went to *Britain* in hope of Pearls. It is obvious therefore to every man, that the gain of such a Voiage into *Britain*, may bee lesſned, and that the abundance either of Pearls themselvs, or of those shell-fishes, which produce them, may through a promis-

[a] *In Alcorano, Azoarâ, 16. in Cod. Arab. 26. in Latino.*

[b] *Azoar.* 55. Sed in *Cod. Latin.* 65.

[c] *Hist. Nat. lib. 9. cap.* 35.

[d] *In Julio, ca.* 47. & videsis *G Camden. in Britanniâ, pag.* 630. & 721.

promiscuous and common use of the Sea, bee diminished in any Sea whatsoever. Where then is that inexhaustible abundance of Commodities in the sea, which cannot bee impaired? There is truly the same reason also, touching every kinde of Fishing. But what need many words about this Matter? Do wee not at this day finde it pressed home to the utmost every where by Lawyers, especially those of the Empire? and was it not a thousand times said of old when the *Romane* Empire was in its prime, [e] *that* Cæsar *is Lord of the whole world?* Thus *Ovid*, according to the *Romane* custom, saith;

[e] *L. 9. ff. tit. ad Legem Rhodiam. &c.*

> [f] *Gentibus est aliis tellus data limite certo:*
> *Romanæ spatium est urbis & orbis idem.*

[f] *Fastorum, lib. 2.*

> **All other States have Limits to their Ground:**
> Rome **and the World, have but one common Bound.**

The Sea (I suppose) is not more inexhaustible then the whole world. That is very much inferior to this, as a part is to the whole, in greatness and plenty. And therefore a Dominion of the Sea is not to bee opposed upon this accompt, unless also wee in like manner affirm, that not onely that saying of the Emperor's Dominion over the world is manifestly fals, (as it must bee) but also contrary to natural reason it self, becaus of the worlds extraordinary greatness and abundance. Therefore they are more justifiable in their Opinion, who, as they say, that the Roman Emperor, according to the antient Law, is Lord of the World or Land, (that is to say, a large part of it) so also [g] they would have him to bee Lord of the Sea.

[g] *Jo. Gripbiander Jurisdictione Insulæ, cap. 14. § 65. &c.*

Nor

Nor is there any difficulty in that expression of the Emperor *Antoninus*, wherein hee call's himself Lord of the World, but the Law (as 'tis commonly understood) Lady of the Sea; which (if it were granted that his Answer ought [h] so to bee understood) doth signifie no other thing, then that the *Rhodian* Laws, where they did not thwart the Romane, were so far in force about Sea-affairs, that (however hee were Moderator and Lord of both) hee would by no means determin ought contrary to those Laws, by any Rescript of his own. [i] *Alcialus*, and other very Learned men also, make almost the same interpretation: But concerning that Answer of *Antoninus*, I shall add more [k] by and by. So that it seem's the Antients, in that so often repeated speech, concerning universal Dominion, conceived the Romane Empire to bee no less or narrower; then it is represented by *Petronius Arbiter*, who set's forth the matter in these words;

Orbem jam totum victor Romanus habebat,
Quà Mare, quà Terræ, quà Sidus currit utrumque.

The Romane Conq'rer then the World,
Both Sea and Land did sway,
Wheresoe're the Moon travel's by night,
Or the bright Sun by day.

And [l] the Ancient Inscription in honor of *Augustus Cæsar* was, ORBE MARI ET TERRA PACATO, IANO CLUSO, &c. *Peace beeing restored to the World by* Sea *and Land, hee shut up the* [m] *Temple of Janus*; according to which sens it is recorded also by [n] Historians, *that hee shut* Janus *his Temple three times, having settled Peace by* Sea *and* Land; whereby they would have

[h] *L. Deprecatio 9. ff. ad legem Rhodiam.*

[i] *Dispunctionum lib. 2. ca. 5.*

[k] In the 25 Chapter.

[l] *Emeritæ; apud Gruterum, pag. 149 4.*

[m] This temple stood open in time of war, but was shut in time of peace.

[n] *Suetonius in Octavio, cap. 22.*

have us to understand (the verie same thing which wee have proved more fully before) that the Seas were comprehended as well as the Land, within the huge Bodie of the *Romane* Empire.

An Answer to such Testimonies as have faln from Writers treating of other subjects, *and which are usually alleged against Dominion of the Sea.*

Chap. XXIII.

IT remain's in the next place, that wee consider of what validitie the contrarie Opinions of Writers are whereof wee formerly made mention. As to what concern's those Passages of the Poëts, *Plautus* and *Phœnicides*; it is clear in *Plautus*, that the lewd slave *Trachalio* was but in jest with *Gripus* the Fisherman: Hee saith in general, that the Sea is common to all, which signifieth a Sea that never was possessed, as well as that which is necessarily and naturally common; and in that place, that, rather then this. Wherefore it may bee understood, that Fishing was common or not yet appropriated; that, is, that the people either of *Rome* or *Greece*, had such a Dominion over any kinde of Sea (for, by what hath been alreadie mentioned, it appear's both of them had a Dominion over som Sea before *Plautus* his time) that either of them might use their respective Seas at their own pleasure, in hindring others from sailing through them, and removing such impediments of Trade and Commerce as should happen therein: And yet that hitherto they had prohibited no man from fishing in that Sea (mentioned by *Plautus* and *Phœnicides*) in such a manner, but that the use of it might remain common either to Natives or Neighbors, as the use of a ground for feeding of Cattel; though there may indeed bee a particular Owner in possession, reserving the other Commodities of it to himself, as it often come's to pass. But afterwards also, especially in the *Eastern* Empire, or among the *Greeks*, it is clear out of what wee have alreadie shewn you, that a peculiar Right of Sea-fishing hath passed into the hands of private persons, as well as of Princes: So that such Expressions as these beeing applied against private Dominion of the Sea, soon vanish and com to nothing.

As to that passage out of *Ovid*, *Quid probibetis aquas?* **Why do yee forbid water? &c.** (then which nothing is more usual in Disputes about this matter) it is not so much an Assertion of the communitie of waters, as a vehement and hyperbolical reproof of the inhumanitie of that rustick Rout in *Lycia*. *Latona* beeing thirstie and wearie, asked for a draught of water; and that out of a Lake. The barbarous people denie her; and therefore shee most deservedly reprove's them. But shee doth it not more earnestly, then *Ampelisca* in [a] *Plautus* did merrily, to *Sceparnio* a slave that denied her water;

[a] *In Rudente*, *Act*. 2.

Cur tu (inquit Ampelisca) *aquam gravare amabò, quam hostis hosti commodat?*

Why (saith Ampelisca) **art thou so loth to let mee have water, which one stranger afford's another.**

For, whatsoever may bee afforded or communicated without

without prejudice of the Owner, hee is concerned many times in humanitie to impart it to a meer stranger that asketh him. For, the word *Hostis* in that place signifie's a Stranger, as wee often finde among the [b] Antients; And it appear's also by the question of *Sceparnio*, whereby hee jeer's the wench,

[b] *Festus in verb.* Hostis, *& Cic. de Offic. lib.* 1.

> *Cur tu* (aït ille) *operam gravare mihi, quam civis civi commodat?*

> **Why** (saith hee) **dost thou denie mee that help, one Citizen afford's another?**

Here hee opposeth *Citizen* to *Stranger*. From the same Office of humanitie those particulars are derived; as *not to denie running Water*; *to suffer one Fire, or one Candle to light another*; and other things of that nature, which are profitable to the Receiver, and not troublesom to him that give's or permit's the Favor. And upon this Rule of Moralitie onely, which is the Rule of Charitie, are those demands both of *Latona* and *Ampelisca* grounded. They denie not the private Dominion of waters: Neither *Latona* of the Lake (whose private Dominion is confess't by all) nor *Ampelisca* of the Well, from whence shee demanded water for the Priest of *Venus*. Moreover, those words of *Latona* are spoken concerning a Lake of little water; as *Ovid* sheweth in that place,

> *Fortè lacum mediocris aquæ prospexit in imis Vallibus.*——

> **By chance a little Lake shee did espie,**
> **Which in the Vallies far beneath did lie.**

And after shee had said that shee came to claim a publick gift, shee add's,

Quæ tamen ut detis, supplex peto.——

Which notwithstanding I humbly beg you would bestow.

Nothing in that place opposeth a Dominion of the waters, more then of any other things whatsoëver, whereto that saying of *Ennius* may have relation,

[c] *Nihilo minùs ipsi lucet, quum illi accenderit,*

c *Cic.de Offic. lib.*1.

His own light is not the less, when hee hath lent light to another.

And as *Cicero* tell's us, all things of the same kinde seem common to men. Which communitie notwithstanding derogate's nothing at all from the Dominion here in Question; unless any will bee so unadvised as to affirm, that the Laws of friendship (wherein Philosophers say all things are common) with those of Charitie and Liberalitie, may overthrow private Dominion.

Nor is there any more weight in that which is objected out of *Virgil.* What is this to the purpose? *Virgil*, or *Ilioneus* speaking of the *Tyrrhen* Sea, said, *That the water is open to all. Ergò*, by Law the water must lie open at all times to all men. A verie trifling Argument! There was no Land that was omitted in the first distribution of things, which did not remain open to all, before it came under particular possession. But in that passage of *Virgil*, there is no demand made of Right, but onely an Office of humanitie requested from the King of *Latium.* Yea, and a promiss made of recompence, saying;

Non

Non erimus regno indecores, nec vestra feretur
Fama levis, tantique abolescet gratia facti. *Æneid.li.7.*

Wee'll not disgrace your Realm, nor lightly set
Your Fame, and so great courtesie forget.

Therefore in the Poëts sens, the benefit was to bee received and acknowledged from the grace and favor of the Prince, not claimed by any Law of nature common to all. Yea, wee know that in many places an excise or paiment is made somtimes for the very use of water. As among the *Hollanders* they have in *Delph-land* a Custom called *Jus Grutæ*; which hath ever been under the care of those Officers called in Latine [d] *Comites Plumarii*, in Dutch, **Pluymgraven**, and whereby the Beer-brewers (as [e] *Hadrianus Junius* tell's us) are bound to pay them the hundreth part for the use of water. Other instances there are to bee found of the same nature.

[d] *Comites Plumarii* or Officers of the Feather; their place is to see that Birds or foul bee not transported thence.

[e] *In Histor. Bat.c.*19.

Lastly, as to that saying of the *Jewish Rabbins* concerning *Alexander*, it shew's onely they were of Opinion that *Alexander* had not gotten a Dominion over the Sea. They do not say at all, that hee could not lawfully get it; nor truly could they say it without gross indiscretion, unless they would renounce their own Right (which wee have alreadie mentioned out of their determinations) in the great or *Phænician* Sea. And whatsoëver those Rabbins may lightly say of *Alexander*; yet truly *Flavius* [f] *Josephus* a Jew, and (if wee may believ himself) the most eminent Lawyer of his time among the Jews, call's the Emperor *Vespasian*, *Lord both of Sea and Land.* And [g] *Julian* saith, that *Alexander* aspired after an Empire by Sea as well as by Land: which hath been mentioned also by [h] *Seneca*.

[f] *De Bello Judaïco,lib.*3.*cap.*27.

[g] *Orat.*3.

[h] *Suasor.*

But all these Objections are brought out of Writers treating of other matters, which ought also to bee consider'd. And therefore in the last place, let us take such opinions of the Lawyers into consideration, as are opposed against it.

An Answer to the Objections taken out of Antient Lawyers.

Chap. XXIV.

Of those Lawyers that are of the contrarie opinion, som are antient, som modern. If wee look into the most notable Testimonies of the Antients, this onely is to bee collected from them touching the Communitie of the Sea, that som of the most eminent were indeed of Opinion, that by the Law natural and of Nations the Sea is perpetually and necessarily common to all men; which neverthelesse, most clearly appear's to bee far otherwise, if a diligent survey bee made of the Laws and Customs, either Civil or Intervenient, of most Ages and Nations; As wee have verie abundantly proved in what hath been alreadie shewn you. And that not onely out of the most approved Historians (whereof there is verie oftentimes most use, in searching out the most common Customs of Nations, and other things relating to the Laws themselvs[a]) but also out of the verie Leagues or *Intervenient Law* of divers Nations, yea, and other Lawyers of no less note, together with the principal Edicts in the Eastern Empire, besides, manie other, from whence any one may easily learn what, according to the *Natural Permissive Law*, ought to bee determined in this matter.

[a] *Vide Gaspar. Knockium, lib. de contributionibus, cap.* 20. §. 463. *& seqq.*

Som

Som of the Antients have been of Opinion, that according to the Law Natural or of Nations, it is lawful to hunt and hauk in another man's [b] wood or Ground, and to Fish in another man's Pond or Lake, much more in a River, except it were prohibited by the Owner in possession. *These things,* saith [c] *Cujacius, were so determined by the prudent* Romans, *who adhered most to the Law of Nations. But Custom hath now over-ruled the Law of Nations, so that it is not lawful to Fish so much as in a publick River, nor to hunt or hauk freely in the Fields.* And saith the same [d] Autor in another place; *The Exchequer is to bee justified onely by Custom, in laying claim to the Fisheries, in a private manner, contrarie to the Law of Nations.* Whereas notwithstanding, in the *Feudal* Laws, the Revenues of Fisheries are counted among the *Regalia* or Royalties of the Prince; and reckoned by learned men among the Antients belonging to the [e] *Romane* Exchequer or Treasurie, who cite *Ulpian* himself for a witness. For, hee among the publick Customs or Revenues numbreth the Revenues [f] *Piscariarum* (as som would have it read) of *Fisheries.* Others instead of it put *Picariarum* **Pitch-pits**, for those places from whence Pitch is digged. Surely, even [g] *Ulpian* himself reckon's Fish-ponds among those things that are liable to assessments. But howsoever the later Customs of Nations have subverted or over-ruled that more antient Law of Fishing, Hunting, and fouling freely, whether it were the Law natural (as they term'd it) or of nations; as sufficiently appear's by the [h] Law of those places which they call

[b] *L. 3. ff. de acquir. rer. dom. & instit. de rer. divis. § Feræ igitur bestiæ & l. Injuriar. 13. ff. de injuriis §. ult.*

[c] *Observat. lib. 4. cap. 2.*

[d] *Ad lib. 5. Feud. tit. de Regalibus.*

[e] *Guid. Pancirol. variar. lect. utriusque Juris, lib. 3. cap. 31.*

[f] *L. 17. ff. de V. S.*

[g] *L. 4. §. 6. ff. tit. de Censibus.*

[h] *Vide Sebastianum Medicem tract. de venatione &c. Edict. & consuetud. de Aquis & Forestis* Galliarum *collect. per Sanctyonium, Andream Gaill. pract. Observat. lib. 2. 67. Matth. Stephani de Jurisdictione, lib. 2. part 1. cap. 7. §. 432. & ejusmodi alios de Venationis Jure in imperio* Romano-Germanico, *&c.*

Forests

Forests De Wildt bahne or *Bannum ferinum*, and of Rivers, as it is variously established in several Countries. And so without any prohibition of the Owner in Possession, that antient Freedom hath been abrogated many Ages since by most received Custom: which may bee said in like manner of the Sea, whatsoêver those Antients and their Followers have written to the contrarie.

Moreover, the Emperor *Leo* hath (as wee have shewn you) expresly declared by Edict, that the antient Right concerning a necessarie communitie of the Sea, was not without injustice pretended in the *Eastern Empire*. Wherefore *Michaël Attaliates* truly did ill, and so hath any other Lawyer of the East (if any there bee) since the daies of *Leo*, that hath opposed its private Dominion. Nor indeed hath that eminent man dealt any better, who write's that *Leo* made a change against reason of Law. And here, especial care must bee taken to avoid that which som have presumed to affirm, touching those most excellent Books of *Justinian*, which make up an entire Bodie of the antient Law; [i] *That the Law prescribed in those Books is not the Law onely of a Citie, but even of Nations and nature; and that the whole is so fitted unto nature,* that after the Empire was extinct, *though the Law was a long time buried; yet it rose again, and spread it self through all the world. And therefore that it concern's even Princes, although it was framed by* Justinian *for private persons.* As if the law natural and of Nations were to bee derived onely out of those Books. For, not to mention, how that not onely very many Decrees, and Custome's introduced in the *Romane-Germane* Empire it self and other places abroad, have extremly alter'd many things conteined in

[i] *Albericus Gentilis de Jure Belli, l.* 1. *cap.* 3.

in thoſe Books; but alſo that wee finde divers Kings both of [k] *Spain* and [l] *France* have ſomtimes heretofore prohibited the uſe of them in any kinde within their Courts of Juſtice; there are truly ſom things in the very Law of the Nations of *Europe* (who receiv thoſe Books, and that upon very good ground, both into their Schools and Courts, ſo far as the particular Laws of their Kingdoms will permit) I mean in their Law Common, or Intervenient, which are not grounded at all upon the Law of *Juſtinian*, but have had their original from Cuſtoms quite contrarie thereto. Priſoners of war are not now made ſlaves, nor are the Laws concerning captivitie or *Remitter upon return from Captivitie*, touching the [m] perſons of men, in any uſe at all, which notwithſtanding take up a Title in the *Digeſts*. Ships driven by wrack upon a Shore do by the [n] Law of *Juſtinian* (which is confirmed alſo in the [o] *Roman-German* Empire) belong either to the former Owners, or as things relinquiſhed and unpoſſeſſed, to the firſt Finders; nor doth the Exchequer interpoſe any Claim, whereas neverthelesſ, according to the Law of divers Nations, intervenient to themſelvs and their Neighbors, it bee moſt certain, that thoſe Ships are very often confiſcated according to the varietie of Cuſtom: As among the *Engliſh*, the [p] *Britains*, [q] *Sicilians*, ſom [r] Borderers upon the Shores of *Italie*, and others. And although it bee accounted crueltie by ſom to perſue profit upon ſo ſad an occaſion, as it was alſo by the [ſ] Emperor,

[k] *Gregor. Lopez in Alphonſin. 3. tit. 4. l. 6. Azevedo ad reg. conſtit. in rubric. tit.* De las leyes.

[l] *Choppinus de Domanio, lib. 2. tit. 15. §. 5. & Bodin de Repub. lib. 1. cap. 8. & vide Guil. Burlæum in Proœm. ad Comm. in Ariſt. Phyſica.*

[m] *Boërius Deciſ. 178. Alvarus Velaſc. Conſult. tom. 1. 30 Fra. Suarez de Legibus, l. 2. cap. 20.*

[n] *C. tit. de Naufragiis, & l. 1. & 3. ff. de Incendio & l. 21. §. 1. ff. tit. de acquir. vel amit. poſſeſſione.*

[o] *Frederic. 2. in C. de Furtis, c. Navigia, & Conſtit. Caroli 5. de Judiciis Capitalibus, cap. 118.*

[p] *Bertrand. Argentræus in Conſuet. Brit. Art. 56. §. 45.* [q] *Choppinus de Domanio, lib. 1. tit. 15. §. 10.* [r] *Luc. de Pennâ ad C. tit. de Naufrag. Matth. de Affliƈt. in Conſ Neapolit. lib. 1. conſuet. 59. vide Garſiam Maſtrillum de Magiſtratibus, lib. 3. cap. 10. §. 393.* [ſ] *Andr. Gail. practic. Obſervat. lib. 1. cap. 18. Bodin. de Repub. l. 1. cap. 10. Stat. Romæ Urbis. l. 3. cap. 85.*

either *Constantine* or *Antoninus*, who made a Law thereupon; yea, and though besides the Decree of the Lateran Councel, the Bull [t] *Cœnæ Domini* do blast those every year with Excommunication that plunder the goods of such as suffer Shipwrack, in [u] any Sea, upon any pretence of Law or Custom whatsoëver; yet the Custom of confiscation in this case derived not its Original from the rude and barbarous Ages, but it flowed first from the most antient Maritim Laws of the *Rhodians* (which were in use among the *Grecians* in their flourishing condition) as shall bee shewn by and by, and from thence was received by divers Princes. Also, *when the Emperor's Ambassador*, as *Bodin* saith, *made complaint before* Henrie *the second King of* France, *that two Ships beeing driven a Shore were seized by one* Jordanes Ursinus, *and demanded a restitution of them*; Annas of *Monmorancie Master of the Horse made Answer, that all things which had been cast upon Shore, did by the Law of all Nations belong to such Princes as have commanded the Shores. So far hath Custom taken place in this particular, that* Andræas Doria *did not so much as complain about those Ships that were cast upon the French Shore, and made prize by the Admiral of France.* So far hee. In like manner, Whales and other Fish of extraordinarie bigness, do not, according to the known Law of *England*, [x] *Portugal*, and other Nations, belong to him that first seizeth them, but either to the Exchequer, or (which is all one) to such as the Prince shall grant a Royaltie of that nature.

[t] *Sub. Alex.* 3. c. *Excommunicationi extr.tit.de Raptoribus.*

[u] *Bartholomæus Ugolinus de Censuris Pontifici reservatis, part.*2. *cap.*4.

[x] *Georg. de Cabedo Decis. Lusitan. part.*2.48.

Other instances might bee brought, sufficiently to shew that the Law natural and of Nations is not wholly to bee drawn out of such Decrees or Determinations as are found in the Books of *Justinian*;

And

And so that what is there inserted touching a Communitie of the Sea, doth not in any wise diminish the Autoritie of the received Customs of so many Ages and Nations. But it is to bee observed, that the Sea is said in those Books to bee common, as the Aër, and as wilde Beasts are common. As if indeed the neighboring Aër it self could not pass into private Dominion, as well as a River that is possess't, and wilde Beasts that are taken. Moreover, those Antients do ordinarily conjoin a communitie of Shores and Ports, not unlike to that which they teach of the Sea: As if the very reason of the Dominion of Ports and Shores, as they belonged either to the people of *Rome*, or (which is all one here) to the Prince himself, were not manifestly drawn, as wee have expresly shewn alreadie out of [y] *Celsus*, from the Imposts and Customs which are frequent enough both in the Shores and [z] Ports of the *Roman* Empire, and in the Books of [a] *Justinian* (as in many other places.) For, as the [b] paiment of that Tribute which is called *Solarium à Solo*, and thence by the Greek Lawyers [c] Σωλάϱιον, for an hous that is built upon the ground of the Common-weal or the publick ground, was a sufficient Argument that the Common-weal or the Prince was Lord of the Soil; so indeed also the Custom paid for the use of Ports, manifested that there was the same kinde of Dominion over Them. Also, Ports themselvs are rightly supposed to bee a part even of the Continent, as appear's in [d] another place. Moreover also, *Justinian* appropriated the *Hellespont* to himself in such a manner, that hee would not permit Merchants and Sea-men to enjoy a freedom of that Sea and the Ports, but at an extraordinarie rate, if wee may

[y] *Cap.* 14.
[z] *Cic. Orat. pro lege Manilia. Symmachus, l.* 5. *Ep.*62. 65. *Tacitus Annal. lib.* 13. Alii *obiter.*
[a] *Tit. de Publicanis, in ff. & tit. de vectigalibus in C.*
[b] *L.* 1. *C. tit. de diversis Prædiis, & l.* 5. *ff. tit. de Operibus publicis, §.* 1.
[c] *Eclog. Basilic. lib.* 58. *p.* 488. *ut etiam simili notione in l.* 15. *ff. tit. Qui potior in Pignore.*
[d] *L.* 15. *Cæsar, ff. tit. de Publicanis.*

may believ [e] *Procopius*, who was his comtemporarie and wrote his Affairs.

[e] *In Arcanâ Historiâ, pag.* 110.

Nor did they imagine there was any difference betwixt the Dominion of the Sea, and that over the Land or People, who about 400 years since put this Inscription upon the Monument of the Emperor [f] *Frederick* the second,

[f] *Georg. Gualtherus in Tabulis antiq. Siciliæ,&c.pag.* 93.

Qui Mare, qui Terras, Populos, & Regna subegit,

Who subdued the Sea, the Land, Nations, and Kingdoms;

To wit, in the Cathedral Church of *Palermo*, in which place notwithstanding, the Imperial Law flourished at that time, as well as in the rest of the *Roman German* Empire. The sum of all is, that those antient Lawyers do deliver many things carelesly touching this matter, not onely such as thwart the most received Customs of Nations through almost all Ages, but such also as do sufficiently contradict one another; especially, whilst they join the Shore it self, and consequently the Ports together, as it were in an equal state of Communitie. So that they are equally refuted as well by their own indiscretion, as by the Autoritie of others.

Touching the Emperor Antoninus *his Answer; that* himself was Soveraign of the world, but the Law (*as 'tis commonly translated*) of the Sea; *in L. Deprecatio, ff. tit. de Lege Rhodiâ.* The true meaning of *the said Answer, and* a new, *but* genuine Exposition *of it. Also, that it comprehend's nothing which may in any wise oppose a* Dominion of the Sea.

CHAP. XXV.

BUt seeing that among those particulars, which are usually drawn out of Antient Lawyers, against *Dominion of the Sea*, that Answer of the Emperor *Antoninus* to *Eudæmon* several times before-mentioned, is of so principal an account; therefore it seem'd meet to treat of it apart by it self, and search into the genuine sens thereof; concerning which, whosoêver shall look into the whole matter with a little more care then ordinarie, will I suppose bee very well satisfied, not onely that most Interpreters have hitherto been wholly ignorant thereof, but also that it in no wise contradict's a Dominion of the Sea.

Eudæmon having been Shipwrack't at Sea, had petitioned the Emperor, for a restitution of those wrack't goods that had been seized by the Receivers of his Customs. The words, according to [a] *Volusius Mætianus* who was one of the Emperor's Privie Coun-

[a] *L. 9. ἀξίωσις ff. de Lege. Rhodiâ.*

Councellors, are these; Κύριε Βασιλεῦ Ἀντωνῖνε· ναυφράγιον ποιήσαντες ἐν τῇ Ἰταλίᾳ, διηρπάγημεν ὑπὸ τῶν δημοσίων τῶν τὰς Κυκλάδας νήσους οἰκούντων; *O Emperor* Antoninus, *our Lord; wee having made Shipwrack, have been spoiled of all by those Receivers of the Customs that inhabit the * Cyclades Islands.* Hee received an Answer from the *Emperor*, pointed for the most part after this manner, in the printed Books. Ἐγὼ μὲν τοῦ κόσμου Κύριος, ὁ δὲ νόμος τῆς θαλάσσης. τῷ νόμῳ τῶν Ῥοδίων κρινέσθω τῷ ναυτικῷ, ἐν οἷς μή τις τῶν ἡμετέρων αὐτῷ νόμος ἐναντιοῦται· τοῦτο δὲ αὐτὸ καὶ ὁ θειότατος Αὔγουστος ἔκρινεν. Which is usually thus translated; *I indeed am Soveraign of the world, but the Law, of the Sea. Let it bee determined by the* Rhodian *Law which is prescribed for the regulation of Sea-affairs, so far as it is not opposed by any of our Laws. For, the Emperor* Augustus *also was of this Opinion.* There never was any Controversie about the reading or Translation of this Answer, unless it were in those words, ὁ δὲ νόμος τῆς θαλάσσης, whereto answereth, *but the Law of the Sea* with a period or full point after it; as for the most part it is taken, and as wee have according to the received translation related it [b] alreadie in the Objections. Of those that would have it so rendred, there have been not a few who were of Opinion, that from the *Adversative* δὲ *autem* is implied, that the Emperor answer'd that himself indeed was Lord of the rest of the world, but not of the Sea; and that the Law onely, not any man was Lord of this. *Andræas* [c] *Alciatus* saith; *Whereas it is said, I indeed am Lord of the world, but the Law of the Sea; som* French *Doctors were of Opinion becaus of that* Adversative, *that a Soveraigntie of the Sea did not appertain unto the Emperors.*

* These Isles are part of those that lie in the *Archipelago.*

b *Cap. 2.*

c *Dispunctionum, lib. 2. cap. 5.*

perors. But hee add's; *which truly is very ridiculous: Although* [d] Baldus *and* [e] Jason *conceived for this reason, that the* Venetians *were not subject to the* Roman *Empire. But the sens of this Law is this* (to wit, that Sea-affairs were to bee determined by the *Rhodian* Law, as hee declare's a little before.) *For, seeing the Emperor is Lord of the world, surely, not the Land onely but the Sea also, ought to submit to his Laws, and hee to appoint Laws therein: though notwithstanding hee do not determine matters by his own Law in the Sea, but by the* Rhodian *Law, which was by him approved. Understand therefore, when it is said,* I am Lord of the world, *becaus I govern the world according to my own Law.* But the Law, *suppose the* Rhodian *Law*; of the Sea; *becaus by it, Justice is administred upon the* Sea. *Add hereunto, that this Particle* δὲ, *that is,* Autem, *is not so opposed, that it alwaies exclude's what goeth before.* And therefore *Alciatus* also rendreth it thus, *But the Law of the Sea, by which Law of the* Rhodians *concerning Navigation, let it bee determined, &c.* And therefore truly, it is upon exceeding good ground that hee call's their opinion very ridiculous, who would have it hence concluded, that a Dominion of the Sea did not belong unto the Emperors. For, suppose the Emperor did answer so, as it is commonly rendred. Doth hee therefore deny himself a Dominion of the Sea, becaus hee affirm's the Law to have Dominion at Sea? was hee not in the mean time Soveraign Lord and Arbitrator of the world (as hee implied indeed by his Answer) and so also of the Law? whatsoever hee pleased, was [f] Law. Therefore to say, that any thing which the Law had Dominion over, was not also under the Emperor's Dominion (to whom the Law it self was subject) is so absurd, as nothing can bee more.

[d] *In rub. de Rer. Divis.*
[e] *L. ex hoc Jure, ff. tit. de Justitiâ.*
[f] *L. 7. ff. tit. de Constitut. Principum.*

Others

Others there are that render the ſenſ of the words after this manner. *Although I my ſelf bee Lord and Emperor of the World, and ſo, free from all Laws, nor bound by any Rule to give any account to my Subjects, yet notwithſtanding the Law ſhall bee Empreſs and Queen at Sea, that is, it ſhall bear ſway by Sea, in ſuch Caſes as have faln out at Sea, ſince it concern's Sea-affairs, nor ſhall my Exchequer bee advanced by the loſs of my Subjects, but Juſtice ought to bee equally adminiſtred between the Exchequer and private perſons, and therefore the Exchequer ſhall bee liable to give an account.* So ſaith, *Franciſcus de* [g] *Amaya*, Advocate in the King's Court of Exchequer within the Kingdom of *Granada*. So you ſee, here is not the leaſt Track admitted of a denial of Sea-Dominion.

[g] *Obſervat. Juris, lib.* 1. *cap.* 1. §. 76.

Som alſo there are, who would have the meaning bee, that *Antoninus* ſhould expreſsly ſay that hee himſelf was as well the Law of the Sea, as Lord of the world. *I indeed am Lord of the World, and I am alſo the Law of the Sea.* So *Joannes Igneus*: And ſom [h] others there are that incline this way: with whoſe opinion if wee ſhall concur, wee muſt needs confeſs alſo, that the Emperor did ſufficiently attribute the very Dominion of the Sea unto himſelf. But [i] *Samuel Petit*, a very learned *French-man* ſaith, Antoninus *doth not deny himſelf to bee Lord of the Sea, that hee cannot give Law and do Juſtice to thoſe which deal upon the Sea; for, you ſee his meaning was, that Right ſhould bee don betwixt* Eudæmon *and the Cuſtomers which dwelt in the* Cyclades *Iſlands, according to the* Rhodian *Law; nor doth hee ſay alſo that hee is ſo tied by this* Rhodian *Law, that hee can by no means reliev* Eudæmon *againſt this* Law, *if any injurie bee don him, but his meaning is, that* Eudæmon *ſhould have Right don him according*

[h] *Forcatulus in Cupidine, Juriſp. cap.* 9. *Mendoza apud Amayam, in loco citato.*

[i] *Miſcellan, lib.* 3 *cap.* 11.

ing to this Law, but yet so that this do not thwart any of the Roman *Laws.* Thus hee interpret's it, though the vulgar reading bee reteined; which hee would rather have to bee rejected, and the name of Law to bee put out there; Beeing of opinion that the words ὁ δὲ νόμος τῆς θαλάσσης *but the Law of the Sea*, are corrupted from ὁ δὲ ἄνεμος τῆς θαλάσσης, *but the winde of the Sea.* As if the Emperor had said, that hee himself indeed was Lord of the Sea, but that the Sea neverthelesse is so subject to the power and alterations of winde and weather, that it was not in his power, though Lord thereof, to prevent Shipwracks. Moreover also, *Petit* correct's the Cosmographie of the Petition. Hee is of opinion, that those words, ἐν τῇ Ἰταλίᾳ *in Italie*, crept in through the negligence of Transcribers in stead of ἐν τῇ Τηλίᾳ (θαλάσσῃ being understood) *in the Telian* or Ægean *Sea*, which is about the Island *Telos. What a monstrous thing were* (saith hee) *that those who were shipwrack't in the Sea upon the Coast of* Italie, *should have been pillaged by Publicans or Customers dwelling in the* Cyclades *Islands? what Cosmographie is this? what relation have the Publicans or Customers of those Isles unto Italie?* which is most judiciously spoken: For, it appear's a manifest error there concerning *Italie.* And it is most certain, that the Island *Telos*, whether it bee one of the * *Cyclades* or *Sporades*, is so placed in the Ægean or *Levant* Sea (as wee finde in [k] *Strabo*, [l] *Plinie*, and *Stephanus de urbibus*) that the matter hang's well together, if wee say that the Customers of the *Cyclades* seized upon wrack't Goods in the *Telian* Sea, which to say of the *Italian* Sea or Shore is too monstrous in reason. Perhaps also, in that Catalogue of Seas summ'd up by *Æthicus*, an antient Cosmographer,

* The *Cyclades* and *Sporades* make up the Isles in the *Archipelago.*
[k] *Lib.* 10.
[l] *Lib.* 4. *cap.* 12.

grapher, the *Ionian* and *Ægean Sea*, the Sea called *Mare Lautades* (which learned men suppose to bee corruptly read for *Leucadium*) and *Mare Tillæ*, the *Telian* Sea it self, beeing taken out of this very Petition, before it was corrupted, was signified by the name of *Tilla*. And thus you have in a manner the opinion of learned men, so far as concern's the matter in hand, touching that Answer, and the Petition of *Eudemon*.

For my part, I most willingly yield my assent to the emendation of the Cosmographie: But do conceiv, that the antient and received reading of the Answer ought not to bee alter'd, save onely in the pointing. Oftentimes no regard hath been had, nor any use of points in antient Books: So that succeeding Generations have been puzzled now and then with a confusion of Syntax. But by a very small alteration of them in this place (for they are the very same with those in the [m] Books that are published) the sens appear's to mee not onely suited to the matter of the Petition, and clear; but also plainly freed, both from that Phansie, as if Dominion of the Sea were denied the Emperor in that place; and also from that fiction there expresly delivered touching the Sea-Dominion of the Law. Nor can I bee perswaded, that Interpreters hitherto have sufficiently hit upon the *Emperor's* meaning. For, what is this to the purpose? *I indeed am Lord of the World, but the Law of the Sea*. If it were spoken of the Law in general, certainly the Law had Dominion as well upon the main Land, The Emperor himself was Lord of every kinde of Law, even by Land as well as by Sea: And so truly, the Answer had hitherto, concerned the Petition nothing at all. If you would under-

[m] *Vide Alciat. Disp. lib. 2. cap. 5.*

understand it of the *Rhodian* Law, in such a sense (as *Alciatus* did) that the Emperor's meaning was that the Law had Dominion over the Sea, what then is the Consequence? that the matter was to bee determined by the *Rhodian* Law, so far as it was not opposed by any of the *Roman* Laws. What, was the *Rhodian* Law simply supreme over the Sea, and yet notwithstanding that high Title subject to restraint by the *Roman* Laws? These things do not cotten well. Let it bee pointed therefore, either after this manner; Ἐγὼ μὲν τοῦ Κόσμου Κύριος. Ὁ δὲ νόμος τῆς θαλάσσης. Τῷ νόμῳ τῶν Ῥοδίων κρινέσθω τῷ ναυτικῷ, ἐν οἷς μή τις τῶν ἡμετέρων αὐτῷ νόμος ἐναντιοῦται, *I indeed am Lord of the World. But of this kinde,* or *this is the Law* or *the Custom of the Sea. Let it bee determined by the* Rhodian *Law concerning Navigation, so far as none of our Laws do oppose the same.* Or let it bee pointed thus; ἐγὼ μὲν τοῦ Κόσμου Κύριος. ὁ δὲ νόμος τῆς θαλάσσης τῷ νόμῳ τῶν Ῥοδίων &c. *I indeed am Lord of the World. But let that Law* or *that Custom of the Sea bee judged or determined by the* Rhodian *Law concerning Navigation, so far as &c.*

The Case was this: *Eudemon Asiaticus*, born in *Nicomedia*, a Citie of *Bithynia*, having suffer'd Shipwrack in the *Telian* Sea (or the *Ægean*, which is about *Telos*) complain's that his Goods were seized by the Customers of the *Cyclades*, petitioning the Emperor for relief, in such a manner as if the Customers had made an advantage by his misfortune in a most injurious manner. Hee salute's him with the style of Lord and Emperor. The Emperor in his Answer readily owneth himself to bee a Lord, and so far a Lord, that hee saith the whole Earth, yea, and the world it self was comprised within his

Lordſhip or Juriſdiction. Therein alſo hee ſignifie's that it belong's to him to reliev Petitioners when wrong is don them: But as to what concern'd the matter of complaint, or the Petition about the wrack't Goods that had been ſeized by the Cuſtomers, that it did not ſufficiently appear whether thoſe Cuſtomers had don it wrongfully. Becauſ (if our former reading, or pointing bee admitted) in general, ſaith hee, and according to Rule, the Sea-Cuſtom, or that Law of the Sea which give's wrack't Goods to the Cuſtomers, hold's good. For, ſo theſe words ὁ δὲ νόμος τῆς θαλάσσης [*but that Cuſtom* or *that Law of this kinde belong's to the Sea*] hath relation to the thing don by the Cuſtomers, as it was in brief ſet forth in the Petition. But in regard that to this Cuſtom or Law of the Sea, there might, either through ſom privilege, or becauſ of the qualitie of the goods, or ſom other Cuſtom no leſs in force, certain Qualifications ariſe, according to circumſtance, in reſpect whereof perhaps either the Cuſtomers ought, in this caſe, to have forborn medling with the goods, or the Complainant might have a ſpecial exception to privilege his goods from Seizure; therefore hee did well to leav it, beeing a matter ſo ſuccinctly and without any addition of circumſtance expreſſed in the Petition, to bee determined by the Naval Laws of the *Rhodians*; but yet ſo far onely as the *Roman* Laws in the mean time were not contrarie thereto. Nor doth the ſenſ much differ, if the latter pointing and tranſlation bee admitted: I indeed am Lord of the world, and the Sea as well as the Land is conteined within my Juriſdiction: in both, I willingly right thoſe that are wronged, according to Law: But truly what the Cuſtom of the Sea may bee in this

this case, and whether the Complainant ought to bee relieved, let it bee determined by the *Rhodian Laws*, which, by my permission, are in use upon the Sea, where they are not contrarie to our own. But it seem's to mee not a little conducing to a confirmation of the fore-going sens, whereby the Maritim Law touching Wrecks and the Right of the Customers (that is, of the Exchequer, whose Right is transferr'd into their hands) is asserted, if it shall bee made appear that such a Law or Custom was in force at that time, which Interpreters are not wont here to grant. It is indeed certain enough according to the Imperial Law (as wee have it now compiled in the Books of *Justinian*) that [n] Wrecks are reserved to the former Owners, and so that both the Exchequer and the Customers are thence excluded: Yea, and that the Custom whereby they are confiscated, is condemned by the received determinations of the *Roman-German* Empire, as well as the Canon Law, as wee hinted in the former Chapter. But it is collected by manifest evidences, that the Law or Custom for Confiscation of Wrecks was in force, in the time of this Emperor *Antoninus* (I mean *Antoninus Pius*) who, as *Julius Capitolinus* write's did in the establishing of this Law, make use of *Volusius Metianus* the Lawyer, out of whose Books the Petition and Answer here spoken of was transcribed into the *Digests* [o]. It is clear, that almost all those Passages that wee finde in the *Digests* for reserving them to the former Owners, were taken out of *Paulus*, *Callistratus*, and *Ulpian*, who lived many years after this *Antoninus*. There is somwhat also to this purpose out of [p] *Priscus Javolenus*, who lived at the same time with this *Antoninus*. But this Emperor

[n] *L.3.& 21. ff.tit. de adquir.& amittend.possess. l. 44.ff.de adquir. rer. dom.l.1.3. & seqq.ff. tit. de Incendio.l.1.C.de Naufragiis.*

[o] *Locis superius citatis.*

[p] *L.21.ff.tit. de adquir. & amit.possess. §.1.*

reigned XXII years, and as appear's out of *Javolenus*, hee did by Decree mitigate the rigor of Confiscation in this Case. From which it might easily com to pass, that under the same Emperor such a Law and Custom as wee have mentioned might bee in force, and under the same it might either bee abrogated, or the rigor of it abated. The principal Constitution, which, according to the [q] Book of *Justinian*, would not have the Exchequer to interpose in this case, is by *Antonius Contius*, a very eminent Lawyer, attributed to the Emperor *Antoninus*, according to the Testimonie of an antient Book in Manuscript; although the name of *Constantine* bee put before those that are published. The words are these; *If at any time a Vessel bee driven a Shore by Shipwrack, or if at any time it run aground, it shall belong to the Owners. My Exchequer shall not interpose it self. For, what right hath the Exchequer by another man's misfortune, that it should seek after profit upon so sad an occasion?* Yea, and *Ulpian* shew's, that such a kinde of Constitution there was also under *Adrian*, who was this man's Father by Adoption. *It is decreed* (so saith [r] *Ulpian*) *that it may bee lawful for every man, to recover his losses by Shipwrack freely; and thus much was ordained by the Emperor* Antoninus, *with the Emperor his Father.* There are in these very clear Evidences, that about that time, there was such a Law or Custom of Confiscation, as wee have mentioned; which wee know very well was wont to take place often, even contrarie to the Autoritie of antient Decrees. For, it may bee concluded from the Shipwrack of *Valgius*, or *Victor*, related by [s] *Paulinus*, that it was in som use even under *Theodosius* the elder. There are the like Examples upon the [t] Shore of the *Roman-German* Empire:

And

[q] *L.* 1. *C. de Naufragiis.*

[r] *L.* 12. *ff. tit. de Incendio.*

[s] *Epist.* 37. *ad Micarium.*

[t] *Chronic. Albert. Stadensis, ann.* 1112. *videsis Frederic. Lindebrog. in Glossario, pag.* 1443.

And others may bee brought, whereas notwithstanding ſom Laws were made to the contrarie.

Moreover alſo, the antient Orators, both Greek and Latin, whilſt they allege Examples about the ſtating of Queſtions in pleading, do mingle this very Law or Cuſtom about Shipwrack with other uſual and antient Cuſtoms in the *Greek* and *Roman* Empire, as a thing that was very frequently received. *Sopater* and [u] *Syrianus in Hermogenem* ſay; *The Law is, that ſpoils which are found, do belong to him that is General of the Army; In like manner the Law is, that Wrecks do belong to the Cuſtomers. In a tempeſtuous Sea, ſpoils are brought into Port. Hereupon ariſeth a controverſie about them, between the Commanders and the Cuſtomers of the Cuſtoms. In this caſe it behove's us not to vex our ſelvs in vain with reading of Laws, but to look into the very nature of things.* For, in truth the Queſtion is, whether the Goods bee now to bee called Spoils or Wrecks. In like manner ſaith, [x] *Curius Fortunatianus; what is a ſimple definition? when wee define a particular thing ſimply. Put caſe, that Wrecks do belong to the Publicans or Cuſtomers. The bodie of a certain man that was loſt by Shipwrack, clothes and all, beeing driven aſhore was cover'd by the Sands. The Cuſtomers came and drew it out. Therefore they are guiltie of the violation of Sepulcre. For here the Queſtion is ſimply, what it is to violate a Sepulcre.*

Moreover, that, *Voluſius Metianus* wrote that Petition and the Anſwer, appear's *in Libris Publicorum ex Lege Rhodiâ*; that is, in his ſummarie of thoſe Laws which belong either to the Excequer or the Cuſtomers, wherein alſo is conteined either the Law or Cuſtom of Confiſcation of Wrecks. It ſuit's very well with theſe Particulars, that in that Anſwer of the

u Εἰς στάσεις, *pag.* 107. *Venetiis*, 1509.

x *Artis Rhetoricæ Scholicæ, lib.* 1. *pag.* 46 *edit. Parij.* 1599.

the Emperor *Antoninus* those words, ὁ δὲ νόμος τῆς θαλάσσης, should bee rendred, *but that Law of the Sea* or *that Custom of the Sea*, which hee meant should bee so examined and determined, according to the *Rhodian Laws*, that in the mean time, those *Rhodian* Laws should not bee of force, if any Rescript or any *Roman* Law were against it. And of what Autoritie *Adrian's* Decree was at that time (whereof *Ulpian* speak's in the places before quoted) perhaps it did not sufficiently appear, no not to the Lawyers themselvs without a more curious examination, whose assistance *Antoninus* made use of in his Answer. But, that wee may at length dispatch this particular; no man whatsoëver, whether hee approve the common Translation, or mine, will (I suppose) unless hee renounce his own reason, conceiv, upon a due consideration of the whole matter, that any denial is made of the Dominion of the Sea in that Answer, or that the least Tittle can bee found in it against the Dominion thereof.

An Answer to the Opinions *of* modern Lawyers, *so far as they oppose a* Dominion *of the Sea; especially of* Fernandus Vasquius, *and* Hugo Grotius.

Chap. XXVI.

Having thus refuted, or upon good ground removed som Opinions of antient Lawyers, which are usually alleged for the mainteining of a perpetual Communitie of the Sea; it is no hard

hard matter in like manner to wave the Autoritie of those of later time, that oppose a Dominion. For, if wee consider the great number of those, who, whether they comment upon the bodie of *Justinian*, or treat apart of this particular, would not have us to recede from that natural Communitie; wee shall finde plainly that they deal in the same manner, as they that have pinn'd their Faith, more then was meet, upon the sleev of *Ulpian*, or som other such antient Autor: Unless wee conceiv that som of them did not so much explain the Law in this point, as recite the opinions of Lawyers, so far as they have been by them deliver'd: Just in the same manner, as if a man should so discours upon *Aristotle's* Astronomie, or the opinion of *Thales* touching the Earth's floating, like a Dish in the Sea, and that of the Stoicks of its encompassing the Earth like a Girdle, with that of the Antients concerning an extreme heat under the Equinoctial, and other opinions of that kinde, which are rejected and condemned, by the observation and experience of Posteritie; that hee might seem not so much to search into the thing it self, as to represent the person of the Autor, thereby to trace out his meaning, onely for the discovering of his opinion. But as the root beeing cut, the Tree fall's, so the Autoritie of those antient Lawyers beeing removed out of the way, all the determinations of the modern which are supported by it, must bee extremely weakned.

Now therefore, as to what hath been formerly alleged out of *Fernandus Vasquius*, it is grounded upon such Arguments as are either manifestly fals, or impertinent. For, what is this to the purpose?

That the Sea, from the beginning of the World to this present day, is, and ever hath been in common, Without the least alteration, as 'tis generally known. Whereas the quite contrarie is most certainly known to those, who have had any insight into the received Laws and Customs of Ages and Nations. That is to say, that by most approved Law and Custom, som Seas have passed into the Dominion and partrimonie, both of Princes and private persons; as is clearly made manifest out of what hath been alreadie shewn you. Moreover also hee [a] would have prescription to ceas betwixt Foreigners in relation to each other, and not to take place in the Law of Nations, but in the *Civil* onely; so that by his Opinion presciption should bee of no force between those (as between two supreme states or Princes) who are not indifferently subject to the Civil Law, which admit's prescription; then which not any thing can bee said or imagined more absurd. Almost all the principal points of the *Intervenient Law of Nations,* beeing established by long consent of persons using them, do depend upon prescription or antient Custom. To say nothing of those Princes, whose Territories were subject heretofore to the *Roman* Empire, and who afterwards became absolute within themselvs, not onely by Arms, but also by prescription (which is every where admitted among the Laws of Nations;) whence is it that Prisoners of war are not now made slaves among Christians, unless it bee becaus that Custom began to grow out of date som Ages since upon a ground of [b] Christian brotherhood, and by prescription ratified betwixt Nations. Whence is it that the ransoms of prisoners are to bee paid, som to the Princes, and som to the Persons that

[a] *Illustrium Controvers. lib.* 1. *cap.* 51. §. 23. *unde & V. Cl. Hugo Grotius in Mari Libero, cap.* 7.

[b] *Suarez de Legibus, lib.* 20.

that take them? As for instance, when the ransom is not above ten thousand Crowns, it goe's to him that took the Prisoner; when it exceed's, it is to bee paid to the Prince. *Becaus* (saith [c] *Nicolaus Boërius*) *if it exceed, as when any one hath taken a Duke, a Count, a Baron, or any other great man, then it belong's to the Prince, and so it is observed in the Kingdoms of* France, England *and* Spain. *It hath by prescription of time been observed among* Princes; *and so it became Law.* And truly, to deny a Title of prescription wholly among Princes, is plainly to abrogate the very intervenient Laws of Nations. As for those other things mentioned by *Vasquius*, concerning Charitie and the inexhaustible abundance of the Sea (whereby hee make's a difference betwixt Rivers and Seas) and other things of the like nature, they have no relation at all to the point of Dominion; as you have been sufficiently told alreadie.

[c] *In Decisionibus Burdegal. decisione* 178. *num.* 4.

In the next place, wee com to the other, to wit, *Hugo Grotius*, a man of great learning, and extraordinarie knowledg in things both Divine and Humane; whose name is very frequent in the mouths of men every where, to maintein a natural and perpetual Communitie of the Sea. Hee hath handled that point in two Books; in his *Mare Liberum*, and in that excellent work *De Jure Belli & pacis.* As to what concern's *Mare Liberum*, a Book that was written against the *Portugals* about trading into the Indies through the vast Atlantick and Southern Ocean; it contein's indeed such things as have been delivered by antient Lawyers touching communitie of the Sea; Yea, and disputing for the Profits and Interests of his Countrie, hee draw's them into his own partie; and so endeavor's to prove that the Sea

 is

is not capable of private Dominion. But hee hath so warily couched this subject with other things, that whether in this hee did hit or miss, the rest howsoever might serv to assert the point which hee was to handle. Moreover, hee discourseth about the Title of Discoverie, and primarie occupation (pretended to by the *Portugals*) and that also which is by Donation from the *Pope*. And hee seem's in a manner, either somtimes to quit that natural and perpetual Communitie, which many Civil Lawyers are eager to maintein, and hee himself, in order to his design, endeavored to confirm; or els to confess that it can hardly bee defended. For, concerning those Seas that were inclosed by the antient Romans; *the nature of the Sea*, saith [d] hee, *differ's from the Shore in this, that the Sea, unless it bee in som small part of it self, is not easily capable of Building or Inclosure. And put case it were, yet even this could hardly bee without the hindrance of common use. Neverthelesse, if any small part of it may bee thus possessed, it fall's to him that enter's upon it first by occupation.* Now, the difference of a lesser and a greater part, cannot take place (I suppose) in the determining of private Dominion. But in express words hee except's even a Bay or Creek of the Sea. And a little after, saith hee, *Wee do not speak here of an In-land Sea, which in som places beeing streightned with Land on every side, exceed's not the breadth even of a River, yet 'tis clear that this was it the* Roman *Lawyers spake of, when they set forth those notable determinations against private Avarice. But the Question, is concerning the Ocean, which Antiquitie called* immense Infinit, *the Parent or Original of things, confining with the Aër.* And afterwards hee saith, *The Controversie is not about a streight or Creek in this Ocean, nor of so much*

[d] *Mari libero, cap.* 5.

much as is within view when one stand's upon the shore. A little farther also, speaking of *Prescription*, hee saith, [e] *It is to bee added, that their Autoritie who are of the contrarie opinion, cannot bee applied to this Question. For, they speak of the Mediterranean Sea, wee of the Ocean. They of a Creek or Bay, wee of the broad and wide Sea, which differ very much in the point of Occupation.* And certainly, there is no man but must conceiv it a very difficult thing to possess the whole Ocean: Though if it could bee held by occupation, like a narrow Sea, or a Creek, or as the whole world was said to bee possessed at first by antient Princes, it might even as well pass into the Dominion or Ownership of him that should enter upon it first by occupation. Howsoëver, there have been [f] som others, who by the same Rule distinguish in like manner the inner and neighboring Seas from the open Sea or main Ocean.

[e] Cap. 7.

[f] Jo. Gryphiander, de Insulis, c. 25. §. 52.

But it is by no means to bee omitted, that they, for whose sakes *Hugo Grotius* wrote that Book, that is to say, the States of *Holland*, did, not unwillingly, but rather (as it seem's) according to their own hearts desire, give ear to the condemnation of that Opinion (especially becaus it was owned by *Grotius*) concerning a Communitie of the Sea and freedom of Fishing therein according to the Law natural and of Nations, by the Embassador of *James* King of great *Britain*, in a speech of his deliver'd openly in *Holland*; and that others were gravely admonished from his misfortune, not to maintein the like. Of which thing *Grotius* himself bear's witness. [g] *I have labored*, saith hee, *as much as any to maintein the Right of Navigation to the* Indies, *and for the preservation of Clothdressing in our Countrie. But for the freedom of Fishing at Sea so much, that* Carleton *the King of great* Britain's

[g] In Apologetico eorum qui Hollandiæ præfuerunt ante mutationem 1618. p. 387. edit. Heidelberg. cap. 19. pag. 257.

Britain's *Embassador, beeing incited by my enemies to speak somwhat in publick against mee beeing at* [h] *that time in Prison, hee had nothing els to say, but that I had begun to make som Discourses in defence of that freedom, as a thing grounded upon the Law of Nations, and Custom, time out of minde; whereas notwithstanding, nothing had been said or written by mee upon that subject, different from those things which the State's Embassadors had mainteined in* Britain *in the year* MDCX; *and our Ancestors before, even for som Ages past. And yet that Embassador said, that others ought to bee terrified by the example of my misfortune, from defending that Opinion.* It is true indeed, that persons in power usually take a libertie to aspers men as they pleas when they are in question: But these things were not spoken so much against *Hugo Grotius*, as against that natural Right of Communitie at Sea (injuriously pretended to) which many men have defended more expresly and plainly then himself; but none, with so much learning and ingenuitie. Nor, did that Speech of the Embassador, for ought wee know, as things then stood, displeas the States of *Holland*.

[h] Hee was imprisoned for having an hand in *Barnevel's* business.

But in his Books [i] *de Jure Belli & Pacis*, having indeed set down the reason of the original of private Dominion to bee upon this ground, that those places which became peculiarly assigned were not sufficient for the maintenance of all men, hee conclude's that the Sea, becaus of its bigness and inexhaustible abundance, beeing sufficient for all, cannot bee appropriated to any. Hee add's other things also, touching the nature of the Seas not beeing distinguishable by Bounds; of both which wee have said enough alreadie. But at length hee betake's himself to the received Customs of Nations and speak's more then once,

[i] *De Jure Belli & Pacis, lib.2.cap.2. §.2.& 3.*

once concerning the proprietie or private Dominion of the Sea, as of a thing somtimes to bee yielded without Controversie. *The Land*, saith [k] hee, *and Rivers, and any part of the Sea, in case it com under the proprietie of som Nation, ought to bee open for such as have need of passage upon just and necessarie occasions.* Afterwards also, speaking of the [l] proprietie of Rivers, *After this example*, saith hee, *it seem's that even the Sea may bee possessed by him that is Owner of the Land on both sides, although it lie open either above, as a Creek; or above and below too, as a streight or narrow Sea: So that it bee not so great a part of the Sea, that beeing compared with the Lands it cannot seem to bee any portion of them. And that which is lawful for one Prince or People, the same seem's lawful also for two or three, if in the like manner they pleas to enter upon the Sea flowing between. For so, Rivers that flow between two Nations, have been entred upon by both, and then divided.* Hee allegeth other things also touching the Right of primarie occupation by Sea; but so, that for the most part hee contein's himself within Creeks and streights. [m] Hee saith, that not by any natural Right or Reason, but by Custom it came to pass, that the Sea was not appropriated, or that it could not lawfully bee entred upon by Right of Occupation. And that the Custom beeing changed, if there were any in the antient Law that might hinder a private Dominion of the Sea, the reason of Communitie must bee changed also. But that it hath been sufficiently changed, appear's abundantly (if I bee not deceived) out of what wee have hitherto shewn you. Yea, the very Laws as well * Civil as Intervenient of most Nations make abundantly to this purpose, as it hath been proved.

[k] *Ibidem.* §.13.

[l] *Ibid Cap.* 3. § 8.

[m] *Ibidem.* §. 19.

* The same with Municipal.

Moreover,

Moreover, that nothing may bee wanting to weigh down the Ballance, therefore, besides the opinions of the Civil Lawyers before-alleged out of *France*, *Spain*, and *Italie*, for a private Dominion of the Sea, let this over and above bee added, which is taken out of that sort of Lawyers also, discoursing in general terms about the Sea. I here give it you as it was composed by a Lawyer, none of the meanest in the *Roman-German* Empire, by name [n] *Regenerus Sixtinus*, who was indeed against private Dominion of the Sea. *The matter in question*, saith hee, *concerning the Sea and its Shore, is, whether as Rivers that are navigable, and by which others are made navigable, they may bee reckoned* inter Regalia **among the Prince's Roialties;** (for, whatsoëver is reputed a part of those *Regalia* or Roialties, is as private or peculiar to Princes, as that is to subjects which is their own; for which caus the Revenues of the Exchequer are private after the same manner;) *so also, whether the Sea it self and its Shore, bee comprised within those* Regalia? *Cacheranus*, *Decis.* 155. *n.* 81. *Ferrarius Montanus*, *de Feud. lib.* 5. *c.* 7. [o] *reckon's the regulation and the very dominion also of the Sea among the* Regalia, *nor doth hee make any difference betwixt the Sea and a publick River.* Mynsingerus *also*, *Resp.* 1. *nu.* 162. *Decad.* 11. *saith*, *that the proprietie of the Sea is a part of those* Regalia. But *Sixtinus* himself, discoursing upon this matter, just as they do that are more addicted than they ought to the words of *Ulpian*, and numbring up those Autors that are of the contrarie opinion, conclude's thus, *But more true it is that a proprietie of the Sea and Shore, is not by the Common Law to bee reckoned among the Regalia.* But upon due consideration of all those particulars, which hither-

n *De Regalibus, lib. cap.* 4. §. 97.

o *Versic. Tametsi Jus piscandi.*

to have been produced out of the Customs of so many Ages and Nations, and as well out of the *Civil*, as the *Common* or *Intervenient Law* of most Nations, no man (I suppose) will question but that there remain's not either in the nature of the Sea it self, or in the Law either *Divine*, *Natural*, or of *Nations*, any thing which may so oppose the private Dominion thereof, that it cannot bee admitted by every kinde of Law, even the most approved; and so that any kinde of Sea whatsoëver may by any sort of Law whatsoëver bee capable of private Dominion; which was the thing I intended to prove.

The End of the first Book.

Touching the

DOMINION,

OR,

Ownerſhip of the Sea.

BOOK II.

The order or Method *of thoſe things that are to bee handled in this Book. The* Britiſh Ocean *divided into four parts.*

CHAP. I.

HAving made it evident, in the former Book, that the Sea is capable of private Dominion as well as the Land, and that by all kindes of Law, whether wee ſeriouſly conſider the *Divine*, or *Natural*, or any *Law of Nations* whatſoëver; it remain's next that wee diſcourſ touching the Dominion of *great Britain* in the Sea encompassing it about, and of those large Testimonies whereby it is asserted and mainteined. Wherein this Method is observed, that in the first place wee premise both the distribution and various appellation of the Sea flowing about it, in order to the Discours. Then it shall bee shewn, from all Antiquitie, down to our times without interruption, that those, who by reason of so frequent alterations of the state of Affairs, have reigned here, whether *Britains*, *Romans*, *Saxons*, *Danes*, and *Normans*, and so the following Kings (each one according to the various latitude of his Empire) have enjoied the Dominion of that Sea by perpetual occupation, that is to say, by using and enjoying it as their own after a peculiar manner, as an undoubted portion either of the whole bodie of the estate of the *British* Empire, or of som part thereof, according to the state and condition of such as have ruled it; or as an inseparable appendant of this Land. Lastly, that the Kings of Great *Britain* have had a peculiar Dominion or proprietie over the Sea flowing about it, as a Bound not bounding their Empire, but (to borrow the Terms used by Surveiors of Land) as bounded by it; in the same manner as over the Island it self, and the other neighboring Isles which they possess about it.

The Sea encompassing great *Britain*, which in general wee term the *British* Sea, is divided into four parts, according to the four Quarters of the World. On the West lie's the *Vergivian Sea*, which also take's the name of the *Deucaledonian*, where it washeth the Coast of *Scotland*. And of this *Vergivian*, wherein *Ireland* is situate, the *Irish* Sea is reckoned to bee a part, called in antient time the [a] *Scythian Vale*, but now the *Channel of* St *George*. So that as well that which washeth

[a] *Gildas, Epist. de Excidio Britanniæ.*

washeth the Western Coast of *Ireland*, as that which flowe's between great *Britain* and *Ireland*, is to bee called the *British* Sea. For, not onely this (which of old was called great *Britain*, and somtimes simply the [b] *Great Island*) but also the Isle of *Ireland*, with the other adjacent Isles, were termed *Britanniæ*: So that many times *Albion* and *Ireland* are equally called *British* Isles and *Britannides*; as you may see in *Strabo*, *Ptolomie*, *Marcianus Heracleötes*, *Plinie*, *Eustathius* upon *Dionysius Afer*, and others. Moreover, *Ireland* is called by *Ptolomie* [c] Μικρὰ Βρεττανία *little Britain*. And, saith *Ethelward*, an antient Writer, [d] *They go to* Ireland, *called heretofore* Britannides *by the great Julius Cæsar*. Perhaps hee had a more perfect Copie of *Julius Cæsar*'s Book: For in none of his Commentaries which wee use, is *Ireland* called by that name. And it hath been observed by [e] learned men, that that book hath been maimed and alter'd by one *Julius Celsus*, whose name wee finde now and then in the Manuscript Copies.

Towards the North this Sea is named the Northern, *Caledonian*, and *Deucaledonian* Sea, wherein lie scatter'd the *Orcades* Islands, *Thule*, and others, which beeing called the *British* or *Albionian* Isles; yea, and * *Britannides*, gave name to the neighboring Sea. And indeed *Thule* (which som would have to bee *Island*; others, and that with most reason, do conceiv it to bee the biggest of the [f] *Shetland* or *Zetland* Isles, called **Thilensel** by the [g] Seamen, and som there are again that think otherwise) was of old not onely termed a *British* Isle, but also by som expresly placed in *Britain* it self. *Mahumedes Acharranides* an Arabian, called likewise *Aracensis* and *Albategnius*, a famous Mathematician, who lived above nine hundred years ago, saith,

[b] *Aristides*, *in Oratione Ægyptiacâ*.

[c] *Magnæ Constructionis, lib.* 2.

[d] *Lib.* 4. *c.* 4.

[e] *Lips. Epistolicar. quæst. lib.* 2. *cap.* 3. & *Elect. lib.* 2. *cap.* 7.

* *Jo. Tzetzes, Chiliad.* 8. *cap.* 218.

[f] *Guil-Camden. in Insul. Brit. p.* 850.

[g] *Gaspar. Peucerus, lib. de Terræ dimensione.*

[h] *De Scientiis Stellarum, lib. cap. 6.*

saith, [h] *Som observing the breadth of the Earth from the Equinoctial Line towards the North, have found it to bee determined by the Isle* Thule *which is in* Britain, *where the longest day is* $\overline{XX}$ *hours*; that is to say, *Ptolomie* and his Followers, who by drawing a Line on the Northside of *Thule* or the *Shetland Isles*, through 63 degrees, and a quarter of Northern Latitude, have set it down for the utmost Bound of the habitable world. Yea, and som have used the name of *Thule* for Britain it self or *England*. In times past, the Emperor of Constantinople was wont to have trustie Guards called *Barrangi*, constantly attending his person; who were taken out of *England*, as appear's out of [i] *Nicetas Choniates*; and *Codinus* also who was keeper of the Palace, [k] write's that they were wont to salute the Emperor with a loud voice Ἰγκλινιστί *in the English Tongue*. But in the Storie of [l] *Anna Comnena*, the Daughter of *Alexius*, it is said expresly, that they came ἐκ τῆς Θούλης νήσου *from the Island of Thule*. In like manner, all the Islands either known or heard of in this Northern Sea, were at length called by the name of *British*; the utmost Bounds whereof, as also of *Thule* it self, som of the Antients would have to reach unto 67 degrees of Latitude, or thereabout. And *Albategnius*, speaking of the Sea as it look's toward *Spain*, saith; [m] *There are* $\overline{XII}$ Brit*ish Isles in it towards the North; and beyond these it is not habitable; and how far it stretcheth, is unknown.*

[i] *Hist. Græc. lib. 2.*

[k] *De Officiis Constantinop.*

[l] *Alexiados, lib. 2.*

[m] *De Scientiis Stellarum, cap. 6.*

Upon the Eastern Coast of *Britain* flow's the *German* Sea (so called by *Ptolomie*, becaus it lie's before the *German* Shore.) On the South, flow's that which is particularly noted by *Ptolomie* to

bee

bee the *British* Sea. But all that was called also the *British* Sea, which extend's it self like a half Moon along the *French* Shore, through the Bay or Creek of of *Aquitain*, unto the Northern Coast of *Spain*. For this wee have the Testimonie of *Mela*, who saith the Pyrenean Promontories do butt out into the British Sea. [n] *The Pyrenie*, saith hee, *run's first from hence into the* British *Sea; then turning towards the continent, it stretcheth as far as* Spain. Yet every man knowe's it is called likewise either the *French*, or *Contabrian*, or the *Aquitanick* Sea, from the several Shores which it washeth. But so far even the name both of the British and *English* Sea was inlarged either by that extraordinarie Command of the people of *Britain* at Sea, or of such as had atteined the Rights of Dominion in Great Britain (which is all one to our purpose.) And it is stretch't likewise by som of the Antients as far as the Promontorie *Nerium*, now called *Capo di St Maria*. The *Arabian* Geographer saith; [o] *Towards the North, Andaluzia* (so the *Arabians* use to call *Spain*) *is environed by the Sea of the people of* England, *who are of the* Romans, that is, who are of the people of *Europe*; for, it is usual with those Eastern Nations to call the people of *Europe*, generally either *Romans* or *French*. And then hee saith, *There are nine Stages from* Toledo *to* St James, *which is seated upon the English Sea.* Moreover, hee call's the Place, where that Citie of St *James* is seated, [p] *a Promontorie of the English Sea*; and hath divers other passages of the same kinde. Thus at length *great Britain*, with the Isles lying about it, and the Sea imbracing it on everie side, became as it were one Civil Bodie, so that the whole together is comprehended in the name of *British* or *Britannick*. Also, this Sea and Great Britain have indeed given mutual names as it were of Dignitie to each other. That is to say, this Island was called by the Antients simply [q] *Insula Cæruli*, **the Isle of the Sea,** as

[n] *De Situ Orbis, lib.* 2. *cap.* 3.

[o] *Climat.* 4. *part.* 1.

[p] *Climat.* 5. *part.* 1.

[q] *In Catalectis Virgilii*, de Sabino.

as that was called *Oceanus Insulæ*, **the Ocean of the Isle**, or the *British Sea.*

Having made this preparation, then wee treat first concerning the Sea-Dominion of the *Britains*, before they were reduced under the *Roman* power; Next, touching a Dominion of that kinde belonging to the *Romans* while they ruled here, continually and necessarily accompanying the Soveraigntie of the Island. Afterwards, it is made evident by such Testimonies as are found among the Antients, that the *English Saxons* and others who enjoied the supreme Power in *Britain*, before the *Norman*'s Invasion, had such a kinde of Dominion. Lastly, according to the fourfold division of the *British* Sea, wee set forth the antient Occupation, together with the long and continued possession of every Sea in particular, since the *Norman*'s time; whereby the true and lawful Dominion and Customs of the Sea, which are the subject of our Discours, may bee drawn down, as it were by a twind thred, until our own times. Moreover, seeing both the Northern and Western Ocean do stretch to a very great Latitude (this to *America*; that not onely to *Island* and the Shores of *Groenland*, but to parts utterly unknown) and so it cannot all bee called the *British Seas*; yet becaus the Nation of great *Britain* have very large Rights and Privileges of their own in both those Seas, even beyond the bounds of the *British* name, therefore it was thought fit to touch a little upon these Particulars.

That the antient Britains, *did enjoy and possess the* SEA *of the same name; especially the* Southern *and* Eastern *part of it, as Lords thereof, together with the Island,* before they were brought under the *Roman* power.

CHAP. II.

IT is true indeed which an eminent man saith; [a] *That the Sea hath been enjoyed by Occupation, not for this reason onely, becaus men had so enjoied the Land, nor is the Act or intent of the minde sufficient thereto; but that there is a necessitie of som external Act, from whence this Occupation may bee understood.* Therefore Arguments are not to bee derived altogether from a bare Occupation or Dominion of Countries, whose Shores are washed by the Sea: But from such a private or peculiar use or enjoiment of the Sea, as consist's in a setting forth Ships to Sea, either to defend or make good the Dominion; in prescribing Rules of Navigation to such as pass through it; in receiving such Profits and Commodities as are peculiar to every kinde of Sea-Dominion whatsoëver; and, which is the principal, either in admitting or excluding others at pleasure. Touching which particular, wee shall make diligent inquirie into those things which concern the Isle of *Britain*, through the Ages past, down to the present time.

[a] *Hugo Grotius, de Jure Belli & Pacis, lib. 2. c. 3. §. 11.*

It is upon good ground concluded, that the most antient

antient Historie, whereto any credit ought to bee given about the affair's of *Britain*, is not elder then the time of *Caius Julius Cæsar*; the Ages before him beeing too obscured with Fables. But at his coming wee finde clear passages of the *Britain*'s Ownership and Dominion of the Sea flowing about them, especially of the South and East part of it, as a perpetual Appendant of the Soveraigntie of the Island. For, they not onely used the Sea as their own at that time for Navigation and Fishing; but also permitted none besides Merchants to sail unto the Island without their leav; nor any man at all to view or sound the Ports and Sea-Coast. And that the Case stood certainly thus, it is no slight Argument which wee shall insert here out of *Cæsar* himself. But allowance must bee given ever to Arguments and Conjectures, touching times so long since past and gon; especially when there is a concurrence in the Customs and Testimonies of following times. And as things beeing placed at too remote a distance, so that they cannot bee certainly discerned by the eie, are wont to bee more surely discover'd by the help of a triangle at hand; So what uncertainty soever may bee in those proofs that are to bee brought out of so remote Antiquitie, I question not but it will bee made sufficiently manifest by the continued and more certain usage and Custom of later times, as shall bee abundantly made evident in the following Discours.

As to what concern's the *Britains* particular use of Navigation, in that antient time, without which an Occupation of this kinde cannot bee had; notwithstanding that at *Cæsar*'s first arival, they were [b] terrified with the sight of that unusal kinde of long Ships; and

[b] *Cæsar de Bello Gallico, lib.* 4.& 5.

and though at his second coming with a multitude of Vessels of all kindes (beeing [c] re-inforced to the number of eight hundred; or, as som would have it, to a thousand) they fled in a great fright from the Shore, not beeing sufficiently provided for such a Sea-fight as was then at hand, and which they had never been acquainted with; neverthelesse, it is most certain, that they had Vessels of their own, wherein they used to coast about the neighboring Sea, and so entred upon it corporally by Occupation. Mention is made indeed by Writers of som of their Vessels more notable then the rest, which they frequently used, beeing framed with twigs (as the fashion hath been in the more antient Nations) and cover'd with Ox-hides after their usual manner. Moreover, *Festus Avienus*, speaking of the antient Inhabitants of the *OEstrymnides*, or the Islands called the * Sillyes, with the rest lying about, thus expresseth himself;

[c] *Guil. Pictaviensis, in gestis Willielmi Regis* 1.

* *Andr. Schot. Observat. Historic. lib.* 3. 22. §. 6.

[d] *In Oris Maritimis.*

——— [d] rei ad miraculum,
Navigia junctis semper aptant pellibus,
Corióque vastum sæpe percurrunt Salum.

Tis strange! There Ships they frame with Oxes-hide,
And scout in Leather through the Ocean wide.

And what hee saith of their continual care of Traffick and Custom of Navigation, concern's others as well that were under the *British* Government. Yet it is not to bee conceived, that these twig and Leathern Vessels of the *Britains*, were all of them unfit for making war by Sea (according to the manner of that Age and of the neighboring Nations)

nor

nor that they were less fit for long journies at that time; seeing [e] *Plinie* write's expresly, that somtimes they sailed through the Sea in the space of six daies. In like manner wee read in the *British* [f] Historie, that about *Cæsar's* time, *Lud* King of *Britain* seized upon many Islands of the Sea in a way of war, which denote's that hee had a very considerable strength at Sea, and a well accomplished Navie. It is true indeed, that there were small Vessels among these (as they are no where without them) which doubtless were unfit to bear the brunt of a Fight or Tempest; that is to say, such as *Cæsar* made to transport his Souldiers over the River, when hee was streightned by *Afranius* his Armie, *as hee had been taught* (they are his [g] own words) *som years before by the Custom of* Britain. *The Keels and Ribs were first made of slight matter. The rest of the bulk of their Vessels, beeing wrought together with Twigs, was cover'd with Hides*; which wee finde mentioned also by *Lucan*,

[e] *Hist. Natur. lib.* 4. *c.* 16.

[f] *Henric. Huntingdon. Hist. lib.* 1.

[g] *De Bello Civili. lib.* 1. *cap.* 54. & videsis *Solinum, ca.* 25.

> [h] *Primùm cana salix, madefacto vimine, parvam*
> *Texitur in puppim, cæsóque inducta juvenco,*
> *Vectoris patiens, tumidum circumnatat amnem.*
> *Sic Venetus stagnante Pado, fusóque Britannus*
> *Navigat Oceano.*———— ————

[h] *Pharsal.* 4.

> ———— ————* Of twigs and willow Bord,
> They made small Boats cover'd with Bullocks Hide,
> In which they reach't the river's farther side.
> So sail the Veneti, if Padus flow,
> The Britains sail on their calm Ocean so.

*Translated by my learned friend Mr *Thomas May.*

Others there are also that write of these small Vessels. But they are not (I suppose) at least in that Age, to bee called small Ships, which sailed through the

Sea in six daies space, nor such as *Cæsar* made onely to transport his Souldiers, and conveied them by Cart above XXII miles, according to his own Relation. It cannot bee doubted therefore, but that the *Britains* had Vessels made even of the aforesaid matter, big enough and very fit for service at Sea. Moreover, there will bee very good ground to conceiv out of what wee shall deliver by and by, about the excluding of their Neigbors from the adjacent Sea, that they were wont to build and set forth Ships of war, of a far more commodious and solid substance, for the guarding of their Sea and the Isles. But their use of frequent Fishing (though [i] som write that the more Northerly *Britains* did never eat fish) may bee collected upon this ground, that the better and more Civil sort of them were wont to embellish the Hilts of their Swords with teeth of the bigger Fishes. So saith *Solinus* [k], *They which endeavor to bee neat, do burnish the hilts of their Swords with the teeth of such great Animals as swim in the Sea, becaus they are as white and clear as Ivorie: For, the men take an extraordinarie pride in the brightness of their Arms.* Now, I suppose, that without an extraordinarie abundance of such kinde of Animals, which could not bee caught without great pains and numbers of Fishermen, there could not have been matter enough of this kinde to serv for the triming of a most warlike Nation; wherein it was a Custom for the Mother of every manchild to put the first Food that hee received into his mouth, upon the point of its Father's Sword, in token of a warlike disposition. And the Mothers usual Blessings were to this effect, that their Sons might die no other death then in War and Arms. I know these words of *Solinus* are commonly taken by Writers,

[i] *Dio Cassius*, *lib.*76.

[k] *Polyhist.* *cap.*25.

Writers, as if they had been spoken onely of the Inhabitants of *Ireland* : wherein, if I understand any thing, they are plainly mistaken. The words of *Solinus* in his Chapter concerning *Britain*, are these; *The extremitie of the* French *Shore had been the utmost bound of the world, did not the Isle of* Britain *deserv the name almost of another world. For it is stretch't above* 800 *miles in length, if so bee wee measure it as far as the utmost point in the North of* Scotland, *where* Ulysses *once arrived, as appear's by an Altar there with an Inscription upon it in Greek Letters. It is encompassed with many considerable Islands, whereof* Ireland *is next to it in bigness. It is a barbarous Countrie, by reason of the rude behavior of the Inhabitants; otherwise, of so rank a pasturage, that unless Cattel bee somtimes driven from the Pastures, they run a hazard by too much feeding. There is no Serpent to bee found, and but few birds; The people are inhospitable and warlike : And after a victorie, they first take a draught of the bloud of the slain, and then besmear their Faces. Right or wrong is all one to them. A woman, when shee bring's forth a male, put's its first food upon her husbands Sword, and stealing it into the little ones mouth with the very point, shee pronounceth her blessing according to the Custom of the Nation; with this wish, That hee may die no other death but in War and Arms. They that endevor to bee neat, do burnish the Hilts of their Swords, & cætera,* as it followeth above. Hee treat's next of som Islands that lie about it; as *Thanet*, the *Hebrides*, *Orcades*, and *Thule*; and as to what concern's their manners, hee conclude's that *Britain* is inhabited in part by barbarous people, who from their childhood, by artificial stripes of divers forms, imprint the likeness of several living Creatures, up and down their bodies : As is sufficiently known out of *Cæsar* and other Writers. But now, if thoſe words which follow that brief deſcription, wherein the firſt mention of *Ireland* is made, were to bee underſtood of the *Iriſh*, not of the people of great *Britain*, then it would follow there, that *Solinus* forgetting what hee had propoſed in the very entrance of his Diſcourſ, paſſed immediately from great *Britain* unto *Ireland* and the neighboring Iſles; and that hee made not any mention of the Cuſtoms of its Inhabitants, beſides the ſtriping of their skins with divers ſhapes, and this at the latter end of the Chapter: which I can not in any caſe believ. Nor is it agreeable to the ſcope of his diſcourſ, that *Ireland* ſhould bee meant in this place, as well as great *Britain*. For, of *Britain* hee ſaith, *It is encompaſſed with many conſiderable Iſlands, whereof* Ireland *is next to it in bigneſs. It is a barbarous Countrie, by reaſon of the rude behavior of the Inhabitants,&c.* Then, this more large deſcription of its manners and Cuſtoms which immediately followeth, is no otherwiſe joined to the mention of *Ireland* in the Edition of *Delrio*, and moſt of the reſt which wee have followed in the place before-alleged. And who ſeeth not that the beginning of that deſcription, and ſo what follow's, ought with much more reaſon to bee referr'd thus to *Britain*, concerning which his purpoſe is to treat, then to *Ireland*, whoſe name is inſerted onely by the way. Nor doth that hinder at all which wee read there about *Serpents*. I confeſs it to bee moſt true indeed, if ſpoken of *Ireland*, wherein there is no venemous Creature; and falſ, if of *Britain*. But yet even this alſo hath been believed of our Countrie of *Britain*, and that in the clearer light of learning in time paſt; As appear's not onely by the Books of *Cardan de Subtilitate*, wherein hee denieth

[l] denieth that *Britain* entertain's any such Creature,) but also out of *Scaliger's* [m] *Exercitations* upon him, who in like manner affirm's this, and spend's Discours to no purpose to finde out the reasons why *Britain* hath not any venemous Creatures: which is strange indeed, since hee wrote so eagerly against the other; yea, and both of them beeing very famous men, and most expert Naturalists, lived som time in Britain. But errors of this kinde (as wee see also in *Solinus* concerning Birds and Bees) are not unusual among Writers: And it was a common cours for a *Roman* Writer to attribute extreme Barbarism (as *Solinus* doth in this place) to such forreign Nations as were not in amitie with the *Romans*. Now, as to this passage which is found in som Editions, [*It is encompassed with many considerable Islands, whereof* Ireland *is next to it in bigness, a* [n] *barbarous Countrie becaus of the rude behavior of the Inhabitants &c.*] as if the following words did by a continued sens and order relate unto *Ireland*; it beeing indeed contrarie to the truth of som antient Copies and the most approved Editions, arose (I think) upon this ground, becaus it was falsly supposed by the vulgar, that *Ireland* alone is treated of in som following Lines. Notwithstanding, even so also those words which follow the word [*bigness*] may as well, and ought to refer unto *Britain*, not unto *Ireland*. Moreover also, *Tacitus* saith expresly of the *Irish* of that Age, [o] *The men in their dispositions and habits do not differ much from* Britain.

But now, that wee may return unto that trimming which was made of Fishes teeth; Auxiliaries were wont (as *Cæsar* saith) to bee supplied out of *Britain*, in almost all those wars that the *Gauls* mainteined

l *De Subtilitate, lib.* 10.
m *Exercitat.* 200.
n *Edit. Claudii Salmasi; Atque ita sanè Cod. Ms. vet. in Bibliothecâ Cottonianâ.*
o *In vitâ Julii Agricolæ.*

against the *Romans*. And therefore it must bee said, either that the *Britains* were for the most part an abject savage people, yea and a dull slothful Generation (which appear's to bee most falſ,) or elſ it must bee conceived that the Nation used Fishing very much, which together with the frequent use of Navigation and Commerce, shew's that they did enter upon the Sea corporally by Occupation. But if to such a corporal occupation, as this, wee add also, that they excluded others from the Sea, shutting it up in such a manner, that they restrained them at pleasure from passage and entrance, what hinder's why wee may not conclude, that they acquired a manifest Dominion of their own, both by an Intentional and Corporal possession? But that the Sea was thus shut up by them, *Cæsar* himself seem's to inform us plainly enough. For, when hee, upon his first attempt to cross the Sea into *Britain*, made diligent enquirie among the *Gauls*, touching the Shore and Situation of the ports, and to this end had summoned the *Gallick* Merchants together from all Quarters, hee was so deceived in his expectation about this matter, that hee was necessitated to send *C. Volusenus* before with a long Ship to sound them, as beeing wholly unknown: For as much as the *Gauls* were utterly ignorant of these Shores, becauſ they were prohibited entrance, and so excluded from a free use of the Sea. For, hee write's expresly, [p] *not a man of them went thither without leav, besides Merchants; nor was any thing known even to those Merchants, besides the Sea Coast, and those parts which lay over against* * Gaul *or* Gallia. Therefore, according to the usual Custom, no man, besides Merchants, could touch upon the Shore, without leav of the *Britains*; nor was it lawful for those

[p] *De Bello Gallico, lib.* 4.

* Now *France*.

those Merchants to make a narrow search or prie into such places ashore as were convenient or inconvenient for landing, or what Havens were fit to entertain Shipping. For, although hee saith they knew the Sea-Coast; yet, as *Cæsar* affirm's, they were utterly ignorant, what ports were fit to receiv a number of the greater sort of Ships. And it seem's, Merchants were permitted to visit the Sea-Coasts, onely by Coasting about, and using Commerce in the very Sea with the Inhabitants of the Island. The old Greek Interpreter of *Cæsar*, saith also upon the place, *None els, besides Merchants, were easily admitted among the Britains*: That is to say, neither by Land nor by Sea, whereof they had (as hath been shewn) a very frequent use, and from which they excluded all Forreigners, except Merchants, as from a part of that Territorie, whereof they were Lords in possession. From whence it follow's also, that they also who were wont to cross the Sea often out of *Gaul* into *Britain*, to bee train'd up in the learning and discipline of the *Druides*, could not do it without rendring themselvs liable to punishment for their boldness, if leav were not first had from the pettie Kings or Lords of the Island. From those pettie Kings, I mean, that ruled upon the Sea-Coast: For, the *Britains* at that time were not subject to the Government of a single Person. They were Lords of the Sea, who governed those Cities or Provinces that lay next to the Sea; *Cingetorix, Carvilius, Taximagulus*, and *Segonax* in *Kent*; others also that ruled over the *Regni*, the *Belgæ*, *Durotriges*, *Damnonii*, *Trinobantes*, *Iceni*, *Coritani*, (being the people that inhabited *Sussex*, *Surrie*, *Hampshire*, *Dorsetshire*, *Devon*, *Cornwal*, *Essex*, *Norfolk*, *Lincolnshire*) and the like. For, even *Cæsar*

himself

himself saith, the inner part of the Island was inhabited by such as were said by Tradition to have been born there; but the Sea-Coasts *by such as had crost't the Sea thither out of* Belgium, *to make war and gain bootie, who were called all for the most part by the names of those Cities from whence they came, and having seated themselvs there by force of Arms, they betook themselvs to Husbandrie.* But hee according to that little knowledg hee had of a small part of the Island, called those onely maritime Cities, or Provinces, which lie South of the River *Thames*; especially *Kent*, the * *Regni*, and the * *Belgæ*. But although the Sea-Coasts were thus divided at that time into several Jurisdictions, neverthelesse it cannot bee doubted, but that they used to consult together in common against an Enemie, or to guard the Sea (the defence whereof belonged to all the Princes bordering upon it;) just after the same manner as they used to do upon other occasions of war against forreign Enemies, as you may see in [q] *Cæsar*, where the principal administration of the Government, with the business of war, was put into the hands of *Cassivellaunus*, by a common Council of the whole *British* Nation. Nor is that any prejudice against such a Dominion of the *Britains* by Sea, which wee finde in *Cæsar* concerning the *Veneti*, a people of *Gallia*, that were seated at the entrance of the River of *Loire*; to wit, that they had a very [r] large command upon the Sea-Coast of Western *Gallia*, and that they were better skill'd then any other of their own Countrimen in the Use and Art of Navigation, and that in the Sea-fight with *Decius Brutus*, they had Ships made all of Oak, very well built, and whether you consider their leathern Sails, or their Iron Chains in stead of Cordage, or their Masts,

* The *Regni* were the Inbitants of *Surrie*, *Sussex*, and the Sea-Coasts of *Hampshire*.

* The *Belgæ*, Inhabitants of *Somerset*, *Wiltshire*, and *Hampshire*.

[q] *De Bello Gallico*, *lib.* 5.

[r] *Cæsar de Bello Gallico*, *lib.* 3. *cap.* 8. & 12.

fitted

fitted to bear the brunt of any assault whatsoever; and that CCXX sail or thereabout in number, went out of the Haven very well manned and provided with all necessaries for War, to oppose the *Roman* Navie. It is very probable, that the most of these were Auxiliaries fetched by the *Veneti* out of *Britain*, or how great soever the *Venetan* strength was at Sea, yet that it was not greater then the *Britains*, may bee collected from the same Author: For, hee write's expresly, that Auxilaries were not onely sent for at that time by the *Veneti* out of *Britain*, but also that they had very many Ships wherewith they used to sail into *Britain*: But yet, as it hath been shewn out of him alreadie, no man might sail hand over head into *Britain*, or without leav of the *Britains*. It is not to bee doubted therefore, but that, besides their Twig or leathern Vessels, they had a stout gallant Navie, which was able even at pleasure to exclude those Ships of the *Veneti* that were best armed. Els, how could it bee, that none but Merchants were admitted out of *Gaul* upon the Sea-Coast of *Britain*? Moreover, the whole Senate of the *Veneti* having been put to death by *Cæsar*, not a man was found among those who remained alive after *Brutus* his Victorie, that could discover so much as one Port of *Britain*; as appear's out of the same Author. Which how it might bee admitted, I do not at all understand, if the strength of those *Veneti* that were wont to sail thither, had been greater then the *British*, or if the *British* had not been much greater then theirs. But the reason why at *Cæsar*'s arrival afterwards, no Ship of that kinde was found upon the *British* Sea or Shore (which [f] *Peter Ramus* wonder's at very much) and why the *Roman* Writers mention

[f] *De C. Julii Cæsaris militiâ, cap. de prælio Navali.*

mention not any other Ships then such as were made of Twigs, seem's evident: For, the *Veneti* had got all the Shipping together into one place from all parts, to maintein the afore-said fight, as *Cæsar* saith expressly. Therefore, if the *British* Navie were called forth to their assistance, as tis probable it was, then questionless it was all lost before *Cæsar's* arrival: For, the whole strength and Forces of the *Veneti* perished in that Sea-fight. Moreover also, *Peter Ramus*, speaking of that great tempest, whereby *Cæsar's* Ships were scatter'd up and down in this Sea with great hazard, saith, *The Sea raised this Tempest, as it were revenging the* British *bounds, and disdaining to bear a new and strange Lord.* As if hee had said, that the Bounds of the *British* Empire were in the very Sea, and the Sea it self angrie, that it should bee tranferr'd into the hands of any other Lord. But as to that which wee finde in a certain [t] *Panegyrist*, touching the time of *Julius Cæsar*; *that* Britain *was not arm'd at that time with any Shipping fit for War by Sea*; it was spoken either in a Rhetorical way onely, and highly to magnifie that Victorie of the Emperor *Constantius Chlorus* (whereby having slain *C. Allectus*, who had invaded *Britain*, hee reduced the Island together with the Sea, as is shewn hereafter) or els it is to bee taken onely of the very time of *Cæsar's* arrival. Otherwise, it is expressly contrarie to those reasons here alleged, and grounded upon good Autors, and therefore not to bee admitted for Truth. But after that the Island was reduced under the *Roman* power, doubtless the *Britains* were prohibited from having any Ships of war, that they might bee the better held in obedience. Which is the reason why Writers afterwards make mention of such onely as were made of Twigs.

[t] *In Panegyrico Maximiano dicto*; si mihi.

That

That the Britains *were Lords of the* Northern Sea, *before they were subdued by the* Romans. *And that the Sea and the Land* made one entire Bodie *of the* British Empire.

Chap. III.

THat the *Britains* were Lords also at that time of the Northern, or *Deucalidonian* Sea, is a thing proved by sufficient Testimonie. They called this part of the Sea *Maris sui secretum*, **The secret or Closet of their Sea.** *Tacitus*, relating the Navigation of *Julius Agricola* into this part, saith, *the Britains, as it was understood by the Prisoners, were amazed at the sight of his Navie, as if upon this opening the Closet or secret part of their Sea, there remained no farther refuge in case they were overcom.* And in that stout Oration of *Galgacus* the *Caledonian*, wherein hee encouraged his Souldiers to fight, [a] *Now*, saith hee, *the Bound of Britain is laid open.* The secret part of their Sea or their Sea-Territorie in the North, they called their Bound. Moreover, saith the same *Galgacus, beyond us there is no Land, and not the least securitie at Sea, the* Roman *Navie beeing at hand*; giving them to understand, that the Dominion hereof was to bee defended as was the Island, as a thing acquired before. Add also, that among the Writers of that Age, *vincula dare Oceano*, and to *subdue the Britains*, signified one and the same thing. So that place of *Lucan* is to bee understood, where hee reckon's what pompous Shews and Triumphs might have usher'd

[a] *Tacit. in vita Agricolæ.*

usher'd *Cæsar* into *Rome*, had hee returned onely with Conquest over the *Gauls* and the *North*;

[b] *Pharsal.* 3.

——————[b] *ut vincula Rheno,*
Oceanóque daret! celsos ut Gallia currus
Nobilis, & flavis sequeretur mista Britannis.

What Stories had hee brought! how the vast Main,
And Rhine, **hee by his Conquests did restrain!**
The noble Gauls **and yellow** Britains **tread**
Behind his loftie Chariot, beeing led!

But for all that, our Sea was not as yet subdued by the Romans. *Julius Cæsar* onely shewed the Island, rather then deliver'd it into the hands of Posteritie: neither was any part of it reduced under the *Roman* power, before the Emperor *Claudius* his time; nor the Soveraigntie of the Sea transferr'd into the hands of any other. And although in *Augustus* his time, *Drusus Germanicus* [c] sailed through that part of the Sea which lie's betwixt the entrance of the River *Rhine* and *Denmark*, and subdued the *Friesland*ers, neverthelefs, not any part of the Sea was added by that Victorie to the *Roman* Empire; for, the *Britains* held it all in possession, they beeing not yet fully subdued. Nor is it unworthie observation here, that *C. Caligula*, beeing near *Britain*, and coming out of *Germanie* to the Coasts on the other side of our Sea, *as if* (saith [d] *Dio*) *hee intended to make War in* Britain, and having drawn up his Armie, made readie all his slings and other warlick Engines, and given the signal or word for Battel, no man knowing or imagining what his intent was, hee on a sudden commanded them to fall a gathering of Cockles, and fill their

[c] *Dio Cassius*, lib. 54. *Plin. lib.* 2. *cap.* 67. *Sueton. in Claud. cap.* 1.

[d] Adde *Aurel. Victorem*, ut emendatur *ab Andræa Schotto, Observat. Historic.* lib. 3. cap. 21.

their Laps and Helmets; Then, saying these Spoils of the Sea belong'd to the Capitol and Mount Palatin, hee vaunted as if hee had subdued the Ocean it self. At last, for a token or Trophie of this mock-victorie, hee rear'd a very lofty Tower hard by, out of which (as if it had been another * *Pharos*) Lights were hung forth by night for the direction of Sea-men in their Courses; the ruins whereof beeing not yet wholly demolished, but for the most part over-whelm'd with water near *Cattwiick*, and very sel-dom discover'd, it is called by the *Hollanders* that dwell near it, **Britenhuis** and **T' Huis te Briten**, that is the *British Hous*, or the *British Tower*. Certain it is out of *Suetonius*, that a Tower was raised by *Caligula* in that place: yea, and it is mainteined by divers learned men, as [e] *Hadrianus Junius* the *Hollander*, [f] *William Camden* our Countriman, and [g] *Richardus Vitus*, that these were the ruins of the same Tower; though others denie it, as *Ortelius*, *Gotzius*, and [h] *Cluverius*: And they make a doubt both about the Original of the name, and also its signification; concerning which wee dispute not. But am extremely mis-taken, if *Caligula*, by this Action of his, did not so much neglect the conquest of *Britain* it self, which hee hoped or at least thought of, as seem to sport himself with the conceit of having found out so compendious a way of Victorie. Hee carried the matter as if hee had had an intent to subdue *Britain*; and supposed those Cockles, which hee called Spoils of the Sea, to bee Tokens of Sea-Dominion, and as a most sure pledg of the *British* Empire.

* *Pharos* was a Tower built in the Island *Pharos* by *Cleopatra* Q. of *Egypt*, where lights were hung out to guide Marriners by night.

[e] *In Bataviâ, cap.* 16.

[f] *In insulis Britann. pag.* 852.

[g] *Histor. lib.* 4. *not.* 56.

[h] *De Rheni Alveis, cap.* 14. & *videsis Ortelium in Thesaur. Geograph. verb. Brittanni.*

Moreover, it is upon good ground to bee conceived, that there was one entire Territorie of the

British Empire, made up of the Land or continent of great *Britain*, with the Isles lying about it, and the Seas flowing between in their respective Channels: which may bee collected, both from that one single name of *British*, comprehending an entire Bodie of such a kinde of Territorie (as was shewn you before) and also from hence, that the very Sea it self is, by *Albategnius* and som others, described by the name of *Britain*, in the same manner as the Island, when as hee placeth *Thule*, an Isle of the Sea, in *Britain*. That is to say, just as *Sicily*, *Corsica*, *Sardinia*, and other Isles in the *Tyrrhen* Sea, have [i] in Law been reckoned parts of *Italie*, yea, and continent thereto: For, *Sicily* (after that the *Romans* became Lords of the adjoining Sea flowing between) was called [k] *Regio Suburbana*, as if it had been part of the Suburbs of *Rome*; and all these together with *Italie* and the Sea it self, made one Bodie or Province; so all the *British* Isles before mentioned, with great *Britain* and the Seas flowing about it, might well bee termed one Bodie of *Britain* or of the *British Empire*, forasmuch as the Seas as well as the Isles, passed alwaies into the Dominion of them that have born Rule within this Nation: From whence perhaps it hapned, that the *Romans* conceived the *British* Empire consider'd apart by it self, to bee of so great a bigness, *that* [l] Britain *did not seem to bee comprehended by the Sea, but to comprehend the Sea it self*, as it is express't by that *Panegyrist*.

i *L.9. ff. tit. de Judiciis & l.99. ff. tit. de V.S.*

k *Cicero Actione 2. in Verrem, & Florus, lib. 3. cap. 19.*

l *Panegyric. Maximiano dict.* Si mihi.

That

That the Dominion of the British *Sea, fol-lowed* the Conquest of great *Britain it self, under the Emperors* Claudius *and* Domitian.

CHAP. IV.

AFter that the more Southerly part of *Britain* had been brought into subjection by the Emperor *Claudius*, and the Isle of *Wight* taken in by surrender, the *British* Sea, as of necessitie following the fate of the Island, was together with it annexed to the *Roman* Empire; at least so far as it was stretched before that part of the Isle which was subdued. Whereupon, a [a] Poët of that Age write's thus to the Emperor *Claudius* touching the Conquest of *Britain*,

[a] *Anonymus, Epigr. vet. lib.* 2. *& in Catalect. vet. Poët. lib.* 1. *tit.* 7.

Ausoniis nunquam tellus violata triumphis,
Icta tuo, Cæsar, fulmine procubuit.
Oceanúsque tuas ultra se respicit aras;
Qui finis mundo est, non erat Imperio.

That Land where Roman **Triumphs ne're appear'd,**
Struck by thy lightning, Cæsar, **down is hurl'd.**
Since thou beyond the Sea hast Altars rear'd,
Thy Empire's bound is larger then the World.

And

And then hee goe's on,

Euphrates Ortus, Rhenus recluserat Arctos,
Oceanus medium venit in Imperium.

Euphrates Eastward did thy Empire bound,
And on the North the Rhene,
The Ocean in the middle beeing plac't,
Did lie as part between.

Here hee saith, that the Sea it self was with Britain subdued to the *Roman* Empire; as afterward also hee speak's more expresly.

At nunc Oceanus geminos interluit Orbes:
Pars est Imperii, Terminus antè fuit.

But now the Sea betwixt two Worlds doth flow;
The Empir's part, which was its Bound till now.

The *British* Sea was the Bound of the *Roman* Empire between *France* and *Germanie*. But immediately after the Conquest of Britain it became a part of the Empire. Hee proceed's again thus;

Oceanus jam terga dedit; nec pervius ulli
Cæsareos fasces, imperiúmque tulit.

The Sea's subdu'd; and though it were till now
Open to none, to Cæsar's Sword doth Bow.

And then,

Illa procul nostro semota, exclusáque cælo
Alluitur nostrâ victa Britannis aquâ.

Though conquer'd Britain far from us do lie
The water's ours that on the shore flow's by.

Hee

Hee call's the Sea *Our water*, beeing no less conquer'd, than the Island it self. From whence also hee write's, that the Roman Empire was begirt with the Roman Sea, to wit, after *Britain* was subdued,

Quam pater invictis Nereüs vallaverat undis.

Which the Sea had fortified with unconquer'd waters.

The Empire of the waters ever followed the Dominion of the Island. And [b] *Seneca*, concerning the same Emperor and this Sea, saith;

[b] *In Octaviâ, Act.* 1.

——————————paruit liber diu
Oceanus, & recepit invitus rates.
En qui Britannis primus imposuit jugum,
Ignota tantis classibus texit freta.

The long unconquer'd Sea obedience gave,
And, though unwilling, did his ships receiv.
Hee first the Britains **to the yoke brought down,**
And with huge Navies cover'd Seas unknown.

Moreover, the same Author *in Apocolocynthosi*;

Jussit & ipsum
Nova Romanæ
Jura Securis
Tremere Oceanum.

Hee gave new Laws unto the Sea, as Lord,
And made it tremble at the Roman **Sword.**

This is plainly to bee understood of the *British* Sea. And *Hegisippus* an old Autor (representing the person of King *Agrippa* speaking to the Emperor (*Claudius*) saith, [c] *It was more to have passed over the Sea to the* Britains, *then to have triumphed over the* Britains *themselvs.*

[c] *De Excidio Hierosolymit. lib.* 2. *cap.* 9.

selves. But what could they do, when the Elements were once subdued to the Roman *Empire? The Sea taught them to bear the yoke of servitude, after that it self had upon the arrival of the* Roman *Shipping acknowledg'd an unusual subjection.* Hence it was also, (as [d] *Suetonius* saith) that in honor of the Prince, the resemblance of a Ship was fixed upon the top of the imperial Palace. But these particulars relate onely to the more Southerly part of the Sea. *Claudius* never had any Navie sail to the *North*; For, his Conquest reached not so far. But the *Romans* sail'd about the Island first in the daies of *Domitian*, and then it was, that they first discover'd and subdued that remotest part of the Sea. *Tacitus*, in the life of *Agricola* who was Lievtenant in the Province of *Britain*, saith, *the* Roman *Navie sailing then the first time* (under *Domitian*) *about the Island, affirmed this Coast of the remotest* (Caledonian) *Sea to bee the Isle of* Britain, *and hee discover'd and subdued also those Isles called the* Orcades, *which had been unknown till that time.* To the same purpose also speak's *Juvenal*,

[d] In Claudio, cap. 17.

[e] Satyr. 2.

——— [e] arma quidem ultra
Littora Juvernæ promovimus, & modò captas
Orcadas. ———

We have born our Arms beyond the Irish Main,
And th' Orcad's Islands which were lately ta'ne.

Lately taken hee saith, that is, in the time of *Domitian.* And therefore it is a manifest error in *Eusebius Hieronymianus*, who saith, *That* Claudius *added the* Orcades *Isles to the* Roman *Empire:* yet hee is followed by *Orosius*, *Cassiodorus*, *Eutropius*, *Bede*, *Nennius*, *Ethelwerdus*, and others. But the contrarie is sufficiently proved

proved out of *Tacitus* alone, a very grave Autor, and one that lived at the same time. But as to those passages found in [f] *Valerius Flaccus*, [g] *Silius Italicus*, [h] *Statius*, and others, touching the *Caledonians* and *Thule's* beeing subdued before the daies of *Domitian*, they are so to bee understood onely, that wee are to conceiv either after the manner of the Poëts, that the name of the more Northerly *Britains*, is, by the figure *Synecdoche*, used for all whatsoëver, and *Thule* it self for any part of *Britain*; or els that the *Caledonians* generally among the *Romans*, signified those *Britains* that were but a little removed from the Southern Shore. For, even [i] *Florus* write's, that *Julius Cæsar* pursued the Southern *Britains* into the *Caledonian* Woods: That is, plainly, into the Woods of the more Southerly part of *Britain*: But when *Julius Agricola* had, in *Domitian's* time, reduced the Isle by force of Arms both by Sea and Land, and sailing round about with a Navie, had discover'd the *Caledonian Sea* properly so named on every side, which the *Britains* (as hath been observed alreadie) called the *secret part or Closet of their Sea*, and had taken in the *Orcades*; wee ought to conclude that then that more Northerly Sea also was added to the Roman Empire, and so that the *Romans* were Lords over all the *British* Sea, no otherwise then of the Island: Which also is confirmed in plain terms by *Tacitus*, who speaking of *Agricola's* design to war upon the *Caledonians*, saith, *hee first provided a Fleet, which attended in gallant Equipage to back his Forces; at which time hee prosecuted the war at once both by Sea and Land, and oftentimes in the same Camp, the Hors and Foot and the Sea-Souldiers mingling mirth and companie together, extoll'd every one their own hazards and Adventures; one while they boasted the heights*

[f] *Argonautic. lib.* 1.

[g] *Punic. lib.* 1.

[h] *Sylvarum, lib.* 5. *in Protreptico ad Crispinum, Vectii Bolani propraetoris, sub Vitellio, Britanniæ filium.*

[i] *Lib.* 3. *cap.* 10.

heights of Woods and Mountains; another while the dangers of Storms and Tempests; som vaunted of their exploits against the Enemie by Land, others of their Conquests by Sea, making comparisons, souldier-like, with many bravado's. The Britains *also, as it was understood by the Prisoners, were at their wits end upon the sight of his Navie, as if upon this opening the Closet or secret part of their Sea, there remained no farther refuge in case they were overcom.* This is a most clear Testimonie touching the Dominion of the *British* Sea, shewing that the *Britains* and *Caledonians* first, and the *Romans* afterward became Lords thereof. A doubt hath been made by learned men, whether *inlargement of Dominion,* or *Conquest by Sea*, should bee read in that place: But both the Readings plainly point out an acquisition of Dominion. And if you read *inlargement of Dominion by Sea*, it signifie's that the *Caledonian* Sea was then annexed to the other Sea, which together with the more Southerly part of the Isle, had by the Emperor *Claudius* been added to the *Roman Empire.* And that the *British Sea* was thus reduced at that time under the *Roman* power, as a perpetual and inseparable appendant of the Island, was perhaps conceited by [k] *Papinius*, when hee thus bespake *Domitian*, in whose time this Conquest was made of the *Britains*;

k *Thebaidos, lib.* 1.

——maneas hominum contentus habenis,
Undarum Terræque potens ——

Long maist thou joy in the Command,
Of men, and sway both Sea and Land.

Truly, a [l] late Writer also saith, that *Julius Cæsar* did *assert to himself a Dominion over* British *Isle and Sea.* And this hee saith upon very good ground, whilst hee join's the Dominion of both together, as undivided

l *Jac. Chifletius, in Epist. Dedicat. ad Libellum,* de Portu Iccio.

vided; but upon none at all, when hee ascribe's onely a Dominion of the Isle to the same *Cæsar*.

Touching the Dominion of the Romans *in the* British *Sea*, as an appendant of the Island, *from the time of* Domitian *to the Emperor* Constantius Chlorus, *or* Diocletian.

CHAP. V.

BUt the *Romans* having (as wee told you before) subdued both the Island and the Sea that roll's about it; as they managed the Government by Presidents and Lieutenants at Land, so by a chief Governor called *Archigubernus*, with a numerous Fleet at Sea. For, by that name was the Commander of the *British* Navie called (or els *Archigubernius*, as it is in the [m] *Florentine* Pandects) which appear's also by the Epistles of *Javolenus*, a Lawyer, that lived under the Emperors *Adrian* and *Antoninus Pius*. Seius *Saturninus*, [n] saith hee, *Archigubernus ex classe* Britannicâ, **chief Governor of the** British **Navie**, *left* Valerius Maximus, *Captain of a three-Oard Gally, his heir or Feofee in trust by Will; requiring him to yield back the inheritance to his* Son Seius Oceanus, *as soon as hee should bee seventeen years of Age*. But the *Romans* foreseeing there would bee a great deal of trouble and but small benefit, in subduing and holding the *Caledonian Britains*, they, leaving the North part of the Isle to the barbarous people, and retiring towards the South, did so limit their Land-dominion by rearing up Mounds or Walls before it, that wee must of necessitie suppose their Dominion was but small likewise by Sea. Those Mounds or Fences are frequently mentioned, in

m *Antoninus Augustin. de nominibus propriis. Pandect. Florentin.*

n *F. tit. ad Senatusconsult. Trebellian. lib. 46.*

in the Histories concerning the Emperors *Adrian*, *Antoninus Pius*, and *Severus*. But by that Fence which *Adrian* made and *Severus* repaired, beeing either a Wall or a Trench drawn through the * North parts, from the Eastern to the Western Shore, the Territorie of the *Romans* was confined almost within the same Limits which had bounded the Conquest of *Claudius*. But the other, which parted the Island in the middle between the *Estuaries* of * *Glotta* and * *Bodotria*, bounded the Roman-British Empire under *Antoninus Pius*, and after that in the time of *Valentinian*, *Valens*, and divers other Emperors their Successors: So that perhaps the *Romans* afterward had not much more of the Northen Sea in their Dominion, then what washed the Borders of these Territories. But after *seius Saturninus*, the afore-mentioned Commander in chief of the *British* Navie under *Adrian* or *Antoninus Pius*, there is a deep silence among Writers touching the Sea-affairs of *Britain*, and almost concerning *Britain* it self, till the daies of *Diocletian*. And under *Diocletian*, the *British* Sea beeing infested, all along the Coast of *Britanie* and *Belgium*, by the *French* and *Saxons*, care was taken to quiet and secure it by sending forth *C. Carausius*, a man indeed of mean parentage, ° but expert both in Counsel and Action. And *Geffrie* of *Monmouth* write's, that hee made suit for this Government of the Sea, and promised *to perform so many and so great matters for the advantage and inlargement of the Commonweal, more then if the Dominion of* Britain *should bee committed to his charge.* *Eutropius* also, speaking of the Infesters of the *British* Sea, over which this man was made Commander in chief by the Emperor as Lord thereof, so far as hee enjoied the Dominion of *Britain*, saith, *that hee oftentimes taking many*

of

* That is to say, *Yorkshire*, *Lancashire*, *Bishoprick* of *Durham*, *Westmerland*, and *Cumberland*.

* *Cluyd* and *Forth*.

° *Eutropius*, *hist.* 9.

of the barbarous people, and not delivering the prizes to the Liutenants of the Province, nor sending them to the Emperors, reserved them to himself; therefore when it began to bee suspected, that hee permitted the barbarous people on purpose to fall upon those that conveyed the Prizes, that by this means hee might enrich himself, a command beeing given by the Emperor Maximianus *to kill him, hee thereupon turn'd Usurper; and possessed himself of* Britain. At length, having fortified himself both by Sea and Land, hee held the joint-Dominion of both for 7 years, as inseparable; beeing slain by his companion *C. Allectus*, who enjoied the same 3 years as his Successor. And then hee also (after hee was brought to so low a pass by the Emperor *Constantius Chlorus*, who had cros't the Sea in person on purpose to reduce him, that hee knew not what to do, and seem'd to bee imprisoned rather then fortified by the Sea, as saith the [p] Autor of the *Panegyrick* to *Maximianus*) was at length, by the valor and conduct of the Pretorian prefect *Asclepiodotus*, overcom and slain: And thus both the Isle and the Sea together was recover'd after ten years time, so far as it flow'd before that part which was under the *Roman* Jurisdiction. Nor was it upon any other ground, then this ten years usurpation in *Britain*, that those Coins were made with the Inscriptions both of *C. Carausius* and *C. Allectus* IMP. C. CARAUSIUS P.F. AUG. and IMP. C. ALLECTUS. P. F. AUG. But wee have placed here a counterfeit of that brass Coin which was made by *Allectus*, that you may observ the three-oar'd Gally on the revers of it, with the Inscription VIRTUS AUGUSTA, whereby I conceiv

[p] *Panegyrick.* Si mihi *Cæsar.*

conceiv hee gave to understand, that this Empire of *Britain* chiefly depended upon the Dominion of the Sea flowing about it. Touching the recovery of *Britain* thus together with the Sea, there is also a notable Testimonie in that Panegyrick, whereof som conceiv *Mamertinus*, others *Eumenius* to bee the Autor. *O how great is this Victorie* (saith hee) *and worthie of innumerable Triumphs! whereby* Britain *is recovered, whereby the* French *are utterly destroyed, whereby moreover those many Nations that were engaged in the same mischievous conspiracie, are forced to a necessitie of yielding; And lastly, for our perpetual peace, the* Seas *are scour'd and rid of Pirats! Glory then, O unconquerable Cæsar* (hee speak's to *Constantius Chlorus*, the afore-named Emperor) *that thou hast purchased another world, and added to the Empire an Element greater then all the Earth, by restoring the glorie of the* Roman *power by* Sea. Hee saith *a greater Element*, in a rhetorical flourish, in stead of the *British* Sea, which hee thus expresly affirm's to have been recover'd together with *Britain* it self. It is observable also, that the *Romans* alwaies so spake concerning the Empires, of *Britain*, and of the Sea called by its name, as inseparable. Making mention likewise of that pest, which consumed onely within the bowels of *Britain*, or of the imminent danger then attending the Roman Empire, *It was bounded* (saith hee) *with no mountain or river, which was not secured by Guards at the place appointed. But although wee shared in your valor and felicitie, yet like a Ship it was exposed in every place to great terrors, wheresoëver the Seas are spred or the winds do blow.* And a little after, saith hee, *By this Victorie not onely your* Britain *is redeem'd from vassalage, but securitie of traffick restored to all Nations, which might have run as great hazard at* Sea *in time of war, as they gain benefit by peace.* Hee expresly call's the

Go-

Government also of *Allectus* a *Force of Rebellion by Sea*, *and it appears*, saith hee, *that the very Isle of* Britain, *which had harbor'd a treason of so long continuance, is made sensible of your Victorie by beeing restored unto it self*. Together with the Conquest of *Britain* it self, all the strength of Shipping was lost, which, upon *Allectus* his usurpation in *Britain*, must needs as a perpetual Concomitant of the Island, have been of very great use against the Emperors. But the *Panegyrist* goe's on; *In other parts indeed som things remain which yee may acquire, as you pleas or see caus; but beyond the Sea what was left except onely* Britain? *which you have so recover'd, that those Nations also which border upon that Island, are wholly at your devotion. There is no occasion to proceed farther, except you design (that which is impossible in nature) to finde out the bounds of the Sea*. What Nations are those here that border upon *Britain*, except those that lie beyond-Sea, whose Shores were conjoined with the British Empire as it was then accounted, or with the Sea-bounds of the Province of *Britain*, that is, in the British Sea? As the *French*, and the other adjoining Nations. For, it is not to bee understood of those little Isles which are next to us; their Inhabitants not beeing worthie the repute of Nations. Nor was it agreeable to the Majestie of a Panegyrick, to aggrandise the Emperor's glorie by such pettie things. But by and by in the following Chapters wee shew, that those Nations adjoining to the bounds of *Britain*, or whose bounds are united to the bodie of the British Empire, were those very Inhabitants of the continent of *France*, whose Shores are contiguous to the bounds of the British Sea, which in a civil sens was accounted a part of the Isle it self, or Territorie united therewith. For, the Panegyrist proceed's thus to the explanation of thoſe words : *By the means of thy Victories, O* Conſtantius, *moſt victorious Emperor, all thoſe parts that lay waſte and deſolate about the Countrie of* Amiens, *and* Beauvois, *and* Troies, *and* Langres, *now thrives again by the labor of the rude Husbandman.* In like manner, *Carolus Sigonius*, out of the ſame Autor, ſaith, * By *this victorie not onely* Britain *it ſelf was recover'd, but the Coaſts of* France *alſo*, Spain, Italie, *and* Africa, *were freed from the perpetual incurſions of Pirats.* That is to ſay, by the taking in of *Britain*, with the Sea, and the naval ſtrength that was its Guard, not onely the neighboring but even the remoteſt Provinces bordering on the Sea, were made ſecure and free, ſeeing they were all threatned by this war or rather rebellion by Sea, *which might have raged and wandred as wide as the Ocean, and into the ſtreights of the Mediterranean Sea*; which are indeed the very words of the Panegyrick. So that you ſee, to reſtore or reduce *Britain*, to recover it, to ſuppreſs a Sea-Rebellion here, and to ſcoure this Sea, were eſteemed under ſuch a conſideration, that, the one beeing don, the other followed, by reaſon of the inſeperable Dominion of the *Britiſh* Iſle and Sea together. And when *Britain* was loſt, the Naval Forces of the *Romans*, whereby the Sea was guarded, were loſt in like manner. But when it was reduced, even theſe alſo were reduced together with the Sea.

* *De occidentali imperio, lib.* 1.

Touching

Touching the Dominion of the Southern *and* Eastern *Sea, as an* Appendant of the British Empire, *from the time of* Constantine the Great till the *Romans* quitted the Island. *That it was all under the Command of the* Count of the *Saxon* Shore throughout *Britain. Also concerning the* British Navie, *under the* Romans.

CHAP. VI.

IN the following Age, the manner of Administration of Government beeing changed about the time of *Constantine*; as the *Pretorian Prefect of Gallia* had a Deputie under him to order the Civil affairs of *Britain*; and as the *Magister Militum occidentis*; Hee that commanded the Militia of the West had an Officer under him called *Comes Britanniarum*, **Count of Britain**, and *Dux Britanniarum*, **Duke of Britain**, who commanded Forces for defence of the Midland parts of the Isle : So the said *Magister Militum* was wont at his own discretion to appoint som person of eminent dignitie to bee his Substitute, by the Title of [a] *Count of the* Saxon *Shore throughout Britain*, with Command over the Garrisons and Fortifications placed upon the South and Eastern Shore of *Britain*, and over all that Sea which flow's between *France, Spain, Holland, Denmark,* and *great* Britain, as over a part or bound, not bounding, but bounded by the *British* Empire, no otherwise then as

[a] *Notitia Dignitatum Imperii Occidentis.*

as a distinct Province of the same Empire; as most eminently appear's by the very Title of the Dignitie or Command. For, the *Duke of* Britain, *and Count of Britain*, were as the *Count of Tingitania*, the *Count of Spain*, and very many others of the like kinde, denominated from those Lands and Countries over which they were put in Command. And such of these Dignities or Commands as were for defence of any Frontiers or Borders, took name ever from the Borders. Upon which account it is, that among the Imperial Offices or Commands wee meet with *Comes limitis Ægypti*, **the Count of the** Egyptian **Border**, [b] the *Prefect of Euphrates*, the [c] *Prefect of the Bank of Danubius*, and *the* [d] *Count of Danubius*, and *those* [e] *to whom the Charge and Defence of the river Rhine was committed*: For these Rivers were Bounds or Limits of the Roman Empire. And it is the opinion of [f] learned men upon good ground, that the Counts or Dukes of *Rhine* are meant by those words concerning the River of R*hine*. But as the Northern and Eastern Bounds of the *Roman* Empire were denoted by the names of the Rivers *Danubius*, *Rhine*, and *Euphrates*, so clearly also the name or Limit of the *Saxon* Shore pointed out the Eastern and more Southerly bound of the B*ritish* Empire, or that which was reduced by the name of B*ritish*, as an entire bodie, under the Roman power. So that whatsoever reached as far as that Limit, lay properly under the command of the *Count of the* Saxon *Shore in* B*ritain*, as Governor of the Sea-Territorie, as an appendant of the Isle. But that Territorie or Province subject to this particular *Dignitie* or Command, reached through the very B*ritish* Sea, from the Shore of B*ritain* to the Shores on the other side

[b] *Notitiâ Dignit. Orient.*

[c] *Inscript. Gruter. fol.* 1090.21. *Ibid fol.* 490.

[d] *Sidonius Apollinaris in Panegyric. Anthemio*

[e] *L.* 9. *C. Theodos. lib.* 7. *tit.* 1.

[f] *Marquard. Freber. Orig. Palatin. part.* 1. *cap.* 3.

of

of the Sea, or those which lie over against our Isle of *Britain*; in *France*, the *Low Countries*, *Holland*, and *Denmark*; so that what Sea or Islands soëver lay between near the *British* Shore, appertained all to the Command of the aforesaid *Count*, as to the charge of an Admiral belonging to a Province or Territorie.

But that those opposit Shores were all known at that time by the name of the *Saxon* Shore, is evident both out of *Ptolomie*, *Marcianus Heracleotes*, *Zosimus*, and the like, and also out of the Register or Breviarie of the Dignities of both the Empires. For, [g] *Ptolomie* and [h] *Marcianus* place the *Saxons* at the entrance of the River *Elbe* which lie's near *Cimbrica Chersonesus* or the West-part of the Kingdom of *Denmark*, as also in *Cimbrica Chersonesus* it self. And that Shore took the name of *Saxon* from their first and most antient habitations. But beeing the most eminent people of *Germanie*, they by driving out their Neighbors enlarged their habitations Southward, all along the *Batavian*, *Belgick*, and *French* Shore. From whence [i] *Zosimus* write's, that about *Constantine*'s time, they possessed themselvs of the *Hollander*'s Countrie at the entrance of *Rhine*. And becaus they seated themselvs near these Shores, and by their frequent excursions thence infested both Sea and Land all along the Sea-Coast of *France*, it was called not onely the Shore of those *Saxons*, or the Eastern bound of the *British* Empire; but also that *Belgick* and the whole *Gallicane* Shore, which lie's over against our Isle of *Britain*, was term'd the *Saxon Shore*, and the *Saxon limit* or Border. Touching the Shore of *Denmark* and *Holland*, where they had more inlarged their habitations, the point is manifest by

[g] *Geograph. lib.* 2.

[h] *In Periplo.*

[i] *Histor. lib* 3.

what wee have alreadie mentioned. And the Register or Breviarie of the Imperial Dignities speak's expresly in like manner touching the *Belgick* and *Gallican* Shores. For, in it wee finde, that under the charge or command of the Duke of the Tract of * *Aremorica* (which reacheth from the *Western Gallia*, or from the mouth of the River of *Loire* to the entrance of *Seine*) there was *a Tribune of the first new band of Souldiers of* Armonica *and* Grammona *upon the* Saxon *Shore*. There, the *French* Shore lying over against our South part of *Britain*, is called in plain terms the *Saxon Shore*. For, in the same *Breviarie*, under the Command of the Duke of that part of *Belgica secunda*, (which reacheth from the entrance of the River *Seine* to that of the River *Maze*, and comprehend's *Flanders*) wee finde *Equites Dalmatas Marcis in littore Saxonico*, Dalmatian **Horsmen at the Borders on the** Saxon **Shore**. And the *Saxon Shore* is evidently set forth in the signal Ornaments of the same Duke. So all that which reacheth from *Cimbrica Chersonesus* or the West-part of *Denmark* to the *Western Gallia*, is expresly call'd in the Breviarie the *Saxon Shore*, which hapned not onely from the frequent depredations made then upon that Sea-Coast by the *Saxons*, but by their Excursions and often acquiring of habitations all along that Shore. So that nothing could have been more plainly spoken, to shew that the whole Sea lying between, was possessed at that time, as an appendant of the Island, by the Lords of the South-part of the Isle; except a man should suppose, that those places which are extended from the proper habitation of a *Count*, *Duke*, or any other Officer in Command for defence of Borders, unto those Borders from whence hee

* *Bretaign* in *France*.

hee was denominated or entitled, were not subject either to his Jurisdiction or to the Dominion of those that bestowed the Command upon him. Which truly is absurd, and wholly different from the usual administration of the *Roman* Empire. But that *Count of the* Saxon Shore in *Britain*, had his proper places of abode onely in B*ritain*; and, under the *Romans*, that Magistrate belonged onely to B*ritain*. Nor were those S*axons* any other then Enemies. And their Shore, so far as they possessed it, was an Enemies Countrie. Moreover, this *Count* had Houses, at his own pleasure, in either of those Garrisons, Towns, or nine Maritim Cities, which beeing seated upon the Shores of *Sussex*, *Kent*, *Essex*, and *Norfolk*, hee alwaies had them painted out near the Sea, and added to his grand Commission, for the signal Ornaments of his Office. The names of these Cities were *Othona*, *Dubris*, *Lammanis*, *Branodunum*, *Garianum*, *Regulbis*, *Rittupæ*, *Anderidos* (or *Anderida*) and *Portus Adurni*. Besides, both the *Deputie of* Bri*tain*, and the *Duke*, and *Count of* B*ritain*, had their signal Ornaments given in like manner with their Commands. This had a pourtraicture of the Isle it self, drawn in the form of a Castle fortified in the Sea. The *Duke* had certain Midland Towns. And the *Deputie* those five Provinces into which the Isle was divided by the *Romans*; as you may see in the B*reviarie of Dignities*. Where the afore-mentioned Arms of the *Count of the Saxon* S*hore* are represented after this manner,

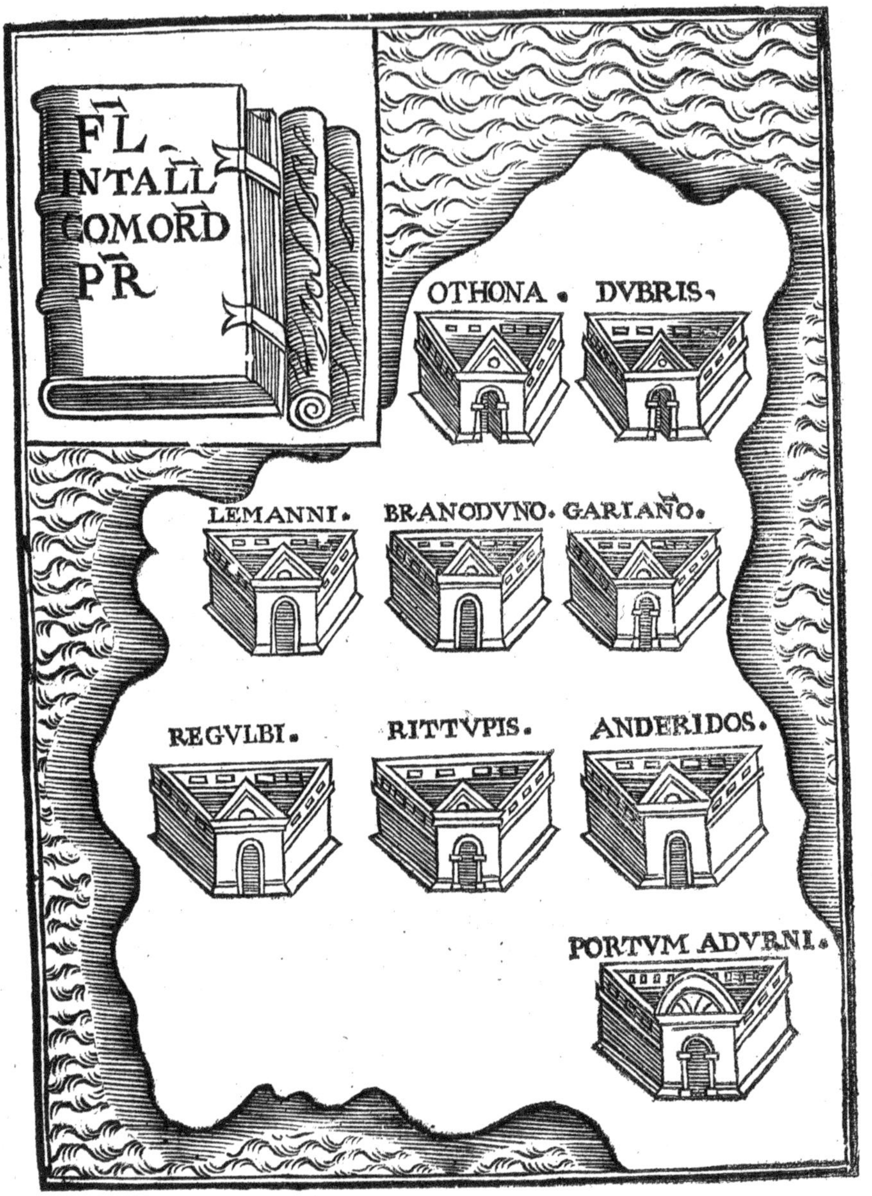

to wit, the very ſame that was wont to bee drawn in his Commiſsion. But as to what concern's thoſe Maritim Cities or Towns in theſe Ornaments; if wee may believ[k] ſuch as are well verſt in the affairs of *Britain*, *Othona* was ſeated upon the Shore of the *Trinobantes* which lie's before **Dengy** hundred in the

[k] *Guil. Camden in Suſſexia, Cantio, Eſſexia, Norfolcia.*

the Countie of *Essex*. *Dubris* is the same with **Dover**. *Lemannis* was placed about **Hith** on the *Kentish* Shore. *Branodunum* was no other but **Branchester** upon the Shore of *Norfolk* near the washes between that and *Lincolnshire*. *Garianum* was either **Gernemutha**, or som place near it. *Regulbium* or *Regulbis* was situate upon the Northen Coast of *Kent*, beeing called now **Reculver**. *Rittupis* or *Rhutupiæ* was seated in *Kent* at the entrance of the River *Wantsum*; Perhaps it was the same with **Richborow**. *Anderidos* stood upon the Bank of the River *Rothermouth*, and is now called **Newenden**. And lastly, *Portus Adurni* became a little Village, now called **Aldrington**, near **Shoreham** upon the Coast of *Sussex*. But the very Form and Fashion of the Book pictured in those Ornaments, which in the Manuscript Copies of the *Breviarie* (as *Pancirollus* saith) is of a purple or yellowish color, did signifie the Instructions of the Emperor. And if wee may believ *Pancirollus*, the Letters inscribed upon it signified in the Notaries language, *Felix Liber injunctus Notariis laterculi, continens Mandata ordine Principis*, seu *Primicerii*, who was the principal Notarie. The very same Inscription is somtimes found in the Ornaments of other Governors. But who they were which the *Count of the* Saxon Shore *throughout Britain* had under his own Command, for defence of the afore-mentioned Dominion by Sea, and what manner of Officers, is expressed in the *Breviarie* after this manner;

1 *Ad Notitiam Dignatum occidentis, cap. 72.*

Sub dispositione viri spectabilis, Comitis litoris Saxonici, per Britanniam.

Præpositus numeri Fortensium, Othonæ.
Præpositus Militum Tangricanorum, Dubris.

Præpositus numeri Turnacensium, Lemannis.

Præpositus equitum Dalmatarum Branodunensis, Branoduno.

Præpositus equitum Stablesiani Garrianensis, Gariannono.

Tribunus cohortis primæ Vetasiorum, Regulbio.

Præpositus Legionis II *Aug.* Rutupis.

Præpositus numeri Abuleorum, Anderidæ.

Præpositus numeri Exploratorum, portu Adurni.

Officium autem habet idem Vir Spectabilis Comes, hoc modo.

Principem ex officio Magistri Præsentalium à parte peditum.

Numerarios duos, ut suprà, ex officio supradicto.

Cornicularium;

Adjutorem;

Subadjuvam;

Regendarium;

Exceptores;

Singulares, & reliquos Officiales.

The names both of the Souldiers and Officers are to bee found in *Pancirollus*; this beeing no place for a Commentarie, to explain them to such Readers as are not well vers't in the Storie of the *Roman* Empire in its declining state. But I shall give an account of their numbers, as it is cast up by *Pancirollus*, that you may the better know what those Garrisons were which were imploied at that time, to guard this Sea-appendant of the British Empire. [m] *Under this Count* (saith hee) *was one Legion or* Regiment *perhaps of a thousand Foot, and six Companies; perhaps one thousand two hundred, and two Troops of Hors almost two hundred. The whole amount's to almost two thousand two hundred* Foot

[m] *Ad notitiam dignit. Occid. cap.* 72.

Foot, and two hundred Horſ. For, [n] Conſtantinus Porphyrogenneta *write's, that at this time there was a Regiment of a thouſand Foot.* So hee. Now, the Ships and Souldiers belonging to the Navie are not mentioned in the *Breviarie,* at leaſt not by this name. But as there were Troops of Horſ diſpoſed againſt the Landings of Enemies (in caſe any ſhould happen;) ſo there is no reaſon to doubt, but that the Souldiers belonging to the Navie were liſted in the Companies and Legion. After which manner likewiſe *Flavius Vegetius* ſaith, *that* [o] *at Miſenus* (now called *Monte Miſeno*) *and at Ravenna, ſeveral of the* Roman *Legions continued with the Fleets, that they might not bee at too great a diſtance from guarding the Citie, and that they might as occaſion required, bee tranſported in Shipping to all parts of the world.* Hee reckon's thoſe Souldiers belonging to the Navie, among the Regiments of Foot, or under their Name. But in the mean time it is to bee obſerved, that the [p] moſt diligent Inquirers into the Roman affairs, whilſt they Treat of their Fleets, do beſides that of *Ravenna* and [q] *Miſeno* (of which this latter lay neareſt to *France, Spain, Barbarie, Africk, Egypt, Sardinia,* and *Sicily*; the other was wont to ſail in a direct courſ to *Epirus, Macedonia, Achaia, Propontis, Pontus,* the *Eaſt, Crete,* and *Cyprus*; which are *Vegetius* his own words; both of them beeing firſt inſtituted and appointed there by [r] *Auguſtus Cæſar,* to guard the Provinces bordering upon the Sea, with the Sea it ſelf, and called alſo *Pretorian,* for the more reputation) they do (I ſay) for the moſt part add onely two more that were ſet forth to Sea, but of leſs account. The one was placed at *Friuli,* in that part of *France* called [ſ] *Gallia Narbonenſis,* The other in the very

n *Lib. de Thematibus.*

o *De Re militari, lib.* 4. *cap.* 21.

p *Lipſius de Magnitudine Romanâ, lib.* 11. *cap.* 5. *ſed & vide Jul. Cæſ. Bullinger. de Imperio Romano, lib.* 6. *cap.* 6.

q *De quibus item Tacitus lib.* 4. *Annal.*

r *Suetonius in Auguſto, cap.* 49.

ſ *Tacit. Annal.* 4. *Strabo, lib.* 4.

very [t] *Euxin* Sea. And it is for the most part agreed, that the *Romans* had onely four constant or more eminent Fleets at Sea. They do indeed rightly add also som other constant Fleets which belonged to Rivers, as that of the *Rhine*, and *Danubius*, of which sort also may bee reckoned that belonging to *Mysia* called *Mæsica*, and another also belonging to *Pannonia* or *Hungarie* called *Pannonica*, and others of the like nature. But among these there were certain Barks or nimble Vessels call [u] *Lusoriæ* or *Lusuriæ* (in *English* wee may call them *Flie-boats*) wherein they scouted out as far as the remotest Banks and the Castles built upon them, to guard the Bounds of the Empire. And under this notion the name of these *Lusoriæ*, was restored by [x] *Claudius Salmasius*, according to two Laws in the [y] Code of *Justinian* which were before sufficiently corrupted. And as in Rivers they for the most part used these *Lusoriæ* or lesser Vessels; so in the Sea they made use of Pinnaces, the least whereof had single Ranges of Ores; those that were a little bigger, double Ranges; and those of a middle size or proportion had three or four, and somtimes five, as wee are told by *Vegetius*. But now, notwithstanding that those diligent Inquirers into the defences and Fortifications of all sorts belonging to the old Roman Empire, are wont, when they mention any Navie of *Britain*, to speak slightly or in terms obscure enough; this neverthelesse is most certain, that there was among the standing Guards of the *Romans*, not onely a particular Fleet of Pinnaces or light Vessels belonging to *Britain*, wherewith they guarded this Sea whereof wee speak, as an appendant of the Isle of *great Britain*; but also that they had not any other Navie in the outer Sea, or

any

[t] *Joseph. Halos. lib. 2. cap.* 26.

[u] *Cod. Theodos.* 7. *tit.* 17. *de Lusoriis Danubii.*

[x] *L.* 4. *C. de Offic. Milit. Judic. & l.* 4. *C. de Offic. Magistri Officiorum.*

[y] *In notis ad Flavium vopiscum, pag.* 475.

any Shipping at all upon the Sea-Coasts of *Spain* or *France*, without the Mediterranean Sea. At least, it is no where mentioned by antient Writers. Which is no slight Testimonie, that the Sea and the Isle together made up one entire Bodie of the *British* Empire, as it was then devolved unto the *Romans*, and also that such a Custom was at that time in force upon the Sea, so far as it belong'd to *Britain*, that the like could no where bee found at least in the more Western parts, there beeing no other Sea-Province among them. There is (besides that ordinarie instance[z] alleged before out of the [a] *Digests* of the Civil Law, concerning *Seius Saturninus* Commander in chief of the *British* Navie under *Antoninus* or *Adrian* the Emperor) express mention made also by [b] *Tacitus* of this *British* Navie, where speaking of the affairs of *Cerealis* and *Civilis* under the Emperor *Vespasian*, *Another fear*, saith hee, *had possessed the minde of* Civilis, *lest the fourteenth Legion beeing assisted by the Navie of* Britain, *should infest the* * Batavians *upon the Sea-Coast*. And therefore that learned man *Lipsius* had no ground to conceiv that this was part of that Fleet of small Vessels called *Lusoriæ*, whereby the River *Rhine* was guarded; to wit, that part of it which guarded the entrance of the River near that place called the *British Tower*, whereof wee spake before in the third chapter of this book. For, it was even the whole Navie of *Britain*, and that which belonged wholly to the Sea, not having any relation at all to the Rivers. And that it belong'd to the Sea, appear's not onely by the thing it self, but also by what hath been alreadie spoken, and what shall bee said in the next chapter touching the *Count of the Saxon Shore*; so far at least as wee may

z *Chap.* V.

a *L.* 46. *ff. tit. ad Senatus consul. Trebellianic.*

b *Historiar. lib.* 4.

* *Hollanders.*

bee able to judg of the former (as wee often use to do) by the latter cours that was taken in ordering affairs, and disposing of Guards and Garrisons. But that this was a compleat Navie, and had a peculiar Prefect or Commander in chief over it, is testified by a fragment of an antient Inscription in a Palace at *Rome*, called *Palatium Capranicense*, [c] wherewith truly that name of Prefect of the *British* Navie was utterly lost. Yet it appear's thereby that such a Prefecture or Command there was, not of the least note among those antient dignities of the *Romans*, and that it was committed to the same man that was likewise *Prefect* of the two Navies called *Classis Moesica* and *Pannonica*; as also Proconsul and President of the *Alps*, Sub-Prefect of the *Pretorian* Navie, and Tribune of the sixteenth Legion. The form of the Inscription stand's thus.

[c] *Janus Gruterus*, p. 493.

. . . .

. . . .

PRAEF. CLASS. BRIT. ET MOESIC.
ET PANNONIC. PROC. ET PRAESIDI
ALPIUM SUBPRAEF. CLASS.
PRAET. TRIB. LEG. XVI.
FL. ECPREPUSA.

Moreover, it is no light Argument to prove, that in those times there was frequent use of that Navie in guarding the *British* Sea, as a part of the Province of *Britain* (as hath been alreadie said;) and that upon this ground, becaus the very name of those scouting Skiphs which were joined with the bigger sort of Pinnaces or light Vessels upon the Guard, was borrowed

borrowed by the *Romans* in their writings from the *Britains*, after the same manner as they took the name of those Boats called *Copuli* from the *Germans*, which [d] were likewise of that sort of Vessels called *Lusoriæ*, imploied in guarding the *Rhine*. The *Romans* observed that the *Britains* called those Vessels *Pyctas*. *Flavius Vegetius*, who in the Reign of the two *Valentinians*, composed his Books concerning the affairs of the *Roman Militia*, out of the Commentaries of *Cato*, *Celsus*, *Trajan*, and *Hadrian*, saith, [e] *scouting Skiphs are joined with the bigger sort of Pinnaces, that had about twentie Rowers in all; which skiphs the* Britains *call* Pyctas. *In these they use to make assaults and inrodes upon a sudden, and somtimes intercept the provision and supplies of their Enemies Shipping, and by diligent watchfulness discover their approaches or counsels. And that their Scouts may not bee discover'd by their whiteness, they die the Sails and Tackling with a blewish color, like the waves of the Sea. They besmear them also with wax as they use to trim their Ships. Yea, and the Seaman or Souldiers put on clothes of the same blewish color, so that they are the less discernable as they scout about, not onely by night, but also by day.* So far hee. And the printed Books do generally render these Vessels here *Pictas* or *Pyctas*. But som Manuscripts, that have been used by *Godescalcus Stewechius*, call them *Picatas*; and also wee read *Picatas* in two Manuscripts belonging to the King's Librarie at S[t] *James*, as I was inform'd by that learned man and my very good friend *Patrick Young*; from whence it is, that, in the old *French* translations of *Vegetius*, it is rendred one while *Picaces*, another *Pigaces*. But saith *Stewechius* upon the afore-mentioned place, *It seem's more probable to mee that they were called* Pincas, Pinks; *For, even at this very day there is such a kinde of*

[d] Videsis *Lips. ad Tacit. Hist. lib.* 5. *num.* 36. & *de Magnitud. Romanâ, lib.* 1. *cap.* 5.

[e] *De re Militari, lib.* 4. *cap.* 37.

Vessel known both in Britain *and* Holland. *And the ordinarie name is* **Een Pincke.** But howsoëver the case hath stood, here wee see in *Vegetius*, that the scouting Vessels were emploied together with the Pinnaces, and their name so observed according to the *British* language of that Age, that there appear's not the least ground to doubt, but that *Vegetius* was of opinion also, that those Vessels were either constantly or very frequently in use among the *Britains*, and in the Sea-Province of *Britain*. So, it is acknowledged by every man, that those words *Gesum* **a Javelin**, *Trimarcia* **Thrée Horses**, *Essedum* **a Chariot**, *Petoritum* **a Wagon of four Whéels**, *Braccæ* **Bréeches**, and others of that kinde, borrowed either from the *Gauls* or *Britains*, and received by the *Romans* into their own Language, do sufficiently set forth the use of those things which they signifie either in *Gaul* or *Britain*. Moreover also, *Vegetius* in this place so join's together the manner of guarding the Sea and the subtile sleights they made use of for that purpose, that there is no reason at all why wee should not believ, that they were then used by the *British* Souldiers which served at Sea, or who had command over the small Vessels called *Pyctæ* or *Picatæ* in those Guards by Sea.

An

An Examination of the Opinion of som learned men, who would have the Saxon Shore, *from whence that* Count *or* Commander *of the Sea* throughout Britain *had his Title, to bee the British Shore* on this side of the Sea; *which is plainly proved to bee fals.*

CHAP. VII.

BUt truly certain learned men, either treating (as it often fall's out) of som other subject, or els beeing too careless in considering the matter, do otherwise interpret that Dignitie or Command of the *Count of the Saxon Shore throughout* Britain; And in such a manner, that if their determination were to bee admitted, the proof or testimonie before-alleged touching a Joint-Dominion of the Sea together with the Isle, in that Command under the *Romans*, would plainly fall to the Ground. These men are of two different Opinions. Som would have the Shore of *Britain* it self or that which is on this side the Sea, to bee called onely the *Saxon*, in the naming of this Dignitie or Command: Others would have it to bee both the Shore of *Britain*, and all that Shore also which fetche's a compass like a half Moon from the Western part of *Denmark* as far as the West of *France*, and lie's over against *Britain*. But truly, they are both extremely mistaken.

The Autor of the former opinion is *Guidus* [a] *Pancirollus*, who write's that the Shore or Limit within the

[a] *Ad Notitiam Dignit. Occid. cap.* 72.

the Island was so denominated from those *Saxons*, who were called in hither by *Vortigern* King of the South part of *Britain*, to his assistance. *The* Saxons (saith hee) *possessed part of the Island, from whence a limit or bound that was rear'd over against them by one that was made Count, was called* Saxon. Then which nothing could have been more ignorantly spoken, if you reflect either upon the thing it self, or the cours of times. For, omitting this, that in the *Breviarie of Dignities* it self no mention is made at all of a *Saxon* Bound or Limit, but of a Shore (notwithstanding that *Pancirollus* in the Inscription of his Commentarie entitle's the Commander that wee speak of, *Count of the* Saxon *Limit throughout* Britain) the Breviarie was written in the Reign of *Theodosius* the yonger, or in the year CCCCX, as learned men do commonly agree. That is to say, of that time, the frame of the whole Government of the Empire, both in the East and West, having been over-grown long before, was with very great diligence digested as it were into one entire Book of Offices and Dignities. But the *Saxons*, as most of the Antients tell us, came first into *Britain* in the year of our Lord CCCCXLIX. But suppose, what upon better consideration may perhaps bee allowed, that their arrival ought to bee reckoned in the [b] year CCCCXXVIII. that is in the XXI year of the Reign of *Theodosius* the yonger, yet in the mean time this is most certain (which is here in the first place to bee observed) that *Britain* was utterly abandoned by the *Roman* Governors, before they were called in. Doubtless they were as [c] *Gildas* write's brought in by King *Vortigern* to *drive back the Northern Nations*, the *Picts*, and *Scots*; not the *Romans*, who had bidden farwel to the Island. Neither

[b] *Apud Guil. Camden. in Brit. pag.* 95. & vide *Tho. Lidiat in Temp. Emendat. pag.* 238.

[c] *In Epist. de Excidio Britanniæ.*

ther had the *Romans* or their Dukes or Counts any thing at all to do within the Isle with the *Saxons*. So that it must needs bee gross ignorance in Histories, and in the Calculation of time, to set down any *Saxon Limit* or *Saxon Shore* in the Island it self, whilst the Roman Empire flourished, or had any kinde of Autoritie in this Countrie. Nothing therefore is more evident then that the Shore lying on the other side of the Sea over against the South and Eastern Coast of *Britain*, as wee described it before, was called the *Saxon* in that Dignitie or Command. Moreover also that *Count of the* Saxon Shore *throughout* Britain was far more antient, and known by an addition thereto of the *Sea-Coast* or of that Sea which was comprehended in the Roman jurisdiction throughout *Britain*, or in the bodie of the *British* Province. For, *Nectaridius* was invested with this Dignitie in the time of *Valentinian* the first, or about the year of our Lord CCCLXX; as is testified by [d] *Ammianus Marcellinus*, where hee saith, information was given by a Messenger, *that* Britain *was reduced to an extreme low condition by a barbarous Conspiracie; and that* Nectaridius *Count of the* Sea-*Coast, and* Buchobaudes *the Duke were surprized unawares by the craft of the Enemy*. Nor is any difference to bee imagined between the Dignitie of the *Count of the Saxon Shore*, in this sens, *throughout* Britain, and that which the fore-named *C. Carausius* received at *Bologne* in *France*, to scour the Sea along the Coast of * Belgica and *Bretaigne*, which (as *Eutropius* and *Orosius* say) *was infested by the* French *and Saxons*. For, that even hee also had places of strength and Mansion-houses belonging to his Government in *Britain*, appear's sufficiently upon this ground; that when *Maximianus* had given order to put

[d] *Histor. lib.* 27.

* *Gaul* was by the *Romans* divided into four parts; of which *Belgica* was one, conteining *Picardie* part of *Champagne*, *Burgundy*, with so much of *Germanie* and the *Netherlands* as lie's on this side the *Rhine*.

put him to death, hee immediately usurp't in *Britain*, and reigned after for the space of seven years. So, the Governor here or *Count of the Sea-Coast*, and the *Count of the Saxon Shore*, beeing ever accounted the same, held the sole Government of *Britain* and the Sea belonging thereto. To whom also wee may add, as differing onely in name, not really, the Prefect or Admiral of the *British* Navie, under the *Romans*, mentioned in the former chapter. Wee confess indeed, that the Duke of *Belgica secunda* and the Duke of the Countrie of *Aremorica* before-mentioned, was by the verie nature of his place to afford supplies for the guarding the Sea and this Shore beyond Sea: For, they also, as hath been observed, had Garrisons seated upon this *Saxon Shore*. But it is chiefly to bee observed here, that these beyond-Sea-Dukes were according to the nature of their Dignitie or Office to take care, not so much of the Shore or Sea, as the Continent; and that from thence, as you see, they took their names. This from the Tract of [e] *Aremorica* and * *Ebroicæ*; which beeing extended through five Provinces, *Aquitania prima* and *secunda*, *Senonia*, *Lugdunensis secunda* and *Tertia* (which comprehend's the lesser *Britain* and *Normandie*) conteined almost all that which was commonly called by the name of *Gallia*; But the other had its name from *Belgica secunda*. Nor was there one Count or Duke of the Midland Countrie, and another of the Shore or Sea-Coast in *Gaul*. But in *Britain*, the Counts or Dukes of the midland parts and the *Count of the Sea-Coast or Saxon Shore*, had distinct charges, distinct Forces, and the signal Ornaments of their Offices wholly distinct. Just as if the *Roman* Emperors would have it signified by this very thing, that as the Sea it self

[e] Præter *Notitiam & Pancirollum*, vide *Joseph. Scaligerum ad Ausonium*, *lib.* 2. *cap.* 6.

* *Ebroicæ* now called *Eureux*.

self did by particular Right alwaies belong unto the Empire of the Island, so the Sea-affairs and their protection to the *British* Command and Jurisdiction of the *Saxon Shore* or that beyond-Sea; but that both the Dukes of the Continent or main Land of *Gaul* lying right before it, were bound so to send relief, as occasion should require, against the *Saxon* Invasions, that in the mean time the sole care of the sea it self, as a particular Province given in charge, lay upon him that was made *Count of the* Saxon shore *throughout Britain.* And if any Duke or Count either of *Aremorica* or *Belgica secunda*, was called by the name of Duke or *Count of the Saxon shore* (as [e] som would have) it was don doutless upon this ground, becaus the *Saxon shore*, lying over against us on the other side of the sea, did bound their Land-Government; as it did also the Sea-Jurisdiction of the aforesaid *Count throughout* Britain.

[f] *Jos. Scaliger. in lect. Auson. lib. 2. cap. 6. &* *Guil. Camden. in Brit. pag. 96.*

Nor indeed is that other Opinion any more to bee admitted, which saith; That our *British* shore was at that time called *Saxon*, as well as that which lie's over against it or beyond sea: And so that the name in the Dignitie or Office of the aforesaid Count, doth signifie the shore on this side the sea. Of this Opinion is [f] *Abrahamus Ortelius*; *I conceiv*, saith hee, *that the* Saxon shore, *in the Breviarie, doth signifie the Eastern part of* Kent, *seeing that* Dubris, Rutupis, *and other Towns of* Kent *are described therein.* Hee hath indeed very eminent men for his Followers, [g] *William Camden*, [h] *Paulus Merula*, [i] *Philippus Cluverius*, and som others. And they add this for a reason; becaus both shores, as well this on this side the sea, as that on the other side, took name from the *Saxons* that used Piracie in very great numbers upon this sea: And therefore that

[f] *In Thesaur. Geograph.*

[g] *In* Kent, *pag. 230.*

[h] *Cosmograph. part. 2. lib. 3. cap. 31.*

[i] *German. Antiqua, lib. 1. cap. 18.*

the *British shore* also is set forth in the Title of that Count. But this is a manifest Error. Wee know indeed the Writers of that time do say, that both the shore over against ours and the neighboring Sea, was infested by the frequent depredations and Invasions of the *Saxons*, and (to say nothing of their antient habitations upon the *Danish* and *Batavian* shore) that they setled their abode there: And therefore that it was thence named *Saxon*, is in a manner out of doubt among learned men. But concerning the *Saxons* thus frequenting that shore, there are testimonies beyond all exception. [k] *Sidonius Apollinaris*, of the Coast of *Bretaign* in *France*, saith,

[k] *Panegyric. ad Avitum August. seu Carm. 7. Adde eum lib. 8. Epist. 6.*

Quin & Aremoricus piratam Saxona tractus
Sperabat.———

———Hope then reviv'd the Bretaigns stout,
The Saxon Pirates beeing driven out.

And [l] *Ammianus Marcellinus* saith, that under the Emperors *Valentinian* and *Valens*, *the Coasts of* Gallia *were wasted by the* Franks *and* Saxons *bordering upon them, every one making excursions as far as they could by Land or Sea, with grievous plunderings, firings, and slaughters of such as they took Prisoners.* Add moreover, that *Saxones* Baiocassini, the Saxons of Baieux are mentioned by [m] *Gregorie* of *Tours*, as antient Inhabitants upon the shore of *Aremorica*: So that the reason is evident, why the name of *Saxon* was given to the shore over against ours. But truly wee read not any where, that the *Saxons* had at that time either setled themselvs upon the shores of *Britain*, or were wont to sail thither, or that they infested any thing of *Britain*, except the Sea. Nor do wee finde so much

[l] *Histor. lib.* 27.

[m] *Lib. 5. cap.* 26.

as the least sign or evidence, whereby to conjecture that the name of *Saxon* was either due or given at that time to the shore of *Britain*. And it was never heard (I suppose) that any shores, which have been of any account or fame, should have taken a new name either from a meer passage, or a bare infesting of the Sea by such as sail along the Coast, without landing. Especially, in the setting forth of a Dignitie or Command, which cannot bee don, except an addition bee made in the mean time of the name of the Land, whereto the shore it self did indeed belong. Run over all the Dignities which are recorded in the *Breviarie* of both Empires, you will finde none set forth by any other denomination, then either from a Bound or Frontier it self, as those that were appointed for the defence of Bounds and Frontiers; or els from a more known and certain name of some Province, as the rest. Wee know indeed, there was a Haven among the * *Morini*, which lay over against us on the other side of the Sea, called heretofore *British*, or, as [n] *Plinie* name's it, *Portum Morinorum Britannicum* **the British Port of the Morini**: which name [o] learned men would have to bee derived from our *Britain*. But (supposing it to bee *Calais*) they would have it so denominated becaus of *Julius Cæsar*'s crossing over from that Port into *Britain*. Now, it doth not appear by the like, or any equivalent reason, that the shore, which belong's to *Britain*, was called *Saxon*, in the time of that *Dignitie* whereof wee speak. And doubtless, there is no improbabilitie in reason, that the *British* Port of the *Morini*, might in the daies of *Plinie*, or of the Emperor *Vespasian* (which is all one) bee denominated from the riding of such Ships as were imploied under the *Romans* to guard the neighboring

* The *Morini* were a people of *Belgica*, bordering upon the Sea, and seated between *Artois* and *Picardie*.

[n] *Nat Histor. lib.4.cap.23.*

[o] *Jacob Chiffletius, in Portu Iccio, cap.6.*

boring Sea, so far as it was *British*, and subject to the Lievtenancie or Jurisdiction of *Britain*. But truly if the very shore of the Island had been meant in the Dignitie of that *Count*, whereof wee speak, whose Office was to guard the Bounds, how compendiously might hee have been called *Count of the British shore*? For, what ground had there been for so singular a circumlocution of words, as *Count of the Saxon shore throughout Britain*, if it had been the very shore of *Britain*? It is plain, that as in the Imperial Offices there was an Officer called *Magister Militum per Orientem*, *Magister Militum per Thracias*, *per Illyricum*, *peditum per Occidentem*; **a Master (or Commander) of the Militia throughout the East, a Master of the Militia over all** Thrace, Illyricum, **and of the Infantrie or Foot throughout the West**; so also that this Officer was called *Count throughout Britain*. That is to say, every where throughout *Britain*, so far as it belonged to his particular charge, that is, as far as was necessarie to guard the bounds of the Empire, placed next to the *Saxon shore*, or that which is on the other side of the Sea. And so the words, whereby this Dignitie is expressed, are to bee distinguished that hee may bee plainly called *Count throughout Britain*; but *of the Saxon shore*, or *Bound beyond-Sea*, upon the same account as other Dukes or Counts in Command over Bounds or Frontiers were wont to bee entitled. And there is an eminent example to this purpose in the Bound of the *German* Empire, which was held by the *Romans*. It was the River *Rhine*. The Guard of the *Rhine* was wont to bee committed to a Lievtenant or Governor; as appear's by [p] Historians, and out of [q] the Code of *Theodosius*. But yet the Bank on the other side of *Rhine* was the bound of

[p] *Zonaras, Tom.2. alii.*

[q] *L.9. C. Theodos. lib.7. tit. 1.*

of this Government, and so of the *German* Empire, not the Bank on this side. From whence also *Posthumius* beeing entrusted with this charge under the Emperor *Gallienus*, is by the Emperor *Valerian*, in an Epistle of his sent unto the *French*, called *Duke of the Bound beyond Rhine*; as wee learn out of [r] *Trebellius Pollio*. Also, the *Bound beyond Rhine*, that is, the Bank beyond the *Rhine* is recorded by [f] *Flavius Vopiscus*. Thus, usually the Proconsul of *Asia* had the whole streight of *Hellespont* under his Command as far as the shores of *Europe*, as is shewn in the fourteenth chapter. And certainly, the *Count of the* Saxon shore *throughout Britain*, is after the same manner to bee reckoned Count of the shore or bound on the other side of the Sea, and so of the whole Sea flowing between, as an established Officer in the Government of *Britain*. And this also is very much confirm'd out of another place of the very *Breviarie of Dignities*, where mention is made of the several Jurisdictions of those Counts which were under the Command of that eminent person entitled *Magister Militum Præsentalis*. In the printed Copies of the Breviarie, wee read it thus;

[r] *In trigenta Tyrannis.*

[f] *In Tacito Augusto.*

Sub dispositione viri illustris Magistri peditum Præsentalis, Comites Militum infrà-scriptorum;

Italiæ,
Africæ,
Tingitaniæ,
Tractûs Argentoratensis,
Britanniarum,
Litoris Saxonici per Britannias.

In the Edition both of *Alciatus* and *Pancirollus*, it is read, as wee render it here, *Militum infrascriptorum.* Yet doubless the word *Limitum* **Limits** ought to bee put in stead of *Militum* **Souldiers**: For it is not agreeable to the nature of the Imperial Offices, that the word *Militum* should bee admitted in that place. And it appear's most certain by those things which follow, that *Italie*, *Africa*, the Tract of *Strasburgh*, *Britain*, and the *Saxon Shore*, had their respective *Counts*, as *Comites Limitum* **Counts of the Limits** or Bounds, no otherwise than those Territories which are added there next after; as *Mauritania Cæsariensis*, *Tripolis*, and other Provinces in like manner, besides *Britain*, which had their respective *Dukes* likewise, by the name of *Duces Limitum* **Dukes of the Limits.** But now both the *Duke* and *Count* of *Britain* had the very Shore of the Island for their Limit or Bound. And therefore seeing it is so, what Limit had that *Count* relation to, was who entitled of the *Saxon Shore throughout Britain*, if you will not yield that hee took his Title from the Shore lying over against us? There was a *Duke*, and a *Count of Britain* (simply so called) besides a *Vicarius* or *Deputie of Britain*, who governed the whole Island according to their several charges; and wee finde in the *Breviarie*, that both the *Duke* and the *Count* and the *Deputie* had for the signal Ornaments of their Offices, the whole Island, but in several Forms, encompassed with the Sea; even as the *Count of the Saxon Shore* had the Isle in like manner, encompassed with Sea-Towns or Ports. Also, it is manifest by those which are set forth in the *Breviarie of Dignities*, that the *Deputie*, *Duke*, and *Count of Britain* had the very Territories of the Isle for the Limits

Limits of their Goverment, and so also that they extended themselvs to the very Shores every where throughout the Jurisdiction of the *Romans*. So that also both the *Duke* and *Count of Britain* ought to have been entitled in like manner from the *Saxon Shore* as from a Limit or Bound, if the Shore of *Britain* had been called by this name at that time. For, wee plainly see, that the Islands of *Britain* themselvs, so far as the Isles about it are comprehended under that name, are expresly described under the notion of Limits, in that Catologue of Dignities relating to *Limits*, which wee have cited out of the *Breviarie*. Therefore from hence also it appear's, that Limit which was the *Saxon Shore* is to bee reckoned without the Island, and so in the Shore over against us or which lie's beyond Sea, according to that which wee proved before in our Discours. Nor truly, is it to bee passed over without observation, seeing there are very many signal Ornaments of Sea-Provinces and Jurisdictions, as well as of those within Land, pictured in the *Breviarie*, and this according to the Form or Fashion received from those that had the supreme power, by the principal Secretaries or others who drew up the Commissions; That not only no Ornaments at all are found in the Dignities of the West, wherein there is any Tract of the Sea, except those which belong to the Government of Jurisdiction of *Britain*, nor indeed in the Dignities of the East, except the Counts of *Egypt* and *Isauria* (both whose Ornaments had a Sea-border about them;) but also that the Sea was ever placed round about in the signal Ornaments belonging to the four several Governments or Jurisdictions of *Britain*, that is to say, that of the *Deputie*, the *Duke*, the *Count*, and lastly, the *Count of the* Saxon Shore *throughout*

out Britain. Just as if the *Romans* would have had it signified thereby, that no other Province at all, nor any other Jurisdiction whatsoëver had either a Dominion of the Sea so amply conjoined, mingled, and as it were incorporated within it self, or a protection and command of a Territorie by Sea.

Som Evidences concerning the Soveraigntie and inseparable Dominion of the Isle of *Britain* and the Sea belonging thereto, *out of* Claudian, *and certain* Coins *of the Emperor* Antoninus Pius.

Chap. VIII.

FRom the Dominion of the *British* Sea, as beeing continually united to the Island, or an inseparable concomitant thereof (as hath been alreadie shewn you) proceeded, as it is very probable, those passages of *Claudian*, who seldom speak's of the quieting, recovering, or subduing of *Britain*, but hee add's also the Sea it self, as that which did necessarily accompanie it. Speaking in honor of the Emperor *Honorius*, touching the original of his Family, which was out of *Spain*, he saith,

[a] *Panegyric, de* 4. *Consulatu Honorii.*

——[a] *Cunabula fovit*
Oceanus. Terræ dominos pelagíque futuros
Immenso decuit rerum de Principe nasci.
Hinc processit avus. ——

The Ocean rock't his Cradle. It became
Those who as Lords both Sea and Land
should claim,

Of

Of nature's mightie Prince deriv'd to bee.
From hence thy Grandsire had his pedegree.

That is to say, *Theodosius*, who after that *Nectaridius* Count of the *Saxon Shore*, as is before related, and *Buchobaudes* Duke of the Island, were slain, was sent into *Britain* by the Emperor *Valentinian* the first. But that which *Claudian* saith, concerning the affairs and actions of this *Theodosius*, relate's very little to the Sea, save that hee call's him *Conquerer of the* British *Shore*, and adds that *having vanquished the* Saxon's, *hee washed the Orcades with their Bloud.* Which is plainly to bee understood of his scouring the *British* Sea that was wont to bee infested by the *Saxons*. A little after also, concerning *Theodosius* the son of this man, or the Father of *Honorius*, that is, the Emperor *Theodosius* the first, hee saith,

Sed laudes genitor longè transgressus avitas
Subdidit Oceanum sceptris.———

His Father did his Grandsir's worth transcend,
And brought the Ocean under his command.

Which without question relate's to the recoverie of *Britain*, after the slaughter of *Maximus* at *Aquileia*, who had tyrannically usurped the Soveraigntie of the Island. The same Autor writing also in commendation of *Flavius Stilico* Tutor or Guardian of *Honorius* the yonger, bring's in *Britain* her self saying, Stilico *hath so fortified and secured mee,*

———[b] *ne Litore toto*
Prospicerem dubiis venturum Saxona ventis,

I could not see throughout the Shore, or stand
One Saxon **readie to cross or'e and land.**

[b] *De laudibus Stiliconis. lib.* 2.

 That

That is to ſay, hee rendred the Sea quiet and ſecure for mee; hee hath guarded and kept it for mee; hee hath driven away the *Saxons* from the uſe of it. In another place alſo, hee bring's in the Goddeſs *Pietie* ſpeaking to *Honorius,*

c In Eutropium, lib. 1.

———[c] *Quantum, te principe, poßim,*
Non longinqua docent: domito quòd Saxone Tethys
Mitior, aut fracto ſecura Britannia Picto.

What progreſs I may make, during thy Reign,
Some late examples tell us; ſince the Main,
The Saxon beeing tam'd, is grown more ſure,
And Britain from the conquer'd Picts ſecure.

The Protection of the Sea is in this place plainly conjoined with that of the Iſland. The ſame Poët alſo, to *Manlius Theodorus* the Conſul, ſaith,

———*Hiſpana tibi Germanáque Tethys*
Paruit, & noſtro diducta Britannia mundo.

Spaniſh and German Seas both yield to thee,
And Britain ſever'd from our World by Sea.

There was the ſame Dominion, the ſame Victorie, and the ſame Guardianſhip or Protection alwaies both of the *Britiſh Tethys*, or Sea, and the Iſle it ſelf. For, the *German Tethys* in this place is that part of the *Britiſh* Sea which flow's between *Belgium*, *Holland*, *Friſland*, the *Jutæ*, and *Britain*.

Add hereunto the form of the Province (which under the more antient Emperors was governed by a *Preſident*)

as it is found among the *Roman* Coins. It is represented in the Figure of a woman, clothed with a Pall or linen frock, sitting somtimes upon *rocks*, somtimes upon a *Globe* in the Sea, with a Militarie Ensign, a Spear, and a Buckler; as you have here pictured according the brass-Coins of *Antoninus Pius*.

Thus they signified, that *Britain* had Dominion over the Sea about it, and the *Roman* Emperor over *Britain*. But we finde not any form of this kinde before the time of *Seius Saturninus*, the first *Prefect* (whereof any mention is made by the Antients) or Commander in chief of the *British* Navie, or of those Naval Forces, wherewith the *Romans* guarded the *British* Sea. Hee held this Command under *Adrian*, or *Antoninus Pius*, as hath been said alreadie. And from hence it is that *Claudian* afterwards, when hee make's a Representation of *Britain* (beeing in a special manner, called the Isle of the Sea) hee clothe's her with a leathern garment so made as it were like waves of water, and died of a blewish color, that it wholly resembled the waves of the Sea; and hee put's the Sea under her feet. Thus hee indeed describe's her, when hee bring's in several Provinces, as *Spain*, *Britain*, and *Africa* demanding the Consulship for *Stilico* at *Rome*. And hee mention's *Britain* in a peculiar manner.

d *De laudibus Stiliconis, lib. 2.*

[d] *Indè Caledonio velata Britannia Monstro,*
Ferro picta genas; cujus vestigia verrit
Cærulus, Oceanique æstum mentitur amictus.
Me quoque vicinis pereuntem gentibus, inquit,
Munivit Stilico; totam cùm Scotus Hibernam
Movit, & infesto spumavit remige Tethys.

In monstrous habit Caledonian-wise
Then Britain came; her cheeks had a disguis
Of divers colors, which, to pleas the view,
In various forms an Iron Pencil drew;
Just at her heels the Sea it self did glide,
Her Mantle mock't the working of the Tide.
Mee and my Neighbors Stilico did save,
Quoth shee, and bravely rescue from the grave;
When as the Scot mov'd Ireland to rebel,
And Pirates made great * Tethys foam and swell.

* *Tethys* signifie's the Sea.

A little before, there hee set's forth the hair of *Spain* with leavs of the Palm-tree, and her mantle imbroider'd with the River *Tagus*; And *Africa* with ears of Corn and Ivorie, after the same manner as it was stampt in the Coins of *Antoninus Pius*. Both these are washed, and almost encompassed by the Sea. But the Poët then understood, that the Dominion of the adjacent Sea belong'd to neither of them, as it did to *Britain*: But as the Palms, and the River *Tagus* were peculiar to *Spain*; as the ears of Corn and Ivorie to *Africa*; so hee would have it understood, that the Province of *Britain* had the Sea of the same name peculiar thereunto. But yet it is to bee conceived,

that

that the Dominion of the *Romans* was ſo limited in this Sea, according to their poſſeſsion of the ſhore, that they had little power in that part of the *Britiſh* Sea, which border'd upon the ſhores of thoſe *Britiſh* Nations, who were not under their obedience: This is to bee taken chiefly of the *Iriſh* Sea, and the reſt that lie's North-weſt. For when the *Romane* Empire began to decline, not onely *Ireland*, but the Iſle of *Man* alſo, and the other Iſles of the Weſtern Sea, and a great portion of the more Northerly part of *Britain*, was poſſeſſed by the *Scots* and *Picts*; ſo that wee have ſufficient ground to conceiv, that they alſo had an antient Dominion of their own in the neighboring Sea. And ſo let this ſerv to have been ſpoken concerning the Empire or Dominion of the *Britiſh* Sea, in the time of the *Romans*, as that which by antient Right no leſs belong'd to the Iſle and the Empire thereof, then either a Wall or Suburbs unto a Citie. Now wee paſs on to the times of their Succeſſors.

Touching the Dominion of the Britiſh Sea, after that the Inhabitants *had freed themſelvs from the Romane power.*

Chap. IX.

WHen the Romane Empire was declining under the Emperors *Theodoſius* the yonger, and *Honorius*, and *Valentinian* the third, inſomuch that they had not Forces ſufficient to guard the Citie it ſelf, then the *Britains* freed themſelvs wholly from their Power, about CCCCLXXX. years after the arrival of *Julius Cæsar*, or in the year of our Lord CCCCXXX. That is to say, as [a] *Zosimus* write's, *They cast off the Roman Government, and settled a Common weal after their own liking.* Then the Dominion of the Sea, as well as of that part of the Isle which was possest before by the *Romans*, returned unto the Natives. In the mean time, the *Saxons* inhabiting the shore over against us, hanker'd after it, who beeing a people extremely given to Piracie, the *Romans* were wont to appoint an Officer to drive them away, called the *Count of the Saxon shore throughout Britain*, as hath been shewn at large alreadie. Neverthelesse beeing sent for by the Southern *Britains* destitute of all manner of succor from the *Romans*, to assist them against the *Scots* and *Picts*, they at length got the whole Power here into their own hands. And so in that famous Heptarchie of theirs, the Kingdom was ever accounted of in such a manner, that even before the time of King *Egbert*, it was under the Power of som one King, which all the rest acknowledged as Supreme. These were driven out by the *Danes*; but questionless, they both had a Dominion by Sea conjoined with that upon Land. For it is not to bee imagined, that they who were so *accustomed to the Sea*, and to whom before that time

> ——[b]*pelle salum sulcare* Britannum
> *Ludus, & assuto glaucum mare findere lembo;*

> **It was a sport to cut the British Main**
> **In Leathern Barks, and plow the azure plain.**

And whose Rowers or Mariners had you beheld, you would have

[a] *Histor. li. 6.*

[b] *Sidon. Apollinaris Panegyric. ad Avitum Aug. seu Carm. 7.*

have thought you had seen so many Arch-Pirats, as [c] *Sidonius Apollinaris* saith of the *Saxons*; And who *did not onely know, but were familiarly acquainted with the dangers of the Sea*; The very same thing is to bee said of the *Danes* also and *Normans*, (for, these names beeing promiscuously used, do very often signifie the same Nation) as is sufficiently attested by *Regino, Dudo,* the Monk of *Malmsburie, Abbo, Gemiticensis,* and others; It is not, I say, to bee imagined, that these people having gotten possession either of the Isle or shore, to which the Soveraigntie of the Sea did so neerly appertein, should not in like manner have possessed the Sea, also lying before it, by right of Dominion. Nor is it perhaps altogether unworthie to bee considered, that these *Saxons* had so great, so singular and admirable an acquaintance with the Sea and Sea-affairs, that by an exquisite observation of the *Tides* and * *Ebbings* of the Sea, they were wont to reckon their months and years, yea, and to frame Computations of years thereby. A thing not to bee parallel'd by any example. And as the more antient Husbandmen used to reckon daies and hours by the time of yoking their Oxen; and as most other Nations measured years and daies by the cours of the Sun and Moon, (as things most to bee regarded before others, in the improvement and various use of those Lands that they possessed): so these alone distinguished their yearly and monthly periods, by the meer reciprocal motion of the Sea, which they were so well acquainted with, and by its various beating upon the shore in Ebbing and Flowing, as that whereof special notice was to bee taken in that kinde of life. Moreover, as they say the *Egyptians* derived their skill in *Geometrie* from the measuring of their Fields, after the Inun-

[c] *Li.8. Epist. 6.*

* The *Ebbs* they called *Ledones* or *Lidunas*; the *Tides* they called *Malinas*.

Inundation of their River *Nilus*; so it is not to bee doubted, but that our *Saxons* derived this strange artifice, never heard of in any other Countrie, from a very frequent use and perpetual observation of the Sea. Concerning which, hee that would know more, may peruse our *venerable* [d] *Bede* first, and after him [e] *Joseph Scaliger*, [f] *Dionysius Petavius*, and *Olaus* [g] *Wormius*. But that the whole Nation was very much accustomed to Sea-affairs, and not onely those that border'd upon the Sea, may bee collected from thence, that otherwise it would hardly bee believed, that the Nation it self could have kept an accompt of Times and Seasons, by the various cours of the Sea: For it could not possibly bee, but that such an accompt would have been either useless, or too difficult for those that were not used to the Sea. Yea, without doubt it was no small caus of their calling the *Saxons* into the Island, that they beeing most expert Sea-men, might guard the Sea, which having been newly deserted by the *Roman* Navie, lay open at that time to the Invasions of Enemies on every side. Thus much indeed seem's to bee signified by [h] *Ethelwerd* an antient Writer, speaking of their coming hither. *In those daies*, (saith hee) *the Britains heard that the* Saxon *was a Nation active in Piracie or Navigation, and strong in all kindes of Necessaries for warr, throughout all the Sea-Coast from the River* Rhine, *as far as the Citie* Donia, *which is now commonly called* **Danemarc.** *To them therefore they sent Messengers with extraordinarie great Presents, desiring aid, promising them a peaceable intercours and amitie.* Thus they that were wont before to infest the *British* Sea, are invited to its protection and amitie. And truly, that the *Britains* had a very special care at that time of the Sea-affairs, and so of the Guardianship of their Sea,

[d] *De Naturâ Rerum, cap.* 28.

[e] *De emendatione temp. lib.* 2, *pag.* 162. *& in Appendice ad conjectan. in Varronem pag.* 181. *Edit.* 1581.

[f] *De Doctrinâ temp. li.* 2. *cap.* 70.

[g] *In Fastis Danicis, lib.* 1. *cap.* 11.

[h] *Lib.* 1.

Sea, appear's from thence; that in the storie of *Britain*, wee read concerning the most famous King *Arthur* and Prince *Malgo*, that by many bloudie Battels they either added or recover'd *six Comprovincial Isles of the Sea*, (which are the very words of *Geofferie* of *Monmouth*) that is to say, *Ireland, and Shetland, Gotland, the Orcades, Norwey, and* * *Dacia, to their Dominion*; yea, and *Groenland, and all the other Countries and Islands of the Eastern Sea as far as Russia, and many other Islands beyond* [i] Scantia, *even to the farthest part of the North.* And that which wee finde in *Nennius* the Scholar of [k] *Elvodugus*, is to bee understood of this time; to wit, that *Cuneda* the Grandfather of *Magolcunus* a Prince of the *Southern Britains*, drave the *Scots* out of all the Countries and Islands of *Britain*. Certainly, for the effecting of this, it was necessarie there should bee a very great strength in shipping, for the guard and securitie of the neighboring Sea.

* By *Dacia*, here is meant *Denmark*.

[i] *Vide Guil. Lambard de priscis Anglorum legibus pag.* 137.

[k] *Ms. in Bibliothecâ Cottonianâ.*

It is proved, both from the *very beginning of the Saxons Reign*, as also from *their Forces and Victories by Sea*, that the *English-Saxons, and Danes*, who ruled the South-part of *Britain*, had Dominion over the Sea.

CHAP. X.

BEsides what hath been alreadie said of the *Saxons*, during their Reign here, there are also in antient Records divers other particulars, which more plainly shew, that both they and the *Danes* had

Dominion over the Sea, whilst they reigned in *Britain*. Those particulars I divide into four parts: The first respect's the *Original of the most Potent Kingdom of the Saxons.* The second, *the Naval Forces and Victories of the following time.* The third, *the Tributes and Duties of fiduciarie Clients or Vassals* belonging to the maintenance of the Navie. Lastly, several plain and *most evident testimonies concerning the Soveraigntie of the English-Saxon Kings* at that time over the Sea.

In the first beginning of the Reign of the *English-Saxons*, I reckon both the coming of *Octha* and *Ebissa*, invited hither by *Vortigern* upon the perswasion of *Hengist*, as also the arrival of King *Ælla* in *Sussex*. Hee possessed himself of the Sea, and the Southern shores; they of the Northern. Concerning the Naval Forces of *Octha* and *Ebissa*, [a] *Nennius* the Scholar of *Elvodugus*, who usually passeth up and down also by the name of *Gildas*, speak's thus; *They sailing about the Picts, with fortie Vessels, called* * Ciulæ, *spoiled the Orcade's Islands, and came and possessed very many Isles and Regions beyond Mare Fresicum,* (meaning *Bodotria* or the Firth of *Edinburgh*) *which lie's between us and the Scots, even as far as the Borders of the Picts. And* Hengist *by degrees drew those* Ciulæ *to himself, so that they forsook the Isles which they inhabited.* It could hardly bee more plainly expressed, that the Nation beeing accustomed to the Affairs of Navigation and Wars by Sea, having thus gotten a great part of *Britain*, did first secure that inseparable Appendant of the Island or the Sea; having brought over a numerous Force, for the accomplishment of this design. As to what concern's *Ælla*, they write, that hee with his sons *Cissa* and *Cimenus*, and a Navie very well appointed with Militarie Forces, arrived upon the shore of *Sussex*,

[a] *Ms. in bibliotheca Cottonianâ, & partim apud Camden. in Britan. p. 91.*

* These *Ciulæ* were full of Saxons, which *Sidonius* call's *Pandos Myoparones*, Vessels built somwhat long and narrow.

neer

neer **Witering**, [b] **Cimenshore**, so called heretofore from this *Cimenus*; and that having driven away the *Britains*, hee possessed the [c] Sea-Coast; and sending daily for new Aids out of *Germanie*, hee at length enlarged his Kingdom along the Eastern shores, as far as the River *Humber*, and was the first of the *English Saxons* that attained here to so large a Dominion. Also, that his posteritie enjoied this Kingdom about LXX years. But truly it could hardly bee, that they who were eminently powerfull in shipping, and had made so happie a Progress upon the shore, should not in like manner bee Masters of the Sea it self; especially seeing wee finde not the least testimonie that any others were at that time, of any considerable strength in shipping upon this Coast.

[b] *Cart. Cedwallæ R. apud Camden in Britann. pag.* 223

[c] *Ethelwerd lib.* 1. & 3. *ca.* 3. *Henric. Huntindon. lib.* 2.

But as for the *Naval Forces and Victories* of the succeeding Kings, both *Danes* and *English-Saxons*, they are to bee seen every where in *Joannes Asserius* Bishop of *Shirburn*, *William* the Monk of *Malmsburie*, *Henrie* Arch-Deacon of *Huntingdon*, *Roger Hoveden*, *Florentius* of *Worcester*, and *Florilegus*; but especially in the Acts of K. *Alfred*, *Edward* the elder, *Athelstan*, *Edgar*, *Ethelred* and *Harold*. And questionless, long after the beginning of the *Saxons* Reign, this Countrie flourisht not a little in shipping, for the mainteining of the Soveraigntie of the Sea, as may bee collected both from the Customs of the Nation alreadie mentioned, and the frequent use of Navigation, from which the Merchants that used to traffick on both the shores were prohibited, upon the occasion of a difference that arose betwixt *Charls* of *France*, (afterwards Emperor) and *Offa* King of the *Mercians* among the *English-Saxons*, to whom the rest were in subjection. Yet a freedom thereof was restored not long after, by an agreement of extraordinarie benefit and advantage to the *English-Saxons*, as wee finde in [d] *Alcuinus*, and *William* of *Malmsburie*. But before K. *Alfred*, their power began to decreaſ by Sea, and that eſpecially in the time of K. *Ethelwolph*, when the [e] *Danes* or *Normans* infeſted not onely the ſhores, but alſo almoſt the whole Iſland, after a moſt grievous manner, and ſeized upon moſt of the Iſles by force, which lie on the weſt of *Britain*. And ſo all was expoſed to the mercie of Pirats. But after that *Alfred* was inveſted in the Kingdom, the defence of the Sea was reſtored, and its Dominion eſtabliſhed; concerning whom, that *Aſſerius* Biſhop of *Shirburn*, his Tutor, write's thus: *Hee gave command for the building of Boats and Gallies,* that is, *long ſhips throughout the Kingdom, that hee might prevent his enemies, and fight them by Sea, and putting Pirats aboard them, hee charged them to guard the paſſages of th Sea.* And a little after, *Hee commanded alſo his Sea-men, to keep all relief of Victual from going to the Enemie by Sea.* Hee uſed the word *Pirats* in this place (as others of that age have don) not for Robbers, as 'tis commonly taken; but for ſuch as beeing skill'd in Sea-affairs, were appointed to ſet upon the Enemie's Fleets, and defend the Dominion by Sea: Touching the derivation of the word, the old Scholiaſt upon *Sophocles* his *Aiax*, ſaith; Πεῖρα Ἀττικῶς δόλος καὶ τέχνη· ὅθεν καὶ Πειραταὶ οἱ κατὰ θάλασσαν κακοῦργοι, That is, *Pira, in the Attick Tongue, ſignifie's craft or art, and hence it is, that they are called Pirats which infeſt the Sea.* But when the *Engliſh-Saxons* and *Danes*, in the time of K. *Alfred*, were ever and anon ſtrugling for the Soveraigntie in *England* (for, *Gurmundus*, or *Guthrunus* King of the *Danes*, was at that time ſetled in *Northumberland* as a *Fiduciarie Client or Vaſſal* to *Alfred*, and had very large Territories in the East-

[d] *In Epiſt. apud Guil. Malmsbur. de geſtis Regum, lib.* 1. *c.* 5 *Et in operibus Alcuini inter Epiſtolas, p.* 1669.

[e] *Geſta Normann. ann.* 840. *Malmsb. lib.* 2. *cap.* 2. *&c.*

Eaſt-part of *England*) their Fights were moſtly by Sea, as if they had both been of opinion, that hee which could get the Dominion of the *Britiſh* Sea, would by neceſſarie conſequence becom Lord alſo of the Land, or of that part of the Iſle which lie's before it. For this cauſ alſo it was, that the *Danes* growing ſtrong at Sea, K. *Alfred* mightily augmented his Naval Forces, by building ſhips twice as long as the *Daniſh* ſhips, deeper, nimbler, and leſs rocking or rolling, and ſo much more convenient for Sea-Fights. *Florentius* the Monk ſaith, *In the ſame year* (that is to ſay, the year of our Lord MCCCXCVII.) *the Forces of the Pagans reſiding in Eaſt-England and Northumberland, uſing Piracie upon the Sea-Coaſts, did grievouſly infeſt the Weſt-Saxon's Countrie, with very long and nimble ſhips, which they had built divers years before. Againſt whom ſhips were built by the Command of K.* Alfred, *twice as long, deeper, nimbler, and leſs waving or rolling by whoſe force hee might ſubdue the aforeſaid ſhips of the Enemie.* It is related alſo in the ſame words by *Roger Hoveden.* But *Henrie* of *Huntingdon*, ſpeaking expreſly of the number of Oars that ſerved for the rowing of theſe ſhips of *Alfred*, ſaith, *King Alfred cauſed long ſhips to bee made readie; to wit, of 40 Oars or more, againſt the* Daniſh *ſhips.* But there are [f] Chronicles written in the *Saxon* Tongue, that ſpeak of ſhips of 60 Oars, and larger, built by him at that time; out of which theſe Writers above-mentioned, and others of the like ſort, have compiled theirs. The words of the Chronicles are theſe, þa het Ælfred Cing timbrian lange ſcipu ongen þa æſcas þa wæron full neah twa ſwa lange ſwa þa oðre. Sume hæfdon XL ara ſume ma. þa wæron ægþer ge ſwiftran ge unwealtran ge eac hearran þonn þa oðre.

[f] Ms. *Codices bini, in Bibliothecâ Collonianâ, anno* 897.

oðþe. næþon hi naþoþ ne on fpiſiſe geſceapen ne on ðeniſe buton ſpa him ſelfum þuhte þ hi nyt ƿeoþhoſte beon mihton, That is to ſay, *King* Alfred *gave command for the building of long ſhips to encounter the* Daniſh. *But they were twice as long as theſe; whereof ſom had ſixtie Oars, ſom more. They were alſo more nimble, leſs rolling, and deeper then the other. Not built after the* Friſian *or* Daniſh *manner; but ſuch as hee conceived moſt convenient for fighting.* So that there is no doubt but the buſineſs of ſhipping was mightily advanced in his Reign, among the *Engliſh-Saxons*, in order to the defence and maintenance of their Dominion by Sea. And wee very often finde, that thoſe Sea fights managed by *Alfred* and his ſon *Edward*, with various ſucceſs, againſt the *Danes*, and *Normans*, were undertaken not without great numbers of Shipping. But in the time of King *Athelſtan*, who was very ſtrong at Sea, upon *the Iriſh Nation* (ſaith [g] *Huntingdon*) *and thoſe that dwelt in ſhips, there fell a fatal deſtruction.* The *Engliſh-Saxon* words in the antient Chronicles, from whence *Huntingdon* tranſlated thoſe, and which agree wth theſe, are, Scotta leoðe ꝛ scypflotan ſæge feollan, which fully ſignifie the ſame thing. For, Scotta leoðe or the *Scotiſh Nation* and *Scots* are by the Antients often taken for the *Iriſh*. *Hee alſo* (ſaith the ſame Autor) *led an huge Armie by* Land *and* Sea *into* Northumberland *and* Scotland, *and in regard there was none appear'd to make any oppoſition, hee marched up and down the Countrie, and waſting it at pleaſure, returned with Triumph;* whereupon ſaith a [h] *Poët* of that time,

Jam cubat in terris fera barbaries Aquilonis;
Jam jacet in campo, pelago, pirata, relicto,
Illicitas torváſque minas Analavus *anhelans.*

[g] *Hiſtor. l. 5.*

[h] *Apud Guil. Malmsbur. de geſtis Regum 2. cap. 6.*

Now

Now is the wilde and barb'rous North
brought down;
Now Analave, the Pirat, is o'rethrown,
Who having left the Sea, on Land doth
lie,
And spightful threats breath's out against
the Skie.

This *Analavus* was King of the [i] *Irish*, and of many Islands, who invading the Coasts of *Athelstan* with a Fleet of DCXV ships, at the mouth of the River *Humber*, received a great overthrow, and was put to a most shameful Flight. But King *Edgar* (as saith [k] *Florentius* of *Worcester*) *sailing about the North of* Britain *with a great Navie, arrived at* Chester, *where his eight pettie Kings met him, as hee had given order, who sware fealtie to him, and that they would assist him both by Sea and Land.* Or, as [l] *Huntingdon* saith of the same thing, *they all did homage to him, declaring themselvs readie at his command to serv him by Sea and Land.* Among these pettie Kings there was one *Maccusius*, whom *Hoveden* and *Florentius* call *a King of very many Islands*; and *Florilegus*, *a King of* Man, *and very many Islands*. *William of Malmsburie* call's him an Arch-Pirat, Moreover, the same King *Edgar*, as if hee intended to set forth the splendor, magnificence, and as it were an Epitome of his whole Empire in Sea-affairs and Shipping, *did* (as say *Florentius* and *Hoveden*, during his abode at *Chester*) *enter into a Boat, wherein hee was rowed by those pettie Kings, himself holding the Stern, and steering it about the River* Dee; *and beeing attended by all his Dukes and Peers in such another Vessel, hee sailed from the Palace to the Monasterie of S.* John Baptist, *where an Oration beeing made to him, hee returned in the same pomp unto the Palace.*

i *Roger Hovedenius, Annal. part.* 1. *Ann.* 937. & *Florent. Wigorn. ann.* 938.

k *In anno* 937.

l *Anno Edgari,* 13. *Huntingdon. l.* 5.

In

In the very Entrie whereof hee is reported to have said to his Lords, that then his Successors might boast themselvs Kings of England, *when they should bee thus attended by so many Kings, and enjoy the state and glory of such honors*; or, as *Malmsburie* write's of the same thing, *when they should enjoy so great a Prerogative of honors*: So many Kings as Vassals, to bee readie alwaies to assist with their Forces, whensoëver they should bee required, both by Sea and Land. There is also a notable testimonie in the same *Florentius*, and the Monk of *Malmsburie*, how that this King sailed round about his Sea every year, and secured it with a constant Guard and Forces. *Every Summer*, saith *Malmsburie*, *immediately after* Easter, *bee commanded his ships upon every shore to bee brought into a Bodie, sailing usually with the Eastern Fleet to the West part of the Island, and then sending it back, hee sail'd with the Western Fleet unto the Northern, and thence with the Northern hee returned to the Eastern, beeing indeed very diligent to prevent the Incursions of Pirats; that is, behaving himself in this manfully* (as say *Florentius* also, and *Hoveden*) *for the defence of his Kingdom against Foreiners, and the training up of himself and his people for warlike emploiments.* Thus the Guardianship or maintenance of the Dominion by Sea is evident.

But as concerning the Fleets aforementioned, they each of them consisted of MCC ships, and these, as Writers say expresly, *very stout ones*; so that in the time of his Reign, the *British* Navie consisted of such ships to the number of *Three thousand six hundred Sail*, as [m] *Florentius* and *Hoveden* speak expresly. But others write, that these Fleets amounted to *Four thousand* ships, as [n] *John Bramton* Abbot of *Jorvaux*, others adding to these Three a *Fourth Fleet*, whereby the number is increased to *Four Thousand Eight hundred Sail*; as you may see

[m] *In anno* 975.

[n] *Ms. In Bibliothecâ Cottoniarâ.*

ſee in *Florilegus*. So, as *Florentius* alſo ſaith, *Hee by the help of God governed and ſecured the bounds of his Kingdom with Prudence, Fortitude, Juſtice, and Temperance, as long as hee lived, and having the courage of a fierce Lion, hee kept all the Princes and Lords of the Iſles in aw.* Wee read alſo in *Ordericus Vitalis*, of King *Harold* or *Herald*, that hee ſo *guarded the Sea with a force of ſoldierie and ſhipping, that none of his Enemies could without a ſore conflict, invade the Kingdom.* So that wee cannot otherwiſe conceiv, but that theſe Naval Forces were at that time diſpoſed, and the Sea-Fights undertaken, for the defence and guard of the Sea, as an Appendant of the *Engliſh-Saxon* Dominion in this Iſland. Eſpecially, if wee duly compare theſe things alreadie manifeſt, with thoſe which are added by and by to this particular, touching the ſame age.

The Sea-Dominion of the *Engliſh-Saxons*, and *Danes*, during their Reigns in *Britain*, obſerved in like manner, from ſuch *Tributes* and *Duties* of their *Fiduciarie Clients or Vaſſals, as concerned the maintenance of the Navie.* Alſo, concerning the Tribute or Paiment called *Danegeld*, which was wont to bee levied for the Guard of the Sea.

CHAP. XI.

HEre follow next the *Tributes* and *Duties of Vaſſals*, concerning the maintenance of the Navie or Guard of the Sea; which are evidences alſo of that Sea-Dominion which was in the time of the *English-Saxons*. I call thoſe Tributes, which were wont to bee levied for the re-inforcing of the Navie, and for proviſion of Victuals for the Sea-men. Of which kinde were thoſe that were levied, according to the value of men's eſtates in Land, for the ſetting forth of ſhips in the time of King *Ethelred*. For, at that time whoſoëver poſſeſſed CCCX. *Caſſatos*, or *Hides* of Land, was charged with the building of one ſhip. And they were all rated proportionably, after this manner, who were owners of more or leſs *Hides*, or of part of an *Hide*; as [a] *Marianus Scotus*, *Hoveden*, and *Florentius* do all tell us in the very ſame words. *Ethelred King of* England (ſay they) *gave* ſtrict command *that one Gallie ſhould bee charged upon* CCCX *Caſſati, but a Coat of Armor and an Helmet upon nine, and that ſhips ſhould bee built throughout all* England, *which beeing made readie, hee victualled and manned them with choice ſouldiers, and appointed their Rendezvous at the Port of* Sandwich, *to ſecure the Bounds of his Kingdom from the irruptions of Foreiners*. But [b] *Henrie* of *Huntingdon*, as alſo *Matthew Paris*, and *Florilegus*, ſpeaking of the ſame thing ſay; *The King charged one ſhip upon three hundred and ten Hides of Land through all* England; *alſo a Coat-Armor and Helmet upon eight Hides*. Then *Huntingdon* tell's what an *Hide* doth ſignifie. *But an* Hide *in Engliſh*, ſaith hee, *is ſo much Land as a man can till with one Plow for a year*. Others there are that determine otherwiſe touching the quantitie of an Hide: And moſt certain it is, that it was very various, according to the different Cuſtom of Countries; but the ſame with *Caſſata* and * *Carucata*. Indeed, the *Engliſh-Saxon* Chronicles of the Abbie of [c] *Abingdon*, do likewiſe mention *Hides* here expreſly. In the year MVIII. Her bebead ſe Cing (ſay they) ꝥ man ſceolde ofer

eall

[a] *Ms. anno* 1008. *in Bibliotheca Cottoniana.*

[b] *Hiſtor. minor. Ms. in Bibliotheca Cottoniana.*

* A *Carue of Land*, *i.e.* as much as may bee tilled by one Plow in a year.

[c] *Ms. in Bibliotheca Cottoniana.*

eall anᵹelcẏn ꞅcipu ꝼæꞅtlice ƿyꞃcan ꝥ iꞅ ðonn oꝼ þꞃim hund hidum ⁊ oꝼ Tynum ænne ꞅceᵹð. ⁊ oꝼ VIII. hidum helm ⁊ byꞃnan, That is to ſay, *the King gave command for the building of Ships carefully throughout all* England; *to wit, that one Gallie ſhould bee charged upon* CCCX *Hides of Land; but a Coat-Armor and Helmet upon eight* Hides. And it was uſual, according to the Laws of that Age, that the richer ſort ſhould bee taxed by the number of *Hides*; as wee ſee alſo throughout that *Breviarie of England* or the Book of Rates called [d] **Domes-day**, which was firſt written in the time of King *William.* Huntingdon add's alſo, *that there never had been ſo great a number of Ships in the time of any one in Britain*; which is teſtified in like manner by the *Saxon* Chronicles before-cited. So that, that moſt numerous Navie of King *Edgar* (mentioned in the former chapter) was not to bee compared with this. But yet that moſt learned man and great Light of our Iſland, Mr [e] *Camden*, hath ſo caſt up the number of H*ides* throughout *England*, out of the antient Records of that Age, that they do not exceed 243600. If this had been ſo, then they could have ſet forth no more then 785 Ships by this Tribute, which is a leſſer number then that of King *Edgar* by ſom thouſands: So that ſom other account is to bee made concerning H*ides*, which is not to bee handled in this place.

[d] *Mss. penes Camerarios Scaccarii.*

[e] *In Brit. pag.* 114.

Hereunto belong's that of *Huntingdon,* touching King *Canutus* and his Son *Harald*. *In the daies of Harald* (ſaith hee) *as alſo in the time of his Father, eight Marks were paid by everie Port for* XVI *Ships*. In the like manner, *Hoveden* ſaith, *there was a Tax impoſed which was paid for the maintenance of the Navie,* when King *Canutus* and King *Edmond* made an agreement in an Iſle in the midſt of *Severn*, called *Oleney*. Moreover, *Huntingdon* write's, *that* 11048 *pounds were raised* by *Hardecanute* King of *England*, before hee had reigned two years, *for thirtie two Ships* (that is to say, for the building of two and thirtie Ships.) *Hee gave Command also* (as [f] *Matthew Westminster* saith) *that eight marks should bee paid to everie Rower of his Navie, and ten marks to each Commander, out of all England.* Hee saith again also of the same King; *that hee appointed Officers through all parts of the Kingdom, to collect the Tax imposed, without favouring any, and therewith to provide all things necessarie for his Forces at Sea.* And *Florentius* saith; [g] *Hee gave command for the paying of eight marks to every Rower of his Navie, and twelve* (so wee read it in that Autor) *to everie Commander, out of all* England; *a Tax indeed so grievous, that scarce any man was able to pay it.* But these things spoken of *Canutus*, his son *Harald*, and *Hardecanute* relate perhaps unto that Tribute or Tax called *Danegeld*: which was paid yearly for the maintenance of the Navie and guarding the Territorie or Dominion by Sea.

[f] *Anno* 1040.

[g] *Anno eodem.*

Among the old Laws of *England* it appear's; *that the paiment of* Danegeld *was first imposed becaus of Pirates* (either Robbers or others invading the Sea.) *For, they infesting the Countrie, wasted it as far as they were able. Therefore for the repressing of their insolence, it was determined that an yearly paiment should bee made of* **Danegeld**; *that is to say, twelve pence upon every hide through the whole Land, for the pay of those that should bee imploied to hinder the eruption of Pirates.* So wee read it in som [h] Copies; [i] others render it *Irruption.* But the other reading seem's to signifie, that this Tax was imposed, for the raising and mainteining of Naval Forces, so to guard the Sea, that Pirates or Enemies might not bee able to make any eruption from the Shore on the other side of the Sea.

[h] *Apud Roger. Hoveden, part.*2.*pag.* 344. *in* Edit. *Londin. pag.* 603.*in* Edit. *Francofurt.*

[i] *Apud G. Lambard. de priscis Anglorum Legibus, fol.* 128. *&* G.*Camden. Brit. pa.*102.

Sea. Nor can the word *Eruption* otherwise bee well put in that place. So that even that antient Dignitie of the *Count of the* Saxon *shore* (whereof wee have alreadie spoken) is therefore not obscurely represented by him who commanded as *Admiral* over the Fleets of that Age. This Tribute or Tax had its beginning under King *Ethelred*. For, hee beeing brought into miserable streights by *Swane* King of *Denmark*, beeing forced to buy a Peace of him, hired XLV *Danish* Ships also by Agreement, for the guarding and securing of his Dominion in the Sea, who were to receiv their pay yearly out of this Tribute for their maintenance. For the right understanding whereof, it is to bee observed out of the *English Saxon* Storie, that the Tribute or Tax usually paid at that time to the *Danes*, was of more kindes then one. There was one Tribute or sum of Monie, wherewith the *English-Saxons* were forced somtimes to buy Peace of such as grievously infested the Island. But another was levied to pay the *Danish* Navie, which was hired to guard the Sea and defend the Sea-Coasts. The first kinde of Tribute appear's by that of *Florentius* and *Hoveden*, in the year MVII. *Ethelred King of* England, *by the advice of his Lords, sending Embassadors to the* Danes, *gave them Commission to declare, that hee was willing to defray their Charges and pay them a Tribute upon this condition, that they would desist from rapine, and establish a firm Peace with him. To which demand of his they yielded. And from that time their charge was defraied by all* England, *and a Tribute paid, which amounted to 36000 pounds.* That is, hee effected this onely for the present, *that hee obteined a peace for a time by monie, which hee could not by Arms*, as *Florilegus* saith well. Four years after also, *all the great Lords of* England *of both Orders, met together at* London *before Easter, and there they staid so long till paiment was made of the Tribute promised to the* Danes, *amounting to fourtie eight thousand pounds*; which wee reade of likewise both in *Florentius* and [k] *Hoveden.* But this was paid to the intent, *that all* Danes *which were in the Kingdom, should in every place dwell peaceably by the English, and that both People should have as it were one heart and one soul,* as it is expressed by *Florilegus*. Other passages of the same kinde there are in the storie of that Age, yea and som of an elder date. Yet this first kinde of Tribute was not wont to bee paid yearly, but levied now and then, as occasion required. Notwithstanding it may bee true perhaps which [l] som write, that *Ethelred* in the aforesaid agreement of the year MVII *yielded to pay every year a Tribute of Thirtie six Thousand pounds to the* Danes , *for a longer continuation of the peace.* Wee read here that hee yielded or granted, but no where likewise that hee paid it. But as for the second kinde of Tribute, which was to bee paid (as wee have told you) for hire of the *Danish* Navie, it was a yearly Tribute, and levied at the same time, at least in the same year, (to wit, of our Lord MXII.) wherein these fourtie eight thousand pounds were paid to procure a peace. Nor was it limited by any set-summe of monie, but so much as would serv for victualling, and clothing the Forces at Sea. *Florentius* and *Hoveden* in the aforesaid year say; *After these things, upon paiment of the Tribute,* (meaning that of fourtie eight thousand pounds) *and a confirmation of the peace by Oaths, the* Danish *Navie which was before in a Bodie, was disposed and dispersed abroad afar off. But* XLV *ships remained with the King, and sware fidelitie to him, and promised to bee readie to defend* England *against Foreiners, upon condition that hee would provide them Victuals and Clothing.* This is related likewise in the *English-Saxon* Chronicles of the Abbie of [m] *Abingdon*; Ða ꝥ gafol gælest wæs ⁊ frið aþas asworene wæron

þa

[k] *Anno* 1012

[l] *Autor Chronici Melrosensis, Ms. in Bibliotheca Cottoniana.*

[m] *In Bibliotheca Cottoniana. Anno* 1012.

þa ꞇo ꝼeꞃde ſe heꞃe ƿide ſƿa he æꞃ ȝeȝadeꞃode ƿæſ. Ða buȝon ꞇo þam cynȝe oꝼ þam heꞃe ꝼiꝼ ⁊ ꝼeoƿeꞃꞇiȝ ſcypa. ⁊ him beheꞇon ꝥ hi ƿoldon þyſne eaꞃd healdan ⁊ he hi ꝼedan ſceolde ⁊ ſcꞃydon; That is, *the Tribute beeing paid, and Oaths of Amitie taken, the Armie* (or Navie) *which was before in a Bodie, was disperſed abroad. But fourtie five ſhips of that Navie remained with the King, and promiſed upon Oath to bee readie for the defence of this Land, upon condition the King did finde them Victuals and Cloathing.* *Swane* was at that time King of *Denmark,* with whom *Ethelred* made this agreement. But both the kindes of paiment aforementioned, were called Daneȝeld, *Danegeld,* or *Danageld,* that is to ſay, *Daniſh Tribute.* The firſt kinde is expreſsly intimated by this name in [n] *Joannes Sarisburienſis*; where hee ſaith, *Swane waſted and ſpoiled the Iſland of* Britain, *the greateſt part whereof hee had in his poſſeſsion, and afflicted the Members of Chriſt with many perſecutions, by an impoſition of Tribute, which in the Engliſh Tongue they call* Danageld. But the ſecond kinde which was paid for the maintenance of the Forces by Sea was called likewiſe by the ſame name, both becauſ it was occaſioned by the agreement with the *Danes,* as alſo becauſ it was wont to bee paid to the *Daniſh Fleet,* that was hired to guard the Territorie by Sea. For which cauſ alſo it reteined the ſame name, not onely under theſe *Daniſh* Kings, *Canutus, Harold* the firſt, and *Hardecanutus*, but alſo under the *Engliſh-Saxon* or *Engliſh.* And that this which wee have ſpoken was the Original hereof, is affirm'd alſo by *Ingulphus* the Abbot of *Crowland*, a witneſs beyond all exception, who lived at that time. Hee ſpeaking of the affairs of *Edward* the Confeſſor, ſaith, [o] *In the year* MLI. (which was the tenth of King *Edward*) *in regard the Earth did not bring forth its Fruits in ſuch plentie as it was*

wont

[n] *In Polycratico, ſeu de Nugis Curialium, lib.* 8. *cap.* 21.

[o] *Edit. Londin. pag.* 510. *Francofurt.* 897.

wont, but devoured very many people by famine, insomuch that many Thousands of men died through the scarcitie of Corn, and want of Bread; therefore the most pious King Edward, *beeing moved with compassion towards the people, released that most grievous Tribute called* **Danigeld**, *to all* England *for ever. It is reported by som, that this most Religious King beeing brought by his Officers into the* Exchequer, *to see the* **Danigeld** *that was collected, and to take a view of so vast an heap of treasure, stood amazed at the first sight, protesting that hee beheld the* Divel *dancing upon the heap of monie, & extremely rejoycing; whereupon hee immediately commanded to restore it to the former Owners, and would not keep one jot of so cruel an exaction; but remitted it for ever, to wit, in the thirtie eighth year after* Swane *King of* Denmark *commanded it to bee paid every year to his Navie, in the time of his Father Ethelred.* By dis-counting 38 years from the year 1051. that year 1012. is sufficiently manifest, wherein the beginning of this *Danegeld* is placed, according to that which hath been alreadie spoken. Nor is it any prejudice at all, that there seem's perhaps to bee one year over and above. For, such as are verst in the Chronicles of the Monks, know well enough, that differences of that kinde are very frequent among them, especially by reason of their careless confounding of the years of our Lord, and of the Kings, whose beginnings do variously differ, as every man know's. Nor is it probable, that they were sufficiently agreed touching the Tribute and Taxes before the next, or one thousand and thirteenth year. For, concerning that year, *Florentius, Hoveden,* and others speak expresly thus; *In the mean time the Tyrant* Swane *gave command to make readie Provisions in abundance for his Navie, and for paiment of an almost intolerable Tribute. In like manner* Turkillus *sent out his commands every where; that it should bee paid to his Fleet,*

which

which lay at **Grenewich.** That Fleet of XLV. ships rode now and then in the Thames neer *Grenewich*, and then first received their promised pay. That is, in that very year, which beeing discounted is the Thirtie eight year, as *Ingulphus* would have it: wherefore its beginning was not ill placed in that year. Without all question, that *Ingulphus* was a Courtier in the time of King *William* the first, or a man of no mean account, at the time wherein that was don which hee relate's: so that especial credit is to bee given him in this particular. Whereas also hee saith, that King *Edward* remitted *Danegeld* for ever, the same thing is affirmed also by *Roger Hoveden*, and *Matthew the Monk of Westminster*; who saith, *In the year of Grace* MLI. *King* Edward *absolved the people of* England *from that most grievous Tribute of 38 thousand pounds, which was usually paid to the* Danish *Auxiliaries, during his Father's Reign.* Whereof wee read also in [p] *Matthew Paris*. But *Hoveden* saith, *K. Edward absolved the people of* England *from that grievous Tribute, in the thirtie eight year after that his Father K.* Ethelred *had commanded it to bee paid to the* Danish *Souldiers.* Others there are also that write to the same purpose. Som of the [q] *English-Saxon* Chronicles place the same thing in the following year, and so affirm, that there intervened 39 years from the beginning of this Tribute (which also they call Heregyld or *Heregild*, that is, a *Militarie* or *Naval Tribute*) to that abolishment of it by King *Edward*; Neverthelesse, as to what concern's its beginning, they agree with *Ingulphus* and *Hoveden*, to wit, in the year MLII those Chronicles render it thus; Alede Eadpard cyng ꝥ Heregyld ꝥ Æþelred cyng ær astealde. ꝥ pæs on þam nigon ⁊ þrittigoþan geare þæs þe he heht on gannon hæfde. That is to say, K. Edward *abolished that Militarie Tribute, or* Heregild,

[p] *Hist. minor. Ms. in Bibliothecâ Cottonianâ.*

[q] *Ms. in Bibliothecâ Cottonianâ. Compacti cum Guil. Gisburnensis Annalibus.*

gild, *which had been formerly imposed by K.* Ethelred , *to wit, in the nine and thirtieth year after it began.* But yet in the Autor of that [x] *Dialogue concerning the Exchequer*, written in the time of K. *Henrie* the second, (commonly supposed to have been *Gervasius Tilburiensis*) wee read it was paid yearly even till the time of K. *William* the first or the *Norman* Conquest; that is to say, for fourteen years compleat, immediately after that abolishment. For, so long K. *Edward* reigned, whom that *William* succeeded. The Autor's words are these; *The Pirats of the adjacent Islands, having made an irruption, and spoiling the Sea-Coasts, carried away Gold, Silver, and all things of any value. But assoon as the King and his Subjects set forth any preparations of Warr, for the defence of their Nation, they presently fled away by Sea. But the chief among them, and ever more inclined to mischief, was that warlike and populous Nation of the* Danes, *who besides their ordinarie desire of prey; pressed on the more furiously, becaus they laid claim to somwhat of antient Right in the Government of the Kingdom, as the* British *Historie relate's more at large. Therefore for the repelling of them, it was ordeined by the Kings of* England, *that two shillings silver upon everie Hide of Land should by a kinde of Custom for ever bee paid for the maintenance of valiant men, who by scouting about continually, and guarding the Sea-Coasts, might repress the Invasion of Enemies. And in regard this Revenue was appointed chiefly becaus of the* Danes, *therefore it was called* Danegeld. *And thereupon it was paid by yearly Custom* (as hath been said) *under the* English *Kings, until the time of* K. William *the first, who was of the* Norman *Stock and Nation.* So that Autor, who would have this Tribute to derive its name from the *Danes*, as if the Navie had been mainteined thereby chiefly to drive them from the Coasts of *England.* But questionless, the first reason of the name, is to bee received, as it hath

[x] *Ms. Penès Camerarios Scaccarii, c. 27. Idem habetur Dialogus etiam in Codice Rubro, penes Rememoratorem Regis.*

hath been alleged out of the passages above mentioned; though afterwards there was a Subsidie raised and Tribute paid for the like Fleet, consisting of such as were not *Danes*, or of *English*, for the repelling of the *Danes* themselvs, which was not improperly called by the same name. Touching the paiment hereof after the *Norman* Conquest, I shall add more [s] by and by. But as concerning what hee saith here, that two shillings silver upon everie *Hide* were wont to bee paid yearly for the raising of this Tribute, the same is affirmed also by other antient Autors, as [t] *Roger* Hoveden, and [u] *Matthew Paris*: So that these men make the paiment double to that which is before alleged out of the Laws of the *English-Saxons*. The yearly paiment of this Tribute is valued also by *Matthew* of *Westminster*, & *Matthew Paris*, at thirtie eight thousand pounds, as appear's by the particulars alreadie cited: which truly was written by them with very little discretion. Nor have they dealt any better, who set down that paiment at the rate of thirtie thousand pounds, as the Autor of the Chronicle called [x] *Chronicum Melrosense*. For, at what rate soever that Tribute was paid to the King, according to the alteration of times, it appear's for certain, that the Stipends usually allowed to the *Danish* Fleet were so uncertain, that they were set somtimes higher, somtimes lower (as wee must suppose it could not otherwise happen) according to the number of Ships and Forces that were necessarie for the Guard of the Sea. Of which also there are examples among Historians. *Florentius* in the year MXIV. saith, K. Ethelred *gave command, that the Tribute amounting to thirtie thousand pounds should bee levied for the Fleet which lay at* **Grenewich**; So also *Hoveden*. But the [y] *English-Saxon* Chronicles of the Abbie of *Abingdon* say of the same year; Se cyng

[s] *Cap.* 15.

[t] *Edit. Londin. pag.* 276. *Edit. Francofurt. pag.* 482.

[u] *Hist. minore Ms. in* Bibliothecâ Cottonianâ; *in Stephani R. initiis.*

[x] *Ms. ibid.*

[y] *Ms. in* Bibliothecâ Cottonianâ.

het ȝyldan þam here ðe on ȝrenaƿic læiȝ XXI. þusend pund. *The King commanded that* 21000[l] *should bee paid to his Armie*; (For so that Fleet is called every where in English Saxon) *which rode at* Grenewich. Here (you see) is no small difference in the number of pounds. But howsoëver, if it bee to bee conceived of the yearly Tax or Tribute, then it was far less this year then it is reckoned by those Monks, who speak of thirtie eight thousand pounds. Four years after, in the Reign of King *Canutus*, (who was a *Dane*) a far greater summe of Monie was raised for the maintenance of this Fleet. That *Florentius*, whom wee have often cited, saith; *In this year*, (that is, MXVIII. *Seventie two thousand pounds out of all* England, *and one thousand and fiftie pounds out of* London, *were paid to the* Danish *Fleet*; *and there remained fourtie ships with* K. Canutus. *But the rest were returned to* Denmark. Of which year *Hoveden* speak's thus; *Out of all* England *seventie two, and out of* London 410 *pounds were paid to the* Danish *Armie or Fleet. And there remained,&c.* They differ about the Summe, not the Thing, wherein they agree with the *English-Saxon* Chronicles before-mentioned. Yet these altogether speak contrarie to that accompt of the certain summes, as it is set down by the aforesaid Monks. But [z] *Matthew Paris* and *Matthew Westminster* say of the same Time, *that* Cnute *sent home the* Danish *Fleet*, *and Stipendarie Souldiers*, (except fourtie ships, as appear's by what hath been said alreadie) *having paid them out of all* England *eightie two thousand pounds in silver*. Also, in the second year of King *Hardecnute*, *a Tax was levied for the* Danish *Armie or Fleet*, *amounting to* 21000 *pounds*, *and* 89 *pounds*, as *Huntingdon* tell's us. All which particulars do, I suppose, sufficiently demonstrate, that the *Danish* Tribute here mentioned was not fixed to any certain

[z] *Histor. Minor. Ms. in* Bibliothecâ Cottonianâ.

certain summe of yearly paiment; and also that an huge summe of monie was wont to bee paid yearly at that time to the Kings of *England*, for the Guard of the Sea, (for, to what purpose els was that Fleet alwaies kept, and so great Taxes levied every year for the maintenance thereof?) But in the Reign of King *Henrie* the second, the name of *Danegeld* grew out of use, Tributes or Taxes beeing usually paid still, notwithstanding by other names that are very well known, for the Guarding of the Sea; as wee shall shew by and by. But they are extremely mistaken, even they who agree either with *John*[a] *Bramton* the Abbot of *Jorvaux*, or som other Autor out of whom hee wrote it, or any others of that kinde, in deriving the Original of that yearly *Danegeld*, so often mentioned every where, from the former kinde of Tribute, which was paid to the *Danes*, for the procuring of a peace; and they also who [b] would have the Warr to have been undertaken by the *Danes* and *Saxons* against the *Britains*, becaus they denied them a freedom of Navigation, and that the end thereof was, that this Tribute was upon that accompt imposed upon the Nation when it was subdued.

Now, as concerning the *Duties of Fiduciarie Clients or Vassals*, wont to bee paid in that Age for Naval Expeditions and the Guard of the Sea, wee have set them down among those particulars which were spoken of King *Edgar* in the former Chapter. The Pettie Kings or Lords of the neighboring Isles were bound to him by Oath to bee readie at his command to serv him by Sea and Land. And in that famous Breviarie or Register of *England* called [c] **Domesday**, (conteining very many Customs in use among the *English-Saxons*, besides the assessment of the Provinces, and written in the

a *Ms. in* Bibliothecâ Cottonianâ, *anno* 13. *Ethelredi Regis*, seu *Christi* 991. *pa.* 57.

b *Apud Jacob. Thuanum. Historiar. li.* 95.

c *Ms.* penes Camerarios Scaccarii.

the time of *William* the first) wee read thus; *It is a Custom at* Warwick, *if the King went by Sea against his Enemies, to send him either* IV. *Batsueins* (Sea-souldiers or Rowers) *or els* IV. *pounds in monie.* And at Excester, *when hee made any Expedition by Land or by Sea, this Citie served after the rate of* V. *Hides of Land.* **Barnestaple, Lydeford,** and **Totenais** *served as far as that Citie.* That is, these three Towns paid as much as *Excester* alone. Moreover, *Glocester* yielded XXXVI. *Dicres of Iron and* C. *iron Rods fitted to make nails for the King's ships. Leicester* also, *if the King went against his Enemies by Sea, sent him four horses from that Town to* London, *to carrie Arms or other necessaries.* Concerning **Lewes** also, a chief Town in *Sussex*; *there* K. Edward (the Confessor) *had* CXXVII. *Burgers at his service. Their Custom was, if the King went not himself in person, but sent others to guard the Sea, then they collected* XX. *Shillings of every man, of what Countrie soëver hee were, and provided men who were to look to the Arms on shipboard.* Here very express mention is made of the defence or Guardianship of the Sea it self. And in *Colchester*, an eminent Town of *Essex*, wee finde it was the Custom of that Age, *to pay out of every hous six pence a year, that was able to pay it, for maintenance of the King's souldiers upon an Expedition by Land or Sea, &c. And this ought to bee the rate, if the King shall entertain souldiers, or make any Expedition.* All these particulars are in that Register: And others there are in it of the same kinde. But an Expedition by Sea signified in these testimonies, not a Warr to bee undertaken for subduing the Dominions of their neighbors lands, but most clearly a preparation and enterprise of Warr, for the guarding, scouring, and keeping the Sea, as a part of the Empire of *Britain*: As it sufficiently appear's out of the Histories of that time. For, wee do not reade, that our *English-Saxons* or *Danes* had any other quarrel at that time, with any of their Neighbors whatsoëver, unless it concerned either the *British* islands or the Sea belonging thereunto. Which also is especially to bee consider'd.

The Testimonies of Edgar *and* Canutus, *Kings of* England, *with others expressly declaring the* Dominion *which they and their predecessors had over* the Sea; *together with an observation touching the Nations which in that age were seated upon the* opposite Shore.

CHAP. XII.

THat wee may at length set an end to that fourfold distribution which wee made of the Testimonies of that Age, let us in the last place add the express determinations of King *Edgar* and *Canutus* concerning their own Dominion over the Sea. As for *Edgar*, the title which hee commonly used, ran thus; [a] *I* Edgar *Soveraign Lord of all* Albion, *and of the Maritim or Insular Kings inhabiting round about.* So hee make's the bodie of the *British* Empire to comprehend all the Maritim Kingdoms that lay about, that is to say, all that are Situate in the *British* Sea. And this hee more plainly declare's in the Charter or Deed by which hee setled revenues on the Cathedral Church of *Worcester*, in the year DCCCCLXIV; if so bee the copie were rightly rendred by those who many years since printed so much of it as concern's this title. The words are these, [b] *Altitonantis Dei largifluâ clementia qui est Rex Regum, Ego Edgarus*

[a] *Apud Guil. Malmsbur. de gest. Regum. lib.* 2. *cap.* 8.

[b] Inspeximus *in Rot. Pat.* 1. Ed. 4. *part.* 6. Sic habetur apud *Joannem Dee in Monarch. Britannic. pag.* 58. & 60. *And in* Purchas *his Pilgrimage, part.* 3. *lib.* 3. *cap.* 19. *pag.* 619.

Edgarus Anglorum Basileus omniúmque Regum insularum, Oceanique Britanniani circumjacentis (so *John* Dee, a man very well seen in most parts of Learning, did read it a good while since, save onely that in stead of (*Britanniam*) hee hath (*Britanniani*) while [c] others reade, *Insularum Oceani quæ Britanniam circumjacent*) *cunctarúmque nationum quæ infra eam includuntur Imperator & Dominus; gratias ago ipsi Deo omnipotenti Regi meo qui meum imperium sic ampliavit & exaltavit super regnum patrum meorum; qui licèt Monarchiam totius Angliæ adepti sint à tempore Athelstani* (*qui primus regnum Anglorum & omnes nationes quæ Britanniam incolunt, sibi armis subegit*) *nullus tamen illorum ultra ejus fines imperium suum dilatare aggressus est. Mihi autem concessit propitia divinitas cum Anglorum imperio omnia regna Insularum Oceani cum suis ferocissimis regibus usque Norwegiam, maximámque partem Hiberniæ cum suâ nobilissimâ civitate Dubliniа, Anglorum regno subjugare. Quos etiam omnes meis imperiis colla subdere* (*Dei favente gratiâ*) *coëgi.*—By the abundant goodness of Almightie God who is the King of Kings, I Edgar King of England, and of all the Kings of the Islands, and of the Ocean lying round about Britain, and of all the Nations that are included within the circuit thereof, Supreme Lord and Governor, Do render thanks to the same Almightie God my King who hath enlarged my Empire thus, and exalted it above the Royal Estate of my Progenitors, who although they arrived to the Monarchie of all England, ever since the time of Athelstane (who was the first that by force of Arms subdued the English, and all the Nations that inhabite Britain) yet none of them ever attempted to promote their Empire beyond the bounds thereof. But the divine goodness hath favored mee

[c] *Edward* Coke, *in his Preface* ad Commentariorum Juris, lib.4. And *James Usher* Bishop of *Armagh, in Epistol.* Hibernicarum Sylloge, pag.121. *ubi vide item, p.*163.

mee so far as beside the English Empire, to enable mee to subdue all the Kingdoms of the Ilands in the Ocean with their most stout and mightie Kings, even as far as Norway, and the greatest part of Irland, together with their most famous Citie of Dublin. All which (by God's grace and assistance) I have subdued and made their necks to stoop under the yoke of my command. Whereas hee saith, that none of his Progenitors had attempted to enlarge their Empire beyond the bounds of *Britain*, it must bee so understood, that it bee taken for the Northern and Western bounds of the *British* Empire, as sufficiently appear's by the mention of *Irland* and *Norway*. So that then more Islands than the name of *Britain* did comprehend, or than the Isles of that Sea, together with the Sea it self, were brought under his Dominion.

But King *Canutus* (or *Cnute*) hath left a testimonie also, whereby hee most expresly asserts the Sea to bee a part of his Dominion. Hee placing himself on a seat by the Sea side as it flowed upon *Southampton* Shore, having a minde to demonstrate to his flatterers, that Kings themselves are but men, is reported to have made trial of the obedience of the Sea (it beeing flood) after this manner, Thou, O Sea, art under my dominion, as the Land also upon which I sit is mine. And there never was any that disobeied my Command without punishment. Therefore I command thee not to ascend up upon my Land, nor do thou presume to wet the feet or garments of thy Soveraign. *But the Tide* (saith *Huntington*, and *Florilegus* who relate this storie) *swelling as at other times, did very unmannerly wet not onely the feet, but legs of his Majestie.* Whereupon the King leaping up

Nn proclaimed

proclaimed with his own mouth none to bee worthy the name of King, but him alone who command's both the Sea and land, and they obey. And from that time hee refused to wear his Crown of Gold; consecrating it to a Crucifix. In the mean time, hee here openly professed himself to bee the Soveraign of the Sea as well as of the land. Hereunto may bee added som testimonies of other Writers, which although they are of a later date than the Kingdom of the *English-Saxons*, yet they are transmitted to posteritie by the hands of such as were perfectly acquainted with the English Historie, and by the Tradition of their Ancestors well informed of the most authentick Opinions and Resolvs concerning the English Dominion over the Sea. *Geoffrie Chaucer* (who was not onely the most famous Poët of his time, but, as Learning went in those daies, a very well accomplisht Scholar) in one of his *Canterburie* Tales, bring's in his *Man of Law* telling a storie which hee would have relate to the time of *Alla* King of *Northumberland*, who reigned thirtie years; and his Reign began in the year of our Lord DLIX. In this Tale there is brought in a Ladie, called *Constantia*, the Daughter of I know not what Roman Emperor, married to the King of *Syria*; driven shee was by weather to a place which lay under the command of a Fortress upon the Shore of *Northumberland*, and there the Ship ran aground; shee was a Christian, banished for her Religion, and there taken Prisoner by the Commander of that Fortress. In this Relation of the sad adventures of *Constantia*, hee saith (what indeed is true) that Christian Religion was not received into any part of that Territorie, but that *Pagans* had over-run and did hold those Northern Countries under their Dominion as well by Sea as Land. His words to this purpose are these,

In

In all that lond durſten non Chriſten rout;
All Chriſten folk been fled from the Countre
Through Paynims that conquer'd all about
The plagues of Northumberland by land & See.

Hee ſaid diſcreetly, that the neighboring Sea fell to the Conquerers of this Iſle as well as the Land, knowing what was the reſolution and generally received opinion of his Anceſtors concerning that matter Hee lived two hundred and thirtie years ago in the time of *Richard* the Second. Nor is it any prejudice to this autoritie, that the other things there related are fabulous; For wee know that out of the Fables of *Heliodorus*, *Achilles*, *Tatius*, *Theodorus Prodromus*, *Euſtathius*, and ſuch others, whether of an amorous or any other ſtrain, ſomtimes many uſeful obſervations may bee gathered concerning the cuſtoms, manners, and received opinions, as well of the men among whom they are feigned to bee acted, as of the times to which they are related. *John Harding* alſo, who, in the time of *Edward* the Fourth, wrote an Hiſtorie of the affairs of *England* in verſ, when hee reckons up thoſe Princes that ſware fealtie to King *Canutus* for the Lands which they held of him, [d] hee adds

[d] *Chap.* 117.

So did the Kings of Wales of high parage,
And all the North-West Ocean
For their kingdoms and for their lands than;

That is to ſay, *the ſame was don at that time by the greateſt Kings of* Wales, *and of all the North-weſtern Sea, for their reſpective Kingdoms and Territories.* Thus *Canutus* was King of the Kings of that Sea, which hee himſelf alſo ſufficiently declares, when hee expreſly affirms in what was before related, that the Sea it ſelf was under his

Dominion. And ſo much for teſtimonies, to prove that the *British* Sea hath been poſſeſſed not onely by the *Britains*, after they had caſt off the *Roman* yoke, but alſo by the *English-Saxon*, and *Danish* Kings.

Moreover, it ſeem's they did uſe to take a kinde of courſ for the ſtrengthning and preſervation of their Dominion, both by Sea and Land, as the antient *Germans* (of whom both *Danes* and *Saxons* are a part) were wont to do for the defence of their midland Cities. *Among them* (ſaith [a] *Cæſar*) *it was the highest glory to make very large depopulations, and lay all the Countrie round about them waste; measuring their honor by their distance from any neighbor, and accounting it the onely token of valor when none durst plant themſelvs within their reach; and besides, they thought by this means to render themſelvs more secure by removing the fear of any sudden incursion.* So it hath been the manner of thoſe that at any time have made themſelvs Maſters of the Kingdom of *Britain*, to extend their Dominion in the circumambient Sea to the largeſt Circuit, ſcouring the Seas about, and keeping other Nations at a diſtance, as it were from the Wall or Precinct of the Iſland. Nor were thoſe *German* Cities more Maſters of that waſte part of the Countrie that lay about them, then the King's of *Britain* were over the Sea of the ſame name. But as wee obſerved before of the *Scots* and *Picts*, in the time of the *Romans*, ſo here alſo it is to bee noted of the *Norwegians* or *Normans*, (for many times they are to bee taken for one and the ſame people) and other Northern Nations, That thoſe *British* Iſles which are ſituated in the Weſt and Northern Sea, were ſomtimes ſo poſſeſſed by the *Scots* and *Picts*, as alſo by the *Norwegians*, and ſuch others as infeſted the Northern Sea, and invaded the Iſles lying between them and *Britain*, that it is not to bee doubt-

[a] *De Bello Gallico, l.* 6.

doubted, but they also according to the various alteration of their Dominions by Land, succeeded one another for that interval of time, in the possession of a proportionable part of the Sea also, as an Appendant to every one of the shores of *Britain* The *Scots* (saith an [f] unknown Autor, speaking of the year DCCCXLVI) *for many years became Tributaries to the* Normans, *who without any resistance entred and setled themselvs in the Isles lying round about.* And as touching the Naval affairs of the *Normans* in our Sea, there are many passages to bee seen in *Regino* the Abbat, *Aimoinus* and other Writers of that Age. But in the mean time it is sufficiently manifest, that as by reason of the tumultuarie & unsetled posture of affairs in those daies, the Dominion of the Island it self was very often tossed to and fro; so also the Dominion of the Sea was in like manner attempted, disturbed, invaded, recovered, and defended, as that which did inseparably follow the Dominion and Soveraigntie of the Island. Wee are not ignorant that in the *French* Histories there are now and then som passages that speak of their Naval power in this Age, which are collected by [g] *Popelinerius.* But there is nothing to bee gathered from them that may set forth the least sign or shadow of a Soveraigntie or Dominion over the Sea. Very few indeed are to bee found, and such as either concern onely the defending the mouths of their Rivers against the *Normans* and *Danes* then roving up and down our Sea, or the subduing of the *Friezlanders*, and som of the Neighbor-Nations. Whereunto also som other passages relate, which wee shall mention by and by, when wee com to speak of the Admirals of *France*.

[f] *In Gestis Normannorum, pag.* 2. Vide *Aimoinum, de Gestis Francorum, lib.* 4. *ca.* 90. & 100. de Normannis.

[g] L'Amiral de France, chap. 6. & 7.

Several Testimonies concerning the Sea-Dominion of the Kings of England, since the Norman Conquest, *set forth in* General Heads.

Chap. XIII.

FOllowing the Order and Method of our Enquirie, in the next place wee treat of the Sea-Dominion of the *Britains*, since the coming of the *Normans* into *England*. And in the first place our Discours shall bee of the Dominion of the *English* Sea, or that which flow's between *England* and the opposite shores or Havens of the Neighbor-Nations. Now whereas it is confessed on all hands, that all Dominion is chiefly founded upon just possession or occupation, and its continuance, and that possession is not supposed to bee had, by the act either of the minde or bodie singly and apart (as [a] *Paulus* long since hath well determined) but is most firmly gotten and retained by the joint concurrence of minde and bodie; whereupon it is distinguished into [b] *Civil*, that is, where there is a right or title by Law, and *Natural* or *Corporal*, and it is requisite that this Dominion receiv a signal confirmation by a long continued assent, a free and publick confession or acknowledgment of such neighbors whom it most concern's: First then, as concerning the *Corporal* or *Natural* possession of this Sea, as well as that which is *Civil* or by *Law*, and is retained by the act of the minde, wee shall give you very ample Testimonies since the time of the coming in of the *Normans*. And in

[a] *L.3.F.tit. de Acquir.vel amitt. possessione.*

[b] *Hugo Donellus, de Jure Civili, l.5. Cujacius, observat.l.9.ca.* 37. *l.10. C. tit. de acquir. possess.& retinendâ.*

in the next place, wee will ſhew how this Dominion of the Kings of *England* hath been acknowledged by thoſe Foreign or Neighbor-Nations, whom it moſt concern's. But foraſmuch as what wee ſhall thus ſpeak of the *Engliſh* Sea in general, will chiefly relate to the *Southern* and *Eaſtern*, or that which hath the *Engliſh* ſhore on one ſide, and *France* and *Germanie* on the other, wee will therefore diſcourſ ſeverally of that which lie's to the Weſt of *England*, and alſo of the *Scotiſh* Sea, or that which lie's more *Northerly*.

As concerning the poſſeſsion of the *Engliſh* Sea, both *Corporal* and *Mental*, or *Civil*, continued for that ſpace of time which wee now ſpeak of, with the like Dominion ariſing and retained thereupon, there are divers notable and very clear teſtimonies thereof, which for Methods ſake wee divide into eight heads; whereof

I. The *Cuſtodie*, *Government*, or *Admiraltie* of the Engliſh Sea, as a *Territorie* or *Province* belonging to the King.

II. *The Dominion of thoſe Iſlands* that lie before the *French* ſhore.

III. The *Leav of paſſage* through this Sea *granted* to *Foreiners upon requeſt*.

IV. The *Libertie of Fiſhing* therein allowed upon courteſie to Foreiners and Neighbors, and the *Protection* given to Fiſher-men.

V. Preſcribing of *Laws* and *Limits* to *Foreiners*, who beeing in Hoſtilitie one with another, but both in amitie with the *Engliſh*, made Prize of each other in this Sea.

VI. The *Records* whereby this Dominion is expreſsly aſſerted by the By, as a moſt undoubtdoubted right; and that not onely by the King, but by the Parlaments of *England*, when they debated of other matters.

VII. *The Commentaries of the Law of the Land, and common customs of the Nation*, which do either assert or at least allow such a Dominion.

VIII. Som antient *Testimonies of inferior note.*

All the testimonies almost that are comprehended in this Division, are indeed domestick; but so publick, and of so approved credit, that hardly any thing can bee imagined, which might give a clearer proof of possession whether *Civil*, as they call it, consisting in the act and intention of the minde, or *Natural*, which require's the presence of the Bodie. As it will appear to any man that pleas to make enquirie. Especially if hee add hereunto the judgment or acknowledgment of such Forein Nations whom it chiefly concerned, whereof wee shall treat also by and by. But of these things severally, and in order.

That

That the Kings of England, *since the coming in of the Normans, have perpetually enjoied the Dominion of the Sea flowing about them, is in the first place proved from the* Guard *or* Government *thereof, as of a* Province *or* Territorie; *that is to say, from the very Law of the* English Admiraltie.

CHAP. XIV.

AS concerning the Guard or Government of this Sea, there are three things therein that deserv special consideration. 1. *The bare mention and nature of the Guard of the Sea,* and of the *Guardians or Admirals* thereof, in publick Records and Histories. 2. The *Tributes and Customs* imposed, demanded or accustomed to bee paid *for, and in consideration of the said custodie.* And lastly, *the tenor and varietie of Commissions* belonging to this *Guard,* and *English Admiraltie,* or Government by Sea. Since the coming in of the *Normans,* there is frequent mention of a Guard or Government instituted for the defence and guarding of the Sea. Here call to minde those observations touching this kinde of Guard, which have been alreadie gathered out of that Record or Breviarie of *England* called **Doomesday.** And King *Henrie* the first, saith *Florentius* of *Worcester, gave order to his* Butsecarli *to guard the Sea, and take care that no person from the parts of* Normandie, *approach the* English *Coasts.* The same saith *Roger Hoveden,* in the very same words almost, save onely that the printed Copies err in putting *Buzsecarlis* for *Butsecarlis*. These *Butsecarli*, or **Butescarles**, in the old English Language, are Officers belonging to the Navie, or Sea-souldiers, as *Hutesecarli*, were Domestick Servants or Officers in Court. And that *to guard the Sea* here signified to secure the Sea it self, not to defend the Sea-Coasts (as somtimes, though seldom it did) with Land-forces, plainly appear's out of *Henrie* of *Huntingdon*, in whom it is clear, that the persons who thus guarded the Sea were emploied by the King, to make Warr by Sea against *Robert* Duke of *Normandie*, who was then preparing an Expedition against *England*. Now those publick Records are lost, wherein the Roial Commissions for the delegation of this Command or Government were wont to bee registred all that space of time betwixt the coming in of the *Normans*, and the Reign of K. *John*. But from thence through all the succeeding ages unto this present time, it is as clear as day, that the Kings of *England* have been wont to constitute Governors or Commanders, who had the charge of guarding the English Sea, and were the Guardians or Governors thereof, in the same manner as if it had been som Province upon Land. First of all there were [a] intrusted with the Government of the Sea, or the *Maritimæ* and *Marinæ*, the *Maritime* and *Marine* part of the Empire (understanding by those words not onely som Countrie lying upon the Sea-Coasts, but comprehending the *British* Sea it self, though I confess it was not alwaies so) such as were to guard and keep it, under the title (somtimes) of *Custodes Navium*, Guardians of the ships, but more frequently *Custodes Maritimæ*, or *Marinæ*, in the sens aforesaid. And in the time of *Henrie* the third, *Thomas de* **Moleton** is styled [b] *Captain and Guardian of the Sea*, and hath autoritie given him

[a] *Rot.Pat.* 6. *Joannis R. Membr*.8.vide *Rot.Pat.* 8 *Hen*. 3. *part*.1. *M*.3. & 4.*Claus*. 9. *Hen*.3. *Membr*.15. *Pat*. 9 *Hen*. 3. *part*.2. *M*. 9.

[b] *Rot. Pat.* 48 *Hen*. 3. *part*.1.*memb*. 3. & *Rot. Claus*. 48 *Hen*.3.*Membran*.3.

him *to guard the Sea and the Maritim parts* of the Eastern Shore. In the same King's Reign also, the Inhabitants of the Cinque-Ports are said *to guard the* [c] *Coast of* England, *and the Sea.* So *Hugh de* **Crequeur** was *Warden of the* [d] *Cinque-ports and of the Sea in those parts.* Afterward the title of Guardians or Wardens very often changed into that of Admirals. *Edward* the First, saith *Thomas* of [e] *Walsingham, for the keeping of the Sea divided his Shipping into three Fleets, setting over them three Admirals, namely over the Ships at* Yarmouth *and the road thereabout* John de **Botetort**; *over those at* Portsmouth, *William de* **Leyburn**; *and over the Western and Irish Ships, a certain Irish Knight.* Moreover also, that *John de* **Butetort** is in the [f] Records of that time styled *custos Maritimæ*; as were others also. After this, in the Reign of *Edward* the Second, *three Admirals of the three several Coasts of England* (saith [g] *Walsingham*) *had the guarding of the Sea, namely, Sir* John **Sturbin**, *Sir* Nicolas **Kyriel**, *Sir* John **Felton**. Wee finde moreover in our [h] publike Records, that the principal end of calling a Parlament in the fourteenth year of *Edward* the Third was, *De Treter sur la gard de la pees de la terre, & de la Marche d'Escoce, & de la Meer,* i. e. That consultation might bee had concerning keeping the peace of the Land, also of the Borders of *Scotland*, and of the *Sea.* The same regard they had to the defence of the Sea, as of the Island or Land-Province: giving us to understand, that the Land and Sea together made one entire bodie of the Kingdom of *England.* Other evidences of the same nature wee finde in the [i] Records of Parlament of the same King's time, or in the consultations of the estates of the Realm had about this matter, that whilst they Treat indifferently *De la saufegard de la terre,* concerning *the safeguard* or *defence of* the

c *Rot. Pat.* 27. *Hen.* 3. *part.* 1. *Membran.* 3. *in dorso.*

d *Rot. Pat.* 19. *Hen.* 3. *Memb.* 14.

e 22. Ed. 1. *seu anno* 1295.

f *Rot. pat.* 23. *Edw.* 1. *m.* 5.

g 18. Ed. 2. *seu ann.* 1326. *& vide Rot. Pat.* 19. *Ed.* 2. *part.* 1. *Mem.* 12. *&* 20. *Ed.* 2. *Mem.* 22.

h *Rot. Parlam.* 14. *Ed.* 3. *art.* 2.

i *Rot. Parlam.* 13. *Ed.* 3. *part.* 1. *art.* 6, 9. *&* 11. *& Rot. Parlam.* 20. *Ed.* 3. *artic.* 21.

the Land or Island, and *de la sausseguard de la Mere, the safeguard of the Sea*, they seem sufficiently to declare, beeing well inform'd by their Ancestors, that the Dominion of this as well as of that, did belong unto the Crown of *England*. For the business debated by them was not onely how to provide a Navie to make resistance against their Enemies by Sea, but for the guarding the Sea it self as well as the securing of the Isle, and so for the maintaining the antient right of their King in both. In the time of *Richard* the Second, *Hugh* **Calverlee** *was made Admiral of the Sea* (saith [k] *Walsingham*) *and* Mr Thomas **Percie** *joined in Commission with him to scour the Roades of the Sea for one year.* And in the Reign of the same King, and likewise of the two succeeding *Henries*, the Fourth and the Fifth, debate was had in [l] Parlament *about the Guard of the Sea.* In the Reign of *Henrie* the Sixth, the *Guard* [m] *of the Sea* was with a numerous Navie Committed to *Richard* Earl of *Salisburie*, *John* Earl of *Shrewsburie*, *John* Earl of *Worcester*, and *James* Earl of *Wilts*, to whom was added Baron *Sturton*; and afterward to *John* Duke of [n] *Excester*. And in those daies it was usual to procure King's Letters commonly called, in the language of the Law, *Protections*; whereby Privilege and exemption from all suits was granted to those that were emploied in this kinde of Guard or Defence of the Sea, or that spent their time *super salvâ custodiâ & defensione Maris*, [o] **For the safeguarding and defence of the Sea**, as the form of the words hath it, which wee frequently finde in the *Archives*. Moreover, in the Acts of Parlament of the same King's Reign, mention is made *of the safeguarding of the Sea*, or *de la saufegard de la mier*, as of a thing commonly known, and for which it was the Custom of the *English* to make as diligent provision as for the Govern-

k 2. *Rich.* 2.

l *Rot. Parlam.* 2. *Rich.* 2. *part.* 2 *art.* 39. & 7. *Rich.* 2. *Membran.* 9. *art.* 13. & 14. & 7. *Hen.* 4. *art.* 18. & 19. & 8. *Hen art.* 6.

m *Rot. Par.* 33. *Hen.* 6. *artic.* 27.

n *Rot. Franciæ*, 32. *Hen.* 6. *m.* 4. & 6. &c.

o *Stat.* 20. *Hen.* 6. *cap.* 1.

… the Protection of … ven-
…gs of *England*. For, … rr'd
…ein by any forrein … vie
…n Harbors, or at the … e-
…tween those Islands … is
…oasts of *Germanie* or … eric
… as far as wee can … ose.
…Testimonies of for- … Se-
…es likewise, there … his
…f Guard, Defence, … chara-
… as will hereafter … the *English*
… speak of … *glish* Merchant of
that … *issions* giv… …ove all things is, that
the Sea be… …er left destitute of such pro-
tection as may keep it safe and quiet. Which hee speak's to set out the whole generation of Merchants in that age, whose custom it was to bee sollicitous for traffick above all things, and consequently about the Sea it self, which would not afford them safe Voyages, did not the Kings of *England*, as Sovereigns thereof, according to their Right and Custom, provide for the securitie of this, as a Province under their Protection. The words of *Chaucer* are these,

p *Rot.Parlam.20.Hen.9.Artic.29.*

> **His reasons spake hee full solemnely,**
> **Shewing alway the encreas of his winning;**
> **Hee would the See were kept for any thing**
> **Betwixe** Middleborough **and** Orewel.

Orewel is an Haven upon the Coasts in *Suffolk*. *Middleborough* is in *Zealand*. The whole Sea that floweth between *Britain* and *Zealand* the *English* Merchants would have secured, this they were wont solemnly and unanimously to pray for, knowing that the Sea

was part of the Kingdom, and [illegible]
them part of the dutie of the Ki[illegible]
as concerning any Protection her[illegible]
Princes, any farther then in their ow[illegible]
most within the winding Creeks be[illegible]
which they possessed upon the C[illegible]
Gallia Belgica, there is nothing, [illegible]
finde, to bee gathered from any [illegible]
mer Ages. In the succeeding Ag[illegible]
is frequent mention of this kinde o[illegible]
and Government of the same Sea, [illegible]
more fully appear when wee com t[illegible] *[illegible]butes*,
and of the *tenor and varietie of the Comm*[illegible] to our
Admirals. But now, it is to bee ob[illegible], that both
the name and nature of this Guard is very well known, not onely by the use of the word both in the [q] *Imperial* and *Canon* [r] Law, wherein it denotes that the Guardian ought to take a diligent care of that thing, whereof hee is owner, who doth either lend it, or commit it to his over-sight, but also by the common and obvious use which the *English* make of the same word in other Offices or Governments. For in those daies of old, when the title of Guardians or Wardens of the Sea was more usual, there were appointed *Wardens of the Ports*, even as at this day there are *Wardens of the Counties* (who are those Commanders of Counties called *Sheriffs*, and in the usual form and tenor of their Writ have *custodiam comitatûs* **the Guard or Defence of the Countie committed to their charge**) *Wardens* or Keepers *of the Marches* or Borders, Keepers of Towers or Castles, Parks, Houses, and the like. Yea, and the Lord Lievtenant of *Ireland* was especially in the time of King [s] *John* and [t] *Henrie* the Third, styled usually Warden or *Keeper of Ireland*, and his Office

q *L. ff. tit. Commodati*, §. 5. & 8.

r *Extr. tit. de Officio Custodis Ecclesiæ.*

s *Rot. Cart. 2. Joann. R. in Dors. & Rot. Pat. 17. Joannis.*

t *Rot. Pat. 3. Hen. 3. Membran. 4. &c.*

or

or dignitie, commonly called the Keepership of *Ireland*; after the same manner as *John* Duke of *Bedford*, and *Humphrey* Duke of *Glocester*, whom *Henry* the fift during the time of his absence in *France*, deputed to govern the Kingdom of *England*, by turns, were called *Custodes Angliæ*, *Keepers of England*, as wee very often finde both in [u] Histories and [x] Records. So *Arthur* Prince of *Wales* was made [y] *Keeper of England*, while *Henry* the seventh was beyond the Seas. So *Piers Gaveston was keeper of England*, while *Edward* the second remained in *France*. So were others also in like manner. The Governors also of the Islands of **Jarsey** and **Garnesey**, and the rest that are situated in this **Sea**, who now are styled *Governors*, *Keepers*, or *Captains*, were in [z] antient times called onely by the name of *Guardians*, or *Keepers*. This then beeing so, what reason have wee to think that our Ancestors did not use the same Notion of Guardian or Keeper, and of guarding or keeping, in the name of the Guardian and the Guard of the Sea, which they were wont to use in the Guard and keeping of the Island, and in the other dignities or offices before mentioned? Doubtless, in all these the peculiar Dominion and Soveraigntie of him that conferr'd the Dignities, is so clearly signified and included, that his Dominion or Ownership of the thing to bee kept and guarded, as well as Autoritie over the person dignified, is plainly implied in this Title. Nor is it to bee omitted, that in antient times before the autoritie of the high Admirals of *England* was sufficiently established by our Kings, and setled so distinct, that the Command and Government of the Sea did belong onely to them, the Governors or Keepers of the Provinces whom wee call *Sheriffs* of the Counties, by virtue of their Office had also som

Custodie

[u] *Th. Walsingham, ann.* 1420, *&c.*

[x] *Rot. Parl.* 8 *Hen.* 5. *&c.*

[y] *Rot. Pat.* 8 *Hen.* 7. *part.* 1.

[z] *Rot. Pat.* 3 *Hen.* 3. *in Junio*; Philippo de Albiniaco, *&c.*

Custodie or Command of part of that Sea which adjoined to their respective Provinces, as of a part of the Kingdom of *England.* Which truly (to let pass other proofs) is sufficiently evident by this, that many times in those daies, they who, by the Common Law of the Land, were wont, as at this day, to put in execution the Commands of the King in those places onely that were committed severally to their charge and custodie, did do the same also in the Sea it self as well as in any Land-Province belonging to him from whom they received their autoritie. For, by virtue of their ordinarie power derived from the King, and such as was founded upon the very same right by which they held the Government of the Countie or Province, they did oftentimes remove the King's Ships and Fleets from one Port to another by Sea, as through the Territorie of the Province that was committed to their charge. Which indeed is a thing wee hear not of in later times; but that so it was in the Reigns of King *Henrie* the third, and *Edward* the first, the Records [a] of those times do testifie. But afterwards, the Universal Custodie of the Sea, excepting onely what was extraordinarie, was committed by our Kings to the *high Admirals of England*, and to them alone or their Deputies, and apperteineth unto them now by an unquestionable right. But when any person is intrusted with that Guardianship or Custodie, the possession and dominion of the King who intrust's or give's him the Autoritie, is comprehended in that Government or Command; which also is confirmed by words most express and home to the business in hand, that are to bee seen in a Libel, or Bill of Complaint [b], hereafter mentioned, which was exhibited by a great number of the neighbor-Na-

[a] *Rot. Claus. 7 Hen. 3. dors. 6. 14 H. 3. Memb. 22. & 17. in dors. Claus. 17 H. 3. Membr. 7. in dors. Rot. Pat. 24 Ed. 1. Membr. 17. & Claus. 25 Ed. 1. Membr. 12. in Dorso &c.*

[b] *Chap.* XXVII. & XXVIII.

tions, to the Commissioners of our *Edward* the first, and *Philip the fair* King of *France*.

The Dominion of the English Sea asserted from those Tributes *or* Customs *that were wont to bee imposed, paid, and demanded, for the* Guard *or* Protection *thereof, after the* Norman *Conquest.*

Chap. XV.

Concerning the *Tributes* or *Customs* that were wont to bee imposed, paid, and demanded, for the *Guard of the English Sea,* there are very ample antient Testimonies, all along since the Reign of the *Normans*: And those things which have been alreadie mentioned touching the Guard of the Sea, do not a little confirm it. It is manifest, that the Tribute imposed, in the time of the *English-Saxons*, for the Guard of the Sea, which was called *Danegeld* (of whose Original and use wee have [a] alreadie spoken) was wont now and then to bee paid heretofore under the *Norman* Kings. After the words there cited out of the antient *Dialogue* touching the Exchequer, about the paiment thereof before the *Norman* Conquest, it immediately follow's thus in the same Dialogue: *In his Reign* (that is to say, the Reign of *William* the first) *the* Danes, *as well as other Robbers of Land and Sea, restrained the Invasions of Enemies, knowing this to bee true which is written,* When a strong man armed keep's his hous, hee possesseth his goods in peace. *For they were not ignorant, that resolute and valiant men would not let injuries pass unrevenged. Therefore whereas the Land had*

[a] Chap. XX.

had paid it a long time in the same King's *Reign, they were unwilling to pay that every year, which had been exacted upon urgent necessitie in time of warr: But yet they would not have it wholly cashiered, becaus of sudden occasions. Therefore it was seldom paid in his Reign, or the Reign of his Successors; that is, onely then, when they either had or suspected a warr with Foreiners.* And among the [b] old Laws of *England* wee finde that *William Rufus requiring aid of the Barons for the regaining of* Normandie *out of the hands of his brother* Robert, *firnamed* **Cortehose**, *who was upon a Voiage to the Holy Land,* Danegeld *was granted to him, not established, nor confirmed by a Law*; that is to say, four shillings upon every *Hide* of Land, which were paid for defending the Dominion by Sea. For, that was the intent and end of *Danegeld*, according to its nature and original.

[b] *Apud Roger. Hovedenium in Annal. part.* 2. *pag.* 344. *Edit. Londin. &* 603. *in Edit. Francofurt. & apud G. Lambard. in Archaeonomia pag.* 128.

Moreover; [c] *Roger Hoveden* saith expresly, that it was usually paid until the time of King *Stephen.* Hee speaking of the promisses which hee made at the time of his Coronation, saith, *Thirdly, hee promissed that hee would remit* Danegeld *for ever, that is, two shillings upon an Hide, which his Predecessors were wont to take every year.* The same also is affirmed by *Matthew Paris*, and [d] *Roger of Wendover*, out of whom the Chronicles set forth by *Matthew* until the nineteenth year of *Henry* the third, or the year of our Lord MCCXXXV. were wholly taken. They say of King *Stephen*, *Tertiò vovit quòd* **Danegeld**, *id est, & qualibet ydâ terræ duos solidos, quos Antecessores ejus consueverant accipere in æternum annis singulis condonaret.* So indeed wee read it in the [e] Manuscript Books of this *Matthew*, whereby the Printed ones are to bee amended, who render it onely thus: *Tertiò vovit, quòd Antecessores ejus accipere consueverant, in æternum annis singulis condonaret.* But this also is added by *Hoveden*; *These especially*

[c] *Annal. part.* 1. *pag.* 276. *Edit. Londin. pag.* 482. *Edit. Francofurt.*

[d] *Ms.* in bibliothecâ Cottonianâ.

[e] In Biblioth. Cottoniana.

especially, and divers other things hee promissed before God, but kept none of them, as wee are told likewise by *Paris* and *Wendover*: So that this Tribute was wont to bee paid in the Reigns of *William* the *first*, and the *second*, *Henrie* the *first*, and King *Stephen* also, for the guard of the Sea. And it appear's by the accompts of the Exchequer, that it was paid somtimes in the time of *Henrie* the second. And after that it grew out of date, another cours was wont to bee taken very frequently, and used as the Custom of the Land, that Pay, and Provisions might not bee wholly wanting, to maintain the Dominion of the Kingdom of *England* by Sea. Mention is made touching this particular in the Court-Rolls of *Edward* the first[f], *Terrarum ad Custodiam Maris agistatarum*; that is, of such Lands as were charged with a Paiment or Tribute for the guard of the Sea. Wee know indeed also, that it was in the same manner collected at that time, under pretence of the Sea, for the pay and maintenance of Land-Forces neer the Shore. But certain it is, that the Sea it self was guarded then with Naval-Forces, as well as the Shore by Land-Forces, and so that that Paiment belong'd either to the Sea it self, or els to the Shore as well as the Sea. Moreover, Subsidies have been demanded of the people in Parlament, *Pour*[g] *la salvation du Royalme & de eux Mesmes & auxint de la Meer, de la March d'Escoce, de Gascoign & des Isles*; that is, *for defence of the* Kingdom, *the Sea belonging thereunto, the Scotish Border, Gascoign, and the Isles.* Thus the Sea, and its defence and Dominion is reckoned in an equal right and condition with that of the Kingdom, the Borders, and the Isles. Several other instances there are of that kinde. But that especially is to bee observed in this place, which wee finde in the Parlamentarie Records of King *Richard* the second, concerning

f *M.* 25 *Ed.* 1. *Comm. Banc. Rot.* 72. *Penès Camerarios* Scaccarii.

g *Rot. Parl.* 13 *Edw.* 3. *Art.* 6.

ing a Tribute or Custom that was imposed upon every ship that passed through the Northern Admiraltie, that is, in the Sea which stretcheth it self from the *Thames* mouth along the Eastern shore of *England* towards the North-East, for the pay and maintenance of the Guard or Protection of the Sea. Nor was it imposed onely upon the ships of such Merchants and Fisher-men as were *English*, but also by the same right in a manner upon those of any Foreiners whatsoever, no otherwise than if a man that is owner of a Field, should impose a yearly Revenue, or Rent for the libertie of Thorow-fare, or driving of Cattel, or Cart, through his Field. Paiment was made at the rate of six pence a Ton upon every Vessel that passed by; except such ships onely as brought Merchandise out of *Flanders* to *London*, or that carried Wooll and Skins from any other place within the Jurisdiction of that Admiraltie to *Calais*. If a Vessel were imploied to fish for Herrings, it paid the rate of six pence a week upon every Ton. If for other kindes of Fish, so much was to bee paid every three weeks; as they who brought Coles hither from *New-Castle*, paid it every three months. But if a Vessel were bound for *Prussia*, *Norwaie*, *Scone*, or any of the neighboring Countries, it paid a particular Custom, according to the weight and proportion of the Freight. And if any were unwilling, it was lawful to compel them to pay. That is to say, there were certain Officers that had autoritie to exact it, having the Command of six ships, Men of War, for this kinde of Guard or Protection. But the whole matter I here faithfully set down out of the [h] Original, in the same language it was written, that is, the *Norman* Language of that time.

[h] *Rot. Parl.* 2 *Rich.* 2. *part.* 2. *art.* 38. *in schedulâ.*

C'est

C'est l' Ordinance & Granté, per l'aduis des Marchaunds de Londres, & des autres Marchaunds vers la North, per l'assent de touz les Communes de Parlement, par devant le Comte de Northomberland & le meaire de Londres, pur la garde & tuicion du mier & costers del Admiralté de North ove deux Niefs, deux Bargis, & deux Ballingers armez & arraiez pur guerre sur les coustagis que s' ensuient.

Primerement, pur prendre de Chescun Nief & Craier, de quele portage q' il soit que passe per la mier dedeinz le dicte Admiralté alant & returnant pur la voiage de chescun tonnetight VI^d. *horspris Niefs chargez ove vins, & Niefs chargez ove marchandises en Flandres qe serront frettez & dischargez à Londres, & Niefs chargez ove leynes & peues à Londres ou ailleurs dedeinz la dicte Admiralté que serront dischargez à Caleis; les quieux Niefs les Gardeins de la dicte mier ne serront tenuz de les conduire sans estre allovez*

Item, de prendre de chescun vesseau pessoner qe pessent sur la mier du dit Admiralté en-

entour harang, de quelle portage q'il ſoit, en un ſemain, de cheſcun tonnetight VI[d].

Item, de prendre des autres Niefs & veſſeauz peſſoners que peſſont entour autres peſſons ſur la mier dedeinz la dicte Admiralté, de quele portage q'il ſoit, en trois ſemaignes de cheſcun tonnetight VI[d].

Item, de prendre de touz autres Niefs & veſſeaux paſſanz par mier dedeinz la dicte Admiralté, chargez ove Charbons ou Novel Chaſtiele ſeur Tyne de quele portage q'il ſoit, en le quarter de un an, de cheſcun tonnetight VI[d].

Item, de prendre de touz autres Niefs, Craiers & veſſeaux paſſanz per mier dedeinz la dicte Admiralté, chargez ove biens des Marchanz queconques en Eſpreux, ou en Northway ou en Scone, ou en aſcune lieu en meſme les parties de pardela, pur le voyage alant & retornant, de cheſcun laſt Squar, viz. *laſtas graves* VI[d].

This

This is the Ordinance and Grant by the advice of the Merchants of London, and other Merchants towards the North, by the Assent of all the Commons in Parlament, before the Earl of Northumberland, and the Mayor of London, for the Guard and tuition of the Sea, and the Coasts of the Admiraltie of the North, with two Ships, two Barges, and two Ballingers, armed and fitted for Warr, at these rates following.

First, To take of every Ship and Bark, of what burthen soever it bee, which passeth through the Sea within the said Admiraltie, going & returning, for the Voiage, upon every Tun VI^d; Except Ships laden with Wines, and Ships laden with Merchandises in Flanders, which shall bee unladen and discharged at London, and ships laden with Wools & skins at London, or elswhere within the said Admiraltie, which shall bee discharged at Calais; which ships the Guardians of the said Sea shall not bee bound to convoy without allowance.

Item, To take of every Fisher-boat that fisheth upon the Sea of the said Admiraltie for Herrings, of what burthen soever it bee, for each week, of every Tun VI^d.

Item, To take of other Ships and Fisher-boats, that Fish for other kindes of Fish upon the sea, within the said Admiraltie, of what burthen

burthen soever they bee, for three weeks, of every Tun VI[d].

Item, To take of all other ships and Vessels passing by Sea, within the said Admiraltie, laden with Coles from New-Castle upon Tyne, of what burthen soever they bee, for a Quarter of a year, of every Tun VI[d].

Item, To take of all other ships, Barks, and Vessels, passing by sea, within the said Admiraltie, laden with Goods of any Merchants whatsoever for Prussia, or for Norway, or for Scone, or for any other place in those Parts beyond the sea, for the Voiage going and returning of every Last VI[d].

So run the Records of Parlament, which in that Age were almost all written in this kinde of Language; Not such as arrived at shore were charged here (as in most other places) with Customs, as upon the Account onely of the shore; but those that passed or sailed by, or used Fishing, as well Strangers as Natives. And this was upon the request also of the Estates in Parlament under *Henrie* the fift in the preferring of a certain Bill, which I have taken out of the Records, and set down at large[i] hereafter. That is to say, they desired it, as beeing very well instructed in the antient Law and Custom touching that particular, and of the King's Dominion. Nor can any thing bee said more expresly, for asserting the Dominion of the King of *England* over the Sea it self. For, it is clearly the interest of him who is Lord or Owner of the place, to impose paiments and services within a Territorie.

[i] *Chap.* 23.

More,

Moreover, in the time of *Henrie* VI, *William de la* **Poole** Duke of *Suffolk* beeing accused in [k] Parlament, the principal head of the Charge was, that hee had converted the Subsidie monie to other uses, which had been imposed and levied for the Guard of the Sea. The words in the *English* are, **For the Defence and tuycion and saufe keeping of the Sea**, as wee reade it in the Records. A demand was made also in [l] Parlament, in the two and thirtieth year of the same King, of fourtie thousand pounds, **For the defence and saufegard of the Sea**; as wee reade likewise in the Records. But why do I cite them here? In those [m] Acts of Parlament which are published abroad in Print, wee very often finde it, as a thing asserted by the Estates of the Realm in Parlament, that the Kings of *England* have time out of minde, by autoritie of Parlament, taken large sums of monie, by way of Subsidie or Custom, upon Merchandise either imported or exported, **For the defence of the Realm, and the keeping and the saufegard of the Seas, for the entercourse of Marchandise safely to come into and to pass out of the same** (which is the usual form of words.) That is to say, these words are part of the Preface or Preamble which was usually placed in the beginning of any Law or Statute, whereby that most known Custom or Impost of *Tonnage* and *Poundage* was wont to bee imposed, **For the keeping and sure defending of the Seas against all persons entending or that shall extend the disturbance of us your said Commons in the intercourse and the invading of this your Realm.** So that the King of *England* hath ever been so accounted the Arbitrator and Lord of Commerce throughout these

[k] *Rot. Parlam.* 28. *Hen.* 6. *art.* 38.

[l] *Rot. Parlam.* 32. *Hen.* 6. *articul.* 30. & 41.

[m] *Stat.* 1. *Edward.* 6. 1. *Mariæ Reginæ*, 1. *Elizabethæ*, 1. *Jacobi Regis.*

theſe Seas, that it could not lawfully bee hindred without his Commiſſion. Which truly is a manifeſt evidence of that Dominion or Ownerſhip, whereof wee treat. And here you ſee alſo that the defence of the Realm, that is, of the Iſland (for ſomtimes the Iſle alone, and ſomtimes the Sea alſo, as I ſhall ſhew by and by, is comprehended in that name) and of the Sea, as of thoſe things which are held and poſſeſſed by one and the ſame Right, is joined together. The Tribute or Cuſtom afore-mentioned, which was wont to bee impoſed, and the uſual form of the ſame Impoſition, may bee ſeen compleat in the printed Acts of Parlament of K. *Kdward* the Sixt, and others following. But it appear's moſt certain by the *Rolls*, that the Predeceſſors alſo of this *Edward*, whoſe Records are yet extant, did enjoy the ſame or the like, according to the various Cuſtom of the Times.

Obſervation

Observations touching the Dominion of the English *and* Irish *Sea, from the* tenor and varietie *of those* Letters Patents *or* Commissions Roial, *whereby the* Admirals of England *were wont to bee put in Autoritie.*

CHAP. XVI.

THe usual form of Commission, whereby the High Admiral of *England* is wont to bee invested with Autoritie for the Guard of the Sea, run's thus at this day, as it hath don also for very manie years past.

Wee give and grant to N. the Office of our great Admiral of England, Ireland, Wales, and of the Dominions and Islands belonging to the same, also of our Town of Calais and our Marches thereof, Normandie, Gascoigne, and Aquitain; And Wee have made, appointed, and ordained, and by these Presents Wee make, appoint, and Ordain him the said N. our Admiral of England, Ireland, and Wales, and our Dominions and Isles of the same, Our Town of Calais and our Marches thereof, Normandie, Gascoign, and Aquitain; as also general Governor over all our Fleets and Seas of our said Kingdoms of England and Ireland, our Dominions and Islands belonging to the same. And know yee further, that Wee of our especial grace and upon certain knowledg &c. Do give and

and grant to the said N. **our great Admiral of** England **and Governor general over our Fleets and Seas aforesaid, all manner of Jurisdictions, Autorities, Liberties, Offices, Fees, Profits, Duties, Emoluments, Wrecks of the Sea, Ejectments, Regards, Advantages, Commodities, Preheminences and Privileges whatsoever, to the said Office our great Admiral of** England **and** Ireland, **and of the other Places and dominions aforesaid in any manner whatsoever belonging and appertaining.**

And afterwards there follow verie many other particulars in the King's Commission, setting forth that most ample Command and Jurisdiction. In former times, as hath been alreadie shewn you, this kinde of Commanders were called *Custodes Maris*, **Guardians or Keepers of the Sea**, who afterward began to bee invested with the name of *Admirals*, in the Reign of *Edward* the First. But their Commands were usually restrained to certain Limits of Coasts; So that particular Commanders were somtimes set over each of the Three, Western, Southern, and Northern Coasts, but for the most part over the Western and Northern. Seldom was one set over both, before that the Title of Admiral of *England, Ireland*, and *Aquitain* was put into the Commissions; of which more by and by. But as the name of *Guardian of the Sea* was taken from the Sea it self, whereof hee was Governor as of a Province; so that of *Admirals* (a word, whose Original is very uncertain; but Ἀμηράλιος or [a] *Amiralius* was used of old for a *Commander of a Fleet or Navie*, not onely in the *West*, but also in the *Eastern Empire*) derived its name of Dignitie, either from the Fleet wherewith hee defended his Jurisdiction at Sea (as

[a] *Georgius Codinus, de Officiis Constantinopolit. cap.* 2.

(as it was usual heretofore) or els from the Land, either bordering upon that Jurisdiction or joined therewith, as it hath been in the later Form of Commissions. Whereupon, from the time of *Edward* the First, unto *Henrie* the Fourth, about one hundred and Fiftie years, they were in solemn manner created **Admirals of the Fleet or Navie of our Ships, towards the Northern Parts, or towards the Western Parts, or the Southern**, or (as it fell out somtimes) of both together. For, the Southern and Western Coast did, as appear's by the thing it self, signifie one and the same: That is to say, the Coast stretched here and there along the Shore from the North of the *Thames*. But as the Dignitie of those Officers called *Comes* and *Magister Equitum* of the West, *Magister Equitum* throughout Gallia, *Magister Militum* throughout the East, *Magister Militum* throughout *Thrace*, and others of that kinde in the Imperial Offices, did no less denote the Autoritie and Jurisdiction of them that commanded in these Provinces, who before were Lords of the Provinces, than if they had been called *Comes* and *Magister* of the West, *Magister* throughout *Gallia*, throughout the *East*, and throughout *Thrace*; so it is evident, that the Admirals of the Fleets and Navies (whereby the Sea is guarded after the same manner, as the Land is possessed by Land Forces) did no less set forth the Command and Dominion, and civil possession of those that had autoritie over the Sea (who before were Lords of the Sea) then if they had been styled Guardians of the Sea, Commanders, or Admirals, in their Commissions. And such as were so constituted Admirals of both Coasts, or of the whole *English* Navie, were somtimes by a general name [b] called *Admirals of England*

[b] *Rot. Pat.* 10. *Rich.* 2. *part.* 2. *Memb.* 19. *&* 11. *Rich.* 2. *part.* 2. *m.* 12. ubi Richardus Comes Arundeliæ sic nuncupatur *in Protectionis revocatione.*

England over the Sea, before that form of words was put into the Royal Commiſsions. And of this ſort of Admirals you have a Catalogue ſet down by that eminent man Sir *Henrie Spelman* in his Gloſſarie, where there are others alſo that follow.

But ſuch a change hapned in the Form of the Commiſsions, in the time of *Henrie* the Fourth, that there was one man appointed Admiral not onely of the Fleets or Navies, but of *England and Ireland* (over whoſe *Fleet of Ships* or Navie for Defence of the *Iriſh Sea*, ſomtimes a particular perſon was made Admiral, as was [c] *Thomas* Percie Earl of *Worceſter*) yea and in expreſs words alſo Admiral of *Aquitain* and *Picardie*; As was *Thomas Beaufort* (who alſo was Duke of *Exceſter* under *Henrie* the Fifth) in the [d] thirteenth year of *Henrie* the Fourth, after hee had ſurrendred the Commiſsion, whereby hee had before been made Commander of the Fleets: And hee was the firſt (for ought wee know) that was created in this manner. But in the next Form of Commiſsion the name of *Picardie* was left out. So indeed in the fourth year of *Henrie* the Sixth, or *Anno Dom.* MCDXXVI. *John* Duke of *Bedford* was by Commiſsion [e] made *Admiral of England*, *Ireland and Aquitain*. That Form continued about 88. years, or throughout the Reigns of *Henrie* VI, *Edward* IV *Richard* III, *Henrie* VII, and the three firſt years of *Henrie* VIII. And about that time, ten others were in like manner made Admirals, for the moſt part perpetual, of *England, Ireland*, and *Aquitain*; the laſt of which was *John* Earl of *Oxon*, who was Commiſſionated in that [f] Form, in the firſt year of *Henrie* the Eight. But there followed another alteration, or addition of Titles, in the fourth year of that King, *Anno*

[c] *Rot.Pat.21. Rich.2.part.2.m.15.*

[d] *Ms. Formularum de Rebus Maritimis*, in Biblioth.Cottonianâ.3. Maii,13. H[illegible].4.

[e] *Rot. Pat. 4.Hen. 6. part.2. Mem. 11.26.Julii.*

[f] *Rot.Part. 1.Hen.8. part.1.*

Anno Dom. MDXIII. At that time, Sir *Edward* **Howard** Knight, son of *Thomas* Earl of *Surrie*, afterwards Duke of *Norfolk*, was made [g] *Admiral of England, Wales, Ireland, Normandie, Gascoign, and Aquaitain.* To which words, [h] *Calais and the Marches thereof* are added in the Commission of *William* **FitzWilliams** (who also was Earl of *Southampton*) beeing appointed Admiral in the twentie eight year of King *Henrie* the Eight. This Form of Commissions held in use afterward, through the whole Reign of that *Henry*, adding (according to antient Custom) the clauses touching Jurisdiction. But in the beginning of *Edward* the Sixt, *Thomas* Baron **Seymour** of **Sudeley**, brother to *Edward* Duke of *Somerset*, was made Admiral [i] almost in the same words, as that *William* Earl of *Southampton*; inserting after the name of *Calais*, *Boloign and the Marches of the same.* After him followed *John* Earl of *Warwick*, who was created by *Edward* the Sixt, in the third year of his Reign, [k] *our Admiral of England, Ireland, Wales, Calais, and Boloign, and our Marches of the same, of Normandie, Gascoign, and Aquitain; as also Governor general over all our Fleets and Seas*; And in the same Commission hee is styled afterwards, *Great Admiral of England and Governor of our Fleets and Seas.* But after a while, the name of *Boloign* being omitted, the next high Admiral of *England* was created in the very same Form of words, as is mentioned before in the beginning of the Chapter. For, in the same [l] Form was *William* Baron **Howard** of **Effingham** Son of *Thomas* Duke of *Norfolk*, made Admiral in the beginning of Queen *Marie*, or *Anno Dom.* MDLIII. And the Command or Government of those Seas, as the principal charge of that Office or Dignitie, is more notably expressed there, as you may see, than in the Commission of the Earl of *Warwick.*

g *Rot. Pat. 4. Hen. 8. part. 2. Augusti. 15.*

h *Rot. Pat. 28. Hen. 8. part. 2. Augusti. 16.*

i *Rot. Pat. 1. Edw. 6. part. 6. 17. Febr. membran. 9.*

k *Rot. Part. 3. Ed. 6. part. 2 Novemb. 28.*

l *Rot. Pat. 1. Mariæ Reginæ, part. 5. 20. Martii. Membr. 3.*

From

From that time forwards, the very ſame Form was kept alwaies; as in the Commiſsion of the high Admiralſhip granted to *Edward* Baron *Clinton* (afterwards Earl of *Lincoln*) in the Reign of [m] *Philip* and *Marie*; alſo in the Commiſsion of *Charls* Baron of *Effingham*, afterwards Earl of *Nottingham*, in the time of Q.[n] *Elizabeth*; and of *Charls* Duke of *York*, in the time of King [o] *James*; beſides *George* Duke of *Buckingham*, who enjoied the ſame Office or Command in the ſame words, in the Reigns of [p] *James* and *Charls*. So that for above eightie years or thereabout (that is, from the beginning of Q. *Marie*) the whole form, as it is ſet down in the beginning of this Chapter, was ever expreſsly reteined in the Commiſsions of the high Admiralſhip of *England*, ſo far as they denote either the Countries, or the Seas, or the Dominion of the ſame. But therein the Admiral is ſtyled *Governor General over all our Fleets and Seas*, (juſt as *John* Earl of *Warwick* was likewiſe expreſsly appointed in general tearms under *Edward* the ſixt) or *over our Seas aforeſaid*. But what were thoſe Seas, or *the Seas aforeſaid*? They are in the fore-going words expreſsly called *the Seas of our ſaid Kingdoms of England and Ireland, our Dominions and Iſlands of the ſame*. That is, in plain tearms, *Mer d'Engleterre, d'Ireland, & Gales*, or the *Sea of England, Ireland, and Wales*; after which manner the Seas belonging to the Dominion of *England*, are ſomtimes alſo deſcribed in [q] our Laws, which are called likewiſe now and then by [r] our Lawyers, *Les quatre Miers d'Engleterre*, or *the four Seas of* England, divided according to the four Quarters of the World. So that in the moſt received form of this Commiſsion, after the beginning of Queen *Marie's* Reign (out of which alſo the ſenſ and meaning of former Commiſsions is

to

[m] *Rot. Pat.* 4. & 5. *Phil. & Mariæ, par.* 1. *Feb.* 10.

[n] *Rot. Pat.* 27 *Eliz. R. part.* 10. 8. *Julii.*

[o] *Rot. Pat.* 9. *Jacobi Regis, part.* 9. *Jan.* 27.

[p] *Rot. Pat.* 16 *Jacobi Regis, part.* 17.

[q] *Stat.* 20 H. 6. *cap.* 1.

[r] 2 Ed. 3. *fol.* 9. *ſeu* 36 *a. pl.* 6.

to bee collected) wee have a continual possession or Dominion of the King of *England* by Sea, pointed out in express words for very many years. And what wee have alreadie spoken by way of Collection out of these that followed the beginning of *Marie*, touching the sens or meaning of former Commissions, wherein a positive Command of the Sea is not expressed, is truly (to omit the thing it self, which sufficiently intimate's as much of its own nature) not a little confirmed upon this ground, that hee also, who before any express mention of *our Seas*, took place in the form of the Commission of the high Admiralship, was next preferr'd to the same dignitie, was immediately after his Creation, according to the whole Title of his Office (as beeing the same title which indeed alwaies belonged to the Admirals of *England*) styled; *Great Admiral of England, and Governor General of the Navie and our Seas.* So verily *Thomas* Baron *Seymour* (whom I mentioned before) is styled Admiral of *England* in the Patent Roll granted to him by *Edward* the sixt.

[f] Rot. Pat. 1 Ed. 6. part. 6. membran. 5. Augusti, 30.

It is proved by words plain enough in the form of the Commissions *for the Government or command of the high* Admiral of England, *from antient to the present time, that the Sea, for whose guard or defence, hee was appointed by the King of England as Lord and Soveraign, was ever bounded towards the South, by the shore of* Aquitain, Normandie, *and* Picardie.

Chap. XVII.

BUT in the Form alreadie shewn, which hath continued in use for so many years, you see mention is made onely *of the Seas of our Kingdoms of* England, *and* Ireland, *our Dominions, and Islands belonging to the same*, as the Province, for whose guard or defence the *Admiral* was appointed; that is, (as wee have told you) the *English*, *Irish*, and *Welch* Sea, all which is conteined under the name of the *British*, as it hath been observed at the beginning of this Book. Yet the names of *Normandie*, *Gascoign*, and *Aquitain*, besides *Calais*, are added, which are Provinces seated upon the shore over against us. As to what concern's them in this place, they are either to bee considered in the same manner as if they had been alwaies held in subjection by the *English* from the time of the first mention of them in the Commission; or as they have alreadie for som Ages past been out of their Jurisdiction.

But suppose in the first place, that they had alwaies remained in the Jurisdiction and Possession of the *English*.

lish. Questionless, howsoëver the Admiral of *England* might then, according to this Form of Commission, have had Courts of Admiraltie in those Provinces (as there is no place almost without Courts of Admiraltie, even where not any Dominion of the Sea at all is pretended to belong unto the place, wherein they are held) yet by no means might hee thence bee called Commander of the Sea it self (if so bee you except the Ports, and such like Creeks of the Sea, which are as it were incorporated within Land) either as it may bee said to belong to *Normandie*, or to *Aquitain*, *Gascoign* or *Picardie*: But by virtue of this form of Commission, hee had exercised Maritim Jurisdiction in those Provinces beyond Sea, no otherwise almost than our Admiral in *England*, and *Ireland*, or others the like do at this day, over men's persons & goods upon the *African*, *Mediterranean*, *Indian*, or any other Sea at a remote distance: For, the extent of such a Jurisdiction by Sea is without bounds. But the extent of his Jurisdiction, or of the Sea, over which hee is placed Admiral, as Warden, Guardian, or President, to defend and keep it under the Dominion of him who is Lord thereof, are bounded. And it sufficiently appear's by express words of the antient form of Commission, that no Sea is conteined therein, as a Province to bee defended, but that which is either *English*, *Welch*, or *Irish*, or relate's to *England*, *Wales*, and *Ireland*, as an appendant. From whence it follow's, that those names of the opposite shores in the Commissions do not at all mention the Sea flowing between as proper to those shores, or belonging to them in any kind, but serv onely as a limit beyond the Sea (so far as concern's the limiting of the *English* and *Irish* Sea;) as those names also of *England*, *VVales*, and *Ireland*, serv in stead of a limit on this side of the Sea, so far as in the Commission they denote the Sea under the Admiral's Charge or Protection: So that, even as that Officer called the *Count of the Saxon shore throughout Britain*, was eminently according to the name of his dignitie, Commander of the whole Sea flowing between *Gallia* and *Britain*, as of a particular Province, (which hath been shewn [a] alreadie) and had the name of the opposite shore for the limit of his Jurisdiction; so the high Admiral of *England*, or Commander of the Sea belonging to the *English* Empire, hath in the King's Commission the shore of *Normandie*, *Gascoign*, *Aquitain*, and *Picardie*, to set forth onely the beyond-Sea limits of his Jurisdiction or Command (so far as hee hath charge of defending the Sea-Province or Dominion belonging to *England*) in those shores which lie over against us. For, if any say, that the case is otherwise, wherefore then is not the sea over which hee hath command, denominated from som of these shores over against us, as well as of the English, Irish, and Welch, or *the Seas of the Kingdoms of* England, Ireland, *and* Wales, *and of the Dominions and Isles belonging to the same?* The Reason is, becaus no other Sea, as it falls under a Civil consideration (for wee speak not here of the denomination given by Geographers) doth flow between the Territories on this and the other side of the Sea which are mentioned in his Commission. Therefore as in that Roman dignitie of the *Count of the Saxon shore throughout Britain*, the shore was the transmarine bound or limit of that dignitie, so also in the Command of the high Admiral of *England* (so far onely as hee hath a Province or Jurisdiction by Sea, as a Governor of a Territorie) those opposite shores or transmarine Provinces, named in his Commission, are to bee reckoned the Bounds of the Sea under his Charge or Protection. And this truly is sufficiently appa-

[a] *Chap. 6. of this Book.*

apparent from the words of the Commiſsion alreadie handled, if ſo bee wee ſuppoſe (as hitherto wee have don for diſcourſ ſake) that the Kings of *England* did, all the while that form of Commiſsion was in uſe, retain thoſe Beyond-ſea Provinces under their Dominion as the *Romans* had don of old. But the matter is made more evident, if wee obſerv how the names of thoſe Provinces have, at leaſt, from the time of Queen *Marie*, been ſo kept in the form of this Commiſsion, that ſince her Reign there remain's not the leaſt ground for any of thoſe in the Commiſsion, to ſignifie any other thing than what wee have alreadie declared: For, in her Reign *Calais* was yielded up to the *French*, and ſince that time, the *Engliſh* have not been poſſeſſed of any Province upon any part of the oppoſite ſhore.

Moreover alſo, in the one and thirtieth year of King *Henrie* the ſixt, or *Anno Dom.* MCCCCLIII. the *Engliſh* were driven out of *Gaſcoign*, *Aquitain*, and the other Provinces of *France*, by the *French* King, *Charls* the ſeventh: Nor was there after the time of this *Henrie*, any Officer or Governor of Note appointed, or that could conveniently bee appointed by the *Engliſh* either in *Normandie*, or in *Aquitain* it ſelf; yea, nor in *Normandie*, either after or long before the loſs of *Aquitain*. It is true indeed, that the Countie of *Guiſe*, *Calais*, and ſom other Towns in *Picardie*, beſides thoſe neighboring ones that *Henrie* the eight gained by force of arms in the ſame Countrie, remained long after in ſubjection to the Kings of *England*; yea, and that a ſmall part of [b] *Aquitain* yielded obedience, though not conſtantly, to the King of *England*, for ſom years after *Henrie* the ſixt; but not the whole Dutchie. Nor doth it make to the contrarie, that ſomtimes under ſom of our later Kings, there was one appointed *Captain General* or *Governor over*

[b] *Rot. Vaſcon. 6. & 7 Ed. 4. &c. in Capellà Rotulorum.*

all our subjects in Normandie, with which Title both *Ambrose* Earl of *Warwick*, and *Adrian Poynings* were honor'd in the time of Queen [c] *Elisabeth*. For, they were meerly Generals of the Forces that were transported thither to assist the King of *France*, not invested at all with any Government or Command of the Dutchie of *Normandie*. But yet, even after the time of *Henrie* the sixt, the name of *Aquitain* was constantly retained in the Commission of the High Admiralship of *England*: That is, for one hundred and fourscore years, or thereabout, after the *English* were driven out of *Aquitain*, as appear's in the former Chapter. Hereto at length was added (as is shewn there also) the name of *Normandie*, in the beginning of *Henrie* the eight: whereas notwithstanding the King of *England*, was not possessed of *Normandie* a long time before, nor in any wise after; nor did hee in that agreement [d] made a little before with the King of *France*, claim any other possession in *Picardie*, besides that of *Calais*, and the Territorie of *Guise*, and *Hammes*. And so it hath continued now for one hundred twentie two years also in the Commission of Maritim Government or high Admiralship of E*ngland*, without any relation at all had to the Government or Command of the Dutchie it self, but onely of the shore, which bounded the Sea under his Master's protection, upon the Coast of *France*. For, although *Aquitain* indeed was first added to the names of *England* and *Ireland*, in that Commission, while the *English* possessed the Dutchie of *Aquitain*, neverthelesse it not onely so remained likewise in that form of Commission constantly, even after the expulsion of the *English*, until our times, but *Normandie* also (which had never been named before in the Commission of high Admiral of E*ngland*) was added, and this som Ages after

[c] Rot. Pat. 4 Eliz. R. part. 1. in dorso.

[d] Rot. Franciæ, 2 Hen. 8.

after that the *English* were wholly deprived of the Dutchie it ſelf : So that either theſe names do ſerv in ſtead of a Limit to the Sea under his protection, or elſ wee muſt perforce admit contrarie to reaſon, that they ſignified nothing in the Commiſsion for ſo many years. For, wee ſee that thoſe names of oppoſite Shore were reteined in the Admiral's Commiſsion, even from the end of Queen *Marie's* Reign until our times, or for the ſpace of 77 years, though the *Engliſh* in the mean time were not poſſeſt of the leaſt part of *France*; as alſo that *Normandie* was added many years before, but yet long after the *Engliſh* were outed of its poſſeſsion. Nor ought any man fondly to imagine that theſe Names were inſerted, becauſ of that right the King of *England* had to the Crown of *France*. For indeed, the Kings of *England* have, by an antient Right, uſually entitled themſelvs Kings of *France*: Alſo the Dutchies of *Aquitain* and *Normandie* and the other Provinces of *France* mentioned in this Commiſsion, are comprehended in that name of the Kingdom, as the leſſer in the greater. But if that had been the cauſ, certainly the name of *France* ſhould have been aſcribed to our Admiral; yea, and other Officers of that Kingdom have been made in the ſame manner by the King of *England* after hee was driven thence : Of which thing there is not the leaſt evidence indeed any where exſtant. And it is to bee obſerved, as ſoon as ever an alteration was made in the Draught of the Commiſsion, from that denomination of the Command of the Admirals of *England*, which was derived from the Fleets and Coaſts over which they had command, unto that which is made up of the Kingdoms and Provinces, that then an Addition was made of *Aquitain*; to the end that the limit or Bound, as well on this as the other side of the Sea, might bee pointed out by the Shores: The name of *Normandie* beeing added afterwards, and reteined still together with *Calais* and the Marches thereof and *Aquitain*, upon the same account. But while that the Kings of *England* were in former times possest of *Normandie*, *Aquitain*, and other Countries in *France*, there are not found in the form of Commission, wherein the Kingdoms and Provinces (as hath been alreadie shewn) are expresly nominated, any other Admirals or Governors of the Maritim Province or Dominion by Sea made by them, besides those to whose care the Fleets and Coasts were committed in the manner alreadie mentioned; that is to say, the whole Sea flowing between our *British* Isles and the Provinces over against them, and the Fleets belonging to any Territories whatsoëver of the Kings of *England*, were at that time by a peculiar right of the Kingdom of *England* in the Sea, so subject to them who were so put in Command over the *English* Fleets and Coasts, that there remained neither place nor use for any other Commanders of that kinde. Which may bee said likewise of those times, wherein som of the Kings of *England* stood possessed also of the Kingdom of *France*; as *Edward* the Third, and the two *Henries* 5th and 6th. Nor is it a bare conjecture, that they did not put any others in command over the Sea and Fleets, besides those to whom, by right onely of the Kingdom of *England*, the power was committed (to wit, according to that right which comprehended the whole Sea flowing between) but it is sufficiently proved also upon this ground, that wee have the antient publick [e] Records of those times, touching the Offices constituted by our Kings in *France*

[e] *Rotuli Franciæ, Normanniæ, Vasconiæ,* Archivo arcis Londinensis, *Regum ferè singulorum annis distincti.*

France, and those Provinces beyond Sea, in most whereof I finde not the least sign of the contrarie.

And if it bee demanded here, wherefore it was that the Shore of *Bretaign* was omitted (which in like manner lie's over against our Isle of *Britain*, and together with the Shore of *Picardie*, *Normandie*, and *Aquitain*, sufficiently take's up that whole Tract which stretcheth it self in the Realm of *France*, before the *English* and *Irish* Sea;) certainly, if the afore-mentioned reason take place, there is little caus to doubt that it hapned thence, becaus the King of *England* was not at any time so possest of *Bretaign*, that beeing outed of it, hee needed to bee very sollicitous touching the Bounds of the Sea-Territorie adjoining. Distinct Lords of Territories confining on each other (as were the King of *England* and Duke of *Bretaign* heretofore; for *Bretaign* had Kings and Dukes of its own before *Charls* the Eight, under whom, *Anno Dom.* 1491. it was united to the Realm of *France*) do for the most part keep their Bounds so distinct, that they may bee the more evidently taken notice of by all; but when of such kinde of Territories there is but one and the same Lord (as the King of *England* was while hee possessed either *Normandie* or *Aquitain* or any other Maritim Province in *France* together with *England*) hee beeing outed of either, ought above all things to take care that the past confusion of possession bee not prejudicial to the future distinction of Bounds. For fear then, lest it might have been pretended that even the Sea adjoining or confining with those Maritim Provinces, which were a long time heretofore possessed by the *English* and afterwards taken away, was taken away together with the Provinces, whenas perhaps, by reason of the past confusion of possession in one and the same Lord, all men might not bee sufficiently instructed touching the Bounds of the *English* Sea placed, as wee have said, upon the Shore over against us; therefore for the setting forth of those Bounds, the name first of *Aquitain* after its beeing lost was reteined in the Admiral's Commission, and then that also of *Normandie* was added. And afterwards both of them, with the name of *Calais* and the *Marches*, in stead of the Shore of *Picardie*, were for the same reason continued down to our times. Which reason truly could not concern *Bretaign* at all; nor *Flanders* likewise, nor any other Shores lying Eastward over against us: All which neverthelesse do, after the same manner, bound the Sea-Territorie of *England*. Moreover, those things that have been hitherto observed, shall bee confirmed, by what wee shall add next, touching the Office of Admiral among the *French*.

Touching the Admirals *of the* Kingdom of France, *or those* constituted upon the opposite Shore; *their* Original, nature, *and* varietie. *That the Sea it self flowing between Britain and France,* is not conteined in that command of his, *as of one that is Governor of a* Territorie or Province; *nor is there any thing in it that may oppose the Dominion of the King of* England *by Sea.*

CHAP. XVIII.

THat there were Admirals also constituted by the *French* King upon the opposit Shore of *France*, is known to everie man. And as there is an Admiral appointed in *Gallia Narbonensis* to over-see maritim Affairs there, so also on the opposite Shore, there are distinct Offices of the Admiral of *Aquitain*, *Bretaign*, and *Normandie* and the adjoining Coasts. But the *French* Lawyers of late are wont to call their Admiral in Latine *Præfectus Maris*, **Governor of the Sea**, as if the Sea were subject to him also as a Governor; whereas notwithstanding, if the thing bee rightly consider'd that Goverment of the Sea by what name soever it bee called, doth not signifie (as among the *English*) any Dominion of one having command in any nearer part of the Sea (for, wee speak not of the Sea of *Marseille*, which hath no relation hereunto

unto) but onely of their Naval Forces in any Sea whatsoëver; together with the Government of the Sea-men and Jurisdiction over their persons and moveables, which may fall under the determination of a Judg *pour raison ou occasion* (as they [a] say) *de faict de la mer*, that is, *by reason or upon occasion of any suit or controversie arising about Sea-Affairs.* For the more plain understanding whereof wee must make farther enquirie.

[a] *Arrest. ann.* 1377. *sub Carolo* 5. *Edict. Franc. Tom.*3.*Tit.*2.

In the more antient times, there were indeed Admirals or Governors of Sea-affairs among the *French*, yet so that their Writers do not a little differ about the original of the dignitie. They for the most part say, that *Rotlandus* is found to have been Governor of the Sea of *Aremorica* or [b] *Bretaign* under *Charlemaign*, whom they fetch out of *Eginhartus* who wrote the life of *Charls* at that time. But in *Eginhartus* he is expresly called *Governor*, not of the *British Sea*, but onely *of the Shore of Bretaign*, as wee told you in the * former Book: In which name there is a description, not of one that govern's the Sea as a Province, but who command's the Shore as the limit of his dignitie. That is to say, of the same kinde as those *Counts* (or officers) were, *who were* [c] *deputed in that Age to guard the Sea-Coast*, and secure it from the incursions of enemies by Sea. There is also a [d] nameless Autor of a Chronicle belonging to a Monasterie called *Monasterium Besuense*, who write's that this guarding of the Shores under the *Caroline* Kings *was given over* a little after the time of *Charlemaign*. But in the following Ages, the Kingdom of *France*, beeing divided as it were by piece-meals into several principalites, that which a long retained this name of the Kingdom of *France*, was reduced into so narrow a compass, that the Province of *Narbon* was held by Sovereign Earls of its own, *Aquitain* or

[b] *Choppin. de Domanio Franciæ, lib.* 1.*tit.*15.§.11. Pasquier en les Recerches, *liv.* 2.*cap.*14. *J.Tilius de de Rebus Gallicis, lib.*2. *Alii.*

* *Cap.* 18.

[c] *Capitular Caroli & Ludovic. RR.lib.*5. *cap.*4.

[d] *In Gest. Normannorum,pag.* 22.

of the Western Shore which lie's more Southerly with *Normandie* by the *English*; *Bretaign* either by Kings or Dukes of the same, aud *Flanders* by Earls: So that whilst the whole Sea-Coast, except *Picardie*, remained separate from that Kingdom, there was Sea little enough lying before it. Yea, and the Naval Forces were small enough, of which (before the accession of a larger Sea-Coast to the *French* Kingdom) there was most use in the expedition of the *holy War*. Nor was any other Governor wont to bee appointed there by the name of Admiral, then hee who as occasion required was put in Command over the Navie and Militarie Affairs by Sea, yea, and was borrowed from som Nation bordering upon the Sea, as the *Genoeses* or others of that kinde. But the Kings themselvs had at that time no Command over the Sea, as it is expresly written by *Johannes Tilius*, a Clark of the Parlament of *Paris*. His words are these, [e] *After that the Kingdom of* France *was lessen'd by divisions, and the Kings confined to more narrow Dominions, becaus they had potent Vassals who enjoied Feuds with absolute Soveraigntie, if you except their homage (for, the King of* England *held the Dutchies of* Normandie *and* Aquitain; Britain *had a Duke of its own; and* Flanders, Tholouse, *and* Provence *had their Earls) the Kings of* France *for a long time had no command over the Sea, and therefore had no need of Admirals, until they undertook the Expedition for the holy Land, at which time they made use of* Genoeses *whom they hired, with* Spaniards, *or other of their neighbors that were well skill'd in Sea-affairs, to under-take the care of transportation, having no office appointed for that purpose; and by this means they had many Admirals in one single Expedition.* But after that the *English* had quitted *Normandie*, and the Kingdom

[e] *De Rebus Gallicis, lib.* 2. *Adde Laurent. Bochel. in Thesauro Juris Gallicani. part.* 1. *pag.* 90.

 of

of *France* had gotten ground upon the Sea-Coast, the use of Sea-Affairs also was somwhat augmented; That is to say, about the times of *John* and *Henrie* the third Kings of *England*. So that the first Admiral that they reckon in the Catalogue of French dignities, of whom any memorie is left to posteritie, was *Enguerandus Coucæus*, in the time of *Philip* the Bold King of *France*, or about the year 1280, as it is related by *Joannes Feronius*. And what kinde of dignitie his was, appear's sufficiently thence, that his next Successors *Matthew Momorancie*, and *John Harcourt* were onely, upon a particular occasion, put in command over the Sea-Forces by *Philip the fair*; as wee[f] understand by their Commission. Yea, and they are mentioned by *William de Nangis*, by the title of Admirals; as others also are by [g] *Joannes de Beka*, in the time of *Philip the fair*. Although [h] *Joannes Tilius* reckon's *Amaurius* Viscount of *Narbonne*, to bee the first that bare the dignitie of Admiral in *France*, as a constant setled Office over the Affairs of the Sea; to wit, in the time of *John* and *Charls* the fift Kings of *France*, that is, about the year 1300; whilest [i] others are too busie in summing up divers other particulars, touching the Antiquitie of this command among the *French*. Afterwards *Aquitain* was added to the Dominion of the King of *France*, in the year 1453. *Henrie* the sixt of *England* beeing driven out. But in the year 1481. the Province of *Narbonne*; in the year 1491. the Dutchie of *Bretaign*; and lastly, in the space of som years, all that the English held in *Picardie*, was added also. So all the Sea-Coast, except *Belgium*, returned into the Patrimonie of the Kingdom of *France*. Hereupon it came to pass, that four Sea-Governments or Admiralships were afterwards in use therein, notwithstanding that somtimes one and the same person

held

[f] *Apud Andræam Chesnium, in Historia Familiæ Momorànciæ, lib.3. pag.183.*

[g] *In Chronic. Episcoporum ultraject. & Com. Hollandiæ.*

[h] *De Rebus Gallicis, lib. & vide Paschasium, en les Recerches, l.2. c.14.*

[i] *Popelliner. en l'Amiral de France.*

held several together. But of these, the Government that belong's to the shore of *Normandie* and *Picardie*, is at this day usually called the *Admiralship of France*, becaus before that the Province of *Narbonne*, *Aquitain*, and *Bretaigne* were annexed to the patrimonie of the Crown; the onely Maritim Government in the Realm of *France*, was that of *Picardie*, whereto *Normandie* was added afterward, as the next Province; the other three beeing denominated from their respective Provinces. The whole matter is very well set forth by *Renatus Choppinus.* [k] *There are* (saith hee) *four Governors of the* French *Sea, who bear an equal command under a different title, and upon several Coasts of the Sea. For, in antient time*, Aquitain *was possessed by the* English, Bretaign *by its Dukes*, Provence *by Hereditarie Earls, not by the Kings of* France. *And therefore at that time, the Admiral of* France *had command onely over the* Belgick *Sea of* Picardie, *and* Normandie, *as far as the Coast of* Bretaign. *But then all the other bordering Princes chose Governors of the Sea, or Admirals. peculiarly for themselvs. And therefore the* English *beeing driven out of* Aquitain, *and the Countries of* Provence, *and* Bretaign, *beeing brought into subjection to the Crown of* France, *the King supposing it not fit to innovate any thing, appointed a Lievtenant and Admiral of* Aquitain; *likewise a Governor of* Bretaign, *with the government of the Sea; as also in the Prouince of* Gallia Narbonensis, *in a manner distinct and apart from the rest. But the chief Courts of Judicature belonging to the* French *Admiral, are setled at* Paris, *and* Roan. So hee. And a little after hee write's, that there were Princes, not a few, who held the Sea-Coasts as *Beneficiaries*, that enjoied the power of Admiral in their Territories. But wee have Edicts and Decrees concerning the Admiral's Jurisdiction over the Maritim Forces, Affairs, and Persons, in the times of [l] *Charls* the

[k] *De Domanio Franc. lib.* 1. *tit.* 15. § 13. *Adde Popelliner.* En l'Amiral de France, *chap.* 12.

[l] *Edict. Regum Franciæ, lib.* 3. *tit.* 5. & *Popelliner. cap.* 10.

the fift and sixt, *Lewis* the 12th, *Francis* the first, *Henrie* the 2[d] & 3[d], and other Kings of *France*; as allso touching the Tenths of Spoils taken from Enemies, and other things of that kinde which relate unto the Goods and Persons of such as are subject to the Crown of *France*, upon the account of any manner of Navigation whatsoëver. And in these Edicts hee is somtimes called by the King, *Nostre* [m] *Lieutenant general per la mer & greves d' icelle*, that is, *our Lieutenant general throughout the Sea and the shores thereof*. But this Lieutenant or Governor (as they pleas to call him) of the Sea, was never at all in command over any part of the Sea flowing between *France* and *Britain*, as over a Province or Territorie to bee defended for the King of *France*, (after the same manner as the Admiral of *England*) but in the Sea onely over the [n] Naval Forces, Persons, and Affairs belonging to the French Jurisdiction; much after the same manner, as a Soveraign Prince take's cognizance of Offendors of his own Retinue in a Forein Territorie, and rule's them as at home; but without any pretence of his to a right of Dominion in that Territorie. Which truly there is no man but will conceiv, that shall in the first place observ the defect and deep silence of antient Testimonies, touching such a kinde of Dominion among the French, besides the Qualitie of that Government among them, and at length the entire and most ample Power alwaies exercised throughout the Sea and the shore lying about it, under the sole command of the English, and will but compare it for so many Revolutions of years, with those so long broken and divided Dominions upon the opposite shore of *France*, and with the late addition of the Sea-Coast to the Kingdom of *France*, according to those things which have been alreadie spoken about

[m] *Edict. Ludovici*, 12. 1480.

[n] *Petrus Gregor. Tholosan. in Syntagm. Juris, lib.* 1. *cap.* 3.

about it. It is clear, that there are no Testimonies before our time, concerning any Dominion of this sea, belonging to the King of *France*. Nor are there any in our time, except certain Lawyers, who speak of it either by the By, or in a Rhetorical flourish onely, not in a way of asserting it by strength of Arguments. Of these things I have spoken alreadie in the former Book; where also other matters are alleged, of special observation, which confirm what is handled in this particular. But now let us add hereunto, that the very French Historians, both of the past and present Age, do affirm, that in antient times the Kings of *France* therefore either had no Admirals at all, or els that they were constituted now and then (onely as occasion required) *becaus they had no Empire over the Sea*, as *Tilius* saith expresly in the place above-mentioned. In vain therefore doth [o] *Popellinerius* reprehend those Historians, in saying it is fals, becaus *Normandie*, *Picardie*, and *Flanders*, were heretofore under the French Dominion. For, not to mention this, that the Kings of *France* reigned a long time without the possession of *Normandie* and *Flanders*, and reteined not any other shore besides that of *Picardie*, (as appear's by what hath been alreadie shewn, and by the frequent Testimonie of Historians) and the consequence doth not appear to bee good, that they had any command over the Sea, becaus they were in possession of som Sea-Coast; no more truly than it may bee concluded, that a man is Lord of a River in *France*, becaus hee hath Lands lying by it: whereas by received Custom according to the [p] Law of *France*, the King is Owner of all Rivers that are Navigable, where they belong not to som subject by a particular prescription of possession, or som other title, besides the possession

[o] L'Amiral de France, chap. 9.

[p] *Sanctyon des Coustomes des Eaus & Forests, liv. 2. chap. 1. cod. Hen. 3. lib. 16.*

of the adjacent Land, as the Custom is not unusual also in other places.

But as to what concern's the Qualitie of this Maritim Government among the French; it is to bee considered, that as every one of the more eminent Offices or Governments, hath a peculiar place in their high Court of Parlament, and that according to the nature of the Government, as it chiefly respect's any Province or Government within the limits of the French Dominion, as the *Constable*, the *Grand Escuyer*, or Master of the Hors, the *Grand Master*, and others; yet the *Admiral of France*, hath no place at all upon that account: As it was determined in the time of [q] *Henrie* the second, when such a place was plainly denied to *Gaspar Collignie* Admiral of *France*, as hee was Admiral, or had the Maritim Government; but it was granted him as Governor of the *Isle of* France (as they call it) under the King. For, by the title of Admiral, hee had no Government in Chief within the limits of the Kingdom; but becaus beeing Admiral of the Fleets and Sea (in the aforesaid sens) which is out of the King's Dominion, hee exercised Jurisdiction over Persons and Affairs onely upon the Accompt of the Sea; therefore in this respect hee was to bee denied any place. For which caus likewise it came to pass (as it seem's) that those four distinct Admirals before-mentioned, have in like manner also a Government of Provinces, from which they are wont to bee denominated, as wee understand by these passages alreadie cited out of *Choppinus*, and others that write of this matter. So they that have any principal command within the limits of the Kingdom, that is, within the shores of *France*, do enjoie an equal privilege with the other more eminent dignities,

[q] *Ann.* 1552. 12 *Jan. ut Notatur in Edict. Regum Franciæ, tom.* 3. *tit.* 5. *in Margine. Jo. Tilius, l.* 2. *Simon Marion in Placit.* 5.

ties of the Realm. Moreover alſo, the Regulation of thoſe Rivers whereof the King of *France* is Lord, are not under the Admiral's Government, but under the ſpecial charge of thoſe Officers, that are called Preſidents or [r] Maſters of the Waters and Foreſts. That is to ſay, the publick Waters which are within the Bounds of the Kingdom, and over which the King hath Dominion, do belong to another dignitie; not at all to the Admiral, who, according to the general nature of his Office, is not appointed to take charge of any Province there, much leſs of the Rivers (as in *England.*) The principal intent therefore of this Office or Dignitie is onely to command the Fleets by Sea; For which cauſ alſo ſom years ſince *Henrie* of *Momorancie* Admiral of *France*, having ſet up a Statue on horſ back at *Chantillie* in honor of his Father *Henrie* Duke of *Momorancie* [s], call's himſelf in Latine onely *Navalis Militiæ Magiſtrum, Maſter of the Militia by Sea*, inſtead of Admiral, So that never any Admiral conſtituted by the French King either of *France*, or *Britain*, or *Aquitain*, had any autoritie in the Sea it ſelf, whereby hee might challenge a Dominion to himſelf as Governor or Commander in Chief; which may bee ſaid in like manner of all the Admirals of the *Belgick* and the neighboring ſhore on this ſide, and of the *Cantabrian* or *Spaniſh* ſhore on the other ſide: For, the autoritie of them all, ſo far as concern's this particular, hath been and is alike. Wee know indeed, that this dignitie was wont to bee ſtyled *Admiral of* France, *and Governor of the Roial Navie*, as the ſame Dignitie among the Engliſh was uſually called in the ſame manner, *Admiral of* England, *and Governor of the Roial Navie*, in [t] ſeveral Leagues that have been made betwixt the Engliſh and French: But it is clear by what hath been ſhewn, that they bare the Office

[r] De quibus volumen grande conſcripſit *Sanctyonius, &* vide *Cod. Hen.* 3. *l.* 16.

[s] *Apud Andræam Cheſnium, in Hiſt. de Familiâ Momoranciacâ, l.* 5. *pa.* 445. *Anno* 1612.

[t] *Rot. Franc.* 10 *Hen.* 8. *ſeu* 1518. 4 *Octob. cum Franciſco primo. Rot. Fœder. & Tract. Jacobi Regis cum Ludovico* 13. *&c.*

fice or Dignitie called by the ſame name upon a different accompt; And the Qualitie of a Dignitie is to bee valued by the nature of the Charge, not by the bare name or title. And let ſo much ſerv to bee ſpoken touching the defect of antient Teſtimonies, and the Nature or Qualitie of the Government.

But now as to what concern's the moſt ample and entire Command of the Engliſh for very many Ages, and the comparing of it with thoſe ſeveral Governments heretofore on the oppoſite ſhore; it is moſt certain, that there was almoſt from the very beginning of the very firſt Times of the *Engliſh-Saxons* one entire Empire throughout *England*, and ſo on the whole ſhore which lie's over againſt *Germanie*, *France*, and that part of *Spain*, called *Biſcay*, and this alſo in the time of that *Heptarchie* which is mentioned by Writers: For, there was alwaies ſom one perſon who had moſt power therein, and to whom the reſt yielded obedience, as wee are told by [u] *Beda*. And touching that particular there is a notable Teſtimonie in *Alcuinus*, where by reaſon of the Quarrels betwixt *Offa* King of the *Mercians*, that is indeed, of the moſt large, and in a manner the moſt midland part of the *Heptarchie*, and *Charls* (ſirnamed the Great) King of *France*, Navigation was ſo [x] prohibited on both ſides, that Trade was wholly obſtructed; which truly cannot bee conceived, unleſs theſe large Territories near the Sea had been under the Dominion of *Offa*; yea, the Inſcription whereby *Offa* was wont to ſet forth his Roial Title, was often expreſt after this manner, [y] Offa, *by the Grace of God, King of the* Mercians, *and alſo of the Nations round about.* But after the time of *Egbert* or the 800 year of our Lord, there is a continued Catalogue plain enough of thoſe Kings whether *Engliſh-Saxons*, or *Danes*, who (unleſs

[u] *Hiſt. Eccleſ. l. 2. cap. 5. & vide Camden. in Brit. pag. 97.*

[x] *Alcuinus apud G. Malmſbur. de geſtis Regum, l. 1. c. 5. & inter Epiſt. Alcuini in operibus ejus, pa. 1669*

[y] *Hemmingus Ms. in Cod. Eccleſ. Wigorn.* in Bibliothecâ Cottonianâ *fol. 44. b. & 150. &c.*

(unless you fondly except *Edmund* the *Anglo-Saxon,* and *Canutus* the *Dane*, by whom the Kingdom was for som little time divided) did Reign without any other sharer in the Dominion upon this shore. No wonder then that the Kings of *England* beeing entire and absolute Lords in command of so ample a shore, for so many Ages, did also take special care to retein the Dominion of the Sea lying before it, as an Appendant of the Island; especially seeing they not onely had so long and large a command likewise on the shore over against us, but also there were not any of their neighbors that could in any wise hinder it, except such as possessed som pettie Countries bordering on the Sea (which truly may bee so called, beeing compared to the spacious shore of the English Empire) and those also that were under distinct Jurisdictions.

The summe of all this is, seeing that about the beginning of our great Grand-Father's daies, there was onely a very small shore conteined within the bounds of the French Kingdom, and the Lords of the Maritim Provinces, by the addition whereof that Kingdom (as wee have alreadie shewn) was afterwards enlarged, did not so much as pretend any Right to the Dominion of the Neighboring Sea, upon the interest of those Provinces; and seeing no Testimonie can bee had in the Monuments of antient Writers concerning such a kinde of Dominion, but that very many are found touching the Sea-Dominion of the Kings of *England*, they having continually possessed the whole *English* shore in its full latitude under one entire Empire for above a thousand years, and concerning the perpetual enjoiment of the Sea, as an Appendant of the Kingdom; Therefore it follow's, that their Right is very manifest in this particular, and so that the Sea it self is a Province under the tuition or protection of the Admiral of *England*, as part of the Kingdom; but that the Admirals of the shore lying over against us are not in reason to bee called Governors of the Sea, in such a sens as may signifie any Dominion of a Commander in Chief in the Sea it self, out of the Ports or other In-lets of that kinde. For which caus also it was, that som Ages since very many of the Neighbor-Nations understanding well enough the Right of *England*, made their Complaint in express tearms against *Reyner Grimbald* Admiral of the King of *France*, becaus that *l' Office del Admiralté en la mier d' Engleterre per Commission de Roy de France tourcenousment* Emprist *&* *usa un an & plux*, &c. That is, *becaus hee had arrogated to himself and for the space of a year exercised the Office of Admiraltie, by the King of* France *his Commission in the English Sea.* The old Records from whence this is taken, are set down entire by and by; where you have more also that make to the same purpose. And so much may serv to bee spoken touching the Guard or Government of the English Sea, as a part of the King's Territorie or Province and Patrimonie of the Crown.

That

That in the Dominion of those Islands *lying* before the shore of ***France***, *which hath ever been enjoied by the Kings of* England, *it appear's that the possession of the* Sea wherein they are situate, *is derived from their Predecessors.*

CHAP. XIX.

THat a Possession and Dominion of this Southern Sea, hath been held also of old by the Kings of *England*, is not a little manifest by the Dominion of those Islands that lie before the shore of *France*. For, 'tis generally known, that after King *John* and *Henrie* the third were driven out of *Normandie* it self, that the Isles *Cæsaria* and *Sarnia* (which wee call **Jersey**, and **Garnesey**) **Aurenev**, and som other Neighboring Isles lying near the shores of *Normandie* and *Bretaign*, yea and situated within that Creek of Sea which is made by the shore of *Bretaign* on the one side, and that of *Normandie* on the other, have in the following Ages, [b] both now and heretofore, remained in the Dominion of *England*. But by the sentence passed against K. *John*, as Duke of *Normandie*, for the murther of his Nephew *Arthur*, the French would have him deprived of all the Right hee had to *Normandie*. And afterwards [c] *Henrie* the third resigned his Right to *Normandie*. But suppose wee grant what is commonly received, that these Islands were of the *Nor-*

[b] *Rot. Claus.* 2 *Hen.* 3. *membr.* 1. *part.* 1. *Pat.* 3 *Hen.* 3. *membr.* 3. & 5.

[c] *Jo. Bucbetus in Annalibus Aquitaniæ, part.* 4. & *Cod. vet. Fæderum, &c. Ms. in Archivo Fiscali, fol.* 1.

Norman Jurisdiction, or belonging to the Dutchie of *Normandie*; yet truly even so, they neither could bee taken away by the sentence, nor did they fall to the *French* by Resignation, forasmuch as the possession of the Sea, and so of the Islands placed therein, was still reteined; after the same manner almost as manie Priories were in *England* it self, who though they were belonging to the *Norman* Government in Church-matters, yet even as they were of the Government of *Normandie*, they ever remain'd under the Dominion of *England*, as long as the Privileges of Monasteries were in force among the *English*; as beeing situate within the undoubted bounds of the *English* Empire. Nor is it easily understood wherefore the Islands could have been so reteined, unless they also had been seated within the bounds of the *English* Empire in the Sea.

But the thing chiefly to bee consider'd here is, that verie manie Foreign Nations, as well as the Estates of *England*, did in a Libel or Bill of Complaint publickly exhibited in the time of King *Edward* the First, and King *Philip the Fair*, before a Court of Delegates specially in that behalf by them appointed, in express terms acknowledg that the King of *England* hath ever been Lord not onely of this Sea, but also of the Islands placed therein, *par raison du Roialme d' Angleterre, upon the account of the Realm of* England *or as they were Kings of* England. Which truly is all one, as in most express terms to ascribe this whole Sea unto them, as far as the Shores or Ports lying over against us. But concerning that Libel, I shall add more by and by. Nor is it to bee omitted, that the addition of a Shore, larger than that of *Picardie*, to the Kingdom of *France*, hapned first at

that

that time, wherein those Isles were so reteined by the *English* after they were outed of *Normandie*: For before, the Shores of *Aquitain*, *Bretaign*, and *Normandie*, were in the possession of other Princes; that of *Aquitain* and *Normandie* beeing possest by the *English*, and that of *Bretaign* by the Duke or Earl of that Countrie: So that the *French* King had neither any shore almost, nor any considerable use of Sea-affairs at that time; by which means also the *English* did with the more ease retain the aforesaid antient possession of the Sea and the Isles, after they were deprived of the *Norman* Dutchie. And this sufficiently appear's also by that Sea-Fight perform'd between the *French* Fleet (commanded by *Eustachius* the Monk, in the time of *Philip Augustus* King of *France*) and the *English* Fleet under the Command of *Philip de Albenie* Governor of the aforesaid Islands, and *John Marshal*, who both carefully guarded the passages of the Sea, in the beginning of the Reign of *Henrie* the Third. That is to say, a *French* Fleet of about 80 Sail was designed to transport Auxiliarie Forces out of *France* for *Lewis* (afterwards the Eight of that name that was King of *France*) who through the Treason of som Conspirators, made War upon the *English* King in *England*. This of the *French* was assailed by an *English* Fleet of 40 Sail. But [d] *Roger of Wendover* and *Matthew Paris* tell us, *that part of the* French, *who had not been used to Sea-Fight, was in a short time wholly defeated.* Observ here, they say that hitherto the *French* were not accustomed to Fights by Sea. But of the *English* they say, *the* English *being warlick and skill'd in Sea-Fight galled them with Darts and Arrows, ran them through with their Lances, did execution with their Swords, sank their Ships, and* blinded

[d] *Ms. in* Bibliothecâ Cottonianâ.

blinded them with Lime (which they did by throwing the Powder of Lime into the Aër, so it might bee driven by the winde into the *French*-men's eies) *They were deprived also of all hope of relief and succor, and know not which way to flie.* The *English* at that time beeing expert in Sea-Fight, did by this means make good the possession of their Sea, and the Isles also that are situate therein: For, even this Fight relate's to the second year of *Henrie* [e] the Third, or the year of our Lord MCCXVIII, that is, at the same time almost when the *English* were first deprived of *Normandie*. But as to that which is commonly said, that these Islands first belonged to the English *Norman* [f] right, or by the right of the Dutchie of *Normandie*, it is as easily denied as affirmed by any. Nor is there any weight in this Reason, that becaus those Islands have and ever had certain Customs like the *Norman*, therefore they do belong to *Normandie*: For, the *Norman* Customs are often used in *England*, as the *Roman* are somtimes by other Nations; yet everie man know's this can bee no ground for such an Argument. Nor is it any more to the purpose, that those Islands were within the Diocess of the Bishop of *Constances* in *Normandie*, until that in our Grand-father's daies they became subject to the Bishop of [g] *Winchester*. Their Ecclesiastick Government was a long time derived out of *Normandie*, with more convenience indeed becaus of the nearness of the place; which began, as it is to bee supposed, in those daies when the *English* possessed the Shores on both sides: But it doth not follow thence, that those Islands belong'd to the Dutchie of *Normandie*, any more then that the many Priories heretofore in *England*, who were of foreign Jurisdicti-

on

[e] *Matth. Paris*, *pag.* 398. Edit. Londin.

[f] Ed. Coke, *in Comm. Juris Anglic. part.* 7. *in Calvini casu*, *fol.* 20. & 21. *Guil. Camden. insulis Brit. pag.* 855. Alii; quod & admittitur in diplomatum aliquot recentiorum proœmiis, veluti *Rot. Pat.* 7. *Elisabethæ R. part.* 3. Herelio de Carteret, *Rot. Pat* 2. *Jacobi, part.* 19. & 19. *Jacobi part.* 24. ubi de Insularum privilegiis.

[g] *Videsis Rot. Pat.* 11. *Elisabethæ, R. part.* 8. *in dorso.*

on in Ecclesiastical matters, did therefore belong to the Dominion of foreign Princes, and not to that of the *English* Kings, as Kings of *England.* That is every jot as weak also which they use to allege about the *Norman* Languages beeing in use among the Inhabitants of those Islands. The people of *Cornwal* in *England* have alwaies used the *Welch* Tongue, at least with a little alteration in the Dialect, as the *Bretaigns* do also in *France*; In like manner the Inhabitants of the *Isle of Man* use the *Irish* Tongue; yet no man will conclude thence, either that this paie's obedience to the Kings of *England*, as Lords or King of *Ireland*, or that the other are subject to their Princes by any right of the *Welch* Principalitie. Wee know indeed, that somtimes slight mention is made not onely in the proëms of som Charters of later times, but also in several antient Petitions of the Islanders, that those Islands belong'd heretofore to the Dutchie of *Normandie*, and upon that account were held by the Kings of *England*: But yet wee know as well, that those Provinces which in Antient time were derived by Inheritance to our Kings in *France* (of which kinde truly these Islands are to bee reckon'd, if they were held as parts of *Normandie*) were alwaies permitted so to use their own Customs and antient Forms of Jurisdiction, that they were not at all subject to the [h] ordinarie Jurisdiction of the Courts of *England.* The same privilege was ever allowed likewise to the people of *Aquitain*, *Anjou*, *Normandie*, and others. Yea, and som Ages since, the Kings of *England* were pleased to order, that such Controversies as hapned there should not bee decided in any other place out of the Islands, but in their own Courts of Judicature: whereas notwithstanding it

[h] *Vide* 11. *Hen.* 8. Keleway, *fol.* 202. *plac.* 19.

it is most certain, that in the Reigns of *Edward* the [i] *Second* and [k] *Third* (times which without doubt made good search into that Right, whereby those Islands were annexed to the Patrimonie of the Kings of *England*) there were *Justices Itinerant*, that is, Officers created of old, who were often by ordinarie right to take cognisance especially of the more heinous crimes through all the Counties of *England*; also of such Rights and Privileges of the Crown as were usurp't and arrogated by any, and of other matters for the most part that are usually brought into Courts of Justice, who beeing [l] somtimes also called *Justitiæ errantes*, **Justices errant**, were wont to bee sent forth into those Islands as well as into the Counties of *England*; though the Inhabitants did indeed exclaim, and somtimes preferr'd their Petitions against this kinde of Jurisdiction. But yet it is most certain that the opinion of those very Officers (who were themselvs learned in the Law) then was, that those Commissions whereby they were so inabled to administer Justice in those Islands were not onely grounded upon Law (which was the opinion also of those who ruled at that time in this Nation) but also that the very Provinces of the Islands were so incorporated one with another, as they are all with *England*, throughout the extent of that Sea which lie's between, after the manner of our *English* Custom in the Provinces or Countries, that, a Caus beeing somtimes inlarged, they might appoint daies of Appearance to any Inhabitants of those Islands, in the *King's Bench* in *England*, as well as to the Inhabitants of any one of the Isles in the other, after the same manner as is used within *England* it self: Which appear's by the Commission of *John de* **Scardeburgh**

[i] *Rot. Placit. de Insulis*, 2. *Ed.* 2 & *Rot. Pat.* 15. *Ed.* 2. *part.* 1. *Membran.* 21.

[k] *Mich.* 5. *Ed.* 3. *rot.* 183. *coram Rege*, & *Mich.* 6. *Ed.* 3 *rot.* 181. *coram Rege*, penès Camerarios Scaccarii, 2. *Ed.* 3. *fol.* 5. *seu* 32. *b.* & *Itin. Tempore Ed.* 3. *fol.* 138. *a.*

[l] *Jo. Saresburiensis*, *de Nugis Curialium*, *lib.* 5. *cap.* 15. & 16.

Scardeburgh and his Fellow-Justices in the time of [m] *Edward* the Third, and [n] others of that Age. But it was never heard, I suppose, that upon such an inlargement, a time of Appearance might by our Common Law bee appointed in any other place but that which is of the same Jurisdiction (as conteined within the Patrimonie of the Crown) whereto also that place belong's out of which any one is so adjourned. Nor do I remember, that any such thing was ever so much as attempted in those Provinces, which were not reckoned in the Patrimonie of the *English* Empire; yet possessed upon another Title by the King of *England*; as the Dutchies of *Anjou*, *Normandie*, *Aquitain*, and the like. Moreover also, in the more antient Charters of som of our Kings, in confirmation of the [o] Privileges of Islanders, they are noted more than once for such Privileges as they *or their Ancestors or Predecessors have enjoied under the obedience of any of our Progenitors beeing Kings of England.* Surely, if it had been then believed, that those Islands were a part of the Dutchie of *Normandie*, it is not to bee doubted but they had added also *or Dukes of Normandie*, which wee finde truly in som Charters of [p] later time, yet so that in these also those Isles are said in express terms, and that upon verie good ground, to bee retained *in fealtie and obedience to our Crown of England.* But, in the time of *Edward* the Third, the Islanders petitioning the King in Parlament for their Privileges and Custom's which had been established time out of minde, annexed the Customs of som of the Islands, among which are these; Item, *that no man ought to bee questioned about his Freehold, after hee hath quietly enjoied it a year and a day, unless it bee by Writ taken out of the Chancerie of our Lord the King, making special mention both of the Tenement it self and of the Tenant.*

[m] *Mich.* 5. *Ed.* 3. *Rot.* 183. *coram rege, & Mich. rot.* 5. *&* 6. *Ed.* 3. *paulo antè citatis*, 181. *coram Rege*, penès Camerarios Scaccarii.

[n] *Rot. Placit. de Insulis*, 2. *Ed.* 2. *rot.* 30. *in dorso*; in Arce Londinensi.

[o] *Rot. Pat.* 2. *Ed.* 6. *part.* 7. *ubi* Inspeximus. 1. *Henrici.* 8. *&c.*

[p] *Rot. Pat.* 2. *Jacobi*, *part.* 19.

Item, *That they shall not bee put to Answer before the* King's *Justices of Assise, until they first give them Copies of their Commissions of Assise under their Seals.* Item, *that the King's Justices assigned by Commission for the holding of Assise, ought not to hold Pleas here longer than the space of three weeks.* Truly, these antient Customs seem so to relish, as if those Islands had been subject to our Kings & their ordinarie Jurisdiction, by the right of English Empire, not by the *Norman*; although the Islanders insinuate also in the same Petitions, that they were a part of the Neighboring Province of *Normandie*. Add hereto also, that the Isle of *Serk* was granted by Queen [q] *Elisabeth* to *Herelie de Carteret*, to bee held *in Capite* by him and his heirs; that is to say, as a *Feud* belonging to the patrimonie of the Crown of *England*; notwithstanding that it bee unawares, or els carelesly admitted in the Charter of this Grant, to bee within the Dutchie of *Normandie*. But in the Treatie held at *Chartres*, when *Edward* the third renounced his claim to *Normandie*; and som other Countries of *France* that border'd upon the Sea, it was added, that no controversie should remain touching the Islands, but that hee should hold all Islands whatsoëver which hee possessed at that time, whether they lay before those Countries that hee held, or [r] others: For, reason required this to maintain the Dominion by Sea. Yea, both *Jersey*, and *Gernsey*, as also the Isles of *Wight* and *Man* are said in divers Treaties held betwixt the Kings of *England* and other Princes, *to belong unto the* Kingdom *of England, and to lie* [s] *near the Kingdom of England.* These Isles also were granted heretofore by King [t] *Henrie* the fift to his brother *John* Duke of *Bedford*, *without any recognition to bee made unto Us or Our Heirs, notwithstanding any Prerogative of the Crown for any other Tenure held of Us out of*

[q] *Rot. Pat. 7 Elis. part.* 3.

[r] *Tho. Walsingham, Anno* 1360. *sub* 34 *Ed.* 3.

[s] *Fœder.* 1542. *inter Cæsarem & Hen.* 8. *& Fæder.* 1585 *inter Elisab. R. & Ordines Fœderatos Belgii*; quorum transsumpta in Bibliothecâ Cottonianâ.

[t] *Rot. Franciæ,* 3 *Hen.* 5. *Membran.* 6. *num.* 12. *Novemb.* 27.

the

the ſaid Iſlands, which may in any wiſe belong unto the ſaid Iſlands, Caſtles, or Dominions. Which words ſeem not in the leaſt meaſure to admit any Right of the *Dutchie.* Perhaps alſo that antient cuſtom was as a token or pledg of the Sea's Dominion beeing conjoin'd with that of the Iſles, whereby *all the Fiſh* (as it is in the Records of [u] *Edward* the third) *taken by the Fiſhermen of our Iſles of* **Gerneſey, Jerſey, Serk**, and **Aureney**, *in the Sea, between* Eaſter *and* Michaelmas, *is according to the Cuſtom of thoſe places acknowledged to belong unto Us at a reaſonable rate to bee paid therefore, and that the ſaid Fiſhermen are bound to carrie all the Fiſh by them taken between the Times aforeſaid, unto certain places in thoſe Iſles appointed, that the Officers under our Governor of the aforeſaid Iſles, may take thence for our uſe, at what price they ſhall think fit and reaſonable.* Nor is that to bee ſlighted, which wee finde in the Chronicles of the Abbie or Monaſterie of *Teuxburie*, concerning *Henrie Beauchamp* Duke of *Warwick*, who was inveſted by *Henrie* the ſixt with the Title and Dignitie of King, not onely of the Iſle of *Wight* but alſo of *Gerneſey*, and *Jerſey*, whereunto the other Iſles in this Tract do in a civil ſenſ belong. The ſame thing is recorded of the Iſle of *Wight* by that Learned man [x] *William Camden*, and that out of the ſame Book. The [y] Book it ſelf ſpeak's after this manner; *But the noble Lord* Henrie *Duke of* Warwick *and firſt Earl of England, Lord* **Le Diſpenſer**, *and de* **Abergeveney**, *King of the Iſles of* **Wight**, and **Gardſey**, and **Jardſey**, *Lord alſo of the Caſtle of* Briſtol, *with the appurtenances thereunto belonging, died* 3 Idus Junii, Anno Dom. 1446. *in the twentie ſecond year of his Age, at the Caſtle of* Hanley, *and was buried in the middle of the Quire at* Teuxburie. And a little before it is ſaid of the ſame man, *that hee was Crowned King of* **Wight** *by the King's own hand*

[u] *Rot. Finium*, 31 *Ed.* 3. *Membran.* 18.

[x] *In Britann.* pag. 200. & 430.

[y] *Ms. in* Bibliothecâ Cottonianâ.

hand, no express mention beeing made in that place of the other islands, but they reckoned in the same condition with this, as they were part of the patrimonie of the Kings of *England*. But it is not to bee believed, that those Isles which lie before the shore of *Normandie*, had been so turned into a Kingdom, though subject to the Crown of *England*, unless even they also who made them a Kingdom, had conceived that they possessed them before by a Title superior to that of the *Dutchie*; that is to say, by a Kingly Title. As King *Richard* the second, when hee had determined that *Robert* Earl of *Oxford* (who also was Marquiss of *Dublin*, and Duke of *Ireland*) should bee created [z] King of *Ireland*, questionless did not doubt but that hee himself in the mean time possessed that Island by no less a Title and Dignitie than of *King*, although the name of *Lord* was wholly used there at that time [a] in stead of *King*, as also until the latter end of the Reign of *Henrie* the eight. So it is conceived upon good ground, that those Isles, and the Sea lying about them did, though they used different Customs, constitute one entire Bodie of Empire with the Kingdom of *England*. Whereunto also that special privilege of theirs doth relate, whereby through the favor of the Kings of *England*, they enjoie the benefit of freedom from hostilitie by Sea, though there bee a Warr on foot between the Neighbor-Nations round about; but of this more [b] hereafter. And in their Court-Records which contain the Acts or Decrees of the aforesaid *Justices Itinerant*, wee very often finde *Pleas of the Crown*, which phrase is an Evidence of the English Government. Also, in [c] their Trials, those Forms [*In contempt of our Lord the King, his Crown and Dignitie*] and [*Our Lord the King was seised of the aforesaid Advousen in time of Peace, as of his Fee, and in Right of his*

[z] *Tho. Walsingham in Rich.* 2. *anno* 1386. *pag.* 352. Edit. Londin.

[a] *Statut. Hibernic.* 33 *H.* 8. *cap.* 1.

[b] *Cap.* 22.

[c] *Rot. Placit. de Insulis*, 2. Ed. 2. Rot. 21 & 30 &c. *in arce Londin.*

his Crown] and others not a few of that kinde wee meet with, which ſavor not of any Right of the *Dutchie*. Add moreover, that the King of *England* ſo held the Right heretofore, not onely of the Iſles over againſt the ſhore of *Normandie*, but of thoſe alſo which are oppoſite to *Aquitain* (as a pledg or concomitant of his poſſeſsion of that Sea, ſo far as it belong'd to the patrimonie of the Kingdom of *England*) that though our *Henrie* the third renounced his claim to no ſmall part of *Aquitain*, yet that Iſle lying before it, called *Oleron*, (no leſs famous in the Weſt for [d] Naval Laws, than *Rhodes* was of old) hee granted to his eldeſt ſon *Edward* to bee held in time to com, as a perpetual Appendant of the *Engliſh* Crown: For, this Clauſ was added to the Grant [*ſo* [e] *that the ſaid Iſle may alwaies remain to the Crown of* England, *and never bee alienated from the ſame.*] Alſo in his Letters granted to the Inhabitants of *Oleron*, hee ſaith, [f] *Wee will not in any wiſe ſever you from the Crown of England.* Som years before alſo, hee in like manner made a Grant of [g] *Gaſcoign* (or thoſe parts which lie upon the ſhore of *Aquitain* near the Sea) to Prince *Edward, upon condition it ſhould remain entirely and for ever to the Crown of England.* So without doubt his intent was, that both the Sea-Coaſts, and this Iſle ſhould in a ſpecial manner bee poſſeſt by the ſaid Prince, but by no means bee disjoined from the Engliſh Empire, any more than the Sea its ſelf, which waſht their ſhores. And although after a while, both this and ſom other neighboring Iſles, did many Ages ſince, for divers reaſons, follow the fate of thoſe *French* ſhores which lie next to them, yet in the mean time the Dominion of the Sea remained entire, as it did before, to the Kings of *England*; as it ſufficiently appear's by thoſe other paſſages which wee have ſhewn.

[d] Of which ſee more in the twentie fourth chapter.

[e] *Cod. vet. Fœderũ, &c. Ms. anno* 1259. *Penes Camerarios Scaccarii.*

[f] *Cod. Vet. Ms.* in Biblioth. Cottonianâ, *de Rebus Aquitanicis, fol* 3.

[g] *Rot. Vaſcon.* 38 *Hen.* 3. *membr.* 8. *Matth. Paris, pa.* 1187. *ſeu* 1207. *Edit. Lond.* Florilegus, *ann.* 1254. *& Cod. Vet. Ms. de reb. Aquitan. in Biblioth. Cotton. fol.* 66.

The Dominion and possession of the Sea asserted on the behalf of the Kings of England, from that leav of præter-Navigation *or* passage which hath been usually *either* granted by them to *Foreiners*, *or* desired from them.

Chap. XX.

THose things which wee have hitherto alleged concerning this possession and dominion, are confirmed by several Passports that have been obteined from the Kings of *England*, for leav to pass through this Sea; whereof wee have clear Testimonies in Records: that is to say, granted at the intreatie of Foreiners. Our *Henrie* the [a] fourth granted leav to *Ferrando Urtis de Sarachione, a Spaniard, to sail freely from the Port of* London, *through our Kingdoms, Dominions, and Jurisdiction, to the Town of Rochel.* It is manifest, that in this place *our Dominions and Jurisdiction* do relate to the Sea flowing between. And when *Charls* the sixt King of *France* sent Ambassadors to *Robert* the third King of *Scots*, to treat about the making of a League, they upon request made to the same *Henrie* obteined Passports for their safe passage *par touz* [b] *noz povoirs, destrois & Seigniories, par Mer, & par Terre*, that is, **through all places under our Power, Territories, and Dominions, as well by Sea as by Land.** There are innumerable other Letters of Passport (called *safe Con-*

[a] *Rot. Franciæ*, 5. *Hen.* 4. *membr.* 11. *Jan.* 5.

[b] *Ibid. mem.* 14.

Conducts) in the Records, especially of *Henrie* the fift and sixt, whereby safe Port and Passage was usually granted *as well by Sea as by Land and Rivers*, that is to say, throughout the whole Dominion of him that made the Grant. And it is worthie of observation, that this kinde of Letters were usually superscribed and directed by our Kings to their Governors of the Sea, Admirals, Vice-Admirals, Sea-Captains, to wit, the Commanders appointed by the King to take care of his Territorie by Sea; whereas notwithstanding wee finde no mention at all of any such Commanders in those Passports of that kinde which were granted heretofore by the *French* King to the King of *England*, when hee was to cross over into *France*. Letters of that kinde were given to our *Edward* the second by King *Philip the Long*, superscribed onely thus, [e] *Phelip par la grace de Dieu, Roy de France, A touz noz Justiciers, & subgies salut. Philip by the grace of God, King of* France; *To our Judges and Subjects greeting.* But the reason is evident, why the K. of *England* was wont to direct his Letters to his Commanders of the Sea, and the *French* King at that time onely to his Judges and Subjects in general: To wit, becaus the King of *England* had his Sea-Commanders throughout this whole Sea, as Lord of the same, and therefore when hee crost over, it was not reasonable that the *French* K. should secure him by Sea, it beeing within the bounds of the *English* Territorie: And yet the King of *France* might perhaps have an Admiral at that time, but onely upon the shore of *Normandie* and *Picardie*; For, that of *Aquitain*, *Bretaign*, and *Narbonne*, were not as yet added to the patrimonie of that Crown: And it was about that time, or a little before, that they are placed, who are first ranked in the Catalogue of the Admirals of *France*. But of later time it is true indeed, that in those Passports of

e *Rot. Claus.* 13 *Ed.* 2. *membr.* 7. *in dorso.*

or Letters of ſafe Conduct, which have been granted even by the [d] French King, and other Princes bordering upon the Sea, *Admirals* are uſually named in expreſs terms among the other kindes of Roial Officers; to the end that they to whom the Paſsports are granted, may bee ſecured in every place and part of their Dominion. But as touching the Engliſh Command over ſuch as paſs or ſail through their Sea, there are many other Arguments taken (as wee ſhall ſhew by and by) from the manner of our King's preſcribing limits to ſuch as ſail in this Sea; as alſo from thoſe paſſages which wee have [e] alreadie cited out of Records, concerning the Tributes or Cuſtoms impoſed by the Engliſh upon ſuch as paſſed through the Sea. And truly it is very conſiderable alſo, that the Kings both of *Denmark* and *Sweden*, together with the *Hanſ-Towns*, very often and earneſtly begg'd of Queen *Eliſabeth*, that they might have free paſſage through the Engliſh Sea with Proviſions towards *Spain*, during the Warr betwixt her and the *Spaniard*. I know indeed that ſuch a Licence was denied them not onely in reſpect of the Dominion of the Sea, but chiefly to prevent the conveying of Proviſions to the Enemie. For which cauſ alſo divers Ships belonging to the *Hanſ-Towns* laden with Corn, were [f] taken by Engliſh men of Warr, in the very Streights of *Lisbon*, without the Sea-Territorie of *England*, which went by the [g] *Scotiſh* Sea, and the Weſt towards *Portugal*; which was don doubtleſs that they might not preſume to uſe the *Engliſh* Sea, without the leav of the Queen. But the *Hanſ-Towns* cried out thereupon, that the Laws of Nations, Commerce, and Leagues, were violated; becauſ their ſhips were ſo taken by the *Engliſh* onely upon this account, that they carried Proviſions to the Enemie; that is, in a Territo-

rie,

[d] *Stilus & Protocoll. Cancellariæ Franc. cap.* de Paſſaiges & Sauf-Conduits.

[e] Chap. 14. of this Book.

[f] 30 Junii, 1589. quâ de re *Declaratio* tunc Londini typis Edita.

[g] *Thuanus, Hiſtor. l.* 95.

rie, where the *English* did not in the least pretend to any Dominion. And concerning this particular, there is a notable Question controverted by very [h] Learned men, *How far they that are not enemies, or would not bee called enemies, may by the Law of Nations afford supplies unto an enemie.* But som years before the taking of these ships, when the *Hamburgers* (who in the name also of the rest of the *Hans-Towns*, desired leav to pass through this Sea to *Portugal* and *Spain*) were more than once denied any kinde of libertie to transport either Corn or Warlike necessaries; they did not at all suggest, that their Petition at that time was grounded upon the Law of Nations or Commerce, nor that the Queen's denial was contrarie to this kinde of Law. That is to say, they were by her first [i] Answer enjoined to abstein from transporting Arms with other Warlike Necessaries and Corn, *but* (saith the Queen) *in transporting other commodities, wee shall not hinder you at all, but shall with all favour permit the ships of your Subjects to abide and pass after the accustomed manner, that they may perform their Voiage.* This Answer they did not seem to take amiss. But two years after they sent into *England Sebastian à* **Berghen** their Ambassador with Petitionarie Letters, desiring that the Exception in the Licence formerly granted might bee taken away, and a freedom to transport all kindes of Merchandise permitted. Their Petition was denied again, and this moreover added, *That such as should presume to do the contrarie, should for their bold presumption suffer the loss of all their Goods and Merchandise so carried against her Majestie's will and pleasure, if they fell into the hands of her Men of Warr, or any other of her Majestie's Subjects.* Thus they ever addressed themselvs by Petitions; and the Queen gave Answers according to her pleasure. They did not so much as pretend the Laws of Nations or of

[h] *Albericus Gentilis, de Jure Belli, li.* 1. *cap.* 21. *Hispanic. Advocat. li.* 1. *cap.* 20. & *Hugo Grot. de Jure Belli & Pacis, l.* 3. *cap.* 1. § 5.

[i] 1585. As you may read in the Queen's Declaration, 1589.

Commerce, before that they understood their ships were seised in another Sea, to wit, that of *Portugal*, which they conceived free for themselvs by the Law of Nations and Commerce, without leav from the Queen of *England*. Then it was they began to plead, that Libertie ought not by any Law to bee denied; even these men who but som years before, had humbly Petitioned the Queen of *England*, more than once for free passage through the English Sea: So that, that principal point (as som would have it) of the Law of Nations, that relief ought not to bee conveyed to Enemies by a Friend, was not onely the ground either of the *Hans-Town's* Petition, or the *Queen's* denial, but her right of Dominion by Sea was concerned also, which the *Hans-Towns* well knew they should violate, if they should pass the Queen's Seas without her leav.

Hereunto for the same reason those particulars relate, which wee finde concerning this matter in those points that were to bee insisted on in the year MDXCVII. by *Witfeldius*, and *Bernicovius*, Ambassadors from *Christiern* the fourth, King of *Denmark*, to the Queen of *England*. [k] *Wee were* (say they) *strictly enjoined by our King, to mediate with her Majestie, that our Countrie men may bee permitted a freedom to transport Corn or Provision towards* Spain, *even as wee have don formerly, and do now again with all earnestness desire, especially since it is supposed, that the same Licence of transporting Corn is granted somtimes both to English and Dutch; that our Countrie-men may not bee used in a worse manner than your own Subjects, and that at least som certain ships might in favor of the King's Majestie, have leav granted them once a year at least, during the Warr, to carrie Provisions; and that wee may bee able to certifie the King our Master, how far wee in this case prevail.*

[k] In the Records of the Embassie in Sir *Robert Cotton's* Librarie.

prevail. But the Ambassadors had this Answer; *that the Queen cannot in reason bee induced to consent it should bee don as they desired. And whereas you allege a supposal, that both English and Netherlanders have Licence given them somtimes to transport Corn, Wee* (to wit, the Chief men of her Majestie's Privie-Council, who gave the Answer) *dare confidently affirm, that never any such matter was granted by the Queen, nor will shee ever incline to grant the like, during the warr.* If the Queen had not in the opinion of the *Danes,* (as well as of the *Hans-Towns* before) been Soveraign of the Sea-Territorie, through which they were to pass, to what end then was this so earnest a Petition, and so imperious an Answer? Here, in this often iterated Petition, no libertie is pretended besides that which depended upon the Queen's pleasure, as Soveraign of the Passage.

For this caus also it was, that *John* King of *Sweden,* in that Letter of his sent to Queen *Elisabeth* in the year 1587. wherein hee desired leav for *Olavus Wormæus* a Swede, to carrie Merchandise into *Spain,* acknowleged, that hee must of necessitie *Maritimas Reginæ ditiones pertransire, pass through the Sea-Dominions of the Queen,* which are the very [l] words of the Letter. Nor is it any new thing, that this kinde of passage should bee denied to Foreiners: For, in very many of those Pass-ports that were granted to the Merchants of Neighbor-Nations by *Edward* the first, during the warr between him and the French, this claus is usually added, [m] *upon condition, that they neither conveie nor caus any thing to bee conveied to the French partie, nor communicate any thing at all to our Enemies there in any manner whatsoever,* as wee read it in the Records, where are many others of the same kinde. From hence it is, that in the same King's instructions, it is required, that his Soveraign-

[l] *In Sir* Robert Cotton's Librarie.

[m] *Rot.Pat.* 24 *Ed.* 1. *memb.* 5. & 25 *Ed.* 1. *par.* 1. *membran.* 2.7.16. &c.

raigntie by Sea bee preserved with extraordinarie care and diligence, as belonging to him by antient right, as Arbiter and Moderator of the Laws or Customs, and Persons, of such as pass therein. The words themselvs, which signifie the same, are these, [n] *Especialment à retenir & maintenir la Sovereigneté qe ses ancestres Royes d'Engleterre soloyent avoir en la dite Mier d'Engleterre, quant à l'amendement, declaration & interpretation des lois per eux faits à Governer toutes Maneres des gentz passanz per la dite mier*, **especially to retein, and maintain the soveraigntie which his Ancestors the Kings of England were wont to have in the said sea, so far as concern's the amendment, declaration, and interpretation of the Laws by them made to govern all manner of Nations passing through the said sea.** Hereunto also belong's that Commission of King *John*, whereby hee required in very imperious terms, that all kindes of ships whatsoëver which could bee found throughout the English Sea (it beeing expressed by the general name of the Sea, as flowing round about) should bee staid and bee brought near his shores: For, it hath been a Custom in all Ages, that the ships of any persons whatsoëver, as well Strangers as Subjects, may somtimes bee staid in the Ports. But it was King *John's* intent, that his whole Sea as well as the Ports themselvs, should bee plainly signified in this Commission. In witness whereof I here set down the Commission it self. *The* [o] KING *to all the Sturemanni and Marinelli and Merchants of* England *that sail by Sea greeting. Bee it known unto you, that wee have sent Alanus Juvo de* **Sorham** *and Walter* **Stattun**, *and Vincent de* **Hastings** *and Wimund de* **Winchelsey,** *and others of our Barons of the Cinque-Ports, and other our faithful Sturemanni, and Marinelli of our Gallies, to arrest all ships that they shall finde, and them*

[n] *Fascic. de Superioritate Maris Angliæ*, in Arce Londinensi.

[o] *Rot. Pat.* 9. *Johann. R. Membran.* 1. *Num.* 3.

safely

safely to bring, with all that shall bee found in them, into England. *And therefore wee command you, that yee bee attending upon them in this business, so that yee bee in* England *with all your Ships and Merchandises at such Port and Coast as they shall appoint you. And if any shall attempt to resist them contrarie to our command, you, our Liege-men, are required to assist them with all your strength, as you tender your selvs and your chattels, and peace and residence in our Land for you or any of your Generation. Witness hereunto William* **Briwr** *at* **Lutegar**, *the eight daie of Februarie.* These *Sturemanni* here do signifie Sea-Captains, and *Marinelli* Sea-souldiers. But to command that all ships should bee *arrested* throughout the Sea, that is, staid or taken, and brought into *England*, what els was it but undoubtedly to declare himself Lord of the Sea through which they passed? Now let no man object, that this Commission extended onely to the Ships of *English* men, or of the Subjects of him that gave the Commission. It is true indeed, that the Commission before cited, was sent and directed onely to the Sea-Captains, Men of Warr, and Merchants of *England*: But yet it is manifest thereby, that the four persons there named, and others Barons of the Cinque-Ports, and the rest that are added, were obliged by the aforesaid Commands *to arrest all the ships that they should finde throughout the Sea, and bring them safely into* England *with all that should bee found in them.* But this part of the Commission was added (as it plainly appear's) that no English Sea-Captain, or Souldier, or Merchant whatsoëver, might bee wanting in their assistance, in staying the ships of Foreiners; *If anie one shall attempt to resist them contrarie to our command, you, our Liege-*

men are required to assist them with all your, &c. Our *Liege-men* in this place, or they that ought to give assistance in making stay of ships, are all the Sea-men and Merchants of *England* that sail up and down throughout this Sea. They therefore whose ships were to bee staid, did not com under the name of *Liege-men*, or Subjects; and that it so appear's to bee by the very Form of this Commission, that there need's not any thing more bee added touching this matter, I suppose no man will doubt, who take's it into his more serious consideration. Nor do the words make mention of the ships of Enemies, but of any whatsoëver; as beeing deliver'd by a Soveraign Prince, who was concerned at that time, for his own occasion, and at discretion, to use not onely his own Sea-Territorie, but also the ships sailing therein, as well as those that were in Port.

Wee finde a Commission of the like nature, and which speak's to the same purpose, in the time of King *Edward* the third, wherein Command is given to make stay of all ships of ten Tuns and upward, that should bee found in the South and Western Sea (except som that were newly designed to cross over into *Bretaign*) that they might bee arm'd and set forth in the King's service. The Title of this Commission is, *De Navibus arrestandis & capiendis*, **For arresting and seizing of ships.** The Form of it run's thus; *The* KING *to his beloved Thomas de* **Wenlok** *his Serjeant at Arms, Lieutenant of our beloved and trustie Reginald de* **Cobham,** *Admiral of our Fleet of ships from the mouth of the River Thames towards the Western parts, greeting. Bee it known unto you, that wee have appointed you with all the speed that may bee used by you, and such as shall bee deputed by*

you,

you, to arrest and seiz all ships, Flie-Boats, Barks, and Barges of ten Tuns burthen and upward, which may happen to bee found in the aforesaid Admiraltie, (that is, in the Sea reaching from the *Thames* mouth toward the South and West) *and to caus the Flie-Boats, Barks and Barges aforesaid, to bee well and sufficiently arm'd and provided for the warr, by the Masters and owners of the same, and to bring them speedily so provided and arm'd to* Sandwich, *except onely the ships that are order'd for the passage of our beloved and trustie Thomas de* **Dagworth** *and his men that are bound for Bretaign; so that you bee readie there in your own person, together with the Ships, Flie-Boats, Barks, and Barges aforesaid, so well provided and fitted for the warr, upon the Saturday next before the Feast of the Apostles* Simon *and* Jude, *next ensuing at the farthest, to go thence upon our Command, according to such direction as shall then on our part bee given, to the Masters and Mariners of the aforesaid Ships, Flie-Boats, Barks, and Barges, and to take sufficient Provision for the enabling of you to do the premises, in such places as you shall see most convenient (except onely Church-Land) you making due paiment for the same; and also to seiz and arrest all those that you shall finde to oppose or resist you in the execution of the premises, and them to commit into our Prisons, there to abide till wee shall think fit to take farther order, &c.* All Officers also in the said Admiraltie are commanded to yield obedience and assistance upon the same occasion. The usual subscription in that Age shewing the Original Autoritie of the Commission was, **By the King himself and his Council.** But that the aforesaid Sea it self was conteined under the name of the Admiraltie, is clearly manifest by what wee have alreadie shewn you. And King *Edward* the third used his antient Right, as other Kings of *England* did also therein, as well as in the Ports themselvs, or Shores of *England* (for, there are innumerable examples of the staying of all Ships whatsoëver, by the King's Command in Port or Shore.) But that which hath been alleged about the staying of Ships, and Listing them for the King's Service, you are alwaies to understand it was so don according to equitie, that competent Pay was to bee allowed them answerable to the proportion of Tuns, and also to the number of Sea-men, that were so taken into emploiment. Touching which particular, there are several Testimonies also to bee found in the [p] Records of Parlament.

[p] *Rot. Par.* 3 *Hen.*5.*par.* 1.*num.*6.*seu* 31.

That

That Licence hath been usually granted *to Foreiners, by the Kings of England,* to fish *in the Sea; Also, that the* Protection *given* to Fisher-men *by them, as in their own Territorie, is an antient and manifest Evidence of their Dominion by Sea.*

CHAP. XXI.

AS a freedom of passage, so also wee finde that a libertie of Fishing hath been obteined by Petition from the Kings of *England.* There is a clear Testimonie hereof in that which was alleged [a] before out of the Records of Parlament, concerning those Tributes or Customs that were imposed in the time of *Richard* the Second, upon all persons whatsoever that used Fishing in the Sea. Moreover, it appear's by Records, that *Henrie* the Sixt gave leav particularly to the *French* and very many other Foreiners, [b] *for one whole year onely* (somtimes for six Months) *&c. to go and fish throughout the Sea at all times and as often, &c.* But this leav was granted under the name even of a Passport or safe conduct; yea, and a size or proportion was prescribed to their Fishing-boats or *Busses,* that they should not bee above XXX Tuns. And it is true indeed, there was a kinde of consideration or condition added, that som others, who were subjects of the King of *England,* might in Fishing enjoy the same securitie with Foreiners: Which was for this caus onely put into the Licence, that if the Foreiners did disturb or molest

[a] *Cap. XV.*

[b] *Rot. Franciæ 38. Hen. 6. Membran. 9. & 14.*

left them, they should lose the benefit of their Licence. The words of that consideration or condition, in the beginning of those Licences, run after this manner; *To the end that the business of the Herring-fishing and of other Fish, may bee advanced, continued, and mainteined for the publick good; yea and that the like securitie may bee yielded and afforded to som certain Fisher-men under our obedience.* I suppose that those certain Fisher-men under our Obedience were also the *French*, who at that time continued in subjection to the *English*; whereas almost all in *France*, except the Shore of *Picardie*, had newly revolted from the King of *England*: That is to say, at the latter end of the reign of *Henrie* the Sixt. But that which wee finde either here touching equal securitie, or in other places somtimes also, about the giving of safe conduct even to the Fishermen of *England*, by Licence granted, either to *French*, or *Flemings*, or *Bretaigns*; that usually hapned when the heat of War was over & a Cessation agreed on to treat of Peace or Amitie. In the mean time, securitie of that kinde was given on both sides now and then by agreement: But by the King of *England* as well in respect of his beeing Lord of the place, as his beeing a partie that was treating about a League or Amitie. By others upon this account onely, not upon that; unless you understand the question to bee about the use of Ports and Shores: For so, no man denie's but these were Lords as well as hee. Moreover also, in our time, leav was wont to bee asked of our Admiral, for *French*-men to fish for *Soles* in the neighboring Sea, for King *Henrie* the Fourth of *France* his own Table; as it is affirm'd by such as have been Judges of our Admiraltie and Commanders at Sea of an antient standing; yea, and that the Ships of those *French* were seized, as trespassers upon the Sea, who

who presumed to fish there without this kinde of Licence.

But in the Eastern Sea, which washeth the Coasts of *Yorkshire* and the neighboring Counties, it hath been an antient Custom for the *Hollanders* and *Zelanders* to obtein leav to fish, by Petition to the Governor of *Scarborough* Castle, situate by the Sea-side in the Countie of *York*; and this for very many years past, as is affirm'd by that learned man Mr *Camden* speaking of those Coasts; *It is worth the while,* saith hee, *to note what an extraordinarie plentiful and gainful Herring-Fishing the* Hollanders *and* Zelanders *use to have in the neighboring Sea, having first obteined leav from this Castle according to the antient Custom. For, the English have ever granted them leav to fish; reserving alwaies the honor and privilege to themselvs, but through a kinde of negligence resigning the profit to Strangers. For, it is almost incredible what a vast sum of monie the* Hollanders *make by this Fishing upon our Coast.* So he. There is another man also of very great skill and knowledg in Sea-affairs, who, in the time of Q. *Elisabeth*, presented a Book to the Parlament, written in the English Tongue, about the Commoditie of Fishing, wherein hee write's, that the *Hollanders* and *Zelanders* every year, toward the later end of Summer, send forth four or five hundred Vessels called **Busses**, to fish for Herrings in this Eastern Sea, [c] **where before they fish they ask leave of Scarborough,** which are his very words. Care was taken also by Proclamation, in the time of [d] K. *James*, that no Foreiner should Fish in the *English* or *Irish* Sea, or that which belong's to the other Isles of the Realm of *England*, without leav first obteined, and every year at least renewed, from the Commissioners appointed for this purpose at *London*. And touching the libertie of fishing granted at other times also to Foreiners by

[c] **Hitchocks New years Gift.** *Edit. Londinens.* 1580.

[d] *Proclamat.* 7. *of King* James, *May* 6.

by the Kings of *England*, there are many Testimonies in [e] other Writers. But the causs why wee do not often meet with the Forms of those *Licences*, granted either for passage or fishing in the *English* Sea, was plainly this; becaus by the Leagues that were made with the neighbor Princes, a Licence or freedom of that kinde (as also of Ports, Shores, Passage, and other things) was so often allowed by both Parties, that, as long as the League was in force, the Sea served, as if it were a common Field, as well for the Foreiner that was in amitie, as for the King of *England* himself who was Lord and Owner. But yet in this kinde of Leagues, somtimes the Fishing was restrained to certain Limits, which is a thing chiefly to bee consider'd. The limits related both to place and time: So that according to agreement, the Foreiner in amitie might not fish beyond these Limits; the K. of *England* reteining a Dominion over the whole adjoining Sea. Touching this, there is a notable Example in the time of our *Henrie* the Fourth. An agreement was made betwixt the Kings of [f] *England* and *France*, that the Subjects of both might freely use Fishing throughout that part of the Sea, which is bounded on this side by the Ports of *Scarborough* & *Southampton*, and on the other side by the Coast of *Flanders* and the mouth of the River *Seine*. The time also was limited betwixt *Autumn* & the *Kalends of Januarie* following. And that the *French* might securely enjoy the benefit of this agreement, our King directed Letters to that end, unto all his Sea-Captains and Commanders. Here you see plainly, those Limits wholly excluded the *French* from that part of the Sea which lie's toward the West and South-west, and also from that which lie's North-east of them, as beeing so limited by our *Henrie*, at his own pleasure, as its Lord and Soveraign. Nor was there so much

as

[e] *Gerard. Malinius in Lege Mercatoriâ, cap.* 35.

[f] *Rot. Franciæ*, 5. *Hen.* 4. 29. *Septemb.*

as the least shadow of right or Prerogative, whereby the *French* King might seem to have any interest as a Lord or Owner in the setting of these Limits; seeing that part of the Sea which was secluded did not touch upon any Shore of his in the North, nor had hee any Countrie lying before the Sea in the South (except *Normandie*) or in the West; the rest beeing held either by the Duke of *Bretaign* or by the King of *England*, as wee have alreadie observed. From hence truly it was a Custom, for the Kings of *England* to give protection to Fisher-men that were Strangers, somtimes by Proclamation, and somtimes with a Fleet of men of War, when they went to Fish either by agreement made upon treatie, or by leav obteined, qualifications beeing added according to the *English* King's pleasure. There is among the Records of the time of *Edward* the First, an Inscription, *Pro hominibus* Hollandiæ *&c. For the men of* Holland *and* Zeland, *and* Friesland, *to have leav to fish near* **Jernemuth**. The King's Letter for their [g] protection follow's thus. *The* KING *to his Beloved and Trustie* John de **Buteturte** *Warden of his Port* de **Jernemuth** *Greeting. Forasmuch as Wee have been certified, that many men out of the parts of* Holland, Zeland *and* Friesland *also, who are in amitie with us, intend now to com and fish in Our Sea near* **Jernemuth**; *Wee command you, that you caus publick Proclamation to bee made once or twice everie week, that no persons whatsoëver imploied abroad in our service presume to caus any injurie, trouble, dammage, hindrance or grievance to bee don unto them, but rather, when they stand in need, that yee give them advice and assistance in such manner, that they may fish and persue their own advantage without any let or impediment. In Testimonie whereof, Wee have caused these our Letters to bee made Patents, to continue in force till after the Feast of S*[t] Martin *next ensuing. Witness the King at* **Wengham**,

[g] *Rot. Patent. 23. Ed. 1. Membr. 5.*

the XXVIII *day of September.* Which was in the XXIII year of his Reign, and of our Lord MCCXCV. The ſame day alſo, in favor of the Earl of *Holland* and his Subjects, hee ſet forth three men of War toward the farther Coaſt of the Sea, **for the ſafeguard** (as hee ſaith in another Letter) **of thoſe Veſſels belonging to your and our own Countrie, that are in theſe daies emploied about the Herring-Fiſhing &c. and to guard your Coaſts near the Sea.** Here hee grant's a Protection to fiſh. And in both the Letters, hee limits it within the ſpace of two Months. Hee alone alſo protected the Fiſher-men upon the *German* Coaſts (which, by reaſon of its nearneſs, hee call's here *your Coaſt near the Sea,* in his Letter to the Earl of *Holland*) as well as upon the *Engliſh.* Nor might the Fiſher-men uſe any other kinde of Veſſels, but that which was preſcribed by our Kings. Upon which account, all kindes of Fiſhing were ſomtimes prohibited, and ſomtimes admitted, this reſtriction onely beeing added, that they ſhould fiſh in ſuch Veſſels onely as were under thirtie Tuns burthen. This appear's by thoſe Letters of King *Edward* the Third concerning the Laws of Fiſhing, which were directed unto his ſeveral Governors of *Yarmouth, Scarborough, Whitby,* and *Donwich,* Towns ſeated upon the Eaſtern Shore. The words are theſe; [h] **Forasmuch as wee have given Licence to the Fiſher-men of the aforeſaid Town, and to others who ſhall bee willing to com unto the ſaid Town for the benefit of Fiſhing, that they may fiſh and make their own advantage with Ships and Boats under thirtie Tuns burthen, any prohibition, or Commands of ours whatſoever to the contrarie notwithſtanding, wee command you to permit the Fiſher-men of the aforeſaid Town, and**

[k] Rot. Clauſ. 11. Ed. 3. Membran. 35.

and others who shall bee willing to com to the said Town for the benefit of Fishing, to fish and make their own advantage with Ships and Boats under thirtie Tuns, without any let or impediment, any Prohibitions or Commands of ours made to the contrarie in any wise notwithstanding, as wee have said. witness the King at the Tower of London, August. X. Which was in the 11th year of the Reign of *Edward* the Third, or of our Lord MCCCXXXIX. But if any heretofore undertook the protection of the Fisher-men in this Sea, without leav of the *English*, they were to bee seized and imprison'd, as Invaders of the Right of Dominion, and to expect to bee dealt with accordingly, for the injurie don to the King of *England*.

This is evident also in the Records of our K. *Edward* the Fourth. For, hee erected a Triumvirate or invested three Persons with Naval Power, whom the Records call *Custodes, Conductores, & Waftores*, **Guardians, Conductors, and Waftors**, whose Office it was to protect and guard the Fisher-men upon the Coasts of *Norfolk* and *Suffolk*. To the end therefore that the expences of the Guard might be defrayed by the Fisher-men, and all others whatsoever bee excluded from medling with this kinde of Guard or protection, hee appointed four men, by name Sir *John* **Hemingham** Knight, *William* **Hopton**, *Edmund* **Pye**, and *John* **Wansfleet** Esquires, *as well* (say the [i] Records themselvs) *to over-see those* Guardians, Conductors, *and* Waftors, *as to give notice to all Fishermen of what Countrie soever they bee, who shall desire to fish in the Parts aforesaid under the protection of the said N.N. that those Fisher-men and everie of them, do contribute to all and all manner of Costs, Charges, and Expenses belonging to the same Guardians and Conductors in the time of fishing, and charge all*

[i] *Rot. Pat.* 22. *Ed.* 4. *Membran.* 2.

ſuch Coſts, Charges, and Expences according to a proportion, and to levie and collect thoſe Coſts, Charges, and Expences, out of this kinde of Fiſhings belonging to the Fiſher-men aforeſaid, whereſoëver they may bee found; As alſo to arreſt and apprehend all others, except the afore named, who preſume or attempt to becom Guardians, Conductors, or Waſtors, and to commit them to our next Gaol, there to bee kept ſafely and ſecurely, till wee ſhall take order for their deliverie. In the very ſame words almoſt, to the ſame purpoſe, wee finde divers Letters Patents of King *Henrie* the [k] Seventh; yea, and of *Richard* the [l] Third, ſave that in the form hereof, after thoſe words [*charge all ſuch Expences according to a proportion*] this conſiderable Clauſ here is inſerted [*Although the ſame Fiſhermen, whether any one or more of them, may have had Letters of ſafe Conduct from any other King, Prince, or Governor of any Kingdom whatſoëver.*] So that by the received and uſual Cuſtom, the Charges of the Guard were to bee defraied by the Fiſher-men of this Sea, at the pleaſure of our Kings, though they might have had Letters of publick ſecurity and protection from any other Princes. Nor were any other perſons to bee admitted to a partnerſhip in this kinde of Guard, except thoſe that were appointed by the King of *England*, leſt by this means perhaps it might derogate from the *Engliſh* Right. Which is a manifeſt ſign or evidence of the Dominion and Poſſeſsion of the place.

k *Rot. Pat.* 3. *Hen.*7. *part.*2. *in dorſo* 15. *Auguſt.* & *part.* 1. *in dorſo.* 18. *Septembris.*

l *Rot. Pat.* 2. *Rich.*3. *part.* 1. *Membran.*2.

The

The Dominion of England made evident from the laws *and* limits usually set *by our Kings in the Sea, to such* Foreiners as were at enmitie with each other, *but in amitie with the* English. *And concerning the King's* Closets *or* Chambers *in the Sea. Also touching that singular privilege of* perpetual truce (*or exemption from hostilitie*) in the Sea *about those Isles which lie before the shore of Normandie.*

CHAP. XXII.

As to what concern's the Laws and Limits that have been prescribed to Foreiners (from whence I derive a fift sort of Testimonies) who beeing at enmitie with each other, and both of them in amitie with the *English*, did mutually make prize and prey upon each other throughout this Sea; Whereas about the beginning of the Reign of *James* K. of *England*, the rest of the Christian world was every where at peace, but the warr waxed hot betwixt the *Spaniard* and the States of the *United Provinces*, and thereby it happened, that both those parties beeing in amitie with the *English*, did infest one another with mutual and very frequent depredations in the *English* Sea, touching the lawfulness whereof divers Questions arose among the King's Officers, in the Court of Admiraltie; Our K. following the examples of his Predecessors, did as lawful Soveraign and Moderator of the Seas, set forth a [a] *Proclamation*, appointing certain limits upon the English Coasts, within which hee ordeined there should bee safe riding for both

[a] *Proclam.* 1. *March* 2. *of K.* James, *or* 1604. *in Rot. Pat.* 2. *Jacobi R. part.* 32.

both parties, with safe passage, yea, and declared hee would give equal protection to both in such manner, that within these limits neither might the *Spaniards* use any hostilitie against the *United Netherlanders*, nor these against them, nor the Subjects of any Nation whatsoever against those of another, without incurring his displeasure. The words of the Proclamation are these; **Our pleasure is, that within our Ports, Havens, Roads, Creeks, or other places of our Dominion, or so near to any of our said Ports and Havens, as may bee reasonably construed to bee within that title, limit or precinct, there shall bee no force, violence, or offence suffer'd to bee don, either from man of war to man of war, or man of war to Merchant, or Merchant to Merchant of either partie. But that all of what Nation soever, so long as they shall bee within those our Ports and places of our Jurisdiction, or where our Officers may prohibit violence, shall bee understood to bee under our protection, to bee ordered by cours of Justice, and bee at peace each with other.** But by the same Proclamation hee declared, that violence should so onely bee permitted betwixt Enemies in that limited part of the Sea, that if any man of war should either bee hovering near hand with an intent to offer violence to his enemie, in the open Sea adjoining, or the Creeks, Ports, and Havens of the same, or should out of any place so prohibited, contrarie to the intent of the Proclamation, fall upon his Enemies ship, setting forth to Sea from the same place, then the English men of war, as well those belonging to Merchants as Commanders in the King's service, should remove and punish such kinde of violence. The words of the Proclamation are these; **Our**

plea-

pleasure therefore and commandement is to all our Officers and Subjects by sea and land, that they shal prohibit (as much as in them lieth) all such hovering of men of War of either side so near the entrie of any of our Havens, or our Coasts; And that they shall rescue and succor all Merchants and others that shall fall within the danger of any such as shall await our Coasts in so near places, to the hinderance of Trade and Traffick outward and homeward, from and to our Kingdoms. The *Prescribed limits* afore-mentioned were set forth in a Table or Map cut in Brass, and published by the King's Command. The manner of it was such, that both the limited part of the Sea, and those Ports and Creeks were pointed out by direct lines draw from one point of land or adjacent Island, to the next Point or Island upon the *English* shore. These points with the Isles fetching a compass round about from the North-Coast of *England*, by the East and South as far as the West, beeing in number *twentie seven*, are ranked thus in their order. Holy Island, the Sowter, Whitby, Flamborough head, the Sporn Cromer, Winterton-nesse, Easter-nesse, Layestof Estnesse, Orfortnesse, the Northforeland, the Southforeland, Dungenesse, Beach, Dunenoze, Portland, the Start, the Ramme, the Dudman, the Lizard, Lands end, Mildford, S. Davids Head, Beardsie, Holy head, and the Isle of Man. Wee have very great Creeks of Sea cut off by these lines from the Sea round about, which they call *Regias Cameras* The Kings Chambers, and the Ports Roial. Even as in an hous the inner private Rooms, or Chambers, or Closets, which in barbarous Latin are wont to bee termed *Cameræ*, are reserved for the Master; and as the Citie of *London* hath of old been called in our Law the *Chamber of the King of England*, whereby the rest of his Dominion

minion round about is set forth, as it were by the use of a more narrow Title: So these Creeks, though very large,

beeing

beeing called by the like name and limited at the pleasure of the Kings of *England*, do in like manner shew his Dominion over the rest of the Sea. But wee have taken a Description of the Points and Islands, whereby those Creeks set forth in the Table here annexed, are wont to bee limited, out of that [b] instrument which was written in *English* by twelve men very well skilled in Maritim affairs, and sworn for this purpose at the time when the Proclamation was published, and it was by them presented to Sir *Julius Cæsar* Knight, at that time Judg of the High Court of Admiraltie, but now Master of the Rolls, and one of his Majestie's Privie-Council, to whom the care of searching after this kinde of antient limits was committed. But in that Instrument, as well the distance of all the Points in respect of each other, as the manner of sailing in a direct cours is explained, from whence the latitude of every one of the *King's Chambers*, may in part bee collected. Those twelv men beginning at the **Holy Iland**, fetch't a compass round from the North by the East and South to the West, in the order hereafter following. The first cours and distance is from that Island to **The Sowter.** And from thence the rest are reckoned in the like manner.

[b] *Martii*, 1604. *seu* 2. *Jacobi R.*

Promontoriorum series.	*Rumbi*	*Leucæ.*
Ad **the Sowter**	in Phœnicem, **S. S. E.**	17 1/3
Ad **Whitby**	in Notapeliotem **S. E.**	12
Ad **Flamborough head**	in Notapeliotem **S. E.** 1/2 versus Austrum.	8

Promontoriorum ſeries.	*Rumbi.*	*Leucæ.*
Ad **the Sporne**	in Phœnicem **S.S.E.** verſus Apeliotem.	$13\frac{1}{3}$
Ad **Cromar**	in Meſeurum **S. E. and by E.**	$24\frac{1}{3}$
Ad **Winterton-nes**	in Hypophœnicem **S.E. and by S.**	4.
Ad **Caſter-nes**	in Phœnicem **S.S.E.**	$2\frac{1}{13}$
Ad **Layeſtof**	in Auſtrum **S.**	$3\frac{3}{4}$
Ad **Eaſt-nes**	in Auſtrum **S.** $\frac{1}{2}$ verſus Occidentem.	$1\frac{5}{6}$
Ad **Orforth-nes**	in Meſolybonotum **S. and by W.**	$6\frac{1}{6}$
Ad **North-fore-land.**	in Auſtrum **S.** $\frac{1}{3}$ verſus Occidentem.	$15\frac{1}{6}$
Ad **South-fore-land.**	in Auſtrum **S.**	$6\frac{8}{3}$
Ad **Dunge-nes**	in Notolybicum **S.W.** $\frac{1}{4}$ verſus Auſtrum.	7
Ad **Beach**	in Africum **W.S.W.** $\frac{1}{4}$ verſus Auſtrum.	13
Ad **Dune-noze**	in Africum **W.S.W.** $\frac{3}{4}$ verſus Occidentem.	$24\frac{5}{6}$
Ad **Portland**	in Hypafricum **W. and by S.** verſ. Auſtrum.	$16\frac{1}{12}$
Ad **the Start**	in Africum **W. S. W.** $\frac{1}{5}$ in Occidentem.	$18\frac{2}{3}$

Promon-

Promontoriorum Series.	*Rumbi.*	*Leucæ.*
Ad **the Ramme.**	in Occidentem **W.** $\frac{1}{4}$ versus Boream.	6 $\frac{1}{2}$
Ad **the Dudman.**	in Africum **W.S.W.** $\frac{1}{6}$ versus Occidentem.	8 $\frac{1}{2}$
Ad **the Lizard.**	in Africum **W.S.W.** $\frac{1}{3}$ versus Austrum.	9
Ad **the Landsend**	in Caurum **W. N.W.** versus Boream.	7
Ad **Milford**	in Boream **N.** $\frac{2}{3}$ versus Orientem.	31 $\frac{2}{3}$
Ad **S. Davids head.**	in Boream **N.** $\frac{1}{2}$ versus Occidentem.	5 $\frac{1}{2}$
Ad **Beardsie.**	in Hypaquilonem **N. and by E.** $\frac{1}{8}$ vers. Orientem.	12 $\frac{1}{6}$
Ad **Holy head.**	in Boream **N.** $\frac{1}{6}$ versus Occidentem.	9
Ad Monam	in Hypaquilonem **N. and by E.** $\frac{1}{5}$ versus Boream.	26

Here you see very large spaces of Sea, intercepted somtimes for above ninetie Miles (for, three *English* miles here go to everie League) whereby those Chambers or Sea-Closets are made. But wee finde the management of that business concerning these *Chambers*, at the time of the aforesaid Proclamation, set forth after this manner, in the subscription of the *twelv men* that were sworn, and added to the aforesaid distances and courses of sailing. *Wee whose names are subscribed, beeing called before the Right Honorable Sir* Julius Cæsar *Knight, Judg of his Majestie's High Court of Ad-*

 miraltie,

miraltie, and there beeing inrolled, admitted, and sworn, for the describing of the limits and bounds of **the King's Chambers, Havens, or Ports**, *in their full extent, do by these presents make answer, and to the best of our knowledg and understanding, declare, that the said Chambers, Havens or Ports of his Majestie, are the whole Sea-Coasts which are intercepted or cut off by a streight line drawn from one point to another, about the Realm of* England. *For the better understanding whereof, wee have made a Table concerning that business; whereto wee have annexed this our Schedule, shewing therein how one Point stand's in a direct line towards another*, according to that Table. *Given the fourth day of* March, *Anno Dom.* 1604. *and in the second year of the Reign of our Soveraign Lord King James, &c.* And then in the Schedule there follow the names of the *twelv men*; who were all persons of very great knowledg in naval or Maritim Affairs. So, the spaces within the streight lines drawn from one point to another, are the Chambers or Ports of the King of *England*, who beeing Lord in like manner of all those parts of the Sea, as farre as the opposite Shores or Ports, whilst hee commanded a keeping of the peace within these Creeks or Closets, did, as *Arbiter*, permit those that were in amitie with him; but enemies among themselvs, to make prize of one another, in the rest of the Sea; yet not without som qualifications or restrictions added concerning the use of the more open part of the Sea. And truly, the *Spaniards* alleged afterward, that themselvs ought to bee protected from hostilitie also, without these limits, in the more open part of the Sea; and that by virtue of the agreement of peace, whereby the Kings of *Spain* and *England* were obliged to protect one another's subjects, in all parts of their Kingdoms: which is as much as to say, that the rest of the

the Sea flowing between com's no less under the name of the Kingdom of *England*. And this appear's also from the dispute held by their Advocate in *England, about the protection of the Territorie by Sea*, against the Hollanders, who *mightily exclaimed* (as [c] hee saith) *that they should bee intercepted and staid by the King's Officer at Sea, with the prize that they had taken from their enemies the Spaniards. That it was an unjust violence; that beeing disturbed and spoiled, they ought to have reparation made them, and to bee heard against those Spaniards, who beeing prisoners were discharged with the goods that were taken.* But that the King of *England* might justly give the *Spaniards* protection against the *Hollanders*, in the *British* Sea, either within or without those limits, hee plead's after this manner. *You see* (saith hee) *how far the Dominion of the King of* England *stretche's toward the South, North, and West. The* [d] *Northern Coasts of* Britain, *having no Countries lying against them, are washed by the main and open Sea. And the Southern Coasts of* Ireland *are bounded upon* Spain; *the Western upon the* Indian *Countries under the Dominion of* Spain; *And so the Jurisdiction of our King by Sea, is of a mightie vast extent. Nor was it restrained or lessen'd by that subsequent Proclamation of the King* (the same above mentioned) *whereby certain limits were appointed, beyond which the* King *declared the power of his Territorie should not bee extended, in these Acts of hostilitie betwixt the* Spaniards *and* Hollanders. *But it's said, that the* Hollanders *were intercepted by the Officer without these limits. Also according to the Articles of Peace lately agreed on betwixt our King and the King of* Spain, *they ought to protect one another's Subjects in all places throughout their Dominions: And therefore both ought to give protection throughout that immens Jurisdiction. For, there are limits* [e] *founded upon right, and there are limits by compact or agreement: And an argument taken from the one, doth not conclude against the other.*

[c] *Albericus Gentilis in Advocat. Hispanica, lib.* 1. *cap* 8.

[d] Tacit. in vitâ Agricolæ. Cæs. de Bello Gallico, l. 5.

[e] *Menoch. Consil.* 14.

And here wee are to follow the limits of right, concerning which certainly the articles of Peace and Agreement ought to bee understood; Becaus the other Bounds beeing set afterward, were not then in imagination. But the autoritie of the Proclamation extend's not to things past. Certain it is, that Laws and Constitutions do give a Beeing to [f] *future businesses, and are not to bee recalled unto things don and past. Nor is this a Declaration of the King's right (therefore the more easily to bee* [g] *admitted) made in the Proclamation, but a disposition and law wholly new. For, a* [h] *Declaration induceth nothing new, and changeth nothing. But this Proclamation would change much, seeing the power of the King's Territorie extend's it self much beyond those limits now constituted. To this an* [i] *Answer may bee given also, which is acknowledged by all, that a Declaration is of no force to another's prejudice, which here might bee don to the ship that was intercepted; for which right was sought according to common Custom, and also according to the special agreement of the peace, that those Princes should suffer no violence to bee don to one another's Subjects in their Territories. And it is much more strong in respect of that express article of the Treatie, for that it could not bee meet to take off from the full force of the Contract; which would now bee lessen'd notwithstanding, if it were granted that the Territorie is so lessen'd, within which onely our King might protect the* Spaniards. *Moreover, it hinder's not which is objected, that these limits which are now expressed in the Proclamation, were observed long before by long Custom in Controversies of this nature. For, to omit those most difficult things which are deliver'd in* [k] *proving the Custom, certainly the intent of our King in the Contract of peace seem's not to have had respect unto that Custom, if any there hath been, or also unto the Statute, which is alleged here to bee antient. For, neither are those things common and understood by the other Prince in amitie, nor perhaps by our King himself; to wit, matters of fact, in his new Kingdom.* All which things I thought fit

f *L.7. C.de Leg. Non. Cons.* 110. 111.

g *Cravetta, Cons.* 641.

h *Decian.* 1. *Consil.* 8. *Oldrad.* 318. *Imol. Cons.* 67. *fin.*

i *Decian.* 1. *Cons.* 7.

k *Riv.* 1. *Consil.* 74. *num.* 10.

fit to add here out of *Albericus Gentilis*, becauſ they belong not onely unto theſe Limits, Creeks, or Roial Chambers in the Sea, but to the Dominion of the whole *British* Sea. And truly *Gentilis* was ill understood by *Joannes*[l] *Gryphiander*, who diſcourſing at large concerning Sea-Affairs, allegeth the place before-cited out of him in ſo brief a manner, as if by that Proclamation of King *James*, his Juriſdiction had been reſtrained ſimply to thoſe limits. *The Juriſdiction of* England *(ſaith Gryphiander) by Sea, although it bee extended to the South, North, and West, yet by a Proclamation of* James *the preſent King, it is circumſcribed by certain limits in the Sea.* Hee quote's *Albericus Gentilis*, for his Autor. But truly, the King had no intent in that Proclamation, that his Juriſdiction ſhould bee circumſcribed ſimply by thoſe Limits, but onely in relation to the acts of hoſtilitie at that time betwixt the *Spaniards* and *Hollanders*; hee beeing Lord and Moderator of the *British* Sea for ever, as well as his Predeceſſors: which is ſufficiently manifeſt out of the Proclamation it ſelf, & out of *Gentilis*. Nor indeed is it eaſily to bee conceived, from whence that ſpecial and perpetual privilege of Truce or Freedom from hoſtilitie had its original, which the inhabitants of *Jerſey*, *Garnſey*, and the other iſles lying before the ſhore of *Normandie*, do enjoy even in this very Sea, though war bee between the Neighbor-Nations round about, unleſs it bee derived from this Sea-Dominion of the Kings of *England*. Concerning that privilege, Maſter *Camden* beeing well inform'd by antient Teſtimonies, ſpeak's after this manner in brief. [m] *By an antient privilege of the Kings of* England, *here is as it were a perpetual Truce, and though a war bee on foot, yet the French and others have a libertie to com hither to and again without danger, and uſe Commerce ſecurely.* But wee finde the ſame more at large

[l] *Tract. de Inſulis, cap.* 14. § 46.

[m] *In Inſulis Brit. p.* 855.

large, in som [n] Kings Patents, expressed thus concerning *Jersey*; *that in time of War, Merchants of all Nations, and others as well Strangers as Natives, Enemies as well as Friends, may freely, lawfully, and without peril, go unto, pass to and fro, and frequent the said Isle and the places upon the Coasts thereof, with their Shipping, Merchandise, and Goods, as well for shelter from foul weather, as upon any other their lawful occasions, and there to use free Commerce and Traffick, and to abide with safetie and securitie, and to com away thence, and return at pleasure, without any damage, trouble, or hostilitie whatsoëver, in their Affairs, Merchandise, Goods or Bodies; and that not onely near the Island and places aforesaid upon the Coasts, and their Precinct, but also within the spaces distant from them as far as a man may ken, that is, so far as the sight of the eie can attain.* And this is called a privilege, which you see extend's so far into the Sea it self, as the sight of the eie can pierce from the shore. And if so bee this privilege did not proceed from the Kings of *England*, as they are Lords both of the Sea and the Isles, (and by the same right that the Isles themselvs belong to them, as hath been said [o] before) it cannot in reason bee imagined from whence it had its original. There is not (so far as wee know) so much as a pretence of a Grant made by any other Princes. But onely by the Kings of *England*, who unless themselvs were Lords of the whole Sea flowing about, by what Title and Autoritie did they ordein such a Truce so far within the Sea on every side, between enemies of all Nations whatsoëver that came unto those Islands? But as our Kings have very often commanded that all manner of persons should ceas from hostilitie, not onely within the aforesaid Creeks, but also throughout the spaces extended thence at pleasure, into their Territorie by Sea; so in like manner they indulged the like kinde of privilege for ever through-

[n] *Rot.Pat.2. Ed.6.part.7. Rot. Pat. 2.Elizab. part.6. & Rot.Pat.2. Jacobi Regis, part. 19.*

[o] *Cap.XIX.*

throughout these Coasts of the French shore, that all manner of persons, though enemies to one another, might securely sail to and fro, as it were under the wings of an Arbiter or Moderator of the Sea, and also freely use the Sea according to such spaces or limits as they were pleased at first to appoint. Which, without doubt, is a clear evidence of Dominion.

Certain publick Records, *wherein of old the Dominion of the Sea is,* by the way, *ascribed to the Kings of England, both by the* King himself, *and also by the* Estates of Parlament, *debating of other matters, and that in* express words, *and* with verie great deliberation, *as a known and most undoubted Right.*

CHAP. XXIII.

I Shall next of all cite several publick Records, which are kept in the Tower of *London,* wherein the Dominion and possession of the Sea is by the way expresly asserted as belonging to the King of *England,* and that both by the King himself, as also by the Estates of the Parlament of *England,* as they were debating about other matters. For, that is the sixt head of the former Division. King *Edward* the third intitle's himself and his Predecessors Lords of the whole Sea flowing round about, in the ſeveral Commiſsions given to *Geoffry de* Say Governor or Commander of the Southern and Weſtern Sea, and *John de Norwich* of the Northern (the limit of diſtinction beginning, as it was uſual, at the Mouth of the *Thames*) out of which Records wee here ſet down theform, which is eſpecially to bee conſider'd, ſo far as it make's to this purpoſe. [a] *The KING to his Beloved and Truſtie* Geoffry de Say, *Admiral of his Fleet of Ships, from the Mouth of the River Thames toward the Weſtern parts, greeting. Whereas Wee have of late commanded you by Our Letters, that you together with certain Ships out of the Cinque-ports, which wee have order'd to bee furniſhed and made readie for war according to our Command, ſhould ſet forth to Sea, to oppoſe and reſiſt certain Gallies, provided and inforced with men of war in divers forein Parts, which, as Wee were inform'd, were ſet out towards the parts of our Dominion to aggriev Us and Our people, or elſ to turn their courſ toward the Coaſts of* Scotland, *for the relief and ſuccor of our Enemies there; And in regard it hath been related by ſom, that Gallies of that kinde to the number of* XXVI *are newly com to the Coaſts of* Bretaign *and* Normandie, *and do ſtill abide there, as it is ſuppoſed, to do what miſchief they can againſt Us and Ours, or to ſuccor Our ſaid Enemies, as is aforeſaid; Wee calling to minde that OUR PROGENITORS THE KINGS OF ENGLAND have before theſe times been LORDS OF THE ENGLISH SEA ON EVERIE SIDE, yea, and defenders thereof againſt the Invaſions of Enemies; and ſeeing it would very much grieve Us, if our Kingly honor in this kinde of defenſ ſhould (which God forbid) bee loſt in our time, or in any ſort diminiſhed; and deſiring, with God's help, to prevent dangers of this nature and provide for the ſafeguard and defenſ of the Realm and our Subjects, and to reſtrain the malice of our Eenemies; Wee do therefore ſtrictly require and charge you, by the duty and* Alle-

[a] *Rot. Scotiæ, 10. Ed. Memb. 16.*

Allegeance wherein you stand bound, according to the special trust reposed in you, that immediately upon sight of these presents and without any farther delay, you do set forth to Sea with the Ships of the Ports aforesaid and the other Ships which are now readie; and that you arrest the other Ships in obedience to our command, which Wee lately requir'd you to arrest (But so that they might bee readie and provided to set forth according to Our aforesaid Command, seeing Wee caused the Masters and Marriners of the same Ships to bee prepared, and gather'd together, whether they were within your Liberties or without, and to caus them, beeing well provided of men of War and other necessaries, to hasten out to Sea with the aforesaid Ships) and that with all diligence you make search after the aforesaid Gallies and other Ships of War abroad against us, and stoutly and manfully set upon them, if they shall presume to bend their cours for the end aforesaid, toward the parts of Our Dominion, or the Coasts of Scotland. *And if they steal away from you, so that you cannot meet with them, then you are with the aforesaid Ships of our Fleet without any delay to follow after the same Gallies and Ships of War set out against Us, if they shall make towards our Kingdom or the Coasts of* Scotland *aforesaid, and courageously to destroy them, for the conservation of our Royal honor. But yet Wee will not that you occasion any hurt or hindrance to Merchants or others passing by Sea, who have no intention to offend Us and our Subjects, or to succour our Enemies.* Then follow's a power to press Seamen, and som other matters of that kinde. The day also and Autoritie is subscribed after this manner. *Witness the King at the Town of S*[t] John, *the sixteenth day of* August. *By the King himself and his Council.* The like Commission was at the same time, and by the same time and by the same Autoritie given to *John de Norwich* Admiral of the Northen part.

In the preferring of a certain Bill also in Parlament

(which was the voice of the Estates of the Realm) in the reign of the same *Edward*, wee finde that hee was usually accounted and styled King or Soveraign of the Sea by all Nations. The words are, [b] *qe XX ans passez & toutdiz adevant, la Navie de dit roialme estoit en touz portz & bones villes sur mier & sur riviers si noble & si plentinouse, qe touz les pais tenoient & appelloyent nostre avantdit Seignieur, LE ROY DE LA MIER, & tout son pays dotoyent le pluis per mier & per terre per cause de la dite Navie &c.* Which beeing translated out of the old *Norman* speak's to this effect; *That the* English *were ever in the Ages past renowned for Sea-affairs in all Countries near the Sea, and they had also so numerous a Navie, that the people of all Countries esteemed and called our King, the King or Soveraign of the Sea.* There is likewise a notable Testimonie touching this business in the Parlament-Records of *Henrie* the Fifth, where the tenor of the Bill ran (as was usual) after this manner; *Item priont les* [c] *Commens que, per lou nostre tressoverain seigneur LE ROY ET SES NOBLES PROGENITORS DE TOUT TEMPS ONT ESTE SEIGNEURS DEL MEER, & ore par la grace de Dieu est venuz que nostre dit seigneur le Roy est seigneur des costes d' ambeparties del meer, d' ordeigner sur touts estrangers passants per my le dit meer, tiel imposition al œps nostre dit seigneur le Roy à prendre que à luy semblera resonable pur la sauvegarde del dite meer.* That is to say, *Item, the Commons do pray, that (seeing our Soveraign Lord the King and his illustrious Progenitors, have ever been Lords of the Sea, and now that through Gods grace it is so com to pass, that our said Lord the King is Lord of the Shores on both sides of the Sea) such a tribute may bee imposed upon all Strangers passing through the said Sea, for the benefit and advantage of our said Lord*

b *Rot. Parl.* 46 *Ed.* 3. *num.* 20.

c *Rot. Parl.* 8 *H.* 5. *memb.* 3. *art.* 6.

Lord the King, as may seem agreeable to reason for the safeguard of the said Sea. The Answer subscribed to this Bill was, *Soit avise par le Roy*, that is, *let the King himself bee advised of it.* For, the King resided in *France* at that time, beeing Lord of that Countrie by Inheritance and Conquest, and *Humphrey* Duke of *Glocester* was President of the Parlament, beeing then Keeper or Lieutenant of *England*, by whom, as the King's Deputie, this kinde of Answer was usually given to Bills, as often as an assent to them was delaied; but when the King was present in person, *le Roy s' advisera, the K. will advise*, served in stead of an Answer from antient down to the present time, in such Bills as were not passed into Acts. That is to say, in those Bills to which the Lords and Commons had given their assent before, that is, the Estates of the Parlament of *England*, which is here especially to bee considered. For, most certain it is, that, according to Custom, no Answer is given either by the King or in the King's name, to any Parlamentarie Bills, before that the Bill, whether it bee brought in first by the Lords or by the Commons, hath passed both Houses, as it is known to all that are verst in the Affairs and Records of Parlament. And when the name of either of them is left out in the draught of the Bill, (as the Lords are in that before alleged) it was wont to bee supplied, as it is also at this day, by the brief form of Assent, which is added by that Hous, to whom the Bill is sent and transmitted. For, that Hous which first prefer's it, transmit's it to the other, who either give's an assent, or reject's it. And when both Houses have so given their assent, then after a while, either the King give's his assent (whereby it becom's an Act or Law) or els hee laie's it aside, and (as I have alreadie shewn) take's time to advise; Neither of which is ever don by the King, according to the cours of Parlament, till both Lords and Commons have first given their assent. But the whole form of the afore-mentioned Bill, which is full of all kinde of storie concerning things transacted in Parlament, is taken out of the very Schedules annexed to the Bill, (wherein the Forms of this kinde of assent were wont expresly to bee added) and register'd according to antient Custom, among the Records of Parlament, in the very same words wherein it was at first exhibited; no express mention beeing made of the assent both of Lords and Commons which is annexed to the Body of the Form (for, the assent of both sufficiently appear's, in that according to the cours of Parlament it was so presented to the King) and the King's assent onely or intent of deliberation beeing added by way of subscription, as I have shewn. But most of those Schedules annexed to that kinde of Bills which relate to the more antient times are lost; whereas notwithstanding the Records wherein they were wont to bee register'd, have been carefully preserved in the *Tower* for above CCC years. All which wee thought meet to mention here, to the end that in the Bill before alleged out of the Parlamentarie Records of *Henrie* the fift, these three things may bee observed, which make very much to the point in hand. *First*, that the Estates in Parlament, according to the Custom of their Ancestors, that is to say, both Houses of Lords and Commons, beeing well-informed of the matter perhaps by som antient Testimonies whereof wee are bereft by the injurie of time, did with one consent affirm it as a thing unquestionable, that the King of *England* is Lord of the Sea: As it appear's also in that former Record which relate's to the Reign of *Edward* the third;

for,

for, both the Bills are placed alike in the aforeſaid Records. *Secondly*, that the Sea whereof they ſpeak is the whole that flow's between *France* and *England*: For, they ſay in expreſs terms, that King *Henry*, beeing Lord of the Sea, was at that time Lord *des coſtes d' ambeparties del meer*, that is, *of the Coaſts* or *Shores on both ſides of the Sea*, or thoſe that include the Sea on both ſides, which cannot bee underſtood of any other or greater Sea, than of that which was mentioned there immediately before: And ſo it is in plain terms to bee taken of that whole Sea. *Thirdly*, that thoſe *Eſtates* did not queſtion but that Tributes might bee impoſed by autoritie of Parlament, upon all ſtrangers whatſoëver, whereſoëver they paſs through this Sea; as well as Cuſtoms in Port; And that they did not at all conceiv, that a Bill ought to bee preſented touching that buſineſs unto the King, as hee was at that time King of *France*, but onely as King of *England*, that is, as Lord of the whole Sea flowing between. And it is very improbable, and not in reaſon to bee admitted, that they would ſo upon deliberation (for both Lords and Commons uſe to debate ſuch matters a long time before they paſs a Bill) that they would, I ſay, ſo upon deliberation require an impoſing of Cuſtoms by the Act of an *Engliſh* Parlament, in a place that was not ſubject, as a part of the Roial patrimonie, to the King of *England*, as King of *England*. From hence it was alſo, that our preſent King *Charls* did this laſt year declare, *that himſelf and his progenitors the Kings of* England *have in all times hitherto, by an antient and moſt juſt title, been Lords of this Sea*; to wit, in his [d] Letters Patents ſent to the Maritim Counties of *England*, whereby ſhip-monie was impoſed for the defence of his Dominion by Sea. Add moreover hereunto, that in the agreement made betwixt our *Edward* the firſt and *Guie*

[d] *Brev.* 10. *Caroli R. Octob.* 20. *ſeu* 1634.

Guie Earl of *Flanders* about the wearing of Colors or Flags in every ſhip, and puniſhing offendors by Sea, *William de* Leyburn is called [e] *Admiral de la mier du dict Roy d'Engleterre*, or *Admiral of the Sea of the ſaid King of England.* Other Teſtimonies of the ſame kinde there are in Records touching the Dominion of the Sea, as it hath been received and acknowledged according to the Common Law and Cuſtom of our Countrie, which I ſhall diſcourſ of in the next place, and after that, concerning the Teſtimonie of Foreiners.

[e] 1286. *ſeu* 15 Ed. 1. *in Faſcic. de ſuperioritate, Maris*, in Arce Londinenſi.

Of divers Teſtimonies in our own Law-Books, *and the* moſt received Cuſtoms, *whereby the Sea-Dominion of the King of* England, *is either* aſſerted *or* admitted.

Chap. XXIV.

THE ſeventh of thoſe Heads, according to the former Diviſion, which manifeſt the aforeſaid Dominion of the Kings of *England*, relate's to our Law-Book's, and the received Cuſtoms therein, which prove it from the moſt antient times. There are alſo in them many Particulars that may relate hereunto, which are explained now and then touching the Guard of the Sea, the *Engliſh* Admiraltie, and other things alreadie handled. But in this Chapter wee ſhall uſe either the determinations and Commentaries of our own Lawyers, or chiefly ſuch Court-Records as explain their opinions. I confeſs indeed in ſom of the

Authors of our Law who wrote above CCCL. years ago or thereabout, after they had (as the manner then was) read through the *Civil Law* also, they were so strict in following those determinations word for word, which they found concerning the Sea in that Law, that when they treated *de acquirendo Rerum Dominio* **of the manner of acquiring the Dominion of things**, they tranferr'd them into their own writings. From thence it is, that *Henry Bracton*, who was a very famous Lawyer at the later end of the reign of *Henrie* the Third, saith, [a] *Naturali jure communia sunt omnia hæc, aqua Profluens, aër, & Mare, & litora Maris quasi Maris accessoria.* **By the Law of Nature all these things are common, running water, the Aer, and the Sea, and the shores of the Sea as accessories or dependants of the Sea.** Also, *ædificia, si in mari sive in litore posita fuerint, ædificantium sunt de Jure gentium*, **If Buildings bee raised in the Sea, or upon the shore, they becom theirs that build them by the Law of Nations.** And a little after, *Jus piscandi omnibus commune est in portu & in fluminibus*, **a Right of fishing is common to all in a Haven and in Rivers.** Which wee finde likewise in [b] som other of our Law-Books of that Age, as a passage that fell from som Writers (of whom I spake at large in the former Book) that were more affected than was meet with the words of *Ulpian* and *Justinian*, in the general division of things. But these very men in other places, shewing the Customs of our Countrie, do sufficiently admit the King's Dominion by Sea. For *Bracton* himself afterward speak's of them that by the King's grace and favor [c] *quieti sint de Theolonio & consuetudinibus Dandis per totum regnum Angliæ in terrâ & mari, & per totum Regnum tam per terram quàm per mare*, **Were exempted from**

[a] *Lib. 1. scil. de Rerum divisione, cap. 12. §. 5. & 6.*

[b] *Autor Fletæ Ms. lib. 3. cap. 1. Breton lib. 2. cap. de* Purchas.

[c] *Bracton lib. 2. cap. 24. § 2. & 5. fol. 56. & 57.*

from paying Tolls and Customs, throughout the whole Kingdom of England **in the Land and in the Sea; and throughout the whole Kingdom both by Land and by Sea.** And in the same King's time a freedom from som paiments was granted to the Citizens of London [d] *per totum Regnum tam per mare quàm per terram*, **throughout the whole Kingdom as well by Sea as by Land.** And so *Bracton*, when hee return's to speak of the Customs of our Countrie, acknowledged that the Dominion of the Sea belong'd to his King no less then the Land. And hence it came to pass also, that *inter Capitula Coronæ* (as they call them) that is to say, those **Articles or chief Heads**, whereof enquirie was to bee made according to the usual custom, by Judges delegated throughout *England* for the conservation of the publick peace, wee finde this also, *de Purpresturis factis super Dominum Regem, sive in Terrâ sive in Mari, &c.* **Of * Pourprestures made upon our Lord the King, either on Land or in the Sea, or in sweet waters, either within the Libertie or without, or in any other place whatsoever.** And it is placed among the Articles of this kinde recited by [e] *Bracton* himself, and in the [f] Autor of the Book called *Fleta*. But in the language of the Law wee call those things *Pourprestures*, whereby detriment is don to any publick place belonging to the Patrimonie of the Crown, as a publick thorow-fare, a River, and the like: So that according to the nature of this ordinarie Article touching *Pourprestures*, in the general form of enquirie, the Dominion or Ownership of the Sea is ascribed to the King, no less than of the Land, or of publick Road or thorow-fare, and River. agreeable hereto is that Article about any kinde of salt-waters beeing inclosed by any subject, or possessed in any

[d] *Rot. Pat. 51 Hen. 3. membr. 11.*

* *Pourpresture* is properly, when a man encroacheth, or when any thing is don to the nusance of the King's Tenants.

[e] *Lib. 3. de Corona, cap. 1. § 3. & cap. 2. § 1. fol. 116b. & 118a.*

[f] *Fleta, Ms. lib. 1. cap. 20.*

any other manner; which in the antient Records of our Court of Admiraltie is said to bee don, *to the disherison of the King*. The words are there, [g] Item *soit enquis de ceulx qui acrochent à eulx eaues salees en desheretison du Roy*. And at this day, enquirie is wont to bee made, about that business, by Autoritie of the high Admiral. *Robert Belknap* also, an eminent Judg in the time of *Richard* the Second, [h] saith that the Sea is subject to the King, as a part of his English Kingdom or of the Patrimonie of the Crown. His words in the *Norman* tongue run thus; *Le Mere est del ligeans del Roy, come de son corone d' Angleterre*. Hee added to his words, in a remarkable way, *as belonging to the Crown of* England, *or as belonging to the Royal Patrimonie of England*, to the end that no man might question, whether the Sea belong'd to his King by the Right of the Kingdom of *England*, or of the Dutchie of *Normandie*, or of any other Province in *France*. Another also, who wrote in the time of *Henrie* the Eighth, saith, it hath been received by antient custom, that it is a dutie lying upon the King of *England*, as Lord of the *British* Sea, to scour the Sea of Pirates, and to render the use thereof as of a publick Road or Thorowfare whose soil is within his Patrimonie) safe for Shipping. For, hee expresseth himself in *English* thus; [i] **The King of the ould Custome of the Realme, as the Lord of the narrow Sea, is bound, as it is said, to scoure the Sea of the Pirates and petit robbers of the Sea.** So much also, as to what concern's Dominion, is without controversie admitted by our [k] Lawyers of later time. And it appear's by publick Records, conteining divers main points, touching which the Judges were to bee consulted for the good of the Common-weal in the time of King *Edward* the Third, that the King's Sea-Dominion, which they called

[g] Cod. Ms. de Admirallatu, fol. 18b. Artic. in Admirallat. inquirend. Edit. anno 1595. num. 33.

[h] 6. Rich. 2. Fitzherbert tit. Protection. 46.

[i] Seingerman. lib. 2. cap. 51.

[k] Ed. Coke part. 5. fol. 108. & in Comm. ad Littleton sect. 439. fol. 260.

led *the antient superioritie of the Sea*, was a matter out of question among our Lawyers of that Age. But consultation was had for the more convenient guarding of it: For, the whole Bench of Judges were advised with *to the end* (so wee read it in the[1] Records; and that is especially to bee observed which wee finde here about the first beginning of the Naval Laws of the *Isle of Oleron*, seated in the Creek of *Aquitain* at the mouth of the River Charente) *that the form of proceeding heretofore ordained and begun by* Edward *the first, grandfather of our Lord the King and his Council, at the prosecution of his Subjects, may bee resumed and continued, for the reteining and conserving of the antient superioritie of the Sea of* England, *and the Autoritie of the Office of Admiraltie in the same, as to the correcting, expounding, declaring, and conserving the Laws and Statutes long since made by his Predecessors Kings of* England, *for the mainteining of Peace and Justice among all people of what Nation soëver passing through the Sea of* England; *and to take cognisance of all attempt to the contrarie in the same; and to punish Offenders and award satisfaction to such as suffer wrong and damage; Which Laws and Statutes were by the Lord* Richard *heretofore King of* England, *at his return from the holy Land, interpreted, declared, and published in the Isle of* Oleron, *and named in* French **le ley Oleron.** Here you have it declared as a thing most received and certain, that the King of *England* hath, by antient right, been Lord of the Sea, of the same name, or that which flow's about it. But that whereof the Bench of Judges were to consult, was onely about the orderly maintenance of this right. Nor is it truly a small sign of this Dominion, that *Richard* the First King of *England*, beeing in the *Isle of Oleron*, which hee possessed as seated in his own Sea, not so much for that hee was Duke of *Aquitain* as King of *England* (whereof wee have alreadie spoken) did, as sole Ruler

[1] *In Fascic. de superioritate maris*, in Arce Londinensi.

Ruler and Moderator of Sea-affairs, first publish those Naval or Sea-Laws in that his Island, which hold in force to this day, and from that time gave them so large and perpetual an Autoritie by that name, that as the *Rhodian* Naval Laws (as the case stand's) do prove, that the *Rhodians* in antient time were Lords of the *Grecian* Sea, so the Laws of *Oleron* having [m] obteined such a kinde of Autoritie by Sea, from their first Institution, must ever declare the King of *England* as the Autor, to bee Lord of the neighboring Sea round about. But som printed Copies of these Laws, make them about sixtie years later than the Reign of that *Richard*; by what autoritie, I cannot tell. For, they relate them to have been made in the year MCCLXVI, which is the fiftieth year of our *Henrie* the third. Also, in the Law of the Land, it is reckoned among the Privileges of such as are absent, that they, who shall bee out of the Realm of *England* at the levying of a *Fine* of any Land, and making Proclamations thereupon, are not so bound either by a yearly prescription, as heretofore, or by a five years prescription, as is usual of later time, but that their Right remain's entire to them upon their return home, if they make their claim, within the like spaces of time. But *intra regnum* **Within the Kingdom** is by the same Law taken, and that in the usual phrase for that which is *intra* (or as it is wont to bee barbarously render'd *infra*) *Quatuor Maria*, **Within the** [n] **four Seas**, to wit, the Southern, Western, Eastern, and that Northen Sea which washeth both the sides of that neck of Land, whereby *Scotland* is united to *England*. That is to say, within the outmost bounds of the *English* Empire in those four Seas, or within the oppcsite Shores of the Eastern and Southern Sea or Ports belonging to other Princes, and within the bounds of the Northern and

[m] *Edict. France, tom.* 3. *tit.* 2. *Juribus & privilegiis Admiralli* §. 19.

[n] *Stat.* 18. *Ed.* 1. *seu de modo levandi Fines. Bracton, lib.* 5. *de exceptionibus, cap.* 30. *fol.* 437. 2. *Ed.* 3. *fol.* 9ª. 4. *Ed.* 3. *fol.* 46. *pl.* 30. **Fitzherbert** 8. *Rich.* 2. *tit.* Continual Claim, 13. **Plowden**, *Comment.* 1. *part. fol.* 359. & 360. &c.

Western Sea, which indeed are to bee bounded after another manner; but yet to bee bounded: that is, accordirng to the extent of possession West-ward beyond the Western Shores of *Ireland*, and by the first beginning of that Sea, which is of the Scotish name and jurisdiction. But that which is opposed to this Particle *intra quatuor maria*, **Within the four seas**, is that [o] *extra quatuor Maria*, **Without the four seas**, or to bee in the parts so beyond the Seas, that they bee beyond the bounds of the Sea-Dominion of the King of *England*; from whence wee are to determine of the bounds or exterior limit of the Seas. And although the *Land of England* bee somtimes used for that which is the whole Realm, or English Empire, as signifying the same, a more ordinarie and indeed more brief expression beeing applied (as is usual) in stead of a more large; yet it certainly appear's, that *extra quatuor maria*, **Without the four seas**, and *extra Regnum*, **Without the Realm**, do in our Law-Books signifie the very same thing (that is to say, so far as the extent and latitude of the whole English Empire is comprehended in the name of Realm, not as the Realm of *England*, is now and then distinguished in [p] our Law from *Ireland*, which also is a distinct Dominion of the same Empire, or from the other Islands which are reckoned in the Roial patrimonie of the Kings of *England*.) For, it is usual in the Language of the Law, so to describe him, who, in that sens, shall bee out of the Realm. And whereas in the Reign of *Richard* the second to an objection made against one that would avoid the yearly prescription as not bound by it, for that hee was not in *England*, it was excepted that hee was in *Scotland*, and so within the four Seas; It was thereupon [q] answer'd and rul'd by the Court,

o *Bracton ib.* & **Coke** 7. *Jacobi R. part.* 8. *fol.* 100. *Cas. Rich.* **Lichford.**

p **Coke**, *part.* 7. *in cas. Calvini, fal.* 23.

q **Fitzherbert**, *tit.* Continual Claim, 13.

Court, that the Exception was of no force, for that *Scotland* was not within the Bounds and Limits of *England*. So that **within the four Seas**, and **within the Realm**, signified one and the same thing; from whence these terms, **out of the Realm**, and **without the four Seas**, becom one and the same also: *To bee out of the Realm*, is very [r] often repeated in this sens also, by *Littleton*, the most excellent of all our Law-Writers, signifying no other thing than what hee render's it in [s] another place, by one who *ala oustere le mere*, **crossed the Sea**, or, **went beyond sea**. From thence also it seem's to have proceeded, that, whereas with us, among the several temporal excuses of Defendants, who are summoned to appear in Court (in our Law wee call them * *Essoins*) there are two alleged, whereof the one is intitled *de ultra Mare*, the other *De Malo veniendi*, and this latter is allowed to him that is hindred by any kinde of misfortune whatsoever, *within the Seas*, or on this side of the more remote bounds of those Seas, which belong to *England*; but the former to him who live's *without, or beyond the Seas*, belonging to the English Empire; From thence it seem's, I say, to have proceeded, that, in former times, when there was a more frequent use in Court of this kinde of excuses, a Defendant beeing absent in *Ireland*, might lawfully make use of the latter form of *Essoin*, but not of the former. Nevertheless, if through ignorance hee did make use of this, it took on the nature of the latter, that is, wholly quitting all its own nature, it depended upon this, that the Defendant, according to the more vulgar sens or acception, lived *beyond-Sea*. For, according to received Custom, the nature of them both was such, that when any one might lawfully use the former, hee might also after

[r] *Sect.* 440. & 441.

[s] *Sect.* 677. & *videsis* **Plowden**, *Comment. part.* 1. *fol.* 359. & 360

* *Essoin* is an alledgment of an excuse for him that is summoned, or sought for to appear, and answer to an action. It is as much as *excusatio* with the Civilians.

after a while likewise enjoy the benefit of the latter. But in the said kinde of *Essoins* or Excuses, the former not beeing lawfully made use of, but yet turned into the latter by construction of Law, lest it should becom of no use, there was no place for the latter; to the end it might not bee iterated contrarie to Custom. The matter it self was thus decided in the time of K. *Henrie* the third, as it is described by *Henrie Bracton*, after this manner. *Esto*, saith [t] hee, *quòd quis se Essoniaverit de Ibernia quasi de ultra Mare; attornatur Essonium illud ad simplex Essonium de Malo veniendi ut coram Martino de* Patteshul *in Banco, anno Regis Henrici Sexto de Gilberto Mariscallo & Ceciliâ uxore ejus & Allano de Hyda, qui vocavit ad Warrantum Willielmum Mariscallum in Comitatu* Pembroke, *& qui se essoniavit de Ibernia, & non fuit allocatum, & postea fecit de hoc quòd aliud essonium de malo veniendi ad alium diem non fuit allocatum.* So much wee finde also in the antient Autor of that Book entitled [u] *Fleta*. Doubtless, *Ireland* is no less seated beyond sea, than either *France* or *Spain*, unless you take that decision, as relating onely to the Civil notion of this kinde of situation; to wit, that it is not situate beyond that Sea which is a part and Territorie of the English Empire, but placed therein, and comprehended under one and the same Supreme Power with *England*; and so that an Excuse or *Essoin de ultra mare*, is not in that kinde to bee admitted. In the antient [x] Records also concerning the Customs of our Court of Admiraltie, wee read it was an usual Custom in the time of King *Henrie* the first (who died *Anno Dom.* MCXXXVI.) and of other Kings both before and after him, That, if any man accused of a capital crime don by Sea, beeing publickly called five times by the voice of the Crier, (after so many several daies asigned) did not make his ap-

pearance

[t] *Lib.5.tract. de Essoniis, cap.8.§.2.*

[u] *Ms. lib.6. cap.8.*

[x] *Ms. fol. 12b.*

pearance in the Court of Admiraltie, hee was banished out of *England & de mer appurtenant au Roy d' Angleterre*, or *out of the Sea belonging to the King of England*, for fourtie years, more or less, according to the pleasure of the Admiral. Other particulars there are that relate hereunto about Actions for matters arising in this Sea, that were wont to bee entred in express terms heretofore, in the [y] ordinarie Courts of our Common Law, whose Jurisdiction was ever esteemed of such a nature, that an Action instituted about a matter arising in any other place than within the bounds of the Realm, was by the antient strict Law, alwaies to bee rejected by them. After which manner as it hath been a Custom now for many years, that an action ought to bee rejected, unless the matter have its rise within the *Bodie*, (as they call it) *of the Countie*, that is, within som Province or Countie of the Island, usually given in charge to certain Governors or Officers, known to us by the name of *Sheriffs*. So also is it in this Sea-Province, belonging, by the antient received Custom, to the high Admiral, or his Deputies, not onely so far as concern's its defence and guard, but also as to matter of Jurisdiction. So that at length it is manifest, that the Sea-Dominion of the King of England, is without controversie admitted and asserted also, both by the Determinations and Customs of the Law of the Land, and by the express words of the Writs and Forms of the Actions themselvs.

[y] *Temp. Ed.* 1. Fitzherbert *tit.* Avowrie 192. *& Placit.* 37. *&* 38 *Hen.* 3. *Rot.* 10. *Devon. Itin.* Sussex. 47 *Hen.* 3. *Rot.* 10. *Trin.* 50 *Hen.* 3. *Rot.* 22. *& Trin.* 24 *Ed.* 3. *in Brevibus Regis inter* Pike *&* Venore; quæ in Arcis Londinensis Archivo. Ejusmodi item sunt alia.

Nor is that of any force at all to the contrarie, which either our Countrie-man *Bracton* the Lawyer, (as hath been said) or som others, of late as well as antient time, that are Followers of him, but in too careless a manner, (while they [z] set down the Institutions of our English Law) have unadvisedly utter'd by the way, touching

[z] *Jo: Cowel. Instit. Juris Anglicani lib.* 2. *tit.* 1. *sect.* 3. *&* 4.

touching that antient communitie of the Sea, and of Fishing also in Rivers, according to the Books of *Justinian*; as if such a kinde of communitie were admitted in our Law. Truly, that which they have so let slip, is not so much to bee taken as contrarie to the known Law of the Land in this particular (for, even *Bracton* himself, as I have shewn, hath divers other passages that signifie this Dominion of the King) as it is to bee reckoned for som of the reliques of *Ulpian*, or of the School of the Imperial Law, too slightly and carelesly added by the way in writing. And the like may bee said of [a] one or two more of our Writers, who after the manner of reasoning, received for the most part in the Imperial Law, touching the middle of a River, and an Island risen therein, do by the way, but ignorantly, make the middle of the Sea flowing between to bee the bound of this Sea-Dominion of our Kings. Moreover, the same may bee said likewise of the [b] Commissioners of Queen *Elisabeth*, who treating at *Bremen* with the Commissioners of *Christiern* the fourth King of *Denmark*, about a freedom of Navigation through the Northern Sea, object a perpetual communitie of every kinde of Sea, from the Law of Nations, denie a Dominion, and wrest other things by way of Argument out of the Writers of the Imperial Law, which are clearly contrarie to our English Right, as also to the *Intervenient Law* of Nations, which hath continued in force for so many Ages about the Dominion of the Sea. Either, I say, the same must bee said of them, or els that they did not so much make choice of Arguments which they thought were true, to serv the present occasion, as of such that might seem to have the greater force and autoritie among those Civil Lawyers with whom they were in Trea-

[a] *Andræus* Horn, *Ms. in speculo Justitiariorum, lib.*2.& *Joannes* Dee *in Monarch. Britan. pag.*21.

[b] *Anno* 1602 *apud Camden. in Annalibus, Tom. pag.* 272. Edit. Londinens.

Treatie. Nor is it a new thing, that *Civilians* should speak of a natural and perpetual communitie of the Sea, even where it is most certain that a Dominion thereof is admitted from all Antiquitie, in the very Territorie wherein they themselvs are comprehended; as I have formerly declared. There are also very many Rights among us, belonging either to the Exchequer, or to such as enjoy the Right of the Exchequer by Grant from the King, which som conceiv to bee grounded upon that Sea-Dominion, whereof wee discours: As the confiscation of Goods derelict in the Sea, and of som of the greater sort of Fish, as Wale-Fishes, Sturgeons, and others. And for the most part that of the Satyrist hold's good,

[c] *Quicquid conspicuum pulchrúmq; ex æquore toto est,*
Res Fisci est ubicunque natat. —— ——

[c] *Juvenal. Satyr.* 4.

Goods in the sea of any worth and note,
Belong to th'Chequer wheresoe're they flote.

Besides wreckt goods cast out ashore, when no living creature belonging to the ship remain's alive. But these things do not onely appertain to him that is Lord of the Sea, but somtimes also to others in other Nations. And they for the most part depend, either upon the Law or Custom of som Land, as in the case of Goods cast ashore, or of such as are found and imported; or els upon a Right over such Persons as shall first possess them, as in the case of any Goods whatsoëver derelict or found in the Sea, and others of that kinde. Therefore I thought it not meet to draw those things here into Controversie.

Som antient Testimonies of less account, *touching the Sea-Dominion, whereof wee Treat.*

Chap. XXV.

THE last head in the afore-mentioned Division is concerning som Testimonies of a lesser account.

There hath been a piece of Gold very often coined by our Kings, called a *Rose-noble*, which was stampt upon one side of it with a ship floting in the Sea, and a King armed with a Sword and Shield, sitting in the ship it self, as in a Throne, to set forth a Representation of the Dominion of the English by Sea. The first Autor hereof was *Edward* the third; when

hee guarded his own Sea with a very numerous Navie, consisting of [a] Eleven hundred Ships; at which, as at other times, hee marched victoriously through *France*. Questionless, our Kings in a manner followed the example of *Caius Allectus* in this particular, who having gotten possession of the *British* Empire, (as was shewn [b] before) expressed his own Dominion by such a kinde of Coin. This patern, which I have placed here,

[a] *Thom. Walsingham* 1359. *seu* 33 *Ed.*3.

[b] *Cap.*5.

here, belong's, I suppose, to *Edward* the Fourth. And in a Book [c] lately set forth in *France* of the Coins belonging to the *French* Kingdom there are som that were stamp't by those Kings of *England* who were also Kings of *France*. But that those *Insignia* of a Ship, the Sea, a Sword, and a Throne, did relate to the right of the Crown of *England*, not at all to that of *France*, cannot bee doubted by any, who shall observ, that there is not the least impress or print of that thing to bee found in those *French* pieces, that were coined by the Kings onely of *France*. And whereas there are in the Coins of *Zeland*, certain representations of Sea-Dominion, as a Lion issuing out of the Sea, and other things of that kinde; yet truly that is but of late time, and in no case a pointing out of Dominion (if you except their Ports and inner spaces of the Sea included within their Islands) but onely of the kinde of life and situation of the people. But the aforesaid *English* Coin had an inscription upon the revers (which is not unusual in the gold Coins of our Countrie) taken out of the Gospel, viz. *Jesus autem transiens per medium illorum ibat*, which [d] som have conceived was a sentence in use among the Chymists, who by a customarie profanation of the name and passage of our Saviour, thought to set forth the majestie and dignitie of that Art of theirs, which refined the gold for these Coins in the time of *Edward* the Third; Others, that it served for an Amulet or Charm to make a man invulnerable or Shot-free. Wee finde indeed in som [e] Lawyers, that these words are placed among those, that are used by men brought under Examination upon the Rack, to ease and drive away their pain: Touching which it is not worth the while to spend any farther Discours. But as for the meaning of the impress on the other side of the Coin, it is thus explained by a certain Versifier, whose

[c] *Figures des monoyes de France, fol.* 131. & 132.

[d] *Apud Guil. Camden* Remains *pag.* 206. *Edit.* 1614.

[e] *Paulus Grillandus, Tract. de Quæst. & Torturâ, q.* 4. *num.* 13. & 14.

name is unknown, but hee wrote in *English* Rythme, in the time of *Henrie* the Sixt, *touching the conservation of the Government of the Sea* [f];

[f] *Ms. in* Biblioth. Cottonianâ, *& vide G. Camden. in loco antè citato.*

For foure things our Noble sheweth to me,
King, Ship, and Sword and Power of the See.

But his intent is, earnestly to perswade the *English* that it is their main interest diligently to guard the Sea (whereof the Kings of *England* are Lords) and to defend it with all their might, as the perpetual prop and support of their Empire. Hee saith also, that the same advice was given by the Emperor *Sigismund*, at his enterview with our *Henrie* the Fifth, for the procuring of on peace betwixt him and *Charls* the Sixth King of *France*. Give mee leav to set down his words.

The true processe of English policie
Of utterward to keep this region
Of our Englond (that no man may denie
Nor say of sooth but it is one of the best) [West,
Is this; that who seeth South, North East, and
Cherish merchandise, keep the Admiraltie,
That we be Masters of the narrow See.

For Sigismund the great Emperour,
(Which yet reigneth) when he was in this lond
With King Henrie the fift, Prince of honour,
Here much glory, as him thought, he found;
A mightie land which had taken in hand
To warre in France, and make mortalitie,
And ever well kept round about the See.

And to the King thus he said, My brother
(When he perceived two towns Calys and Dover)

Of

Of all your towns to chuse, of one and other,
To keep the Sea and soon to com over
To werre outwards and your reign to recover,
Keep these two towns sure, and your Majestie,
As your tweyne eyne, so keep the Narrow See.

For if this See bee kept, in time of warre
Who can here passe without danger and wo?
Who can escape? who may mischief differre
What marchandie may for by be agoe?
For needs hem must take trewes every foe,
Flanders and Spaine, and other, trust to me,
Or else hindred all for this Narrow See.

What is conteined more at large in these Rhythmes, you have the sens of it contracted above in few words. It is not worth while to render the words themselvs. The same Versifier also proceeds thus;

But King Edward made a siege royall
And wanne the town; and in speciall
The Sea was kept, and thereof he was Lord;
Thus made he * Nobles coined of Record.

* By *Nobles* here are meant the *Rose-Nobles* that hee coined.

Wee have also divers other very large Domestick Testimonies of this thing, which are added in the next place, beeing mingled together with the antient Recognition or acknowledgment of forein Nations concerning the same.

That

That the Sea-Dominion of the Kings of England *is acknowledged by* Foreiners, whom it most concern's, *by their* usual striking of Sails, *according to antient Custom. Also concerning two Edicts or Ordinances that were set forth about this Thing, by the Kings of* France.

Chap. XXVI.

WEe are com now to Foreiners. And it is clearly evident, by what wee have discoursed before, either touching the limits set for Navigation by the King of *England*, or the Licence of passage through this Sea often desired by Petition, that som of them have indeed acknowledged this Dominion. But there are two Testimonies more notable than the rest, which shew (if you consider chiefly, as you ought, their bee-ing Neighbors, and such whom it concerned) that they generally did the same. The one is the usual striking of the Top-sails, by every Ship of any Forein Nation whatsoêver, if they sail near the King's Navie or any Ship belonging to the same Navie in the Sea. The other is a *Libel* published of old, or a *Bill of complaint* instituted, wherein very many forein Nations heretofore, in the time our *Edward* the First, did all together, and by common consent with the *English*, acknowledg the Dominion of the Kings of *England* by Sea. Whereto I shall add also a particular declaration of that kinde, made by the *Flemings*, in an Ambassie to our *Edward* the Second.

But

But that the striking of Sails is don, not onely in honor of the *English* King, but also in acknowledgment of his Soveraigntie and Dominion in this Sea, is, I suppose, a thing out of question. Certainly, the *French* cannot doubt of it, who, by such a kinde of striking, would have had themselvs heretofore acknowledged Lords of our Sea; but in vain. That is to say, they were as much over-seen in the former Age, in setting forth two Edicts or Ordinances, to require and ratifie such a kinde of striking Sail to themselvs by all Foreiners; as they were in so rashly vindicating the Sea-Dominion of the King of *England*. Concerning those Edicts wee spake before in the [a] former Book; Neither of which was received as valid in any Court of Justice, according to a decision made in the [b] supreme Court of Parlament, which wee have observed also in that place. Yea, and here I shall set down the very words used by *Ludovicus Servinus* Advocate general to the King of *France*, to magnifie the Autoritie of those Edicts or Ordinances, at the time of that Decision. The one of them beeing set forth by King *Henrie* the Second of *France*, or in the year MDLV; the other by *Henrie* the Third, or in the year MDLXXXIV, they were both objected by those, who required a striking of Sail to them in the name of the *French* King, even without the bounds of *France* (for, the words of the Edicts did not relate onely to the Sea confining upon *France*;) upon which ground also they offer'd violence to certain *Hamburgers* who refused to do this, and seized them as guiltie of contempt against the dignitie and Dominion of the *French* by Sea. But as to this thing, saith *Servinus*, it may bee said on the contrarie, *That the* (Edicts or) *Ordinances of the Realm making injunction to strike and com aboard, have not been observed and are not to this day; And it doth not appear that of the* year

[a] *Cap.* 18.

[b] *Ludovic. Servin. Placit.* 11. *Tom.* 2. 1592. *pag.* 262. *Edic.* 1609.

year 1555. *hath been verified in the Court of Parlament, but the Defendants do report onely an extract out of the Register of* Broüage (which indeed is evident enough when that *Edict* is objected by the [d] same man.) *Moreover*, it was an old obsolete Law, *and that which prove's it, is the new Ordinance of the year* 1584. *For, there had been no need of a new Law if the old one had been kept; And notwithstanding that the last hath not been verified simply, but as it was promoted by persons in Power at that time, it did not pass without resistance, but was Registred and Published with the Qualification required by the Procurator General, at the charge of the Executor, according to the antient Forms, and such as the Officers of the Admiraltie had made in former time, without doing any thing anew.* The former *Edict*, which was objected, was never admitted by the Estates of the Realm; for, nothing of that matter is to bee found in the Records of Parlament, which is the proper place for a Testimonie of its admission. But the later was indeed admitted, though as to any effect of a Law, either at that time to bee enacted or introduced, or as received before into Custom, it was plainly rejected, and that at the instance of the King's Procurator; who desired it might bee so qualified, as you see, that what was grounded upon antient Custom, it onely might bee ratified, even after this Edict was so admitted in favor of som great Ones. Which was discreetly don; seeing both the Edicts were extremely contrarie to the Custom of their Neighbors, yea, and of all Foreiners. But as to the business of striking sail, which they would have to bee a special Sign or Pledg of their Soveraigntie and Dominion in those Edicts, which notwithstanding, upon second thoughts, were rejected afterwards in Law (as hath been shewn;) truly, it having been usually and perpetually acknowledged due for so many Ages to the

[d] *Servinus, placit. citat. pag.* 254.

English,

English, and performed accordingly both by stranger, and by the *French* themselvs (as a matter grounded upon long prescription) can bee no slight argument among the *French*, to confirm that Dominion of the *English*, whereof wee treat.

Moreover, it is affirmed by all that are used to the Sea as a thing out of Question, that this intervenient Law or Custom of striking sail hath been very usual to the *English* and other Nations; And that it is very antient and received for above four hundred years, appear's by this, that at *Hastings*, a Town situate upon the Shore of *Sussex*, it was decreed by King *John*, (in the second year of his Reign, or of our Lord MCC) with the assent of the Peers, that if the Governor or Commander of the King's Navie in his Naval Expeditions (which were all in that Age upon the Southern Sea) shall *encontre sur la mer* (so the words run in the [c] Norman Tongue) *aucunes Nefs ou vesseaulx charges ou voide, qui ne vevillent avaler & abeisser leurs triefs, au commandement du Lieutenant du Roy ou de l' Admiral du Roy ou son Lieutenant, mais combatant encontre ceulx de la flote, que, silz puent estre pris, quils soient reputez come enemies, & leurs Nefs vesseaulx & biens pris & forfaits come biens des enemies, tout soit que les Maistres ou possessours d' iceulx voudroient venir apres & alleguer mesmes les Nefs vesseaulx & biens estre des amies du Roy nostre seigneur; & que la menye estant en iceulx soient chastiez per emprisonement de leur corps pur leur rebelleté par discretion*; That is to say, *shall meet any Ships whatsoëver by Sea, either laden or empty, that shall refuse to strike their Sails at the command of the King's Governor or Admiral, or his Lievtenant, but make resistance against them which belong to his Fleet; That then they are to bee reputed enemies if they may bee* taken,

[c] *Ms. Commentar. de rebus* Admiral, *fol. fol.* 28. a.

taken, yea and their Ships and Goods bee confiscated as the Goods of Enemies. And that, though the Masters or Owners of the Ships shall allege afterwards that the same Ships and Goods do belong to the friends and Allies of our Lord the King. But that the Persons, which shall bee found in this kinde of Ships, are to bee punished with imprisonment, at discretion, for their Rebellion. It was accounted Treason, if any Ship whatsoëver had not acknowledged the Dominion of the King of *England* in his own Sea, by striking Sail: And they were not to bee protected upon the Account of Amitie, who should in any wise presume to do the contrarie. Penalties also were appointed by the King of *England*, in the same manner as if mention were made concerning a crime committed in som Territorie of his Island.

A Recog-

A Recognition or Acknowledgment of the Sea-Dominion of the King of England, made by very many of the Neighbor-Nations round about, *in an* antient Libel publickly exhibited, *or in a Bill of Complaint instituted by them, together with the English,* against *Reyner Grimbald* Governor of the *French* Navie. *Also, touching a Recognition of this kinde implied in his Defence.*

CHAP. XXVII.

THe other Testimonie concerning the Recognition of most Forein Nations in this particular, is that *Libel* or *Bill of Complaint* heretofore instituted by very many Nations together, wherein they unanimously declared the King of *England* and his Predecessors to bee Lords of the Sea flowiug about, and brought them to give an acompt in a Court of Judicature, who presumed to violate that Right: For the well understanding whereof, I shall relate the whole matter more at large.

A war being on foot between our *Edward* the First, and King *Philip the Fair* of *France*, it was so concluded somtimes by agreement, that there might notwithstanding bee a Freedom of Commerce on both sides, and so a Truce with all Merchants whatsoëver on either side; but as to other things, hostilitie proceeded in the mean time (as it was wont) betwixt both the Nations.

This special kinde of Truce was called [a] *Sufferentia guerræ*, **sufferance of War**, and during war, there were certain persons appointed by both Princes, to take cognisance of things don contrarie to this Truce, and pass their Judgments, *according to the* [b] *Law or Custom of Merchants, and the Form of Sufferance.* After a revolution of som years (wherein this kinde of Truce took place, and somtimes not) a League was made in the year of our Lord MCCCIII. which is the one and thirtieth of *Edward* the first. The first Article of that League is, [c] that those Kings should not onely bee at amitie with each other, but also that they should defend one another in all manner of Rights, against any others whomsoëver, except the Church of *Rome*, and on the part of the King of *England*; his son in law *John* Duke of *Brabant*; but on the part of the King of *France*, *Albertus* King of the *Romans*, and *John* Earl of *Henault*. But the third Article thereof (for the first and third is of singular use in that *Libel* or Bill of Complaint, as will appear by and by) is this, *Item il est accorde qe l' un ne receptera, ne sustendra, ne confortera, ne fera confort, ne aide as Enemies de l' autre, ne soffera qu' ils eient confort, souccors, ne aide, soit de gent d' armes, ou de vitailes, ou d' autres choses queles q' eles soient de ses terres ou de son poiar, mais adiondera sur peine de forfature de corps & d' avoir & empeschera à tot son poair loiaument en bon foi qe les dits enemies ne soient resceipts ne confortes es terres de sa seigneurie ne de son poiar, ne q'ils en aient confort soccours ne aide soit gents d' armes, des chevaux, d' armeures, de vitails, ou d' autres choses queles q' eles soient*: which is in English to this effect; that, according to this contract of amitie, they were neither of them in any wise to cherish the enemies of the other, nor suffer any kinde of aid or relief to bee afforded them in their Territories. The war beeing thus at

an

[a] Rot. Claus. 25 Ed. 1. in Sched. annex. Membranæ 26. Rot. Alemanniæ à 22 Ed. 1. ad 31 Ed. 1. &c.

[b] Rot. Pat. 26 Ed. 1. part. 2. mem. 24. in dorso.

[c] Fœdus integrum habetur in Rot. Alemanniæ, 31 Ed. 1. Membranâ 2.

an end, becauſ there aroſe very many complaints concerning injuries don up and down, as well in the more open as in our own Sea, during the ſpecial Truce afore-mentioned, but alſo it was probable that others of that kinde might ariſe perhaps after the League was made, eſpecially by reaſon of the differences at that time betwixt the *French* King and the Earl of *Flanders*; therefore Commiſsioners were appointed by both Princes to hear and decide them. And thoſe at that time on the behalf of the King of *England* were *Robert de* **Burghershe** Conſtable of *Dover* Caſtle, and *John de* **Banquell** Steward of *Pontoiſe*, *Baraldus de* **Sescas**, and *Arnaldus* **Ayquein** Knights; on the French King's behalf were appointed the Lord *Saquilly*, *Mittonius Blanvillius*, *Bertrandus Jordanus*, and *Gulielmus Rala-ſtanſius*, Knights alſo: To the end that they might take cogniſance (ſo it is in the King of *England*'s Commiſsion) *des enterpriſes, meſpriſes, & forfaites en Treve ou en Sufferance, entre nos & le dit Roy de France, d'un part & d'autre, es coſteres de la mer d'Engleterre & autres per decea & auſint per devers Normandie & autres coſteres de la mer per de la*; that is, *of encroachments, injuries and offences committed on either ſide in time either of the League or Sufferance*, or, *of the Truce agreed on between Us and the ſaid King of* France, *for freedom of Commerce onely, either upon the Sea-Coaſts of* England, *or any other neighboring Coaſts of the Sea, either towards* Normandie, *or others more remote*. But the aforeſaid parties were autoriſed by two Commiſsions, in ſuch manner, that the one Commiſsion contained four, and the other alſo four, an equal number beeing appointed by both the Kings. They both bear date the laſt day of *June*, MCCCIII. To theſe Commiſsioners or others of that kinde, the *Libel* was jointly exhibited by Procurators, on the behalf of the Prelates

d *Rot. Pat. 31 Ed. 1. membr. 16. ult. Junii.*

lates and Peers of *England*, also of the high Admiral of *England*, yea, and of the Cities and Towns throughout *England*; and lastly, of the whole English Nation, and others subject to the King of *England*; and how this could bee don otherwise than by autoritie of the Estates in Parlament, is not to bee imagined. With these in like manner were joined the Procurators of most Nations bordering upon the Sea throughout *Europe*, as the *Genoëses, Catalonians, Spaniards, Almains, Zelanders, Hollanders, Frieslanders, Danes, and Norwegians*, besides others under the Dominion of the *Roman-German* Empire. All these together instituted an Action or Complaint against *Reyner Grimbald*, who beeing Governor of the French Navie, had, during the war between King *Philip* of *France*, and *Guie* Earl of *Flanders*, intercepted and spoiled Merchants of their Goods in this Sea, that were bound for *Flanders*. And all these *Complainants* jointly say, that the King of *England* and his Predecessors, have time out of minde, without controversie, *enjoied the Soveraigntie and Dominion of the English Sea, and the Isles of the same, by right of their Realm of England, that is to say, by prescribing Laws, Statutes, and Prohibitions of Arms, and of Ships otherwise furnished than with such necessaries as belong to Merchants, and by demanding suretie, and affording protection in all places where need should require, and ordering all other things necessarie for the conservation of Peace, Right and Equitie, between all sorts of people passing through that Sea, as well Strangers, as others, in subjection to the Crown of* England. *Also, that they have had, and have the Soveraign Guard thereof, with all manner of Conisance and Jurisdiction in doing Right and Justice, according to the said Laws, Statutes, Ordinances, and Prohibitions, and in all other matters, which may concern the exercise of Soveraign Dominion in the said places.* To wit, such matters as concern'd the

office

office and jurisdiction of the Admirals, that were wont to bee appointed by the Kings of *England*. Then, adding the first Article afore-mentioned of the League made but a little before, whereby both Kings were obliged to defend one another's right, they proceed in their Accusation against *Grimbald*, saying; *That hee is onely Master of the Navie of the King of* France; *but call's himself Admiral of the said Sea; and pretend's that hee was autorised under that title by the King of* France, *upon occasion of his making warr against the* Flemings. *And that after the making of the said League, and contrarie to the intent and meaning of the same, hee had for above a years time unjustly assumed and usurped the office of Admiral in the said Sea, by autoritie of the King of* France *his Commission; taking the People and Merchants of* England, *and other Nations passing through that Sea, imprisoning and spoiling them of their Goods, and delivering them up to the King's Officers, as Goods forfeited and confiscate. And whereas hee hath in a very insolent manner justified these actions of his in writing, as don by autoritie of the King his Master's Commission, as also according to a Prohibition made by the King of* England, *and proclaimed, according to the intent of the aforesaid third Article of the Treatie, throughout his Dominions,* (that is to say, a *Prohibition* which forbade a giving any relief to the *French* King's enemies within the Dominion of the King of *England*) *and so endeavored to defend himself before the Commissioners;* it was alleged to bee don to the great damage and prejudice both of the King of *England*, and of the Prelates, Peers, and all the rest, who jointly preferr'd the *Bill*, as aforesaid. Therefore they all with one consent pray, that the persons so imprisoned beeing set at libertie, and restitution made of the Goods injuriously taken, they might bee referred to the Jurisdiction of the Admiral of *England* (to whom alone this kinde of Jurisdiction, both in respect of Things and Place, as well as Persons, did appertein) and that, by order of the Commissioners, *Reyner Grimbald* himself might bee enjoined to repair the losses of the *Complainants*, in case hee were able to make satisfaction; or otherwise, that the King of *France*, who gave him Commission for that Command, might bee adjudged to do the same. But after reparation made, that then also the said *Reyner* might receiv such punishment for violating the League, as might deter others from the like attempt in time to com.

Now what was don by the *Commissioners*, is not very well known: It seem's it was a matter of such moment, that it was thought more convenient to make an end by agreement, than bring the matter to a trial. But in the mean time, nothing is more evident, than that a right of Dominion over the Sea, and that antient and confirmed by long Prescription, was in express terms here acknowledged by almost all the Neighbor-Nations, to belong to the King of *England*; and so, that hee might, at his own pleasure, give protection, and set Laws and Limits to all that sailed through this Sea, and used it in any manner whatsoever; nor could this kinde of Right bee altered or diminished by the differences of the Neighbor-Nations between each other, or by any Right of war belonging to others, otherwise than in any other Territorie of his Dominion. And it is to bee observed, that the *Flemings* themselvs, betwixt whom and the *French* there was a war on foot at that time, were not, nor could they rightly have been parties in that Charge or Accusation: For, by virtue of the aforesaid League made between the *English* and *French*, they were to assist one another by Arms to defend each other's Rights; so that according to the League, the *French* King was permitted to use the Sea, to infest the *Flemings* beeing his enemies, but not to intercept such as passed this way from any other Nations, or that were bound with Merchandise for *Flanders.* And *Paulus*[e] *Æmilius,* speaking of this very time, saith; *The French King threatned ruine to* Flanders. *The King of* England *protected the* Flemings. *For,* Edward *was so far onely a friend of the King of* France, *that yet hee would not have the* Flemings *ruined.* Thus our King order'd the matter, both as a Defender of his own Right, and supreme Moderator also of Navigation in respect of others. Nor truly is it to bee omitted, that *Grimbald* himself here, beeing Governor of the French Navie, did not onely arrogate this power in this Sea from the Autoritie granted him by his King's Commission, but in express terms also made use of that *Prohibition* of the King of *England,* which was in force according to the Third Article of the said League, thereby to defend himself; as if hee had also acknowledged, that himself could not have lawfully held that office of Admiraltie in this Sea, without such a Permission as hee conceived himself to enjoy, by virtue of that *Prohibition.* For, by that *Prohibition,* it was required that no relief should bee given to the French King's Enemies, nor any aid afforded them within the Dominion of the King of *England,* (that is, *per my son poere,* which were the very words of *Grimbald,* as you may see in the *Libel* it self set down hereafter.) And so *Grimbald* expresly objected the Autoritie of that *Prohibition,* together with the power of his Master's Commission in defence of himself: As if hee had said, I use this power, it beeing given mee by the King of *France,* who put mee in Command over his Navie, and Affairs belonging to the Sea: But besides this, the King of *England* having set forth his *Prohibition,* commanded that no kinde of relief should

e *De gestis Franc. li.* 8.

bee given to any Enemie of the French, within his Dominion, according to the League made between both the Kings. And therefore, seeing I have not taken either the Persons or Goods of any but such as are Enemies, or at least such as according to the *Intervenient Law* of Nations, are to bee reckoned upon an hostile Account (for, doubtless hee pretended, that they were to bee taken as Enemies of what Nation soëver they were, who relieved the *Flemings* by Merchandise or otherwise) I conceiv it a sufficient ground of defence in my behalf, that the King of *England*, according to the League made, did by publick Proclamation require, that no succor or relief should bee given to the Enemies of *France* in any part of his Dominion. Upon which account, not to these, whom I took at Sea. The summe of all in brief is this; That *Grimbald* did not so much as imagine, that his office of Admiraltie or Power given him by Commission depended upon any Dominion of the King of *France* by Sea, but altogether upon the Autoritie of his Kings Commission, the League, and the King of *England's* Prohibition: As if the English King had openly declared by that *League* and *Prohibition*, that hee would not take it for any injurie to himself, during that kinde of League and Prohibition, although the *French* should fall upon any of their Enemies in his Dominion, or though they, which is all one here, should bee taken in his Sea, by the French King's Officers. Certainly, unless you so understand *Grimbald*, I do not see wherefore he should at all join that *Prohibition* together with the King his Master's Commission, in defence of himself, as it is expressed in the *Libel*, or why mention was made there of the Dominion of the King of *England*, throughout which that *Prohibition* was proclaimed, seeing the controtroversie arose touching things don onely by Sea. But if hee bee so to bee understood, certainly then hee did not onely forbear to oppose the antient right of the King of *England* by Sea, but also sufficiently acknowledged it, while hee seem's to affirm that a temporarie restriction onely was added thereto, by an accession of the *League* and the *Prohibition*: So that wee have a tacit acknowledgment even of the French themselvs at that time, in this their *Admiral*. But how the principal points of the League ought to bee expounded, it is no place here to discours; for, wee observ onely that the Sea-Dominion of the Kings of *England* was acknowledged, in that *Libel*, by so many Nations.

Moreover truly, it is worthie observation; that about the very same time, to wit, a little before the making of the League, the King of *England* did homage to the French King for the Dutchie of [f] *Aquitain*, the Earldom of *Pontois*, and other Provinces that hee held in *France*; that hee was also wholly deprived of them som time before by decree of the Parlament of [g] *Paris*; yea, and that about one hundred years before, King *John* was outed of *Normandie*; and yet afterward that the King of *England* now and then regained a possession of it, and that before the time of the League, and of the publication of this *Libel*; which serv all to this end, that wee may observ, that when the aforesaid famous controversie arose about the use and Soveraigntie of the Sea flowing between *France* and *Britain*, and the absolute Dominion thereof was asscribed by so many Nations, upon a Title derived time out of minde, to the King of *England* and his Predecessors, yet in the mean time no title at all was pretended in right to their possession either of *Normandie*, or *Aquitain*, whereupon a Dominion of any part of the Sea might in any

[f] *Rot. Alemann.* 30 & 31 Ed. 1. *Du Tillet en le recueil des Traictes, &c. fol.* 40 b.

[g] *Florilegus, ann.* 1293. 3. *Thomas Walsingham, ann.* 1294. *Alii.*

ſort bee grounded, but claimed upon the ſole right of the Engliſh Empire. And it appear's evident by the thing it ſelf, that the things complained of by thoſe Nations in the *Libel*, were don by that Governor of the French Navie, chiefly in the Sea near the ſhores of *France* and *Flanders*, which were in hoſtilitie with each other: And ſo certainly they all unanimouſly affirm, that the whole Sea, whereof they ſpeak, is under the Dominion of the King of *England*, and that upon the ſole Account and right of the Engliſh Empire. And as for *Grimbald*, hee did not defend himſelf, either by a pretence of any Dominion of the King of *France*, or by diſproving of that Preſcription; whereupon the Engliſh Title depend's, as a thing not declared according to Truth or antient Right; nor did hee at all pretend, that the Right which the Kings of *England* had in the Sea bordering upon *France*, did belong to them either upon the account of *Normandie*, or any other French Province whatſoëver, as Fiduciarie Clients or Vaſſals of the King of *France*, though it had been convenient and very ſeaſonable for him to have alleged all theſe Particulars, if the Truth had been ſo indeed. Whereby alſo that is not a little confirmed, whereof wee diſcourſed before, about taking the names of the ſhore over againſt us, in the later Commiſsions of the Office of high Admiral of *England*, for limits onely of the Sea-Dominion of the Kings of *England*, and of the Province thereof under their protection. Moreover alſo, about ſeven years before the exhibiting of the aforeſaid *Libel* to the Commiſsioners, when as the King of *France*, by reaſon of divers heinous injuries don to his Subjects by the Engliſh in this Sea, required that the King of *England* (as

hee

hee was the Fiduciarie Client or Vassal, becaus of *Aquitain* and other Provinces that hee held under him in *France*) should bee questioned not onely for wrong don, but also for his right to those Lands which hee held, and bee summoned to appear in the Parlament of *Paris*; the matter beeing set down at large in the Letter of Summons, hee inserted nothing therein whereby hee might seem to arrogate any Sea-Dominion at all to himself, or diminish that which belong'd to the King of *England*; as you may see in [h] *Florilegus*, who hath set down an entire Copie of them in his Annals. The same Autor also, speaking of the same Time, saith, [i] *At that time, there was neither Lord, nor Law over the Sea men; but what every man was able to catch, or snatch, hee called his own*; which plainly denote's an extraordinarie Licence or of Depredation, and infesting the Sea; yet so to bee understood, that in the mean time the incomparable power of the English in Shipping, which guarded their Dominion by Sea according to the Custom of their Ancestors, was chiefly signified thereby, the King very freely permitting his Subjects to use depredations by Sea, as long as the war continued. For, *Florilegus* himself relate's, that great numbers both of *French* and *Spaniards*, were then taken at Sea by the *English*. Yea, and about [k] that time, *Thomas* of *Walsingham* write's, that either a *French* or *Norman* Navie of two hundred Sail, which roved about this Sea to rob the English, were overcom by a Fleet of sixtie English Ships, and brought into *England*. There is also another *antient Autor* of the same time, when these affairs were acted, who saith, [l] *That in the Month of May*, MCCCXCIV. *there fell out a Quarrel between the Sea-men of the Cinque-Ports of* England, *and the Sea-men of* France, *and it was determined*

[h] *Anno* 1293.

[i] *Anno* 1294.

[k] *Anno* 1297

[l] *Ms.*

determined by a fight at Sea, wherein the English *with a Fleet of one hundred Sail, took two hundred Ships of* France, *and drowned or killed almost all the Sea-men of* France, *for which caus,* Philip *King of* France, *endeavored to take away Gascoign from the King of* England. Others there are likewise, that have other expressions touching these things, whereby it is easie to collect what is meant by that of *Florilegus*, when hee saith, *that there was neither Lord, nor Law, over Sea-men, at that time*; that is to say, the King of *England* had let the reins loos to his Subjects, as Moderator of this Sea, and this hee did, that they might not onely restrain his enemies, but them also that should reliev his enemies in any manner whatsoëver, or that should use the Sea otherwise than at his pleasure, who was Lord thereof. But as concerning the like acknowledgment, made singly and apart by the *Flemings*, of the Dominion of the Kings of *England* over the Sea, I shall Treat by and by; after that I have in the next place set before you the *Libel* it self in its own, that is, the *Norman* Tongue, as it stand's recorded in the Tower of *London*.

A

A Copie, *or* Transcript *of the* Libel *or* Bill of Complaint, *mentioned in the former Chapter.*

Chap. XXVIII.

IN the Archives of the Tower of *London*, where Records of above four hundred years are kept, there is a bundle of Parchments, which contein som affairs relating to the times of *Henrie* the Third, and of *Edward* the First and Third. The first contein's an agreement made between *Edward* the First and *Guy* Earl of *Flanders*, touching their Ships bearing of Colors about this Sea, to the end that they might bee the more easily known. Then there are annexed three either Originals or Copies of the said *Libel* written at the same time. For (as it seem's) the several Procurators of those Nations, that were parties in the Complaint, had their several *Libels*, though expressed in the name of all together. So that one is endorsed thus, *De Baiona*, as if that *Libel* had been exhibited singly by the men of *Bayonne*; but the title run's thus, *De Superioritate Maris Angliæ, & Jure Officii Admirallatûs in eodem*, that is, **Of the Superioritie** (or Soveraigntie) **of the Sea of** England **and the right of the Office of Admiraltie in the same**, as it is also in the said agreement between the King and the Earl of *Flanders*. Also, in one of the *Libels*, to those words is added *retinendis & confirmandis*; All beeing very plainly written in the usual Character of that Age, whereunto the matter relate's. And there can bee no scruple touching the realitie and truth of them to any one that

 seeth

ſeeth them, who is but a little acquainted with the antient writing and ſuch kinde of Records. I gave you the whole ſenſ, yea and partly the words before; but now have thought fit to ſet down an entire Copie of the *Libel*, as it was written at that time in the *French* or *Norman* Tongue; which run's after this manner.

A vous, Seigneurs, Auditours Deputez per les Rois d' Engleterre & de France, a redreſſer les dammages faits as gentz de lour Roiaulmes & des altres terres ſubgitz a leur ſeignuries, per mier & per terre, en temps de Pees & Trewes, monſtrent les Procurors des Prælatz et Nobles, & del Admiral de la mier d' Engleterre, & des Comminalties des Citties, & des Villes, & des Marchaunz, Mariners, Meſſagiers, & Peleringes, & de tous autres du dit Roiaulme d' Engleterre & des autres terres ſubgits a la ſegnurie du dit Roy d' Engletterre & d' aillours, ſi comme de la Marine de Genue, Cateloigne, Eſpaigne, Alemaigne, Seland, Hoyland, Friſe, Denemarch, & Norway, & de pluſours autres lieux del Empire, *que come LES ROYES D' ENGLETERRE PAR RAISON DU DIT ROYALME, DU TEMPS D' ONT IL NY AD MEMOIRE D DU CONTRARIE, EUSSENT*

ES-

ESTE EN PAISIBLE POSSESSION DE LA SOVVEREIGNE SEIGNVRIE DE LA MIER D' ENGLETERRE ET DES ISLES ESTEAVNS EN YCELLE, par ordinance & establisement des lois, estatutes, & defenses d' armes, & des vesseaux autrement garnies que vesseaux de Marchandise, et de seurté prendre et savegarde doner en tous cas que mestier serra, et par ordinance de tous autres faits necessaries a la garde des pees, droiture, et equite entre toute manere des gentz taunt d' autre seignurie come leur propre par illeque's passanz, et par soveraigne guarde et tote manere de conisance et Justice haute et basse sur les dites lois, estatuts, ordinances et defenses et par toutz aaltres faitz queux à le governement de soveraigne seignurie appertenir purront es lieux avant ditz. Et *A. de B. Admirall de la dite mire deputez per le Roy de* Engleterre, *et touz les autres Admiralls per meisme celui Roy d' Angleterre et ses Auncestres jadis Rois d'* Engleterre, *eussent este in paisible possession de la dite soverein garde ove la conisance et Justice et toutz les aultres apertenances avantdites (forspris en cas d' appell et de querele fait de eux à lour sovereigns Roys d'*

Engleterre de deffault de droit, ou de malvais juggement) et especialment par empechement metere, et Justice faire, seurte prendre de la pees de toute manere des gentz usaunts armes en la dite mier, uo menans niefs aultrement apparallez ou garniez que n' appartenoit au nief Marchande, et en toutz aultres points en queux home peut aver reasonable cause de suspection vers eaux de robberie ou des autres mesfaits. Et come les Maistres des Neifs du dit Royalme d' Engleterre, en absence des dits Admiralls, eussent este en paisible possession de conustre et jugger des touz faicts en la dite mire entre toute manere des gentz solonc les lois estatuts et les defenses et Custumes. Et come en le pimier article de l' Alliance nadgairs faite entre les dits Roys, en les traitz sur la darrain pees de Paris, soient comprises les paroles que s'ensujent en un cedule annexe à yceste (At non in schedulâ annexâ, sed in eâdem membranâ descriptum est quod sequitur; unde non tam ipsos libellos, qui cognitoribus edebantur, quàm sive formulas eorum archetypas sive exemplaria descripta hæc esse conjiciendum fortè est; utì etiam ex eo quòd Admiralli Angliæ nomen aliter ac per A. de B. non inseratur; quæ prima elementa non sunt

ſunt nominis alicujus tunc temporis Angliæ Admiralli in ſacris Scriniis reperti) *Primierement il eſt traict & accord entre nous & les meſſagers & les procurers ſuſdits, en nom des dits Roys, que iceux Roys ſerront l'un à l'autre, deſores enavant, bons, vrayes, & loyaux amys, & eydans contre tout home (ſauve l' Eſgliſe de Rome) en tiele manner que ſi aſcun ou pluſieurs quicunques ils fuiſſent voloient depointier, empeſcher, ou troubler les dits royes es franchiſes, es liberties, privileges, es drois, es droitures, eu es cuſtumes de eux & de leur royalmes q'ils ſeront bons & loyaux amys & aydans contre tout home que puiſſe viure & morir à defendre gardir & maintenir les franchiſes, les liberties, les privileges, les droitures, et les cuſtumes deſuſdites; Except pur le dit Roy d' Angletterre, Monſieur Johan Duc de Braban en Brabant, et ſes heirs deſſendans de lui et de la fille le roy d' Angleterre, et excepte, pur le dite noſtre ſeigneur le roy de France l' excellent Prince Monſiur Aubert Roy d'Alemaigne et ces heirs royes d' Alemaine, et Monſieur Johan Count de Henau en Henau. Et que l'un ne ſerra en conſail ne en aide ou l' autre perde vie, membre, eſtate ou honor; Monſieur Reyner Grimbaltz Maiſtre de la Navie du dit Roy de France,*

France, que se dit estre Admiral de la dite Mier deputez per son seignure avantdit per sa guerre contre les Flemminges, apres la dite alliance faite et affirmee, contre la forme et fource de mesme alliance et l'entencion de ceaux que la firent, l'office de Admiraulte en la dite Mier d'Engleterre, per commission du dit Roy de France, torcenousement emprist et usa un an et pluis, en prenant les gentz et marchaunts du Royaulme d'Engleterre et daillours per la dite mier passaunts ovesque lour biens, et les gens ainsi prises livere à la prison de son dit Seignur le Roy de France, et leur biens et Marchandises à les Resceivors per mesme celui Roy de France à ceo deputez en les ports de son dit Royalme come à lui forfaits et acquises, fist amesner per son juggement et agard, et la prise et detenue des dits gents ove leur dits biens et marchandises, et son dit juggement et agard sur la forfait de eaux et acquest, ait justifie devant vos, Seignours Auditours, en escripts par my l'autorite de sa dite commission sur l' Admiraulte avantdite, per lui aussi usurpee, et per my un defence communement faite per le Roy d'Engleterre per my son poere (solonc la forme de la tiers article de l' Alliance avant dite, que content les

les paroles desussecripts) en requerant que de ceo il en fuisse quitz & absolutz, en grand damage & prejudice du dit Roy d'Engleterre & des Prelatz & Nobles & anltres dessussnomes, per quoi les dites procurours en les nounes de leur ditz Seigneurs, à vous Seigneurs Auditors avantdits, prient que deliverance deune & hastive des dits gents, ovesque leur biens & marchandises ainsi prises & deteinues faites estre faite al Admiral du dit Roy d'Angleterre à qi la conisance de ceo appartient de droit, si come dessus est dist, ainsi q'il saunz destorbance de vous & d' altri puisse de ceo conustre & faire ceo que appertient à son office avant dit, & que le dit Monsieur Reyner soit condemne & destreint à faire deuue satisfaction à tous le dits damages si avant come il purra suffre, & in sa defaulte son dit seigneur le Roy de France, per qi il estoit deputez al dit office, et que apres deuue satisfaction faite as dites damages le dit Monsieur Reyner soit si duement puniz pur le blemissement de la dite alliance que la punicion de lui soit as aultres example pur temps avenir.

In

In *English* it run's thus:

** Or Commissioners.*

To you, our Lords, * Auditors deputed by the Kings of *England* and *France*, to redress the wrongs don to the People of their Kingdoms, and of other Territories subject to their Dominion, by Sea and by Land, in time of Peace and Truce.

The Procurators of the Prelates, Nobles, and of the Admiral of the Sea of England, and of the Commonalties of Cities and Towns, and of the Merchants, Mariners, Messengers, Inhabitant strangers, and all others belonging to the said Realm of England, and the other Territories subject to the Dominion of the said King of England, and of others under the Jurisdiction of the same; As also of divers other Nations, Inhabitants of the Sea-Costs of Genoa, Catalonia, Spain, Almaign, Zeland, Holland, Friesland, Denmark, and Norway, and of divers other places of the Empire, do declare; That whereas THE KINGS OF ENGLAND, By Right OF THE SAID KINGDOM, FROM TIME TO TIME, WHEREOF THERE IS NO MEMORIAL TO THE CONTRARY, HAVE BEEN IN PEACEABLE POSSESSION OF THE SOVERAIGN LORDSHIP OF THE SEA OF ENGLAND, AND OF THE ISLES WITHIN THE SAME, with power of making and establishing Laws, Statutes, and Prohibitions

hibitions of Arms, and of Ships otherwise furnished than Merchant-men use to bee, and of taking suretie, and affording safeguard in all cases where need shall require, and of ordering all other things necessarie for the mainteining of Peace, Right, and Equitie among all manner of people, as well of other Dominions as their own, passing through the said Seas, and the Soveraign Guard thereof; And also of taking all manner of Cognisance in Causes, and of doing right and Justice, to high and low, according to the said Laws, Statutes, Ordinances, and Prohibitions, and all other things which may appertein to the exercises of Soveraign Jurisdiction in the places aforesaid. And whereas A. de B. deputed Admiral of the said Sea by the King of England, and all other Admirals appointed by the said King of England, and his Ancestors heretofore Kings of England, have been in peaceable possession of the said Soveraign Guard, with power of Jurisdiction, & other the aforesaid appurtenances (except in case of appeal, and complaint made of them to their Soveraigns the Kings of England, in default of Justice, or for evil Judgment) and especially of making Prohibitions, doing Justice, and taking surety of the peace of all manner of people using arms in the said Sea, or carrying Ships otherwise furnished and set forth than Merchantmen use to bee; and in all other points where a man may have reasonable caus to suspect them of Robbery or other Misdemeanors. And whereas the Masters of the Ships of the said Kingdom of England, in the absence of the said Admiral, have been in peaceable possession of taking cognisance and judging of all Actions don in the said Sea, between all manner of people, according to the Laws, Statutes, Prohibitions and Customs. And Whereas in the first Article of the League lately made between the said Kings, in the Treatie upon the last peace at Paris, there are comprised the words here following, in a Schedule annexed to these Presents. (But that which follow's is not written in a Schedule annexed, but in the same Parchment; from whence it may perhaps bee conjectured, that these are not so much the very *Libels* themselvs, which were exhibited to the Commissioners or Auditors, as antient Copies taken from the Original; as also from this, that the name of the Admiral is set down A. *de* B. which two first Letters do not agree with the name of any one that wee can finde in Record, to have been Admiral of *England* at that time.) First, it is concluded and accorded between Us and the Agents and Procurators aforesaid, in the names of the said Kings; that the said Kings shall from this time forward, becom to each other good, true, and faithful friends, and bee aiding to one another against all men (saving the Church of Rome) in such manner, that if any one or more, whosoever they bee, shall intend to disturb, hinder, or molest the said Kings, in the Franchises, Liberties, Privileges, Rights, and Customs of them and their Kingdoms, They shall bee good and faithful friends to each other, and aiding against all men living, and readie to die, to defend, keep and maintein the Franchises, Liberties, Privileges Rights, and Customs aforesaid; Except on the behalf

behalf of the said King of England John Duke of Brabant in Brabant, and his heirs descending from him and the daughter of the King of England; and except on the behalf of our Lord the said King of France, the excellent Prince Monsieur Albert King of Almaign, and his heirs Kings of Almaign, and Monsieur John Earl of Henault in Henault; and that the one shall not bee of Counsel, nor aiding, where the other may lose life, member, estate, or honor.

Monsieur Reyner Grimbald, Master of the Navie of the said King of France, who call's himself Admiral of the said Sea, beeing deputed by his aforesaid Lord, in his War against the Flemings, did, after the said League made and confirmed, against the tenor and obligation of the said League, and the intent of them that made it, wrongfully assume and exercise the office of Admiraltie in the said Sea of England, above the space of a year by Commission of the said King of France, taking the people and Merchants of the kingdom of England, and of other places, passing through the said Sea with their Goods, and committed them so taken to the prison of his said Lord the King of France. and delivered their Goods and Merchandises to the Receivers of the said King of France by him deputed in the Ports of his said kingdom, as forfeited and due unto him, to remain at his Judgment and award. And the taking and deteining of the said people with their said goods, as also his said Judgment & award, for the forfeiture & acquest of them, he hath iustified before you, Lords, Auditors, in Writing, by virtue of the autoritie of his said Commission of Admiraltie aforesaid,

said, by him usurped after this manner, and during a Prohibition or Restraint generally made and proclaimed by the King of England, in right of his Dominion (according to the tenor of the third Article of the League aforesaid, which contain's the words above-written) requiring that hee may thereupon bee acquitted and discharged of the same, to the great damage and prejudice of the said King of England, and of the Prelates & Nobles, & others above-mentioned.

Wherefore, the said Procurators, in the names of their said Lords, do pray your Lordships Auditors, that you would caus due and speedie deliverance of the said people, with their Goods and Merchandises so taken and deteined, to bee made to the Admiral of the said King of England, to whom the cognisance of the same of right apperteineth, as is before expressed; So that, without disturbance from you or any other, hee may take cognisance thereof, and do what belong's to his office aforesaid; And the said Monsieur Reyner bee condemned and constrained to make satisfaction for all the said damages, so far forth as hee shall bee able, and in his default his said Lord the King of France, by whom hee was deputed to the said office; and that after satisfaction given for the said damages, the said Monsieur Reyner may bee so duly punished for the violation of the said League, that his punishment may be an example to others in time to com.

So far the *Libel* of so many Nations, manifestly acknowledging the Soveraigntie and Dominion of our Kings over the Sea, and thereupon demanding protection for themselvs. And whereas no mention is made of this thing in the Histories either of the *French*, *English*, or others

others, it is no wonder since the proceedings of Courts of Judicature are very seldom set down in Histories. But wee understand by the French Historie, that this *Grimbald* was Governor of the French Navie at the very same time. *Paulus Æmilius* writing of *Philip* the Fair, saith, [a] *Hee hired sixteen Gallies from* Genoa, *over which* Reyner Grimbald *was Governor or Commander. Hee sailing about by Sea, infested the* Sea-Coast *of* Flanders. Regimerus, Reginerus, or *Reynerus Grimbaldus*, is one and the same man; and among the *Genoëses*, there is an eminent Family of that name: But becaus hee was a Foreiner and Mercenarie, therefore (it seem's) *Joannes Feronius* left him out of the Catalogue of the Admirals of *France*; yet [b] *Joannes Tilius* placing him among the Governors of the French Navie, call's him *Rovertus Grimaldus*. Hee also is that Admiral of the King of *France*, who, as *Joannes de* [c] *Beka* saith, had command of three hundred and fiftie Gallies, that were sent by *Philip* the Fair, in the year MCCCIV. to aid the *Hollanders* against the *Flemings*. There are also several particulars in the Records of *France*, which relate to the differences then on foot between the *English* and *French*: And although that Libel or any Copie of it bee not found therein (if wee may credit *Tilius*, who set forth a Catalogue of that kinde of Records) yet there is that Commission among them, whereby the aforesaid *Auditors* or *Commissioners* were autorised to determine of things don contrary to the League. It is described by [d] *Tilius* after this manner; *Pouvoir donè par le Roy Edovard à deux nommez & accordez de sa part pour avec les deux eleuz de la part du dit Roy* (Phelippe) *d'enquerir & amendir les forfaictes durant lour tresue, le Dernier Juin* MCCCIII. *Ou tresor; layette Procurationes, posse, & potestates Angliæ*; K. **Power was given by King**

[a] *De Gestis Francorum, lib.* 8.

[b] *De rebus Gallicis, li.* 2.

[c] *Chronic. Episcop. Ultraject. & Comit. Holland. pag.* 93.

[d] *Recueil des Traictes, &c. fol.* 40.

Edward **to two persons named and appointed on his part, to meet with two persons chosen on the behalf of the said King** (Philip) **to make enquiry and give remedy touching Injuries committed during the Truce betwixt them the last of June** MCCCIII. **in the Treasury; in the Box intituled,** *Procurationes, posse, & potestatess Angliæ*; *K*. The Commissions bear date the same day and year; whereby these *Auditors* or *Commissioners* were appointed for this purpose, as wee observed before out of our own Records. Nor is it of any force here to the contrarie, that *Commissioners* were somtimes [e] deputed in the same manner by the Princes of the shores on both sides of the Sea, as also by the aforesaid Kings, to determine complaints about robberies and other injuries usually don by private persons to one another by Sea and Land. For, if any one will collect thence, that the Princes which deputed them had both an equal right in the Sea, it may as well bee concluded upon the same ground, that they were but part-owners of their own Countries, and had an equal interest in each other's Land. Besides, in such a kinde of deputation as that, there is more regard had of the persons offending, that are to bee tried, than of the Dominion of Territories; which truly is wholly to bee discovered som other way.

[e] *Rot. Claus. 21 Ed. 3. par. 1. membran. 25. dors. Rot. Franciæ, 10 Hen. 8. &c.*

A

A Recognition *or acknowledgment of the Sea-Dominion of the Kings of* England, *made by the* Flemings *in an* Ambassy *to* Edward *the* Second.

CHAP. XXIX.

TO these let us add now the assent and voluntarie acknowledgment of the *Flemings* in the Parlament of *England*, in the Reign of *Edward* the Second. When as the Ambassadors of *Robert* Earl of *Flanders* complained of the taking of their Goods away at Sea, imploring remedie of the King of *England*, they said more than once that they were taken upon the English Sea towards the parts about **Crauden**, within the power of the King of *England*, and brought into *England*; but that it appertained to the King of *England* to take cognisance of the crime, *for that hee is Lord of the said Sea, and the aforesaid depredation was committed upon the aforesaid Sea within his Territorie and Jurisdiction*; which are the words of the Record; but I shall set down the [f] whole, so far as it relates to this business.

[f] *Rot. Pat.* 14 *Ed.*2. *part.*2. *Membran.*26. *in dorso.*

Memorandum, **That whereas for the reformation of certain injuries in an amicable way, don by the Subjects of the Earl of** Flanders, **to the Subjects of the Kingdom of** England, **and by the Subjects of the said Kingdom to those of** Flanders, **since the time that our said Lord the King undertook the Government of his Kingdom, several Treaties had been held between the Council of our said Lord the King, and the Ambassadors of the said Earl often sent into** England

England, upon the aforesaid occasion, which Treaties, by reason of som impediments that happened, did not attein the desired effect; at length in the Parlament of our said Lord the King, held at Westminster in octabis Sancti Michaëlis, in the fourteenth year of his Reign, there appeared certain Ambassadors of the said Earl, to treat about reforming the aforesaid injuries in the form aforesaid. And when as the said Ambassadors had been admitted by our said Lord the King to treat anew of this kinde of Injuries, these Ambassadors, as other Ambassadors of the aforesaid Earl, in the aforesaid Treaties, did, among other particulars that they required, before all things make supplication; That the said Lord the King would at his own suit, by virtue of his Roial Autoritie, caus enquirie to bee made, and do Justice, about a certain depredation lately made by the Subiects of England (as they said) upon the English Sea, of Wines and divers other Merchandises belonging to certain men of Flanders, towards the parts about CRAUDEN, within the Territorie and Jurisdiction of our said Lord the King; alleging that the aforesaid Wines and Merchandises taken from the said Flemings, were brought within the Realm and Jurisdiction of the said Lord the King, and that it belong'd to the King himself so to do, for that HEE IS LORD OF THE SAID SEA, and the aforesaid depredation was made upon the said Sea within his Territorie and Jurisdiction. In conclusion, after diligent consideration had of the Premisses in the same Parlament, with the Prelates, Earls, Barons, and other Peers of the

the said Realm beeing there present, it was concluded upon their advice by the said Lord King, that, to preserv the benefit of Peace between the Subjects of England and Flanders, the said Lord King do by his Roial Autoritie caus enquirie to bee made about the Goods taken at that time upon the aforesaid English Sea towards the said place of CRAUDEN, and brought within the said Realm, in those places where the Malefactors went with the goods so taken to the said Land of England, and caus the same depredation to bee heard and determined according to Law and Reason, and that the Owners of the Ships who had a hand in the said depredation, and others, who knowingly received the said Offendors with the Goods so taken in whole or in part, may bee charged and punished thereupon, as partakers, of the aforesaid depredation.

So far that *Record.* And Commissioners were appointed with power of Jurisdiction by the King's Commission, through most of the Maritim Counties, to make reparation of damages. But becaus there are upon the shores over against us (especially those of *Zealand*, and there are also upon other neighboring shores) besides Inlets of Rivers, very many windings and turnings of the Sea flowing in, whereby the land is so interwoven up and down, that it cannot well bee but that the Sea also which flow's in, and oftentimes remove's Banks and make's Harbors there in the same manner almost as a River or Brook, must bee conteined under the same Jurisdiction, as an entire Bodie with the Land; therefore somtimes mention is made also of this kinde of Sea flowing in, as of a

Sea reckoned within the Juriſdiction & Current of the Sea of the oppoſite ſhores; as for example, *of the Sea Flanders*, or (as I finde it in ſom antient [b] Manuſcripts which ſeem to bee the Originals of certain Letters of King *Henrie* the Fift to the Earl of *Carolois*, and to the Governors of *Ypres*, *Gaunt*, and *Bruges*) *deins la Juriſdiction & l'eſtrem de la meer de Flandres*, *within the Juriſdiction and ſtream of the Sea of Flanders*, which is all one. For, ſetting aſide the Sea ſo flowing in or making an in-let or harbor before the oppoſite ſhore, all that which remain's, or the Sea flowing between thoſe oppoſite Countries and *England*, was ever eſteemed to bee of the Engliſh Dominion, according to what I have formerly ſhewn. So that a late Writer doubtleſs was in a dream, when, upon the repairing of the Dock at *Mardike*, hee write's, [c] *that hee ſaw the Empire of the Britiſh Sea reſtored to the King of Spain.* And ſo I have don with this point, touching the Declaration and acknowledgment of the Sea-Dominion of our Kings, made by thoſe Forein and Neighbor-Nations, who were moſt concerned in the Buſineſs.

[b] *Ms.* in Bibliothecâ Cottonianâ 3 *Hen.* 5.

[c] *Jacobus Chiffletius*, in EpiſtolâDedicatoriâ ad Comitem *de Olivares*, *Portui Iccio præfixâ.*

Of

Of the Dominion of the King of Great Britain in the Irish *and* Western Sea, *considered singly and apart by it self.*

Chap. XXX.

I have alreadie spoken in general, of the *English* or *British* Sea, which is a part of the Patrimonie of the Crown of *England*, but chiefly as it lie's either East or South. It rest's now, that wee treat of the *Western*, as also the *Scotish* and Northern, and in a word of the whole *British* Sea that remain's. It is evident to all, that part of the Western Sea, lying before *England*, is understood as well in that *Libel* which was exhibited by so many Nations to the Commissioners deputed by the Kings of *England* and *France*, above three hundred and thirtie years ago, wherein wee so often read *le mer d' Angleterre* or **the sea of England**, as in the King's Commission before mentioned, wherein our Kings are expresly declared Lords of the *English Sea* on every side; and therefore I shall forbear to repeat what is [a] cited out of *Bracton*, about the *Essoyning* or excusing of a man absent in *Ireland*, and other things of that kinde alleged before, which make to this purpose. Moreover also, wee read every where, that all the Isles in this neighboring Sea were called *British* (as wee observed at the beginning of this Book) just as if the narrow Seas flowing between, like Rivers or turnings of Rivers, did disjoin those Banks or Shores from great *Britain*, as

[a] *CAP.* 24.

* Ἀποῤῥῶγας. * *Fragments* of the same. Whereby it appear's, that the narrow Seas themselvs with the Isles, even as Rivers with their Banks, are to bee reckoned a part of the *British* Territorie. And hereunto especially relate's also that expression in the *Libel* so often cited; to wit, that the Kings of *England* have ever been Lords both of the *English* Sea (or of the *British*, so far as it stretcheth before *England*) and also of the Isles situate therein, *par raison du Royalme d' Angleterre*, **by right of the Realm of England.** So that the *Isle of Man*, which (as *Giraldus Cambrensis* saith) stand's in this Sea, in the very midst betwixt the Northern Parts of *England* and *Ireland*, was (if I understand any thing) reckoned of old among the Land-Provinces of *England*, even as the Isle of *Wight*, *Lundie*, and others of that kinde. Nor doth it seem to bee understood otherwise by those men of antient time, who, upon occasion of a dispute, whether this Isle ought by right to bee taken for an appendant of *England* or *Ireland* beeing placed in the midst of the Sea flowing between, determined the controversie on this manner. They brought venemous serpents; and observing that the Isle did entertain and cherish them, as well as *England* and the rest of *great Britain*, but on the contrarie that *Ireland* destroied them, *it was concluded* (saith [b] *Giraldus Cambrensis*, who lived under *Henrie* the Second) *by the common censure of all, that it ought to bee ascribed unto England.* For, if they had so thought the Territorie either of *Ireland* or *England*, as it consisted of Land and Sea, to bee dis-joined from this *Isle of Man*, that they had conceived the Sea lying between, either common to all men, or by antient right subject to other than the Kings either of *Ireland* or *Britain*, they might seem to have raised a very ridiculous Contro-

[b] *Topograph. Hiberniæ, dist.2.cap.15.*

versie;

versie: For, I suppose, the Question could bee no other, than touching the bounds of *England* or *great Britain*, and *Ireland*. But that a Question about bounds may bee admitted between Owners that are Neighbors, where the Territories of both are not continual or contiguous, is beyond my understanding. It is well said by [c] *Paulus*; that if a publick Thorowfare, or publick River intervene, which belong's to neither of the neighboring Owners, an Action cannot bee brought upon that Title of the Law, *Finium Regundorum*. And truly, after that *Quintus Fabius Labeo*, beeing [d] appointed Arbiter by the Senate betwixt the *Nolans* and *Neapolitans* about the bounds of a Field, had so craftily perswaded both of them to retire backwards apart from each other, that a portion of the Field was left in the middle which hee adjudged to the people of *Rome*, there could not any Controversie arise farther between them about the bounds of this Field; becaus there ceased to bee any confine betwixt them: But if any Question arose afterwards, they were both to contend with the people of *Rome*. Even so it is to bee conceived of that Question, *to which of the two Countries the Isle of Man ought by Right to bee ascribed*; it arising chiefly upon this ground, becaus it lay in the midst between the Territories belonging to *Ireland* and *Britain*, and at the confine of both. For, by an Argument drawn from the nature of the very soil onely, without a civil consideration of Dominion (though they would have here the very nature of the soil to bee the evidence thereof, as a Lot for decision) it ought no more to bee ascribed either to *Britain* or *Ireland*, than to *Norway*, *Spain*, or *France*, where every man know's that venemous Creatures are bred as well as in *Britain*. Therefore, to bee ascribed to *England* or *Britain* in that

[c] *L.*4. § 11. *l.* 5. & 6. *ff. tit. Finium Regundorum.*

[d] *Cicero de Officiis, lib.* 1.

antient Decision, is, so immediately to bee annexed to the *British* Territorie, that the *Isle of Man* may truly, and in a civil sens, bee called a Land-Province of *England* or *Britain*, seeing the *English* Territorie is so continually extended as far as its Western Coasts; that which bend's Westward from the very Confine, beeing ascribed to *Ireland*. And therefore Queen *Elisabeth's* Commissioners let fall those words too unadvisedly in the [d] Treatie, held at *Bremen*, with the *Danish* Commissioners, about free Navigation and Fishing in the *Norwegian* Sea; *That the Kings of* England *never had prohibited Navigation and Fishing in the Irish Sea between England and Ireland*; as if they would have had it proved from thence, that the *Dane* ought not to bee prohibited Fishing or Navigation between *Island* and *Norway*, becaus neither were Lords of the Sea, but had possessed the Shores onely on both sides by an equal Right. There were other particulars also no less rashly spoken touching a communitie of the Sea, as wee observed before. Concerning Navigation and Fishing in the *Norwegian* Sea, I shall add more by and by. But as it was ill don of those Commissioners in that Treatie to make use of an Argument drawn from a necessarie communitie of the Sea, so there is no truth in that which they let fall concerning the *Irish* Sea. For, wee know, that not onely those pettie Potentates bordering near the Sea heretofore, that were in Rebellion and had usurped the Kings Right in many places of *Ireland*, did exact grievous Tributes of Foreiners for the very libertie of Fishing; but also it was expresly provided by Act of [e] Parlament, that no Foreiner should Fish in the *Irish* Sea, without leav first obteined to this purpose from the Lord Lievtenant, or som other lawful Deputie or Officer of the King of *England*; yea, and that all

[d] 1602. *apud G. Camden. in Annalib. tom.* 2. *pag.* 273. *Edit. Lond.*

[e] *Stat. Hibernic.* 5. *Ed.* 4. *cap.* 6.

all Foreiners should pay yearly, for every Fisher-boat of XII Tons or upward, *thirteen shillings and four pence*, and for everie lesser Vessel *two shillings*; upon pain of forfeiting their Vessels, Furniture, and all Goods whatsoëver, if so they refused this kinde of paiment or did not acknowledg this Soveraigntie of the Lord of the Sea. But I shall insert the whole Act touching this business, that wee may understand what was the most received Opinion of all the Estates of *Ireland*, touching this Right here of the King.

Item, at the requeste of the Commons, that where divers vessells of other landes fro one daie to other goynge to fish amongst the kings Irish enemies in divers partes of this sayd land by which the kings said enemies bee greatlye advanced and strengthened aswell in victualles, harneys, armor, as dyvers others necessaries, also great tributes of money given by every of the said vessells to the said enemies from day to day to the great augmentation of their power and force against the King's honor and wealth, and utter distruction of this said land, thereupon the premisses considered, it is enacted and ordeined by aucthoritie of the said Parliament, that no manner vessell of other landes shall bee no time nor season of the yeere from henceforth, from the feast of the Nativity of our Lord Jesus Christe next comming, go in no part of the said land betwixt the said Irish enemies to no manner fishing without one special licence of the Lieutenant, his deputy or Justice of the land for the time being, or licence of another person having the

the Kings power to grant such licence, upon paine of forfaiture of the shippe and goods to the King. And that whatsoever person or persons that find or impeche any of the said vessells, rumpants or forfaites against this act by the auctoritie of the same, it bee lawfull to them so making any claime in behalfe of the King, and approving the said forfaytures by any of the said vessels to be made, that the King shall have th'one moitye of the said forfeyture, and the said person or persons shall have th'other without anye impechment, and that all manner vessells of other lands comming in the said land of Ireland a fishing, being of the burden of twelue tunnes or lesse, haveing one Drover or boate, everye of them to paye for the maintenance of the Kings warres there xiii. s. iiii. d. by the yeer. And all other small vessells as scarfes or boates, not haveing Drover nor lighter being within the said burden of twelve tunnes, every of them shall paye twoe shillings goings a fishing in the like manner. Provided alwayes that no vessell fyshing in the North parte of Wicklo, be charged by reason of this act; and that the Lieutenant, his deputy or Justice of the land for the time being, shall have the foresaid summes and duties of mony so paid to be imployed in the Kings warres for the defence of the said land, and that the Customers and Collectors of the same summes shall accoumpt before the said Justice, Lieutenant, or Deputy for the time being, or such Auditors that shall be for the same appointed by the King or them, and not before the

Barons

Barons of th'exchequer in the said lande; and that none of the saide vessels so comming from other parts in the saide lande shall not depart out of the saide lande, till every of them pay their said duties upon pain of forfeiture of the vessels and goods to the King.

There are som allso who affirm, that the King of *Spain*[f] obteined leav by request from our Queen *Marie*, for XXI years, to fish in the more Northerly part of the *Irish* Sea, and that thereupon a Revenue of one thousand pounds *per annum* was advanced to the Exchequer in *Ireland*. A Proclamation allso was set forth by[g] *James* King of great *Britain*, prohibiting any foreiner, without leav first obteined, to fish in this *Irish* Sea. But as to what concern's that Controversie about the *Isle of Man*, although it bee remember'd by *Giraldus* (who wrote in the Reign of *Henrie* the Second) nevertheless it is to bee conceived, that it arose in the more antient times of the *English-Saxons*, when all that lie's betwixt *England* and *Ireland*, was in subjection either to the Kings of *Ireland*, or *Britain*, that is, when both of them had in this Sea distinct Territories of their own, whose Bounds were in question. Certain it is, as[h] *Beda* write's, that *Edwin* the most potent King of the *Northumbrians*, or rather of all the *English-Saxons*, *subdued the* Mevanian *Isles to the Dominion of England*, about the year DCXXX. That is to say, both that *Mevanian* which wee call *Anglesey*, & the other also which is *Man*, whereof wee discoursed. But in the later time of the *Anglo-Saxon* Empire, the *Norwegians* or *Danes*, who exceedingly infested both this and the North-east Sea with very frequent Robberies, at length seized both this Isle and the *Hebrides*, and held them almost two hundred years: So that in the mean time, this of *Man* could not in a Civil sens bee

f *Gerardus Malinius, in Lege mercatoriâ cap.* 35 *pag.* 189.

g *Proclam.* 7. *Jacobi* 6. *Martii.*

h *Hist. Eccles. lib.* 2. *cap.* 9.

ascribed either to *Ireland* or *Britain*. But that the Kings thereof were at that time Lords as well of the neighboring Sea as of the Isles, may bee collected out of their Annals, where we find that *Godred*, whose sirname was **Crovan**, *King of Man*, in the year of our Lord MLXVI *brought Dublin and a great part of* **Laynster** [i] *under his subjection. And so throughly subdued the Scots, that no man, who built a Ship, durst drive in more than three Nails* : So that hee gave both limitation and Law to the Shipping of his Neighbors ; which is all one, as to enjoy the very Dominion of the Sea, as I have shewn in what hath been alreadie spoken. And from hence perhaps it is, that the more antient Arms of the Kings of *Man* were a Ship with a Sail folded together, and this Inscription added, *Rex Manniæ & Insularum*, **King of Man & of the Isles** ; as Mr [k] *Camden* observ's from their Sails : For, the three legs of humane shape, now every where known, are but of later time. But afterwards, when *Ireland* was subdued by *Henrie* the Second, and King *John*, and *Reginald* King of *Man* [l] brought into the power of King *John* (the *English* possessing this Sea at that time with a very numerous Navie) there is no reason at all to doubt, but that the neighboring Sea round about was taken also into the Dominion of the *English*. For, in that Age the *King of Man* was no absolute Prince; but beeing subdued, hee paid homage to the King of *England*, & yielded under his subjection. But in a short time after *Alexander* the Third, [m] King of *Scots*, annexed it to the Dominion of *Scotland*, and put in a Governor, who was to assist him upon occasion with thirteen Gallies & five hundred Seamen. Hee recover'd the *Hebrides* also, by driving out the *Norwegians*, & transmitted it to his posteritie. Then, *Man* returned again to the *English*; who enjoied *Ireland* a long time together with it & that sea-territory. But the Kings of the

[i] *Chronic. Regum Manniæ, pag.* 840.

[k] *Britanniâ, pag.* 847.

[l] *Chronic. Manniæ, anno.* 1210 *& Ret. cart.* 14. *Joannis R. membran. in dorso.*

[m] *Hector Boëtius, hist. Scot. lib.* 13.

Hebrides

Hebrides and of *Scotland* enjoied the Northern part of this *Western* Sea, after that they had expell'd the *Norwegians* who were Lords here of the Sea. And from hence it is, that, as *Scotland*, *England*, this *Isle of Man*, the *Hebrides*, and *Ireland* with other adjacent Isles, so even the *Vergivian* and *Deucaledonian* Sea it self washing the West of *Scotland*, and surrounding these Isles with windings and turnings, ought now also to bee accounted the antient Patrimonie of the King of *great Britain*.

But there is moreover, in the more Westerly part of this open and main Sea, another Right belonging to the King of *Great Britain*, and that of a verie large extent upon the Shore of *America*. Whenas S[r] *Humfery Gilbert* Knight, did by Autoritie of Queen *Elisabeth* transport a Colonie into the *New World*, with design to recover certain Lands in the East parts of the Northern *America*, which of Right belong'd to the *English* Dominion, the *Queen* was by him, as her *Procurator* put into a possession, for ever to bee held by her and her heirs, both of the Port, called by the name of S[t] *John* (which is in the Island of *Baccalaos*) and also of the whole Sea as well as Land on every side, [n] for the space of six hundred miles. Then hee received this new Kingdom of the *Queen*, as her Beneficiarie, having a Branch and a Turf deliver'd in his hands, according to the usual cerimonie of *England* in transferring the Ownership of Lands and Possessions. Nor truly was it necessarie, that hee should otherwise get the Possession, from whence this Dominion of the Queen and her Posteritie had its Original. For (as *Paulus* saith well) there is no necessitie that *hee who* [o] *intend's to take possession of a Field, should walk about the whole, but tis sufficient if hee enter any part of that Field, so long as hee doth it with a* minde,

[n] Hackluit, in his Voyages, *Tom.* 2. *pag.* 151.

[o] *L.* 3. *ff. tit. de acquir. Rer. Dom.*

minde, thought and intent, to possess the Field to its utmost extent and Bound: Which saying may relate to Seas, as well as Lands, that were never taken into possession. So that as [p] *Siculus Flaccus* Treating of *Occupatorie Lands*, saith, *Men did not possess so much land as they were able to till, but they reserved as much as they were in hope they might bee able to till*, the like also may bee said of a Sea so taken into possession. Look how much was reserved in hope of using and enjoying, so much also was bounded. But perhaps the first original of the Dominion of this main Sea of *America*, did not proceed from the Possession that was acquired by *Gilbert*. Hee rather restored and inlarged the Right of the Crown here: For, that Island called *Baccalaos*, was added to the *English* Empire by [q] *Sebastian Chabot*, in the time of *Henrie* the Seventh. And it is certain, that afterwards it grew to be a Custom, for the Officers belonging to the *High Admiral* of *England* (in whose charge are all the Seas subject to the King of *England* and *Ireland*, as King of *England* and *Ireland*) to demand Tributes of such as fish't also in this Sea; which was (I suppose) a most evident token of the King's Dominion. But it was [r] provided by an Act of Parlament, in the Reign of *Edward* the Sixth, that no Tributes of that kinde, to the grievance of Fishermen, should bee paid any longer. How far our *English* Colonies, lately transported into *America*, have possessed themselvs of the Sea there, I have as yet made but little enquirie.

[p] *De Conditionibus Agrorum.*

[q] His Commission you may finde, *Rot.Franc.* 12.*Hen.*7.

[r] *Stat.* 2. & 3. *Ed.* 6. *cap.*6.

Touching

Touching the Dominion of the King of Great Britain in the Scotish Sea, *especially toward the* East *and* North.

CHAP. XXXI.

THose particulars which were cited before out of the [b] Proclamation of *James* King of *Great Britain*, about the Prohibition of Fishing, relate as well to the *Scotish Seas*, on every side; from whence also you must acknowledg their possession hath been reteined together with an antient Sea-Dominion. That is to say, all Foreiners were prohibited to Fish in these Seas, without leav first obteined at *Edenburgh*. And in those *Scotish* Acts of Parlament, they are not so much new Laws made, as old ones revived, wherby it was ordeined, **That all manner of [c] Fischeres, that occupies the Sea, and otheres persons quhat sumever that happenis to slay Hering or quihte Fish upon the Coast, or within the Iles or out with the samen within the Frithes bring them to free Ports, &c. where they may bee sold to the Inhabitants of the same Kingdom, quhairby his Majesties Customes bee not defrauded, and his Hienes Lieges not frustrat of the Commoditie appointed to them be God under the pain of confiscation and tynsel of the veschelles of them that cumes in the contrair hereof, and escheiting of all their movable guddes to our soveraine Lords use.** So that use and benefit is claimed hence, by a special right in that Sea: otherwise truly, that use and bene-fit

[b] *Proclam. 7. Jacobi & Martii, 6.*

[c] *Parlam. 4. Jacobi R. 6. cap. 60. & Parlament. 6. ejusdem cap. 86.*

fit would of right no more appertein either to the King of *Scotland* or his Subjects, than to any other whomsoëver. But the Law was made concerning all Fisher-men, as well strangers as *Scotch-men*; as beeing ordeined by all the Estates of that Kingdom, who so well understood both the King's Right, and also their own (as subordinate to the King's) by Tradition from their Ancestors, or by long-continued possession and Dominion, that there remained not the least ground of scruple touching that business. And a *Scotish* Lawyer speaking about Fishing in the Eastern Sea of Scotland, *I cannot*, saith [d] hee, *omit to tell you, that in the past Age, after a most bloudie quarrel between the* Scots *and* Hollanders *about occasions belonging to the Sea, the matter was composed after this manner, that in time to com the* Hollanders *should keep at least fourscore miles distance from the Coasts of* Scotland. *And if by accident they were driven near through violence of weather, they paid a certain Tribute at the Port of* Aberdene *before their return, where there was a Castle built and fortified for this and other occasions; and this was duly and really paid still by the* Hollanders *within the memorie of our Fathers, until that by frequent dissentions at home, this Tribute, with very many other Rights and Commodities, came to nothing, partly through the negligence of Governors, and partly through the boldness of the* Hollanders. So you see, how limits were by agreement prescribed heretofore in this Sea, to the Fishing of Foreiners. But the more Northerly Sea, which lie's against *Scotland*, was for the most part in subjection heretofore to the *Norwegians*, and *Danes*, who were Lords of the Isles there: So that the people of the *Orcades* speak the *Gothish* Language to this day. *Robertus de* [e] *Monte* tell's us, that hee, who was called *King of the Isles*, was possest of XXXII Islands

[d] *Guil. Welwodus, de Dominio Maris, cap* 3.

[e] *In Append. ad Sigebert. Gemblac. Anno* 1197.

ſlands in that Sea above four hundred and ſixtie years ago, *paying ſuch a Tribute to the King of* Norway, *that at the ſucceſsion of every new King, the King of the Iſles preſent's him ten marks in Gold, and make's no other acknowledgment to him all his life long, unleſs another King ſucceed again in Norway.* And [f] *Giraldus Cambrenſis*, writing of theſe things ſaith, *that in the Northern Sea, beyond* Ulſter *and* Galloway, *there are ſeveral Iſlands, to wit, the Orcades and Inchades* (or *Leucades*, which ſom would have to bee the *Hebrides*) *and many other, over moſt of which the* Norwegians *had Dominion and held them in ſubjection. For, although they lie much nearer to other Countries, yet that Nation beeing more given to the Sea, uſually preferr's a Piratick kinde of life above any other. So that all their Expeditions and Wars are performed by Sea-Fight.* This hee wrote in the time of *Henrie* the ſecond. So that ſomtimes thoſe Sea-Appendants of the Dominion of *Britain*, in the Northern parts, were invaded by Foreiners. Hence alſo it is, that [g] *Ordericus Vitalis*, ſpeaking of *Magnus* the ſon of *Olaus* King of *Norway*, ſaith; *hee had a great power in the Iſles of the Sea*; which relate's unto the time of *William* the Second King of *England*. The ſame *Ordericus* alſo ſaith, *that the* Orcades, Finland, Iſland *alſo and* Groënland, *beyond which there is no other Countrie Northward, and many other as far as* Gothland, *are ſubject to the King of* Norway, *and wealth is brought thither by ſhipping from all parts of the world.* So wee have here a clear deſcription of the Dominion of the *Norwegians* heretofore, as well in this neighboring Sea of *Scotland*, as in the more open. But in after time, when as by [h] agreement made between *Alexander* the third King of *Scots*, and *Magnus* the fourth of *Norwaie*, as alſo between *Robert Bruce* King of *Scotland*, and *Haquin* of *Norwaie*, it was concluded touching theſe Iſles,

[f] *Topograph.Herniæ, diſt.* 2. *cap.* 11.

[g] *Hiſtoria Eccleſiaſtica, lib.* 10. *pag.* 767.

[h] *Ex Tabulis publicis, Ferrerius, in Appendice. Hiſt.* Hectoris Boëtii ſubjunctâ, *pag.* 388.

Isles, that they should bee annexed to the *Scotish* Dominion; this could not bee don, but there must bee a Cession also of that Sea-Dominion, which bordered round upon the Coast of *Norwaie*. Yet the *Norwegian* King possessed it for the most part; and afterwards the *Dane*, by an union of the two Kingdoms of *Denmark* and *Norwaie*; until that *Christiern* the first, King of *Norwaie* and *Denmark*, upon the marriage of his daughter *Margarite* to *James* the third King of *Scotland*, made an [i] absolute Surrender of these Islands; and in the year of our Lord MCDLXX. transferr'd all his right both in the Isles of *Orcades* and *Shetland*, and the rest lying in the hither part of the Northern Sea, upon his Son in law, and his Successors. And as concerning this business, I shall here set down the words of *Joannes Ferrerius*, who was indeed Native of *Piedmont*, but supplied with matter of Historie out of the Records of *Scotland*, by *Henrie* **Sainclair**, Bishop of *Ross*. *Moreover in the Deucaledonian Sea toward the North-East, there are the Isles of* Orcades, *seated next to the Coast of* Scotland, *whereof onely twentie eight are at this daie inhabited; and above an hundred miles beyond the* Orcades *towards* Norway, *are the* Shetland *Isles in number eighteen, which are at this daie inhabited, and in subjection to the King of* Scotland; *concerning which, there was a great quarrel in former Ages between the* Scots *and* Danes, *yet the* Dane *kept possession. All these Islands did* Christiern *King of* Denmark *peaceably surrender, together with his daughter in marriage to* James *King of* Scots, *until that either hee himself or his posteritie paid to the* Scotish *King or his Successors, in lieu of her Dowrie, the summe of fiftie thousand Rhenish Florens, which were never discharged to this daie. For, so much I my self have seen and read in the Deeds of marriage betwixt Ladie* Margarite *daughter of the King of* Denmark

[i] *Munster. Cosmograph. lib.2.& Guilielm. Camden. in Insulis Brit. pag.849.*

mark *and* James *the third King of* Scotland, *drawn up and fairly signed with the Seals of both Kingdoms* Anno Dom. 1468. *&c. But afterwards, when Ladie* Margarite *beeing Queen had been delivered of her eldest son* James *Prince of* Scotland, *the* Danish *King willing to congratulate his daughter's good deliverie, did for ever surrender his right in the Islands of the* Deucaledonian *Sea, to wit, the Isles of* Orcades, Shetland, *and others, which hee deliver'd in pledg with his daughter, upon her marriage to the* Scotish *King. I hear the deeds of this surrender are kept among the Records belonging to the Crown of* Scotland. And so at length those Isles, and the Dominion of this Sea, returned to the Kings of *Scotland*, which they enjoy at this day. The Kings of *Scotland* have a pledg of Dominion also in this Sea, that is to say, Tributes or Customs imposed upon Fisher-men, for Fishing; of which by the way you may read in their [k] Acts of Parlament.

[k] *Parlam.6. Mariæ, Reginæ Scot.c.54.*

Touching that Right which belong's to the King of Great Britain, in the main and open Sea of the North. *And the Conclusion of the Work.*

Chap. XXXII.

Concerning that Neighboring Sea, which is a Territorie belonging to the *Scots*, I have spoken in the former Chapter. But I must not omit to treat here of that Sea, which stretcheth it self to a very large extent toward the North, washing the Coasts of *Friesland, Island*, and other Isles also under the Dominion of the King of *Denmark*, or of *Norway*. For, even this

Sea also is ascribed by som to the King of *Great Britain*. *Albericus Gentilis*, applying that of [b] *Tacitus*, *The Northern Coasts of* Britain, *having no Land lying against them, are washt by the main and open Sea*; *you see*, [c] saith hee, *how far the Dominion of the King of* Great Britain *extend's it self toward the South, North, and West*. As if almost all that which lay opposite to the *Isles of Britain*, in the open Sea, were within the Dominion of the King of *Great Britain*. And concerning the Northern Sea also, which reacheth there to parts unknown, the very same thing in a manner was acknowledged by a subject of the King of *Denmarks*, no mean man, in a Letter that hee wrote som years since to a friend of his in *England*, his name is *Gudbrandus Thorlacius*, Bishop of *Hola* in *Island*, who in a Letter [d] sent hither *Anno* MDXCV, to *Hugh Branham* Pastor of *Harwich*, call's the *Britains* almost Lords there of the whole Sea. *There is*, saith hee, *a report now at this day, that you of* Britain *(whom I had almost called Lords of the Sea) have Negotiations every Year in Groenland*. But the Kings of *Denmark* deny it here; and this more Northerly Sea which belong's to *Island*, they challenge to themselvs, as they are Kings of *Norway*; and that by antient right, if not unjustly pretended. To this purpose let us observ, that passage which I finde in a speech of the Ambassadors of *Erricus* the tenth King of *Norway* and *Denmark*, delivered unto our *Henrie* the fift, which run's to this effect. [e] *Most victorious King of* England, *may it pleas your Majestie to understand, that our most gratious Lord the King of* Norway, &c. *aforesaid, hath certain Islands, to wit*, Island, **Feroy, Hietland**, *and manie more belonging to his Kingdom of* Norway, *whereunto of old no persons were wont to repair out of other Countries, upon any occasions whatsoever either of Fishing or Merchandising, under peril of life and* limbs;

[b] In the life of *Agricola*.

[c] *In Advocat. Hispanic. lib.* 1. *cap*. 8.

[d] **Hackluit** in his Voiages. *Tom*. 1. *pag*. 590.

[e] 3 *Hen*. 5. *seu Anno Dom*. 1453. *in Schedis vetustis* Bibliothecæ Cottonianæ.

limbs; nor might the men of the Kingdom of Norway, *more than those of other Countries, without special licence from his Majestie. Nor might they after Licence obteined, set forth out of any other place than the Citie of* Bergen, *nor return to the same place but upon inevitable necessitie, or when they ought to paie Customs and other Duties to the King's Exchequer, according to the most antient Custom of* Norway, *which hath been constantly observed time out of minde in that Kingdom.* Also, in the year MCCCCXLV. *Christophor* King of *Denmark* and *Norway*, [f] granted the Inhabitants of *Zirickzee* in *Zealand* a freedom of Navigation into his Kingdom, *Island and other Isles beeing excepted and prohibited*, which are the very words of the Grant. Moreover, out of the League made at *Koppenhagen* in the year of our Lord [g] MCDXXXII. between our *Henrie* the sixt and the same *Erricus* King of *Norwaie*, and *Denmark*, the Commissioners of the King of *Denmark* who held a Treatie at *Bremen* with the Commissioners of our Queen *Elisabeth*, in the year MDC II about the free use of this Sea, alleged this Article almost to the same sens; *It is provided, that all Merchants, and all other men whatsoëver in subjection to the King of* England *and* France, *do not presume hereafter, under peril of loss of life and goods, to visit the Countries of* Island, Finmarck, Halghaland, or *anie other prohibited places and unlawful Ports whatsoëver, in the Kingdoms of* Denmark, Sweden, *and* Norway. Yea, and som years before, the use of this Sea was prohibited both to Merchants and Fisher-men, unless they were bound with Merchandise to *North-barn*, the most eminent Town of Traffick under the King of *Norwaie*. And touching that particular, there is an Act of Parlament of *Henrie* the sixt, whereby [h] such a kinde of Prohibition continued in force for certain years, in favor of the King of *Norwaie*. So that there were many Let-

[f] *Isaacus Pontanus in Hist. Danicâ, &* Zuer. *Boxhorn. in Apologiâ pro Navigatione Holland.*

[g] *Fœd. Hen. 6 Angliæ, & Errici* 10. *Daniæ R.* 1432. *art.* 6. Ex Tabulis Legationis Danicæ seu Dissertationis Bremensis, 1602. in in Bibliothecâ Cottonianâ.

[h] *Stat.* 8 *H.* 6 *cap.* 2. & *Rot. Parlam.* 8 *Hen.* 6. *num.* 35.

[i] *Rot. Franciæ*, 18 *H.* 6. *membran.* 16. *Rotul. Franc.* 12 *H.* 7. *Rot. Franc.* 1 *Ed.* 5. *&c.*
[k] *Stat. Hen.* 8. *cap.* 1.
[l] *De Gestis Scotorum, l.* 1.

ters Patents afterwards granted by [i] our Kings to their subjects of *England*, whereby they had Licence to go unto *Island*, *Finmark*, and other Dominions of the King of *Norway* and *Sweden*. But that Statute, the rigor whereof was dispensed with at the King's pleasure, by such kinde of Grants, became [k] repealed at the beginning of the Reign of King *Henrie* the eight. And *Joannes Maior* making mention of that time, saith, [l] *A Fleet of* English *went everie year to* Island, *beyond the Arctick Circle to catch Fish.* But what manner of determination soever ought to bee made touching the Dominion of this more Northerly Sea; yet certain it is, such a perpetual servitude at least was, by several agreements betwixt the Kings of *England*, and *Norwaie*, imposed upon it, that to this day also the subjects of *England* enjoy a perpetual right of sailing unto *Island*, and of using and enjoying this sea. For, by a League made at *Koppenhagen* in the year MCDXC. betwixt *Henrie* the seventh of *England* and *John* the second King of *Denmark* and *Norwaie*, it was concluded, [m] *that all Merchants and Liege-men, Fisher-men, and any other persons whatsoever beeing subjects of the King of* England *and* France, *might for ever in time to com sail freely to the Island* Tyle, *that is to saie,* Island (for, in that age it was generally taken for *Thule*, as it is now also by som) *thither to have recours and to enter with their ships and goods, and merchandise, victuals, and any other commodities whatsoever, upon occasion of buying, selling, fishing, or merchandising; and there to abide and convers after the manner of* Merchants, *and from thence freely to return as often as they pleas, without any Prohibition, molestation, or impediment of Us or our heirs and successors in the Kingdoms of* Denmark *and* Norway, *or of any of our Officers; they paying the due rights and usual Customs as well in that Island as also in the Ports belonging to*

[m] *Fœd. Danic.* 11 *Hen.* 7 *art.* 4. quod in Tabulis Legationis 1602. etiam habemus.

the

the same where they shall happen to arrive. Provided alwaies, that seven years immediatly after the date of these presents, they do Petition to renew their Licence from us and our successors Kings of Denmark *and* Norway, *to the end that so from seven years to seven years*, Merchants, *and all other persons aforesaid, may for ever acknowledg us and our successors Kings of* Denmark *and* Norway, *in the renewing of their Licence.* But that this League was not limited by any time, but concerned the heirs and successors of both the parties, appear's not onely in part by what hath been alleged alreadie, but by the very form of the Preface, which I thought meet to add in this place. *VVee* John *by the Grace of God King as aforesaid, by the unanimous advice and consent of our beloved Counsellors, and others the Lords and Nobles of our Kingdom of* Denmark, *have caused a Treatie to bee had, with the Orators of the most illustrious Prince* Henrie, *by the Grace of God, King of* England, *and* France, *our most dear Brother*, James Hutton, *Doctor of the Civil Law*, Thomas Clarentieux *King of Arms*, Thomas Carter, *and* John Beliz, *Merchants of* Lyn, *about the restoring of peace, and establishing a perpetual concord between our Kingdoms; which Counsellors of ours, and the Orators, autorised in our Citie of* Koppenhagen, *by special Commission of the afore-named King of* England, *our most dear Brother, and with full power, whereof wee are assured by the Letters of the said King of* England, *have concluded, that between us, our heirs, and successors, well willers, friends and allies, and the most illustrious Prince* Henrie *King of* England *and* France, *our most dear Brother, his heirs and successors, well willers, friends, and allies, there bee and shall bee for ever in time to com, a perpetual peace, inviolable friendship, and firm concord, in the following form.* Yea, and that League was renewed in the year MDXXIII. by *Henrie* the eight of *England*, and *Christiern* the second King of

Denmark and *Norway*, in the ſame form. The right therefore is perpetual, and tranſmitted to the heirs of the K. of *England*, that the Engliſh ſhould have a free uſe of this more Northerly Sea belonging to *Iſland.* But frequent Ambaſsies notwithſtanding paſſed on both ſides about that buſineſs, in the Reigns of *Frederick* the ſecond, and *Chriſtiern* the fourth, Kings of *Denmark*, and of *Eliſabeth* Queen of *England.* The *Danes* alleged, that the Engliſh had no right to uſe this kinde of libertie, without leav firſt obteined of the Kings of *Denmark*, and that renewed every ſeven years, according to that league made in the time of *John* the ſecond and *Henrie* the ſeventh. Moreover, *Nicolas Craig*, who was ſent Ambaſſador into *England* by *Chriſtiern* the fourth in the year MDXCIX. pretended the agreement at *Haderſlabe*, in the year MDLXXXIII. between *Frederick* the ſecond and Queen *Eliſabeth*, as if it had therein been expreſsly provided, that this ſervitude in the Sea of *Iſland*, eſtabliſhed by the Engliſh, might bee limited by a denial of Licence at the pleaſure of the King of *Denmark.* But it was anſwer'd both by the Lords at home in *England*, as alſo by the Queen's Commiſsioners ſent to *Bremen* for the tranſacting of this buſineſs, that this right or Sea-ſervitude is ſo confirmed to the Engliſh, as well by Preſcription of time, as by perpetual agreements of Leagues, that that particular which occurr's in the agreements of King *John* the ſecond, and *Henrie* the ſeventh about asking of Licence, doth in no wiſe relate to this effect; that whether it were denied or not requeſted by Petition, that right or ſervitude could bee diminiſhed, but to this end onely, that the Engliſh, by a cuſtomarie Petitioning every ſeven years, might acknowledg the *Norwegian* right in this Sea. There was neither manner, nor condition, nor time annexed to the ſervitude, but it

took

took place there onely to this end, that the memorie meerly of the benefit of the League or of the Original of the servitude established, might bee renewed now and then by Petition. Yea, *Frederick* the second in his letters to Queen *Elisabeth*, dated the fourth of *Maie*, MDLXXXV, most expresly disclaim's this Claus of the League, which concern's Petitioning for Licence. And truly the whole right of the English in that Sea, was not first claimed by them upon the account of that League at *Koppenhagen*, whatever they of *Norway* may pretend to the contrarie. For, when the Ambassadors sent heretofore by *Erricus* the tenth to our *Henrie* the fift, made complaint about English men's fishing in this Sea, the King of *England* (I suppose) intimate's plainly enough, that hee had som right before in that Sea, while at that time hee granted this onely in favor of the King of *Norwaie*, that the English should no otherwise use Fishing there for the year immediately ensuing, *than as it had been usual in antient time*, and this hee commanded by publick Proclamation made in the more eminent Ports and Cities. The time limited, and the antient Custom of Fishing, do plainly import som former right. But here I give you the form of the Proclamations; [n] *It is required, that none of the Lieges of our Lord the King, for certain causes specially moving our Lord the King himself, do, for one year next ensuing, presume to go unto the Islands belonging to the kingdoms of* Denmark *and* Norwaie, *and especially towards the Isle of* **Islande**, *for the caus of Fishing or any other occasion, to the prejudice of the King of the aforesaid kingdoms, otherwise than they were wont in antient time.*

[n] *Vet. Sched. de Temp. Hen.* 5. in Bibliothecâ Cottonianâ. & *Rot. Claus.* 3 *Hen.* 3. *Membran.* 5. *in dorso.*

It appear's also by Parlamentarie [o] Records of the same King's Reign, that the English used Fishing in that Sea very many years before. But that League made at *Haderslabe*

[o] *Rot. Parl.* 3 *Hen.* 5. *par.* 1. *membr. n.* 33.

Haderslabe (pretended before by *Craig*) doth not relate unto Fishing either in the Sea of *Island*, or in this of *Norwaie*, but to the Traffick and Merchandise used then by our Merchants of the *Moscovie*-Companie. For, this onely was agreed, that the Merchants of that Companie, beeing constrained by Tempests, or otherwise, might freely have access to the shores and Ports both of *Island* and *Norwaie*; *but with this Reserv, that they do not in any kind Traffick, and use Merchandise, in the Ports of* Norwaie *or* Island *before prohibited, nor molest the Subjects of the King of the said places in any thing against the Laws of Hospitalitie, and that they wholly abstein from all manner of injurie*; which is the summe of that Answer which was given to *Craig*, by the Peers of *England*. But all things are clearly explained about this business, and that right of the English defended at large in the Letters sent by Queen *Elisabeth* to *Christiern* the fourth bearing date *Cal. Septembris Anno* MDXCIX. So much whereof as concern's this particular, I think meet to insert. *At the request of the most excellent Prince your Highnesse's Father, wee sent* (say the Queen's Letters) *an Ambassador into* Germanie, *Anno* MDLXXVII. *who Treated with his Commissioners about all matters in controversie, and especially about the Fishing of* Island *and* Norway, *where it was found, that the King insisted onely upon a former Treatie of two years*[p] *Truce, wherein it was at that time agreed, that the English should not sail beyond* Hagaland. *But there were several Treaties with the Kings* John *and* Christiern *alleged on our part, wherein, all former controversies beeing composed, it was otherwise agreed and concluded; and both parties were to stand to this Treatie of general peace made afterwards, not to the preceding two years Truce. Which the most excellent Prince your Father, acknowledging, desired by his Letters, that that controversie might bee referr'd to another disqui-*

[p] Sub Edwardo IV. Angliæ R.

disquisition. But since that time, no such disquisition hath been made. Nevertheless wee understand that our subjects fishing have been taken, tormented, and handled in a hostile manner. Whether this bee justly don, all men will bee able to judg who shall weigh our Reasons with an impartial minde. Wee do not deny, but that the Lord Chancellor **Whitfeld** *and* de **Barnico**, *when* [q] *they came unto Us, did in words pretend that the fishing of* Island *and* Norway *was used by the* English, *contrarie to the Leagues and Agreements of the Kingdoms. But seeing they neither did nor could produce any proof, and wee have authentick evidences attested by the Kings* John *and* Christiern *to the contrarie, whereto more credit ought to bee given than to bare Allegations, the matter was put off to another time. It was answer'd also to* Dr Craig, *that the Transaction which was concluded with King* Frederick *at* Haderslabe *in the year of our Lord* MDLXXXIII *belong's nothing at all to this Business*, for the reason before mentioned. And a little after the Letters speak thus. *But that which is pretended from the Treatie with King* John, (the aforesaid Treatie at *Koppenhagen*) *that licens for fishing ought to bee renewed by petition from seven years to seven years (as a thing which for very many was not omitted) Wee answer, that the fault of its omission proceeded not from the* English, *but from the* Danes. *For, that seven years Licens was petitioned for till the time that King* Christiern *was expelled, about the year of our Lord* MDXXI. *But afterward it ceased to bee renewed, becaus of the uncertaintie to whom the succession of the Kingdom did lawfully belong. And since the time of the said expulsion of* King Christiern, *neither King* Frederick *your great Grandfather, nor* Christiern *your Grandfather, nor* Frederick *your Highnesse's Father, ever urged any such petition for Licens. But concieving former Treaties sufficient, which*

[q] They were Ambassadors in *England anno* 1597.

were made between the Kings and Kingdoms, they would not innovate any thing after a prescription of verie manie years, seeing they were otherwise sufficiently secure that the same thing would never bee attempted, which was the first occasion of ordaining such a Licens. And to this end, the Letters of King Frederick *your Highnesse's Father written to Us, and bearing date the fourth of* May, *Anno* MDLXXXV *were shewn to Doctor* Craig, *purporting that if the* English *absteined from doing injuries, they should enjoy the wonted libertie and favor, without any mention or requiring of a Petition for Licens; whereas neverthelesse Wee offer'd you, that our Merchants should hereafter petition you from seven years to seven years, according to the antient and long continued Custom, which offer Wee understand your Highness would not admit.* For, the most excellent Queen would not otherwise acknowledg the Jurisdiction and Empire of the King of *Denmark* and *Norway* in this Sea, than that the whole servitude or right of fishing afore-mentioned, there established (as afore-said) might (as a considerable part of the antient Patrimonie) bee reteined to her and her Successors. There were other Letters and Treaties also about this businesse, in the year [r] MDCII. But the Controversie beeing deferred, nothing was concluded. But it appear's the King of *Great Britain* hath Empire and Dominion also in the Sea which lie's far more Northerly than *Island*. To wit, in that of *Groënland*. For, this Sea having never been enter'd by occupation, nor used in the Art and Exercise of Fisherie, was first in the memorie of our Fathers rendred very gainful, through a peculiar fishing for Whales, by those *English* Merchants of the *Moscovie*-Companie who sailed that way. The use of a Sea never enter'd by Occupation and such a kinde of profit beeing first discover'd, doth

[r] *Camden. in Annal. Elisabeth tom.* 2.*anno*.1602.

doth according to the manner of the claim, give a Dominion to the discoverer who claim's it in the name of another (as here in the name of the Soveraign of *England*) as well by a corporal as intentional possession, no otherwise than doth the first both natural and civil possession of any other things whatsoëver that were never yet possessed. Upon which ground it was, that King *James*, in his Letters of credence given to the worthie and most accomplished S[r] *Henrie Wotton* Knight his Ambassador in *Holland*, and others emploied by him to treat about that business, did verie justly call *the Fishings in the North Sea near the Shores of Groenland*, [f] *acquired for Us onely and Ours by right.*

[f] 29 *Septemb.* A Copie of which Letters is in S[r] *Robert Cotton's* Librarie.

But that wee may at length conclude; whatsoëver hath been discoursed hitherto touching the Right and Sea-Dominion of the Kings of *Great Britain*, and the antient extent of their Royal Patrimonie in the Sea, give mee leav to sum up the whole in certain Verses of the most excellent *Hugo Grotius* (of whose Law-writings, so far as they concern etther a private Dominion of the Sea, or a Communitie, wee have spoken in the former Book) which were very elegantly written heretofore to K. *James*, upon his Inauguration in the Kingdom of *England*. Saith hee,

——[t] *Tria sceptra Profundi*
In Magnum coiere Ducem.——

[t] *Sylvarum, lib.*2.

Three Scepters of the Deep their pow'rs do bring,
To make a Trident for a mightie King.

And then addresſing his Speech to the Sea, that is wont to receiv its motion from the Moon,

Sume animos à Rege tuo, meliore levatus
Sidere, nec cela populos quocunque calentes
Sole, per immenſum quem circumvolveris orbem,
Quis det Jura Mari.——

Take courage from thy Roial Governor,
As by the influence of a better Star,
And in thy courſ about the World explain
To all mankinde, Who tis that rule's the main.

And in another place,

——*licèt omnia caſus*
Magna ſuos metuant, Jacobo promiſſa poteſtas
Cum Terris Pelagóque manet.——

Though all great things a fall do fear,
Yet James **his power muſt ſtand,**
Beeing enlarged and compoſ'd
Both of the Sea and Land.

A little after alſo, hee proceed's thus;

——*Rerum Natura creatrix*
Diviſit populos, & metas ipſa notavit.
Sic juga Pirenæ, ſic olim Rhenus & Aſpes
Imperiis menſura fuit: Te flumine nullo
Detinuit, nullâ nimboſi verticis arce;
Sed Totum complexa parens hic terminus ipſa
Subſtitit, atque uno voluit ſub limite claudi.
Te tibi ſepoſuit, ſupremo in gurgite, Nereus.
Finis hic eſt, qui Fine caret. Quæ meta Britannis,
Litora ſunt aliis; Regníque acceſſio tanti eſt,
Quod ventis veliſque patet.——

Nature

Nature her self the mistress of mankind
Hath sever'd Nations, and their bounds design'd.
So the Pyren'ean Tops, Aspes, and Rhine,
As bounds to Empires Shee did once assign.
Yet Thee Shee with no River hath confin'd,
Nor loftie Tow'er that dare's the stormie wind.
But having thrown her wide imbraces round
The Univers, here fix't her self thy Bound,
And mean't one limit should you both contain,
Thee Nereus hath secluded in the main.
This Bound unbounded is. Great Britain stand's
Confined by the Shores of other lands;
And all that may by Winds and Sails bee known
Is an accession of so great a Crown.

And without question it is true, according to the Collection of Testimonies before alleged, that the very Shores or Ports of the Neighbor-Princes beyond-Sea, are Bounds of the Sea-Territorie of the *British* Empire to the Southward and Eastward; but that in the open and vast Ocean of the North and West, they are to bee placed at the utmost extent of those most spacious Seas, which are possest by the *English*, *Scots*, and *Irish*.

FINIS.

Prais and Glorie bee to God our Saviour.

ADDITIONAL EVIDENCES,

Concerning the

RIGHT OF SOVERAIGNTIE and Dominion of *ENGLAND* in the SEA;

Collected

Out of certain publick Papers, relating to the Reigns of K. *JAMES*, and K. *CHARLS*.

LONDON,

Printed by *William Du-Gard*. *An. Dom.* 1652.

ADDITIONAL EVIDENCES

Concerning the

RIGHT OF SOVERAIGNTIE and Dominion of *ENGLAND* in the SEA;

Collected

Out of certain publick Papers, relating to the Reigns of K. *JAMES*, and K. *CHARLS*.

THE Learned Autor having fully evinced the Right of this Island in the Sea, and that from all Antiquitie, it were superfluous to seek after any farther Testimonies relating to elder times, wherein hee himself hath been so abundant, and alreadie set down the most material; And therefore it is conceived requisite to add a few such Evidences onely, as are found among several Papers of publick Transaction, which are still to bee produced, and will serv to shew how that claim which hath been made successively by all our Kings of the *English* Race, was continued down to the present Times, by the two Princes of the *Scotish* Extraction.

In the seventh year of the Reign of King *James*, this Right was stoutly asserted by *Proclamation*, and all persons excluded from the use of the Seas upon our Coasts, without particular Licence; the Grounds whereof you have here set down in the *Proclamation* it self.

A Proclamation
TOUCHING
FISHING.

JAMES by the Grace of God King of Great Britain, France, and Ireland, Defendor of the Faith, &c. To all and singular persons to whom it may appertein, Greeting. Although Wee do sufficiently know by Our Experience in the Office of Regal Dignitie (in which, by the favor of Almightie God, Wee have been placed and exercised these many years) as also by the observation which Wee have made of other Christian Princes exemplarie actions, how far the absoluteness of Soveraign Power extendeth

is

it ſelf, and that in regard thereof, Wee need not yield accompt to any perſon under God, for any action of Ours, which is lawfully grounded upon that Juſt Prerogative: Yet ſuch hath ever been, and ſhall bee Our care and deſire to give ſatisfaction to Our Neighbor-Princes, and friends, in any action which may have the leaſt relation to their Subjects and Eſtates, as Wee have thought good (by way of friendly premonition) to declare unto them all, and to whomſoever it may appertain, as followeth.

Whereas Wee have been contented ſince Our coming to the Crown, to tolerate an indifferent and promiſcuous kinde of libertie to all Our Friends whatſoever, to Fiſh within Our Streams, and upon any of Our Coaſts of Great Britain, Ireland, and other adjacent Iſlands, ſo far forth as the permiſſion or uſe thereof might not redound to the impeachment of Our Prerogative Roial, nor to the hurt and damage of Our loving Subjects, whoſe preſervation and flouriſhing Eſtate Wee hold Our ſelf principally bound to advance before all worldly reſpects: So finding that Our continuance therein, hath not onely given occaſion of overgreat encroachments upon Our Regalities or rather queſtioning for Our Right, but hath been a means of daily wrongs to Our own People that exerciſe the Trade of Fiſhing, as (either by the multitude of ſtrangers which do pre-occupie thoſe places, or by the injuries which they receiv moſt commonly at their hands) Our Subjects are conſtrained to abandon their Fishing, or at least are becom so discouraged in the same, as they hold it better for them, to betake themselvs to som other cours of living, whereby not onely divers of Our Coast-Towns are much decayed, but the number of Mariners daily diminished, which is a matter of great consequence to Our Estate, considering how much the strength thereof consisteth in the power of Shipping and use of Navigation; Wee have thought it now both just and necessarie (in respect that Wee are now by God's favor lineally and lawfully possessed, as well of the Island of Great Britain, as of Ireland, and the rest of the Isles adiacent) to bethink Our selvs of good lawful means to prevent those inconveniences, and many others depending upon the same. In consideration whereof, as Wee are desirous that the World may take notice, that Wee have no intention to denie Our neighbors and allies, those fruits and benefits of Peace and Friendship, which may bee justly expected at Our hands in honor and reason, or are afforded by other Princes mutually in the point of Commerce, and Exchange of those things which may not prove prejudicial to them: so becaus som such convenient order may bee taken in this matter as may sufficiently provide for all these important considerations which do depend thereupon; Wee have resolved first to give notice to all the World, that Our express pleasure is, That from the beginning of the Month of August next coming, no person of what Nation or Qualitie soever, being not Our natural born Subject, bee

bee permitted to Fish upon any of Our Coasts and Seas of Great Britain, Ireland, and the rest of the Isles adjacent, where most usually heretofore any Fishing hath been, until they have orderly demanded and obteined Licenses from Us, or such Our Commissioners, as wee have autorised in that behalf, viz. at London for Our Realms of England and Ireland, and at Edenborough for Our Realm of Scotland; which Licenses Our intention is, shall bee yearly demanded, for so many Vessels and Ships, and the Tonnage thereof, as shall intend to Fish for that whole year, or any part thereof, upon any of Our Coasts, and Seas as aforesaid, upon pain of such chastisement, as shall bee fit to bee inflicted upon such wilful Offendors.

Given at our Palace of Westminster *the 6 day of* May, *in the* 7th *year of Our Reign of* Great Britain, *Anno Dom.* 1609.

Notwithstanding this Proclamation, the *Netherlanders* proceeded still in their way of encroachment upon our Seas and Coasts, through the whole Reign of that King, and were at length so bold as to contest with him, and endeavor to baffle him out of his Rights, pretending, becaus of the long connivence of himself and Queen *Elisabeth*, that they had a Right of their own by *immemorial possession*; which som Commissioners of theirs that were sent over hither, had the confidence to plead *in Terminis*, to the King and his Council. And though the King, out of his tenderness to them insisted still upon his own Right, by his Council to those Commissioners, and by his Ambassador to their Superiors, yet they made no other use of his Indulgence, than to tire out his whole Reign, and abuse his Patience by their artificial delaies, pretenses, shifts, dilatorie addresses, and evasive Answers. And all that the King gained by the tedious disputes, overtures, and dispatches to and again, was in conclusion onely a verbal acknowledgment of those Rights; which at the same times that they acknowledged, they usually designed to invade with much more insolence than before. But you have the main of what passed in those daies in this particular, with their insolent demeanor, lively described in these following Collections, taken out of several Dispatches that passed betwixt Secretarie *Naunton*, and *Dudley Carlton* Lord Ambassador from the King, to the States of the *United Provinces*.

In a Letter of Secretarie *Naunton's* to the said Ambassador, dated at *White-Hall*, the 21 of *December*, 1618. I finde these passages.

I Must now let your Lordship know, that the State's Commissioners and Deputies both having attended his Majestie at New-Market, *and there presented their Letters of Credence, returned to* London *on Saturday was a sevennight, and upon Tuesday had Audience in the Council-Chamber, where beeing required to communicate the points of their Commission, they deliver'd their meditated Answer at length. The Lords upon perusal of it, appointed my* Lord Bining *and mee to attend his Majestie for directions, what Reply to return to this Answer of theirs; which I represented to their Lordships yesterday to this effect; That his Majestie found it strange, that they*

they having been so often required by your Lordship his Majesties Ambassador, as from himself, in their publick Assembly, to send over Commissioners fully autorised to treat and conclude, not onely of all differences grown between the Subjects of both States, touching the Trade to the East-Indies, *and the* Whale-Fishing, *and to regulate and settle a joint and an even Traffick in those Quarters, but withall to take order for a more indifferent cours of determining other Questions growing between our Merchauts and them about their Draperies and the Tare; And more especially to determine his Majesties* Right for the sole Fishing upon all the Coasts of his Three Kingdoms, *into which they had of late times incroached farther than of Right they could; And lastly, for the reglement and reducing of their Coins to such a proportion and correspondence with those of his Majestie's and other States, that their Subjects might make no Advantage to transport our Monies by inhansing their valuation there. All which they confessed your Lordship had instanced them for in his Majestie's name, that after all this attent on his Majestie's part, and so long deliberation on theirs, they were com at last with a Proposition to speak onely to the two first points, and instructed thereunto with bare Letters of Creance onely, which his* Majestie *take's for an Imperious fashion of proceeding in them, as if they were com hither to Treat of what themselvs pleased, and to give Law to his* Majestie *in his own* Kingdom, *and to propose and admit of nothing but what should tend meerly to their own ends.*

To the second; Whereas they would decline all debate of the Fishings upon his Majestie's *Coasts, first by allegations of their late great losses and an* Esmeute *of their people, who are all interessed in that Question, and would bee like to break out into som combustion to the hazard of their State which hath lately scaped* Naufrage, *and is not yet altogether calmed; What is this but to rais an advantage to themselvs out of their disadvantage? But afterwards they profess their lothness to call*

it

it into doubt or question, claiming an immemorial possession seconded by the Law of Nations; To which his Majestie will have them told, that the Kings of Spain *have sought leav to Fish there by Treatie from this Crown; and that the King of* France *(a nearer Neighbor to our Coasts than they) to this day request's leav for a few Vessels to Fish for Provision of his own houshold; And that it appear's so much the more strange to his* Majestie, *that they beeing a State of so late date, should bee the first that would presume to question his Majestie's antient Right so many hundred years inviolably possess'd by his Progenitors, and acknowledged by all other antient States and Princes. That themselvs in their publick Letters of the last of* June, *sent by your Lordship, seemed then to confirm their immemorial possession (as they tearm it) with divers Treaties, as are of the year* 1550; *and another between his Majestie's Predecessors and* Charls *the fift, as Prince of those Provinces, and not by the Law of Nations. To which their last Plea, his Majestie would have them told, that hee beeing an Islander-Prince, is not ignorant of the Laws and Rights of his own Kingdoms, nor doth exspect to bee taught the Laws of Nations by them, nor their* Grotius, *whose ill thriving might rather teach others to disavow his Positions; And his honestie called in question by themselvs, might render his Learning as much suspected to them, as his person. This his Majestie take's for an high point of his Soveraigntie, and will not have it slighted over in any fashion whatsoëver.*

Thus I have particulated unto you the manner of our proceeding with them. Let them advise to seek leav from his Majestie, and to acknowledg him his Right, as other Princes have don, and do; or it may well com to pass, that they that will needs bear all the world before them, by their Mare Liberum, *may soon com to have neither* Terram & Solum, *nor* Rempublicam liberam.

And

And in a Letter of the said Ambassador *Carlton* to Secretarie *Naunton*, of the 30 of *December*, 1618, from the *Hague*, wee finde this Return, touching the busines of *Fisherie*.

Whether the final resolution here will bee according to his Majestie's desire, in that point concerning the Fishing upon the Coasts of his three Kingdoms, I cannot say; And by somwhat which fell from the Prince of Orange, *by way of Discours when hee took leav of mee on* Monday *last, at his departure, I suspect it will not, in regard the Magistrates of these Towns of* Holland, *beeing newly placed, and yet scarce fast in their seats, who do autorise the Deputies which com hither to the Assembly of the States in all things they are to Treat and resolv, will not adventure, for fear of the people, to determine of a Busines, on which the livelihood of fiftie thousand of the Inhabitants of this one single Province doth depend. I told the Prince that howsöever his Majestie, both in honor of his Crown and Person, and Interest of his Kingdoms, neither could nor would any longer desist, from having his Right acknowledged by this State, as well as by all other Princes and Commonweals, especially finding the same openly oppugned both by their States-men, and men of war, as the writings of* Grotius, *and the taking of* John Brown *the last year may testifie; yet this acknowledgment of a Right and a Due was no exclusion of Grace and Favor; and that the people of this Countrie paying that small Tribute upon every one of their Busses, (which is not so much as disputed by any other Nation whatsöever) such was his Majestie's well-wishing to this State,*

Ooo *that*

that I presumed of his permission to suffer them to continue their cours of Fishing; which they might use thereby with more Freedom, and less apprehension of molestation, and let than before, and likewise spare the Cost of som of their Men of War, which they yearly send out to maintein that by force, which they may have of courtesie.

The Prince *answer'd, that for himself at his return from* Utrecht, *hee would do his best endeavor to procure his Majestie contentment, but hee doubted the* Hollanders *would apprehend the same effect in their paiment for Fishing, as they found in the passage of the* Sound, *where at first an easie matter was demanded by the King of* Denmark, *but now more exacted than they can possibly bear: And touching their Men of War hee said, they must still bee at the same charge with them, becaus of the Pirats. Withal, hee cast out a question to mee, whether this freedom of Fishing might not bee redeemed with a Summe of monie? To which I answered, it was a matter of Roialtie more than of Utilitie, though Princes were not to neglect their profit.*

And in another Letter of the said Ambassador from the *Hague* to Secretarie *Naunton*, of the 14 of *Januarie* 1618. Hee give's him to understand, That *having been expostulated with, but in friendly manner, by certain of the* States *about his late Proposition, as unseasonable and sharp,* they said, *they acknowledg their* Commissioners *went beyond their limits in their terms of* Immemorial Possession *and* immuable Droict de Gens; *for which they had no order. Then,* saith hee, *I desired them to consider what a wrong it is to challenge that upon right, which these Provinces have hitherto enjoied, either by connivence or courtesie, and yet never without claim on his* Majestie's *side, &c.*

In

In another Letter of Secretarie *Naunton's* to the Lord Ambaſsador *Carlton*, of the 21 of *Januarie*, 1618. wee read thus:

AS I had dictated thus far, I received direction from his Majeſtie to ſignifie to the State's-Commiſsioners *here, That albeit their earneſt entreatie and his gracious conſideration of the preſent trouble of their Church and State, had moved his Majeſtie to conſent to delay the Treatie of the great Fiſhing, till the time craved by the Commiſsioners; yet underſtanding by new and freſh complaints of his Mariners and Fiſhers upon the Coaſts of* Scotland, *that within theſe four or five laſt years, the Low-Countrie-Fiſhers have taken ſo great advantages of his* Majeſtie's *Toleration, that they have grown nearer and nearer upon his Majeſtie's Coaſts year by year, than they did in preceding Times, without leaving any Bounds for the Countrie-People and Natives to Fiſh upon their Prince's Coaſts, and oppreſſed ſom of his Subjects of intent to continue their pretended poſſeſsion; and driven ſom of their great Veſſels through their Nets to deter others by fear of the like violence from Fiſhing near them, &c. His Majeſtie cannot forbear to tell them, that hee is ſo well perſwaded of the Equitie of the* States, *and of the Honorable reſpect they bear unto him, and to his Subjects for his ſake, that they will never allow ſo unjuſt and intolerable Oppreſsions; for reſtraint whereof, and to prevent the inconveniences which muſt enſue, upon the continuance of the ſame, his Majeſtie hath by mee deſired them to write to their Superiors to cauſ Proclamation to bee made, prohibiting any of their Subjects to Fiſh within fourteen miles of his* Majeſtie's *Coaſts this year, or in any time hereafter, until order bee taken by*

Commissioners to bee autorised on both sides, for a final settling of the main business. His Majestie hath likewise directed mee to command you from him, to make the like Declaration and Instance to the States *there, and to certifie his Majestie of their Answer, with what convenient speed you may.*

Thus far Secretarie *Naunton* to the Ambassador.

Now what effect the Ambassador's Negotiation with the *States* had, appear's by a Letter of his from the *Hague*, of the 6 of *Februarie*, 1618. to King *James* himself; where, among other passages hee hath this:

I finde likewise in the manner of proceeding, that treating by way of Proposition here, nothing can bee exspected but their wonted dilatorie and evasive Answers; their manner beeing to refer such Propositions from the States General *to the States of* Holland. *The States of* Holland *take advice of a certain Council residing at* Delph, *which they call the Council of the* Fisherie. *From them such an Answer commonly com's, as may bee exspected from such an Oracle. The way therefore (under correction) to effect your Majestie's intent, is to begin with the Fishers themselvs, by publishing, against the time of their going out, your resolution, at what distance you will permit them to Fish, whereby they will bee forced to have recours to their* Council of Fisherie; *that Council to the States of* Holland; *aud those of* Holland *to the States-General, who then in place of beeing sought unto, will for contentment of their Subjects seek unto your* Majestie.

By these you may perceiv how earnestly the antient Rights of *England* were asserted, and the old Claim made and renewed, and a recognition made also in the Reign of that King by the *Netherlanders* themselvs, though all proved to no purpose; the King and his Coun-

Council beeing afterward lull'd again into a conni-vence one way or other. And it give's sufficient caus to suspect, that the men in Power at that time might bee charm'd with monie; since it was a *Quære* put by the Prince of *Orange* to the Ambassador *Carlton*, in the heat of all the Controversie, *Whether the Freedom of Fish-ing might not bee redeemed with a summe of monie?* For, turning over the Papers of Transactions of the Time immediately following, I perceiv the dispute was let fall on a sudden, and thereupon an opportunitie gi-ven the *Netherlanders*, to encroach more and more every year, upon the Seas and Shores of this Island. And so far they proceeded in this presumptuous Cours, through the Toleration given them in the later end of the Reign of King *James*, and the begining of the late *Tyrant* his son, that at length they fell to a down-right impeachment of our Rights, not in words one-ly, but by contemning the commands of the King's Officers, prohibiting us free Commerce within our own Seas, abusing and disturbing the Subjects at Sea, and the King himself in his very Ports and Chambers; and by many other actions of so intolerable a nature, that in the year 1635 hee was awakened and constrai-ned to see to the preservation of our Rights at Sea, and give order for the setting forth of a powerful Fleet, to check the audacious designs and attempts of those un-grateful Neighbors. And the following year, in pro-secution of his purpose, hee set forth this ensuing *Pro-clamation*, entituled,

A Proclamation

For restraint of Fishing upon His Majestie's Seas and Coasts without LICENCE.

Whereas Our Father of Blessed memorie King James, did in the seventh year of His reign of Great Britain, set forth a Proclamation touching Fishing; Whereby for the many important reasons therein expressed, all persons, of what Nation or Qualitie soever (being not His natural born Subjects) were restrained from Fishing upon any the Coasts and Seas of Great Britain, Ireland, and the rest of the Isles adjacent, where most usually heretofore Fishing had been, until they had orderly demanded, and obtained Licences from Our said Father, or His Commissioners in that behalf, upon pain of such chastisement as should bee fit to bee inflicted upon such wilful Offendors: Since which time, albeit neither Our said Father, nor Our Self have made any considerable execution of the said Proclamation, but have with much patience expected a voluntarie conformitie of Our Neighbors and Allies, to so just and reasonable Prohibitions

ons and Directions as are contained in the same.

And now finding by experience, that all the inconveniences which occasioned that Proclamation, are rather increased then abated: Wee beeing very sensible of the premisses, and well knowing how far wee are obliged in Honor to maintain the rights of Our Crown, especially of so great consequence, have thought it necessarie, by the advice of Our Privie Council, to renew the aforesaid restraint of Fishing upon Our aforesaid Coasts and Seas, without Licence first obtained from Us, and by these presents to make publick Declaration, that Our resolution is (at times convenient) to keep such a competent strength of Shipping upon Our Seas, as may (by God's blessing) bee sufficient, both to hinder such further encroachments upon Our Regalities, and assist and protect those Our good Friends and Allies, who shall henceforth, by virtue of Our Licences (to bee first obtained) endeavor to take the benefit of fishing upon Our Coasts and Seas, in the places accustomed.

Given at Our Palace of VVestminster *the tenth day of* May, *in the twelfth year of Our Reign of* England, Scotland, France, *and* Ireland.

This Proclamation beeing set forth in the year 1636. served to speak the intent of those naval preparations made before in the year 1635. which were so numerous and well-provided, that our *Netherland*-Neighbors

bors beeing touched with the apprehension of som great design in hand for the Interest of *England* by Sea, and of the guilt that lay upon their own Consciences, for their bold Encroachments, soon betrayed their Jealousies and Fears, and in them a sens of their offences, before ever the Proclamation was made publick: As I might shew at large (if it were requisite) by certain Papers of a publick Character yet in beeing. But there is one, *Instar omnium*, which may serv in stead of all; and it is an acute Letter of Secretarie *Coke's*, that was written to Sir *William Boswel*, the King's Resident then at the *Hague*, the Original whereof is still reserved among the publick Papers: In which Letter, hee set's forth the Grounds and Reasons of preparing that gallant Navie, with the King's resolution to maintain the Right derived from his Ancestors, in the Dominion of the Seas; and therefore I here render a true Copie of it, so far as concern's this business, as most pertinent to our purpose.

(SIR!)

By your Letters and otherwise, I perceiv many jealousies and discourses are raised upon the preparations of his Majestie's Fleet, *which is now in such forwardness, that wee doubt not but within this Month it will appear at Sea. It is therefore expedient both for your satisfaction, and direction, to inform you particularly what was the occasion, and what is his Majestie's intention in this work.*

First, wee hold it a principle not to bee denied, That the King of Great Britain *is a Monarch at Land and Sea to the full extent of his Dominions, and that it concerneth him as much to maintain his Soveraigntie in all the British Seas, as within his three Kingdoms: becaus without that these cannot bee kept safe; nor hee preserv his honor and due respect*

with

with other Nations. But commanding the Seas, hee may caus his Neighbors and all Countries to stand upon their guard whensoëver hee think's fit. And this cannot bee doubted that whosoëver will encroach upon him by Sea, will do it by Land also, when they see their time. To such presumption Mare liberum *gave the first warning piece, which must bee answered with a defence of* Mare Clausum: *not so much by Discourses, as by the lowder Language of a powerful Navie, to bee better understood, when overstrained patience seeth no hope of preserving her Right by other means.*

The Degrees by which his Majestie's Dominion at Sea hath of later years been first impeached and then questioned, are as considerable as notorious.

First, to cherish, and as it were to nurs up our unthankful neighbors, Wee gave them leav to gather wealth and strength upon our Coasts, in our Ports, by our Trade and by our People. Then they were glad to invite our Merchant's Residence with what privileges they would desire. Then they offered to us even the Soveraigntie of their Estates, and then they sued for Licence to fish upon the Coasts, and obtained it under the Great Seal of Scotland, *which now they suppress. And when thus by leav or by connivence, they had possessed themselvs of our Fishings, not onely in* Scotland, *but in* Ireland *and* England, *and by our staple had raised a great stock of Trade; by these means they so encreased their shipping and power at Sea, that now they endure not to bee kept at any distance: Nay, they are grown to that confidence to keep guards upon our Seas; and then to project an Office and Companie of Assurance for the advancement of Trade; and withal, prohibit us free commerce even within our Seas, and take our ships and goods, if wee conform not to their* Placarts. *What insolencies and cruelties they have committed against us heretofore, in* Ireland, *in* Groënland, *and in the* Indies, *is too well known to all the world. In all which, though our sufferings and their wrong may seem forgotten, yet the great*

 interest

interest of his Majestie's honor, is still the same, and will refresh their Memories as there shall bee caus. For, though charitie must remit wrongs don to private men, yet the reflection upon the publick may make it a greater charitie to do Justice on crying crimes. All this notwithstanding, you are not to conceiv that the work of this Fleet, is either revenge or execution of Justice for these great offences past, but chiefly for the future to stop the violent current of that presumption whereby the Men of War and Free-booters of all Nations (abusing the favor of his Majestie's peaceable and gratious Government, whereby hee hath permitted all his Friends and Allies, to make use of his Seas and Ports in a reasonable and free manner, and according to his Treaties) have taken upon them the boldness, not onely to com confidently at all times into all his Ports and Rivers, but to conveie their Merchant's ships as high as his chief Citie, and then to cast Anchor close upon his Magazins, and to contemn the commands of his Officers, when they required a farther distance. But which is more intolerable, have assaulted and taken one another within his Majestie's Chamber, and within his Rivers, to the scorn and contempt of his Dominion and Power; and this beeing of late years an ordinarie practice which wee have endeavored in vain to reform by the waies of Justice and Treaties, the world I think will now bee satisfied, that wee have reason to look about us. And no wise man will doubt that it is high time to put our selvs in this Equipage upon the Seas, and not to suffer that Stage of action to bee taken from us for want of our appearance.

So you see the general ground upon which our Counsels stand. In particular, you may take notice, and publish as caus require's, That his Majestie by this Fleet intendeth not a Rupture with any Prince or State, nor to infringe any point of his Treaties; but resolveth to continue and maintein that happie peace wherewith God hath blessed his Kingdom; and to which all

all his Actions and Negotiations have hitherto tended, as by your own Instructions you may fully understand. But withal considering, that Peace must bee mainteined by the arm of power, which onely keep's down War by keeping up Dominion, his Majestie thus provoked, finde's it necessarie even for his own defence and safetie to re-assume and keep his antient and undoubted Right in the Dominion of these Seas, and to suffer no other Prince or State to encroach upon him, thereby assuming to themselvs or their Admirals, any Soveraign command: but to force them to perform due homage to his Admirals and Ships, and to pay them acknowledgments, as in former times they did. Hee will also set open and protect the free Trade both of his Subjects and Allies: And give them such safe Conduct and Convoie, as they shall reasonably require. Hee will suffer no other Fleets or Men of VVar to keep any guard upon these Seas, or there to offer violence or take prizes or booties, or to give interruption to any lawful intercours. In a word, his Majestie is resolved, as to do no wrong, so to do Justice both to his Subjects and Friends, within the limits of his Seas. And this is the real and Roial design of this Fleet, whereof you may give part as you finde occasion to our good neighbors in those parts, that no Umbrage may bee taken of any hostile act or purpose to their prejudice in any kinde. So wishing you all health and happiness, I rest

Your assured friend

and Servant,

JOHN COOK.

Whitehall,
16 *April*, 1635.
our style.

In this Letter you see first, how it was held for an undeniable principle, that the King was King by Sea as well as by Land; That neither the honor nor safetie of this Island and *Ireland* could bee maintained, but by preserving the Dominion by Sea; and that it is an argument, that they that encroach upon us by Sea, will do it also by Land when they see their time. Hee declare's also, how our unthankful neighbors are risen to this hight and insolence, partly by grant, partly by connivence, but principally through their many injurious abuses of our Patience and Indulgence. And lastly, you may observ here what resolutions were then taken to prevent the like injuries, and preserv our *English* Interest in time to com. But how those Resolutions were followed in the succeeding part of his Reign, I shall not stand to examine; onely it sufficeth here to take notice, that the Claim of Sea-Dominion was made by him, as well as by his Father, and for a time strenuously asserted; though afterward hee slackned his hand in the prosecution; whereof the *Netherlanders* taking advantage, and of our late commotions (which were their *Halcyon*-daies, and time of Harvest) are now advanced to such a monstrous pitch of pride, malice, and ingratitude, that they dare bid defiance to those antient Rights which wee have received from all Antiquitie, and justifie their actions by a most unjust and bloudie war, in the view of all the world. What remain's then, but that the Parlament and People of *England* should lay these things to heart, with an indignation answerable to so prodigious violations and invasions? They have now an opportunitie and strength given them by God (O let not hearts bee wanting!) to make good the Claim, and accomplish that work of establishing our Interests by Sea, beyond the posibilitie

of

of future impeachments. Let it not bee said, that *England*, in the state of *Monarchie*, was able to hold the Soveraigntie of the Seas so many hundred years, and then lost it in the state of *Libertie*. It is, as now established with its Appendants, the greatest and most glorious Republick, that the Sun ever saw, except the *Roman*. God hath made it so by Land, and will by Sea; for, without this, the Land is nothing. It was ever so apprehended by Kings, yea by the last and worst of our Kings: And shall the Founders of this famous structure of Government now in beeing, who have cashiered Kings, and vindicated the Rights and Liberties of this Nation upon his head and his whole posteritie and partie, not assert them against perfidious Neighbors? It were unpardonable in any to harbor a thought of that nature, or to yield that such a blemish should bee brought upon all those glorious actions and atchievments, whereby God hath freed and innobled our Land and Nation.

But that the people of *England* may bee excited to a valuation, maintenance, and improvement of their interest by Sea, it is necessarie to let them understand what advantages are to bee made thereby, and are made by others, who of *Usufructuaries* by permission, have in design now to make themselvs absolute Lords of the Fee. And therefore it is very convenient here to set down an excellent Discours which was written in the time of the late King, and presented by the following Title.

The inestimable Riches and Commodities of the British *Seas.*

THE Coast of Great *Britain* do yield such a continual Sea-harvest of gain, and benefit to all those that with diligence do labor in the same, that no time or season in the year passeth away without som apparent means of profitable imploiment, especially to such as apply themselvs to Fishing, which from the begining of the year unto the latter end, continueth upon som part or other upon our Coasts, and therein such infinite sholes and multitudes of Fishes are offered to the takers as may justly move admiration, not onely to strangers, but to those that daily bee imploied amongst them.

The Summer-Fishing for Herring, beginneth about *Midsommer,* and lasteth som part of *August.*

The Winter-Fishing for Herring, lasteth from *September* to the mid'st of *November*, both which extend in place from *Boughones* in *Scotland*, to the Thame's mouth.

The Fishing for Cod at *Alamby Whirlington,* and *White Haven,* near the Coast of *Lancashire*, from *Easter* until *VVhitsontide.*

The Fishing for Hake at *Aberdenie, Abveswhich*, and other places between *VVales* and *Ireland*, from *VVhitsontide* to Saint *James tide.*

The Fishing of Cod and Ling, about *Padstow*, within the Land, and of *Severn* from *Christmas* to *Mid-Lent.*

The Fishing for Cod on the West part of *Ireland* frequented by those of *Biscay, Galicia,* and *Portugal,* from the begining of *April* until the end of *June.*

The

The Fishing for Cod and Ling on the North, and North-East of *Ireland*, from *Christmas* until *Michaël-mas*.

The Fishing for Pilchers on the West coast of *England* from Saint *James*-tide until *Michaëlmas*.

The Fishing for Cod, and Ling upon the North-East of *England*, from *Easter* until *Midsummer*.

The Fishing of great Staple-Ling and many other sorts of Fish lying about the Island of *Scotland*, and in the several parts of the *British* Seas all the year long.

In *September*, not many years since upon the Coast of *Devonshire* near *Minigal*, 500 Ton of Fish were taken in one day. And about the same time three thousand pound worth of Fish in one day were taken at St *Ives* in *Cornwal* by small Boats, and other poor provisions.

Our five-men-Boats, and cobles adventuring in a calm to launch out amongst the *Holland* Busses, not far from *Robinhood's* Bay returned to *VVhitbie* full fraught with Herrings, and reported that they saw som of those Busses take ten, twentie, twentie four lasts, at a draught, of Herrings, and returned into their own Countrie with fortie, fiftie, and an hundred Lasts of Herrings in one Buss.

Our Fleet of Colliers not many years since returning from *New-castle*, laden with Coals about the Well, near *Flanborough* head, and *Scarborough*, met with such multitudes of Cod, Ling and Herring, that one amongst the rest with certain ship-hooks, and other like instruments, drew up as much Cod, and Ling in a little space of time, as were sold well near for as much as her whole Lading of Cole. And many hundred of ships might have been there laden in two daies and two nights.

Out of which wonderful affluence, and abundance of

of Fish swarming in our Seas, that wee may the better perceiv the infinite gain which Forein Nations make, I will especially insist upon the Fishing of the *Hollanders* in our Coasts, and thereby shew how by this means principally they have increased.

1. *In Shipping.*

2. *In Mariners.*

3. *In Trade.*

4. *In Towns and Fortifications.*

5. *In Power extern or abroad.*

6. *In publick Revenue.*

7. *In private wealth.*

8. *In all manner of Provisions, and store of things necessarie.*

1. *Encreas of Shipping.*

BEsides 700 Strand-Boats, 400 Evars, and 400 Sullits, Drivers and Tod-boats, wherewith the *Hollanders* fish upon their own Coasts, every one of those imploying another Ship to fetch salt, and carrie their Fish into other Countries, beeing in all 3000 sail, maintaining and setting on work at least 4000 persons, Fishers, Tradesmen, Women, and Children; They have 100 Doyer Boats, of 150 Tuns a piece, or thereabouts, 700 Pinks and Well-Boats from 60 to 100 Tuns a piece, which altogether fish upon the Coasts of *England* and *Scotland* for Cod, and Ling onely. And each of these employ another Vessel for providing of salt, and transporting of their Fish, making in all 1600 ships, which maintain and employ persons of all sorts, 4000 at least.

For the Herring-season, they have 1600 Busses at the least, all of them Fishing onely upon our Coasts from *Boughonness* in *Scotland* to the mouth of *Thames*. And every one of these maketh work for three other ships that attend her; the one to bring in salt from Forein parts, another to carrie the said salt, and cask to the Busses, and to bring back their Herrings, and the third to transport the said Fish into Forein Countries. So that the total number of ships and Busses plying the Herring-Fair, is 6400; whereby every Buss, one with another, imployeth fortie men, Mariners and Fishers within her own hold, and the rest ten men a piece, which amounteth to 112000 Fishers and Mariners. All which maintain double, if not treble so many Tradesmen, Women, and Children a land.

Moreover, they have 400 other Vessels at least, that take Herring at *Yarmouth*, and there sell them for readie monie: so that the *Hollanders* (besides 300 ships before-mentioned fishing upon their own shores) have at least 4800 ships onely maintained by the Seas of Great *Britain*, by which means principally *Holland* beeing not so big as one of our shires of *England*, containing not above 28 miles in length, and three in breadth, have encreased the number of their shipping] to at least *ten thousand sail*, beeing more then are in *England*, *France*, *Spain*, *Portugal*, *Italy*, *Denmark*, *Poland*, *Sweden*, and

Rusia. And to this number they add every day; although their Countrie it self afford's them neither materials or victual, nor merchandise to bee accounted of towards their setting forth.

Besides these of *Holland*, *Lubeck* hath 700 great ships, *Hamborough* six hundred, *Embden* fourteen hundred, whereunto add the ships of *Bremer*, *Biscay*, *Portugal*, *Spain*, and *France*, which for the most part fish in our Seas, and it will appear that ten thousand sail of Forein Vessels and above are employed and mainteined by fishing upon our Coasts. So that in *Holland* there are built a thousand sail at the least to supply shipwracks, and augment their store, which as the Prince, and common Nurserie, is the chiefest means onely to encreas their number.

2.
Encreas of Mariners.

THE number of ships fishing on our Coasts, as beeing aforesaid 8400. If wee allow but twentie persons to every ship one with another, the total of Mariners and Fishers, amounteth to 168000, out of which number they daily furnish their longer Voiages to all parts of the world; for by this means they are not onely enabled to brook the Seas, and to know the use of the tackles and compass, but are likewise instructed in the principles of Navigation, and Pilotage, insomuch as from hence their greatest Navigators have had their education and breeding.

3. *Encreas*

3.
Encreas of Trade.

BY reason of those multitude of Ships and Mariners, they have extended their Trade to all parts of the world, exporting for the most part in all their Voiages our Herring, and other Fish for the maintenance of the same. In exchange whereof they return the several commodities of other Countries.

From the Southern parts, as *France, Spain,* and *Portugal*, for our Herrings they return Oils, Wines, Prunes, Honie, Wools, &c. with store of Coin *in Specie.*

From the Straits, Velvets, Sattins, and all sorts of Silks, Alums, Currans, Oils, and all Grocerie-ware, with much monie.

From the East-Countries for our Herrings, and other *French* and *Italian* commodities before returned, they bring home Corn, Wax, Flax, Hemp, Pitch, Tar, Sope-Ashes, Iron, Copper, Steel, Clap-board, Wainscot, Timber, Deal-board, Dollers, and *Hungarie*-Gilders.

From *Germanie*, for Herrings, and other salt Fish, Iron, Steel, Glass, Mil-stones, Rhenish wines, Button-plate for Armor, with other Munition, Silks, Velvets, Rashes, Fustians, Baratees, and such like *Franckford*-commodities, with store of Rix-dollers.

From *Brabant* they return for the most part readie monie with som Tapestries, and Hull-shop. Yea, som of our Herring are carried as far as *Braseil.*

And that which is more strange and greatly to our shame, they have four hundred Ships with Fish, which our men of *Yarmouth*, within ken almost at land do vent our Herrings amongst us here in *England*, and make us pay for the Fish taken upon our own Coast readie monie, wherewith they ſtore their own Countrie.

4.

Encreaſ of Towns and Forts.

BY this their large extent of Trade, they are becom as it were Citizens of the whole world, whereby they have ſo enlarged their Towns, that moſt of them within theſe four hundred years are full as great again as they were before; *Amſterdam*, *Leyden*, and *Middleburgh* having been lately twice enlarged and their ſtreets and buildings ſo fair, and orderly ſet forth, that for beautie and ſtrength, they may compare with any other in the world, upon which they beſtow infinite ſummes of monies, all originally flowing from the bountie of the Sea, from whence, by their labor and induſtrie, they derive the begining of all that wealth and greatneſs, and particularly for the Havens of the aforeſaid Towns whereof ſom of them coſt fortie, fiftie, or an hundred thouſand pound. Their Fortifications alſo both for number, and ſtrength, upon which they have beſtowed infinite ſummes of monie, may compare with any other whatſoëver.

5.

Encreaſ of power abroad.

SUch beeing then the number of the Ships and Mariners, and ſo great their Trade, occaſioned principally by their Fiſhing; they have not onely ſtrengthned, and fortifieed themſelvs at home to repel all Forein Invaſions, as lately in the war between them and *Spain*; but have likewiſe ſtretched their power into

into the East and West-Indies, in many places whereof they are Lords of the Sea-Coasts, and have likewise fortified upon the main, where the Kings and people are at their devotion. And more then this, all Neighbor-Princes, in their differences, by reason of this their power at Sea, are glad to have them of their partie. So that, next to the English, they are now becom the most re-doubted Nation at Sea of any other whatsoêver.

6.

Encreas of publick Revenue.

MOreover how mightie the publick Revênue, and Customs of that State are encreased by their fishing, may appear in that above thirtie years since, over and above the Customs of other Merchandise, Excises, Licences, Waftage, and Lastage, there was paid to the State, for Custom of Herring, and other salt-Fish, above three hundred thousand pound in one year, besides the tenth Fish, and Cask paid for Waftage, which cometh at the least to as much more among the *Hollanders* onely, whereunto the tenth of other Nations beeing added, it amounteth to a far greater summe.

Wee are likewise to know, that great part of their Fish is sold in other Countries for readie monies, for which they commonly export of the finest gold, and silver, and coming home recoin it of a baser allay, under their own stamp, which is not a small means to augment their publick treasure.

7.

Encreas of private Wealth.

AS touching their private wealth, if wee consider the abundant store of Herrings, and other fish by them taken, and the usual prices that they are sold for, as also the multitude of Tradesmen and Artizans, that by reason of this their Fishing are daily set on work, wee must needs conclude that the gain thereof made by private men must of necessitie bee exceeding great, as by observing the particulars following will plainly appear.

During the wars between the King of *Spain*, and the *Hollanders* before the last Truce, *Dunkirk* by taking, spoiling, and burning the Busses of *Holland*, and setting great ransom upon their Fisher-men, enforced them to compound for great summes that they might Fish quietly for one year, whereupon the next year after the Fisher-men agreed amongst themselvs to pay a doller upon every last of Herrings, towards the maintenance of certain Ships of War to waft and secure them in their Fishing, by reason whereof there was a Record kept of the several lasts of Herrings taken that year, and it appeared thereby that in one half year there were taken thirtie thousand lasts of Herrings which at twelv pound *per* last, amounteth to 3600000, and at sixteen, twentie, thirtie pound the last, they are ordinarily sold, then transported into other Countries, it cometh at least to 5000000 *l.* Whereunto if wee add the Herrings taken by other Nations together with the Cod, Ling, Hake, and the Fish taken by the *Hollanders*, and other our neighbors upon the British

British Coasts all the year long, the total will evidently arise to bee above 10000000 l.

The great Trade of Fishing imploying so many men and ships at Sea, must likewise necessarily maintain as great a number of Tradesmen, and Artizens on Land, as Spinners, and Hemp-winders to Cables, Cordage, Yarn-twine for Nets and Lines, Weavers to make Sail-Cloaths, Cecive Packers, Tollers, Dressers, and Cowchers to sort and make the Herring lawful merchandise. Tanners to tan their Sails and Nets; Coopers to make Cask, Block, and Bowl-makers for ships, Keel-men, and Laborers for carrying and removing their Fish, Sawyers for Planks, Carpenters, Ship-wrights, Smiths, Car-men, Boat-men, Brewers, Bakers, and a number of others, whereof many are maimed persons, and unfit to bee otherwise imploied. Besides the maintenance of all their several wives, and children, and families. And further every man and maid-servant, or Orphant, having any poor stock, may venture the same in their Fishing-Voiages, which afford's them ordinarily great encreas, and is duly paid according to the proportion of their gain.

8.

Encreas of Provisions.

AND to conclude, it is manifest that *Holland* only affording in it self som few Hops, Madders, Butter and Chees aboundeth notwithstanding (by reason of this Art of Fishing) in plentiful manner with all kinde of provisions as well for life, as in Corn, Beef, Muttons, Hides, and Cloaths,

Cloths; as for luxury, in Wines, Silks and Spices; and for defence, as in Pitch, Tar, Cordage, Timber. All which they have not onely in competent proportion for their use, but are likewise able from their several Magazines to supply their Neighbor-Countries.

The premisses considered, it maketh much to the ignominie and shame of our English Nation, that God and Nature offering us so great a treasure even at our own doors, wee do notwithstanding neglect the benefit thereof, and, by paying monie to strangers for the Fish of our own Seas, impoverish our selvs to make them rich. Insomuch that for want of industrie and care in this particular two hundred twentie five Fisher-Towns are decaied and reduced to extreme povertie; whereas on the contrarie by diligent endevoring to make use of so great a blessing, wee might in short time repair these decaied Towns of the Kingdom, and add both honor, strength, and riches to our King and Countrie, which how easily it may bee don, will appear by som few observations following.

By erecting two hundred and fiftie Busses of reasonable strength and bigness, there will bee emploiment made for a thousand Ships, and for at least ten thousand Fisher-men and Mariners at Sea, and consequently for as many Tradesmen and Laborers at land.

The Herrings taken by the Busses will afford his Majestie two hundred thousand pound yearly custom outward, and for commodities returned inward thirtie thousand pound and above.

Wee have Timber sufficient, and at reasonable rates, growing in our own Kingdom for the build-

ing

ing of Busses, every Shire affordeth hardie and able men fit for such emploiment who now live poorly and idle at home.

Wee have victuals in great plentie sold at easie rates without paiment of Excises, or Impost.

Our shores and harbors are near the places where the Fish do haunt.

For drink, or nets, salting and packing our Fish; and for succor in stress of weather, wee may bring our Fish to land, salt and pack it, and from som part of his Majestie's Dominions bee at our Markets in *France*, *Spain*, or *Italy*, before the *Hollanders* can arrive in *Holland*.

Wee have means to transport our Fish into som Northern Countries, where the *Hollanders* seldom or never com. And though wee had as many Busses as the *Hollanders*, yet is there vent for all, or more, for in the East and Northern Countries, and in many other places, Herrings are every daies meat, Winter and Summer, as well to draw on drink, as to satisfie hunger, and in most places the greatest part of the year they bee scarce to bee had; for presently after *Michaël-mas* the Sound and Rivers are frozen up so as no Herrings can bee transported into twentie several Kingdoms, and free States until *July*, which is for thirtie weeks space together, so that when Lent com's, there are few to bee bought for monie.

Lastly, since by care and industry wee gained from the *Flemmings*, doubtless so by the means wee may as easily grow expert in the Art of Fishing, and in time make it a staple-commoditie of our own.

But this wee shall the better and sooner do, if wee consider

consider and endeavor to reform certain wants and abuses which hitherto have hindred us from effecting that good and great work, whereof these that follow are none of the least.

1. General libertie of eating flesh contrarie to old custom, and the Statute-Laws provided for observing Fish-daies, from whence our scarcitie and dearth of Fish proceedeth; for where Flesh is ordinarily spent, Fish will not bee bought, and want of sale decaieth all Trade, gain beeing the Nurs of Industrie.

2. Want of order and discretion in our Fishing, every man beeing left to himself and permitted to Fish as best liketh him: whereas amongst the *Hollanders* two of the best experienced Fisher-men are appointed to guide the rest of the Fleet, all others beeing bound to follow them, and to cast their lines according to their direction.

3. The *Hollanders* and other Nations set forth with their Busses in *June*, to finde the shole of Fish, and having found it, dwell amongst it till *November*, whereas wee stay till the Herring com home to our rode-steads, and somtimes suffer them to pass by ere wee look out, our Herring-Fishing conteining onely seven weeks at the most, and theirs twentie.

4. The *Hollander's* Busses are great and strong, and able to brook foul weather, whereas our Cobles, Crayers, and Boats beeing small, and thin sided, are easily swallowed by a rough Sea, not daring to adventure far in fair weather by reason of their weakness for fear of storms.

5. The

5. The *Hollanders* are industrious, and no sooner are discharged of their lading, but presently put forth for more, and seek for Markets abroad as well as at home; whereas our *English* after they have been once at Sea, do commonly never return again until all the monie taken for their fish bee spent, and they in debt seeking onely to serv the next Market.

6. The *Hollanders* have certain Merchants, who, during the Herring-season do onely com to the places where the Busses arrive, and joining together in several companies, do presently agree for the lading of thirtie or fortie Busses at once, and so beeing discharged, they may speedily return to their former shipping; whereas our Fisher-men are uncertain of their Chap-men, and forced to spend much time in putting off their Fish by parcels.

These and other defects would carefully bee taken into consideration, and certain orders made to make our Fishing prosperous, and successful, especially considering the fearful mischiefs the neglect hereof hath brought to the King and Kingdom in general, and to many good Towns and Corporations in particular, as by autoritie even of Parlament it self in the Statute of 33 *Hen.* the eight, is plainly testified, which I have summarily here set down, to avoid the prolixitie of the original.

Becaus the English Fisher-men dwelling on the Sea-Coasts did leav off their Trade of Fishing in our Seas, and went the half-Seas over, and there upon the Seas did buie Fish of *Pickards*, *Flemmings*, *Normans*, and *Zelanders*, by reason whereof many incommodities did grow to the Realm, *viz.* the decaie of the wealth and prosperitie as well of the Cinque-Ports, and Members of the same, as of other Coast-Towns by the Sea-side, which were builded, and inhabited by great multitudes of people by reason of using and exercising the craft and feat of Fishing. Secondly, the decaie of a great number of Boats and Ships. And thirdly, the decaie of many good Mariners, both able in bodie by their diligence, labor, and continual exercise of Fishing, and expert by reason thereof in the knowledg of the Sea-Coasts, as well within this Realm as in other parts beyond the Seas. It was therefore enacted, that no manner of persons English, Denizens, or strangers at that time, or any time after dwelling in *England*, should buie anie Fish of any strangers in the said Ports of *Flanders*, *Zealand*, *Picardie*, *France*, or upon the Sea between shore and shore, &c.

This act by many continuances was continued from Parlament to Parlament, until the first of Queen *Marie*, and from thence to the end of the next Parlament, and then expired.

For conclusion, seeing, by that which hath formerly been declared, it evidently appeareth, that the Kings of *England*, by immemorable prescription, continual usage, and possession, the acknowledgment of all our Neighbor-States, and the Municipal Laws of the Kingdom, have ever held the Soveraign Lordship of the Seas of *England*, and that unto his Majestie, by reason of his Soveraigntie, the supreme command and Jurisdiction over the passage, and Fishing in the same rightfully ap-

perteineth,

perteineth; considering also the natural site of those our Seas that interpose themselvs between the great Northern Commerce of that of the whole world, and that of the East, West, and Southern Climates, and withal the infinite commodities that by Fishing in the same is daily made; It cannot bee doubted, but his Majestie, by means of his own excellent wisdom and virtue, and by the industrie of his faithful subjects and people, may easily, without injustice to any Prince or person whatsoever, bee made the greatest Monarch for Command and Wealth, and his people the most opulent and flourishing Nation of any other in the world. And this the rather, for that his Majestie is now absolute Commander of the British Isle, and hath also enlarged his Dominions over a great part of the Western *Indies*; by means of which extent of Empire, (crossing in a manner the whole Ocean) the Trade and persons of all Nations (removing from one part of the world to the other) must of necessitie first, or last, com within compass of his power and jurisdiction.

And therefore the Soveraigntie of our Seas, beeing the most precious Jewel of his Majestie's Crown, and (next under God) the principal means of our Wealth and Safetie, all true English hearts and hands are bound by all possible means and diligence to preserv and maintain the same, even with the uttermost hazzard of their lives, their goods and fortunes.

Thus you see what wondrous advantages may redound to the Felicitie, and Glorie of this Nation, if God give hearts and resolutions to vindicate those rights which are now most impiously and injuriously invaded. And so much for what concern's *England*.

Now that I may reflect a little upon the point of Sea-Dominion in general, to shew how far it hath been asserted, and mainteined by others, who have enjoied a Dominion in other Seas, when they have been concerned in the like Case with *England*, having their Soveraigntie at Sea impeached and questioned by encroaching neighbors; it was thought meet here to annex an ingenious and learned Plea touching the Dominion of the Sea; which was very succinctly written in *Italian*, but faithfully rendred in English by an honorable Member of this Common-wealth, and published som time since, under the following Title.

Dominium

Dominium Maris:
OR, THE
DOMINION
OF THE
SEA.

Expreſsing the Title, which the *Venetians* pretend unto the ſole dominion, and abſolute Sovereigntie of the *Adriatick Sea*, commonly called

The Gulf of Venice.

Manifeſted in a Pleading or Argument, betwixt the Republick of *Venice*, and the Emperor *Ferdinand.*

Whereby is ſufficiently proved, That the Sea as well as the Land, is liable to the Laws of Proprietie, and may bee brought under the juriſdiction and protection of particular Princes and States. Contrarie to the Aſſertion of thoſe, who affirm, the Sea to be free, and under the Dominion of no man.

Tranſlated out of Italian.

LONDON,
Printed by *William Du Gard.* *An. Dom.* 1652.

AN ADVERTISEMENT TO THE READDER.

I *Thought it fitting not to instruct, but rather to remember the Reader, that this Sea, over which the* Venetians *challenge Sovereigntie and Dominion, beeing commonly called the* Gulf, *is nothing els but a large Bay or inlet of the Sea, which entering in betwixt two lands, and severing them for many miles countinuance, in the end receiv's a stop or interruption of further passage, by an opposite shore, which join's both the said lands together. It is called the* Gulf of Venice, *from the Citie of* Venice, *situated upon certain broken Islands near unto the bottom thereof. It is also called the* Adriatick Sea, *from the antient Citie of* Adria, *lying not far distant from the former. From the entrance thereof unto the bottom, it contein's in length about 600 Italian miles: where it is broadest, it is 160 miles over, in others but 80, in the most 100. The southwest shore of it is bounded by the Provinces of* Puglia, *and* Abruzzo *in the Kingdom of* Naples, *the Marquisate of* Ancona *and* Romagnia *in the Pope's State, and the Marquisate of* Trevisana *in the* Venetian *State. The North part of it, or bottom, hath* Friuli *for it's bounds, the North-East is limited by* Istria, Dalmatia, Albania, *and* Epirus: *whereof* Istria *doth not so entirely belong unto the* Venetians, *but that the Arch-Duke of* Gratz, *of the Austrian family, who at this present is Emperor, doth possess divers Maritim Towns therein. In* Dalmatia, *saving* Zara, Spalato, *and* Cattaro, *they have nothing of importance, the rest belonging to the Republick of* Ragusa, *and to the Turks. In* Albania *and* Epirus, *they possess nothing at all, it beeing entirely the Turk's. So that hee, who shall examine the circuit of this Sea, which must contein above 1200 miles, shall finde the shores of the* Venetian *signorie, not to take up intire 200 of them, omitting som scatter'd towns and dispersed Islands, lying on the Turkish side of the Adriatick shore.*

ſhore. For the ſecuring hereof from the depredation of Pirates, and the pretenſes of divers Potent Princes, as the Pope, Emperor, King of Spain, *and the great Turk, who have each of them large territories lying thereupon; alſo to cauſ all ſuch ſhips, as navigate the ſame, to go to* Venice, *and there to pay custom and other duties, the Republick maintein's continually in action a great number of ſhips, gallies and galliots, whereto they alſo add more, as there may bee occaſion, whereof ſom lie about the bottom of the Gulf in* Iſtria, *others about the Iſlands of* Dalmatia, *to clear thoſe parts of Pirates, who have much infeſted thoſe ſeas: others, and thoſe of moſt force, have their ſtations in the Iſland of* Corfu, *and in that of* Candia: *in the first of which commonly reſide's the Captain of the Gulf, whom they call by the name of* Proveditor, *or* Proviſor general, *whoſe office it is to ſecure the Navigation of the Gulf not onely from the* Corſari *or Pirates, but to provide that neither the Gallies nor Ships of the Pope, the King of* Spain, *or great Turk, do ſo much as enter the ſame, without permiſſion of the* Signorie, *or Republick, and upon ſuch conditions as beſt pleaſeth them; which they are ſo careful to effect, that in the year* 1638 *the Turkiſh Fleet entring the Gulf without licence, was assailed by the Venetian General, who sunk divers of their vessels, and compelling the rest to flie unto* Valona, *hee held them there besieged, although the same Citie, and Port whereon it stand's, bee under the jurisdiction of the Grand Signor. And notwithstandiug that a great and dangerous war was likely to ensue thereupon, betwixt the Grand-Signor and the Republick, becaus the Venetian General, beeing not content to have chased them into their own Ports, did moreover then that, sink their vessels, and landing his men, slew divers of their Mariners who had escaped his furie at Sea: yet after that a very honorable peace was again concluded betwixt them, wherein, amongst other things, it was agreed, that it should bee lawful for the* Venetians, *as often as any Turkish vessels did without their licence enter the Gulf, to seiz upon them by force, if they would not otherwise obey. And that it should likewise bee lawful for them so to do, within any Haven, or under any Fort of the Grand-Signor's, bordering on any part of the Venetian Gulf. Out of all which, when I considered the real and absolute* Sovereigntie, *which this Republick doth actually enjoy over this sea, which they have ever defended, as well by the sword as the*

the pen; and withal how that ſom neighboring Nations of late years, did ſeem to envie the title of England *to the narrow ſeas, affirming in ſom of their writings, the* Sea to bee free; *that* it neither ought, nor could bee under the juriſdiction of any; *that* it was a wilde beaſt which could not bee ruled; *that,* poſſeſsio *beeing* Pedis poſitio, *there* could no poſſeſsion bee either taken or kept of it; *that* the limits thereof, beeing a fluent element, could not bee ſcored out, *or* certainly determined, *that* it was as free for all mankinde to uſe, and as common as the aër, *with many other things to that purpoſe; I chancing ſom years paſt to bee at* Venice, *upon conſideration of the premiſſes, did labor with a great deſire, to know the grounds of that title, whereupon the* Venetians *founded their* Dominion of the Sea; *and after much ſearch, even to the deſpair of obteining of it, I hapned upon this enſuing argument, conteining a* Plea *or* Diſpute, *betwixt the* Auſtrians *and* Venetians, *touching the* Dominion of the Adriatick Sea, *not fictitious or deviſed onely to color the cauſ, but faithfully tranſcribed from out the publick Regiſters of that Citie, which I offer herewith to the Reader in Engliſh, and withal theſe two conſiderations,*

First, *that hereby it will appear, that the Common-wealth of* England's *challenge to the Dominion of the Sea, is neither a Noveltie or singularitie; especially, when it is besides most apparant that the King of* Denmark, *doth not onely pretend to the Sovereigntie of the Sound, but causeth all such Ships as pass through it, to pay what toll hee pleaseth. The great Turk prohibit's all Nations, saving his own Vassals, to enter the black Sea, or* Pontus Euxinus; *the like hee doth to the red Sea, whch contein's at the least* 1200 *miles in length, beginning from the streits of* Babelmandel, *which give's entrance thereinto, and ending at the Town of* Sues, *which is seated at the bottom thereof. The King of* Portugal *opposeth, to the utmost of his power, any, but his own subjects to sail into the East-Indies, affirming those Seas to bee intirely under his dominion, as well by Conquest, as the Pope's donation, insomuch as the smallest vessel, even of the natives of those parts, cannot sail from Port to Port, without the pass-port of the* Vice-Roy of Goa, *or of som other by him deputed thereto, styling himself, amongst others his Titles, to bee King of the Conquest, Navigation, and Commerce, or Traffick of* Æthiopia, Arabia, Persia, India, *&c. which hath*

hath been hitherto so punctually observed, as no Castilian, *or Spaniard, might at any time, or for any occasion, sail into the East-Indies, though both those Nations were for many years together united under one King.*

Secondly, *if the Dominion of these Seas do truely and properly belong to the Commonwealth of* England *(as hath been so sufficiently cleared and proved to the whole world, by that learned Book entituled* Mare Clausum*) why may not, or ought not the People of* England, *by all lawful waies procure, that the Dominion of these Seas that so justly appertein's unto them, may bee secured from any force, violence, or opposition, how great soëver, of their most powerful neighbors; whenas wee see the* Venetians *to bee so jealous in preservation of the title they pretend to their Seas, as rather then to suffer it to bee in the least sort questioned, they do upon all occasions oppose themselvs by force, or otherwise, against the most potent Princes of* Europe *and* Asia. *Vale.*

Κλαρεσάμοιλοσ.

Dominium Maris:

OR,

THE DOMINION OF THE SEA.

AFter a long peace, betwixt the Progenitors of the Emperor *Maximilian* the firſt, and the Republick of *Venice*, in the year 1508, there began certain ſlight differences, which concluded in a notable, and moſt memorable war: inſomuch as the Republick, for 22 years following, were with the ſaid Prince, and with his Poſteritie, for divers reſpects, ſomtimes in war, ſomtimes in peace, and ſomtimes in truce, until in the year 1529 all differences betwixt them were compoſed, and a peace concluded in *Bolonia*, which continued all that Age, with the Emperor *Charls* the Fifth, together with his brother *Ferdinando* King of *Hungarie*, and Archduke of *Auſtria*. But becauſ by the diviſion, made betwixt the ſaid brethren, ſeven years before, all the *Auſtrian* lands which confined with the *Venetians*, were laid by agreement unto the part which belonged unto King *Ferdinand*, the confines of which as they had conjuncture with the lands of the Republick, were very intricate; and of great difficultie to conclude, unto whether partie they did belong, as well for the publick reaſons of the ſaid Princes, as for thoſe of their private ſubjects; To end all which in quiet, it was agreed that there ſhould bee an arbitrarie Tribunal erected in *Trent*, for the deciding of theſe doubts, which in the year 1535, pronounced ſentence, whereby all the differences (beeing more then an hundred) were definitively concluded.

Here notwithſtanding the difficultie ceaſed not, becauſ ſom did traverſ the execution of the ſentence, ſo, as in progreſs of time, new

new quarrels did ariſe from both ſides, each one pretending new wrongs offered by the adverſ partie. Whereupon to put an end to all theſe differences, there was by the common conſent, as well of *Ferdinando* (who ſucceeded in the Empire by the reſignation of his brother) as of the Republick, a convention appointed in *Friuli* 1563, of five Commiſſaries, one Procurator, and three Advocates, for each part, who ſhould treat of the differences, as well old as new, and ſhould have power to conclude them, under the ratification of the ſeveral Princes. And this ſo great a number of Judges, was deſired by the Emperor, the better to give ſatisfaction to his ſubjects, of ſeveral Provinces, intereſſed in the cauſ.

Of the Imperial ſide, the Commiſſaries were *Andrew Preghel* a Baron of Auſtria, *Maximilian Dorimbergh, Elenger de Goritia, Stephen Sourz*, and *Anthonie Statemberger*: the Procurator was, *Giacomo Campana*, Chancellor of *Goritia*: the Doctors or Advocates were *Andrea Rapicio, Gervaſio Alberto*, and *Giovan Maria Gratia Dei*. For the Venetians the Commiſſaries were, *Sebaſtian Venier, Marino de Cavalli, Pietro Sanudo, Giovan Baptiſta*

 Contarini,

Contarini, and *Augustin Barbarigo*: The Procurator was, *Giovan Antonio* a secretarie: the Advocates *Marquardo Susanna*, *Francesco Gratiano*, and *Giacomo Chizzola*.

At this Convention the complaints on both sides were opened, which beeing argued, and the other publick differences partly composed, and partly decided, there was taken into consideration a Petition of the Imperial Procurator, in this form, *Ejusdē Majestatis nomine requiritur, ut posthac illius subditis, atque aliis in sinu Adriatico tutò navigare, ac negotiari liceat. Item ut damna, Tergestinis Mercatoribus atque aliis illata, restituantur.* It is required in the name of his Majestie, that hereafter it may bee lawful for his subjects, and others, to traffick and navigate safely in the Adriatick Gulf. Likewise that recompence bee made for the damages susteined by the merchants of *Trieste*, and others. And *Rapicio* the advocate did accompanie this demand with saying; that *this was not a caus to bee handled with any subtiltie, it beeing a thing most notorious, that navigation ought to bee free, notwithstanding the subjects of his Majestie had been constrained to go with their ships to* Venice, *and there to pay custom,*

custom, at which his Majestie was aggrieved, and made instance that it might bee remedied.

To this *Chizzola*, Advocate of the Republick made Answer, saying, that it was a clear case indeed, that *Navigation ought to bee free*; but yet those things, whereat they were aggrieved, were no waies repugnant to this freedom; forasmuch as in countries which are most free, those who have the dominion thereof receiv *custom*, and order by which way all Merchandise shall pass; and therefore no bodie should bee grieved, if the *Venetians*, for their own respects, did use so to do in the Adriatick Sea, which is under their dominion; and hee added, that if they intended to dispute of the business in question, hee was to advertise them, that this caus could not by any pretens bee brought into judgment, at that convention, which was onely instituted, for the execution of such things as were formerly sentenced, and for righting of such new wrongs, which succeeded after the sentence; it beeing besides a thing most notorious, that the *Republick*, as Lord of the Adriatick Sea, did exercise that dominion at the present, which from time out of minde, it had alwaies

waies don, without any interruption, as well in receiving of customs, as in asigning of places for the exaction of it, and that the pretens now alleged was new, and never before used by any predecessor of the Emperor, either as King of *Hungarie*, or as Arch-Duke of *Austria*, or the countries thereto adjacent, or of his Majestie then beeing, for many years, until this present time. Hee challenged the Imperialists to shew, when ever any such thing was before pretended; certainly not before the peace of *Bolonia*; for then such a difference as this (if there had been any such) had been there determined, or referred over to the Arbitrarie Tribunal, wherein were handled above 120 controversies; but of this not any mention made, neither, from that time to this, was there any such pretension once set a foot. But if this were a new wrong, succeeding after the sentence of T*rent*, they should shew what it was, and when it had beginning, becaus hee was prepared to shew unto them, that any thing concerning the same, was of most antient use and continuance, without the least noveltie in the world; and therefore they ought not to bee heard, who came with demands,

demands, which could take no original either from the ſentence of *Trent*, or from any innovation of wrongs ſucceeding thereupon.

To this *Rapicio* replied, that hee intended not to lay his principal foundation upon that, which to all is ſo well known, which is to ſay, *that the Sea is common and free*, and that by reaſon thereof, not any might bee prohibited, to ſail unto any place, which beſt pleaſed him: and if any Doctors ſhould happen to ſay, that the Republick hath a preſcript Dominion over the Adriatick Sea, with a long poſſeſsion, notwithſtanding they prove it not: and to Doctors who affirm a thing barely out of fact, without any manner of proof, little belief is to bee given; for which cauſ, hee would not dwell upon that; but would com to his principal reaſon, which was, that admitting the Republick to bee Patron of the Sea, yet the Emperor's Subjects might navigate freely by the Capitulations, which were eſtabliſhed betwixt the Princes on both ſides, and therefore the Petition propoſed was pertinent to bee handled by the ſaid Convention; to which (hee beeing ſo required by the *Venetians*) added this for a foundation, *Quia libera navigatio Maris Adriatici cùm Majestatis suæ Cæsareæ, tum subditorum damno & incommodo, ab Illustrissimi Domini Veneti triremium Præfectis impedita fuerit, contra Capitula Vormatiæ, Bononiæ, Andegavi, & Venetiis inita*: Forasmuch as the free navigation of the Adriatick Sea, hath been hindred by the Captains of the Venetian's Gallies, to the loss and prejudice of his Imperial Majestie, and of his subjects, against the Capitulations of *Worms, Bolonia, Angiers*, and *Venice*. And here hee produced a passage of the Capitulation of *Bolonia* which spake as followeth; *Quòd communes subditi liberè, tutè, & securè poßint in utriusque statibus & dominiis tam terrâ, quàm Mari, morari & negotiari cum bonis suis, ac si essent incolæ, & subditi illius Principis, ac Dominii, cujus patrias, & Dominia adibunt; provideatúrque, nè vis aut aliqua injuria, ulla de causa, eis inferatur, celeritérque jus administretur.* That the subjects of either partie may freely, safely, and securely abide, and traffick with their goods, in the States and Dominions of one another, in like manner as if they were inhabitants, and subjects of that Prince and State, into whose

whose Countrie or Dominion they do com: and that it bee provided, that no violence or injurie, bee for any caus whatsoëver offered them; and moreover that justice bee speedily administred. Hee also recited the capitulations of the truce of *Angiers* and *Worms*, and of the peace of *Venice*, which is not necessarie here to repeat, beeing of the same tenor. Hee did rest much upon the word *liberè*, considering that *liberè* is joined to the word *Navigare*: by which it ought to bee understood, according to the common construction of Law, *That everie one might navigate freely*; but hee cannot bee said to bee *free*, who is constrained to go to *Venice*. Hee added moreover, that the word *liberè* could not bee imagined to bee superfluous, but must of necessitie operate somthing; that the two words, *tutè & securè*, could import nothing els, but *without impediment*, or *molestation*, or *paying of Customs*; to this hee added, that there were then 400 complaints of his Majestie's subjects, whose vessels were compelled to go to *Venice*, and there made to pay Custom, for happening onely to arrive in the ports of the *Venetians*, either by fortune or ſom other occaſion. Hee read the ſentence of a Rector of *Lieſina*, who freed a ſhip, which touched upon that Iſland by chance; and hee made a narration, that certain barks with ſalt were ſuffered by the Venetian Fleet, to paſs upon their Voiage, without ſending them to *Venice*. Hee concluded, that his requeſt extended to theſe three points. 1. That the *Auſtrian* ſubjects might Navigate whither it pleaſed them. 2. That arriving in any Port of the Republick, onely *per tranſitum*, they ſhould not pay any thing. 3. *Laſtly*, that coming to Trade in any of them, they ſhould not pay more then the ſubjects of the Republick. *Chizzola* anſwered hereto, promiſing clearly to ſolv all the objections introduced by the other, ſo as there ſhould not remain any place of reply, and to ſhew with true and lively reaſons, that what was don by the Miniſters of the Republick in the *Gulf*, was don by lawful Autoritie. And reſerving himſelf, to ſpeak of the *Dominion of the Sea* afterwards, howſoëver preſuppoſing it in the firſt place, hee began with the Capitulations; and *firſt* hee ſaid, that the word *liberè*, was not joined, as *Rapicio* ſaid, to any

ſuch

such word as *Navigare*, but to the words *Morari & negotiari tam terrâ, quàm Mari*: & therefore by *liberè* is to bee understood as the common construction of Law intend's, when one doth either dwell, or do business in the hous, or land of another, that is to say, *observing the Laws, and paying the Rights of the Countrie*. Hee added also, that those Capitulations, betwixt the hous of *Austria*, and the *Republick*, were equally reciprocal, and not made more in favor of the *Austrians*, in the State of the *Venetians*, then of the *Venetians* in the State of the *Austrians*; neither was there greater libertie granted to the Sea, then to the Land; and that the words were clear enough, which import, that the subjects on both sides might stay, trade, and merchandise, in the state of one another, as well by Land as by Sea, and bee well intreated; insomuch as the subjects of the *Venetians* were to have no less libertie in the Lands of the *Austrians*, then the *Austrian* subjects in the Sea of *Venice*; And that by virtue of those words, what his Majestie would have in the State of the *Republick*, it is fitting that hee allow to them in his own State; and if his Imperial Majestie within his own State, upon the Land, will not yield that the ſubjects of the *Republick* ſhall go which way they liſt, but couſtrain's them to paſs by ſuch places onely, where Cuſtom is to bee paid, hee cannot with juſtice demand, that his ſubjects may paſs by or through the Sea of the *Republick* which way they liſt, but ought to content himſelf, that they go that way onely, which ſhall beſt ſtand with the commoditie of thoſe who have the Dominion over it; and if his Majeſtie cauſ Cuſtom to bee paid, upon *his* Land, why may not the *Venetians* likewiſe do it, upon *their* Sea? Hee demanded of them, if by the Capitulation they would have it, that the Emperor was reſtrained, or hindred, from taking of Cuſtom? and if not, why would they have the *Venetians* tied thereunto by a Capitulation, which ſpeak's of both Potentates equally with the ſame words? Hee ſhewed by particular Narration, that from the Peace of *Venice* 1523, until that preſent, the Emperor had increaſed his Cuſtoms, to the grievance of the *Venetian*'s ſubjects, in victuals and Merchandiſe, which paſſed from the one State unto the other; inſomuch as that which formerly

formerly paied but one, was now increased in som to 16, and in others to 20. and hee instanced in iron and other commodities, which were wont to pay little or nothing, were now raised to such an excessive Custom, as proved much to the damage of the *Venetians*, besides they were forced to pass onely by such places, where they should pay Custom, out of which to pass, it was *Contra banda*, and their goods confiscated. And if his Majestie think's it lawful to do what it pleaseth within his own estate, without breaking of the Capitulations, hee cannot think that the *Venetians* doing but the same, should, contrarie thereunto, any waies offend. Hee added, that in every Peace established betwixt two Princes, after a war, it is necessarie that their subjects may live and trade together, not to the excluding of Customs, although there bee excluded the violences, hostilities, and other impediments of trade, which were formerly used in time of war, neither is the autoritie of the one, or other Prince, thereby taken away or restrained by Sea or by Land.

At the force and clearness of this discours, the *Austrians* remained as it were in a trance, looking

looking one upon another, insomuch that *Chizzola* judging it not to bee necessarie to dwell longer upon this, passed to the proof of the presupposed truth, viz. *That the Republick had the Dominion of the Sea*, and said; that the proportion was most true, that the *Sea was common and free*, but yet no otherwise that could bee understood, then as it is commonly said, *The high-waies are common and free*, by which is meant, that they cannot bee usurped by any private person, for his sole proper service, but remain to the use of everie one : not therefore that they are so free, as that they should not bee under the protection and government of som Prince, and that every one might do therein licentiously, all that which it pleased him, either by right or wrong; forasmuch as such licentiousness or Anarchie is abhorred both of God and nature, as well by Sea as by Land. That the true libertie of the Sea, exclude's it not from the protection and superioritie of such as maintain it in libertie, nor from the subjection to the laws of such, as have command over it, rather necessarily it include's it. That no less the Sea, then the Land, is subject to bee divided amongst

amongſt men, and appropriated to Cities and Potentates, which long ſince was ordained by God from the beginning of mankinde, as a thing moſt natural, which was well underſtood by *Ariſtotle*, when hee ſaid, that unto Sea or maritim Cities, the Sea is the Territorie, becauſ from thence they take their ſuſtenance and defenſ; a thing which cannot poſsibly bee, unleſs part of it might bee appropriated in the like manner as the Land is, which is divided betwixt Cities and Governments, not by equal parts, nor according to their greatneſs, but as they have been, or are able to rule, govern, and defend them. *Bern* is not the greateſt Citie of *Switzerland*, and yet it hath as large a Territorie, as all the reſt of the twelv Cantons together. And the Citie of *Norimberg* is very great, and yet the Territories thereof hardly exceed the walls. And the Citie of *Venice* for many years was known to bee without any poſſeſsion at all upon the firm Land. Upon the Sea likewiſe, certein Cities of great force and valor have poſſeſſed a large quantitie thereof, others of little force, have been contented with the next waters; neither are there wanting Examples of ſuch, who notwithſtanding they are Maritim, yet having fertile Lands lying on the back of them, have been contented therewith, without ever attempting to gain any Sea-dominion; Others, who beeing aw'd by their more mightie neighbors, have been conſtrained to forbear any ſuch attempt; for which two cauſes, a Citie, notwithſtanding it bee Maritim, may happen to remain without any poſſeſsion of the Sea.

Hee added that God did inſtant Principalities, for the maintenance of Juſtice, to the benefit of mankinde, which was neceſſarie to bee executed, as well by Sea as by Land. That S. *Paul* ſaid, That *for this cauſ there was due to Princes, Cuſtoms and Contributions* : that it ſhould bee a great abſurditie to praiſ the well governing, regulating, and defenſ of the Land, and to condemn that of the Sea : that if the Sea in ſom parts for the ampleneſs and extreme diſtance thereof from the Land, was not poſsible to bee governed and protected, that proceeded from a diſabilitie and defect in mankinde; as alſo there are deſerts ſo great upon the Land, as it is impoſsible to protect

protect them; witness the many sandie parts of *Africa*, and the immens vastities of the new world. And as it is a gift of God, that a Land by the Laws and publick power, bee ruled, protected and governed; so the same happen's to the Sea: that those were deceived by a gross equivocation, who said, that the Land by reason of its stabilitie might bee governed, but not the Sea, for beeing an unconstant element, no more then the aër; forasmuch as if, by the Sea and the Aër, they intend all the parts of those fluent elements, it is a most certein thing, that they cannot bee governed; becaus, whilst a man serv's himself with any one part of them, the other escape's out of his power; but this chanceth also to Rivers, which cannot bee reteined. But when it is said to rule over a Sea or River, it is not understood of the Element, but of the site, where they are placed. The water of the *Adriatick* Sea continually run's out of it, neither can it all bee kept in, and yet it is the same Sea, as well as the *Tiber*, *Po*, or the *Rhine* are the same Rivers now, which they were 1000 years past. And this is that which is subject to the protection of Princes.

Hee asked the *Austrians* if their pretens were, that the Sea should bee left without protection, so that any one might do therein well or ill, robbing, spoiling, and making of it un-navigable; this would bee so absurd, as hee durst answer for them, *no*: therefore hee concluded, that by a necessarie consequence his Majestie would acknowledg, that it should bee kept, governed and protected by those unto whom it did appertein by divine disposition: which if it were so, hee desired to know, if it seemed to them a just thing that such should do it, with the expence of their own pains, charges, and bloud; or rather that such should contribute towards it, who did equally enjoy the benefit: To this also hee durst answer for them, that they would say the doctrine of St *Paul* is too clear in the point (not to allege matter of Law) that *all such who are under government and protection, are thereby bound to pay Customs and Contributions*. And thereupon hee concluded, that if the Republick were that Prince, to whom it did appertein to govern and protect the Adriatick Sea, it followed necessarily, that whosoëver Navigate's gate's it, ought to bee ſubject to their laws, in the ſame manner as ſuch are, who travel through a Countrie upon the Land.

From thence hee went on to ſhew, that this Dominion over the Sea, from time out of minde, did belong to the Republick, and thereupon cauſed to bee read out of an Abſtract which hee had taken, the Opinions of thirtie Lawyers, who, from the year 1300, until that preſent time, did ſpeak of the Dominion which the Republick had over the Sea, as of a thing moſt notorious, and of which, even in their times, the minde of man knew not the contrarie: ſom of them affirming, that the Republick had no leſs Dominion over the Sea, then over the Citie of *Venice*; others ſaying, that the Adriatick Sea is the Territorie and demeaſnes of the ſaid Citie, making mention of the lawful power which the *Venetians* had to eſtabliſh laws over Navigaon, and to impoſe Cuſtoms upon ſuch as navigate thoſe Seas; and hee added that hee never read any Lawyer, which ever ſaid the contrarie. And turning himſelf to *Rapicio* hee ſaid, that if hee would not believ thoſe Writers which teſtified that the Sea belonged to the *Venetians*, whereof they had possession from time out of minde, before the age wherein the Autors lived, although they prove it not, yet hee could not denie to receiv them for testimonies of such things which they saw and knew in their times, and to hold them as witnesses, far above all exception, beeing famous men, and dead so many years ago, as they could not bee any waies interessed in the present differences. And becaus more then 250 years were past, from the time that the first Autors, which hee alleged as witnesses hereof did write, to the time of those, which hee last cited in that behalf; by their attestation it was sufficiently proved, that for long time more then so many years, the Republick hath commanded the Sea, and therefore hee could not denie the immoveable possession thereof to the present.

Afterwards turning himself to the Judges, hee praied them, that upon the Autorities alleged, they would bee pleased to listen unto a short consideration of his, which hee did not doubt, but would leav in them a full impression of the Truth. And *first* hee desired them to consider, that notwithstanding

ſtanding ſom of the aforeſaid cited Autors ſpeak with general words, ſaying, the Sea of the *Venetians*, neither declaring the qualitie nor quantitie thereof; yet others do ſpecifie it, uſing the name of the *Gulf*; and others with terms more expreſsive, ſaying, the *Adriatick Sea*; which clearly demonſtrate's, not onely the ſite, but alſo the quantitie of the Sea poſſeſſed; and ſo ſhewed, that thoſe who ſpeak more expreſsively, ought to clear the paſſages of thoſe, who write more generally, according to the common precept, that *with clear places the more obſcure are to bee illuſtrated*. Hee conſidered alſo, that the divers manner of ſpeaking of the ſame Doctors, ſom deriving the Dominion of the Republick over the Sea, from Cuſtom, ſom from preſcription, others from an induced ſubjection, and others from a privilege, did ariſe all out of this reaſon, becauſ as they were moſt aſſuredly informed of the poſſeſſion and juriſdiction of the ſaid Seas, which they both ſaw and heard to belong to the Republick from time out of minde; ſo they writing upon that matter, not at the inſtance of any one, but of their own proper motions, and by way of Doctrine onely,

each

each one of them judged it moſt convenient to expreſs the title of that juriſdiction, ſom with one term, ſom with another, without coming to uſe the ſole and true proper term, as they would have don, if they had been put to write for the intereſt of any one; in which caſes the Counſellors are alwaies conformable, receiving from the perſon intereſted equally the like inſtructions.

Hee added, that, through the varietie of expreſsing themſelvs, the truth of the cauſ was no waies diminiſhed, but rather increaſed; as St *Auguſtine* ſaith, ſpeaking of the diverſitie which is obſerved to bee betwixt the holy Evangeliſts; becauſ by the diverſ manner of expreſsion, uſed by the ſaid Writers, every one may reſt aſſured, that none of them did write *nè pagato*, *nè pregato*, neither paied, nor praied. In which caſes they are never wont to varie, from the ſingle form preſcribed unto them by the partie intereſſed; but rather hee that ſhall well examine it, ſhall ſee amongſt the Doctors a wonderful concord in this one point moſt true, that after the declination of the Conſtantipolitane Empire, the Adriatick Sea was found to bee for many years abandoned

abandoned, (as alſo many Iſlands and Cities of that State) in ſuch manner, as it remained unguarded and without the protection and government of any Prince, and under the juriſdiction of no bodie, until by the *Venetians*, who, to receiv their livelyhood thereby, were conſtrained to maintain it in freedom; and thereupon taking it into their protection, got thereby the government and dominion over it, in like manner as by the law of Nature and of Nations, the Land, the Sea, and other things, which are not under the Dominion of any other, com juſtly unto thoſe who firſt get the poſſeſsion of them; by which reaſon the firſt Empires were founded, as well upon the Land as at Sea, and daily there are new ones in the ſame manner formed, when any of them, either through age or vice, becoming weak, wanteth force, and ſink's of it ſelf. The which coſtodie and government of the Sea, ſo acquired, the Republick hath daily advanced, by the keeping of potent Fleets and greater Armadoes every day then other, with the expence of a great deal of Treaſure, and the profuſion of a world of bloud, both of their

Citizens and Subjects, continuing without interruption, in ſight of all the world, the ſaid begun Dominion and cuſtodie, overcoming and removing all ſuch impediments, as either by Pirates or Potentates, as well of *Italie* as of the oppoſite ſhore, at divers times have been raiſed. And for the clearing of ſuch doubts, as might ariſe by the ſubtil conſtruction of words, hee added; that although thoſe who took upon them to ſpeak in the ſtrict terms of the Law, were wont to ſay, that ſuch things onely were gained by Cuſtom, which by the Civil Law, beeing to bee common, were notwithſtanding converted to a private benefit, yet without any impeachment of the publick profit, as to fiſh in a River without impeachment of Navigation; yet for all that, the Title of Cuſtom cannot bee unproperly given, where there ſhall bee gained and continually kept in poſſeſsion and Dominion, a quantitie either of Sea or Land abandoned, and of no man poſſeſſed, as *Bartholus, Baldus, Caſtro*, and others do affirm. And although that by title of *Preſcription* a thing cannot poſsible bee ſaid to bee poſſeſſed, unleſs, by the occupation of it, another

bee

bee thereof ſpoiled and diſpoſſeſſed, which title come's not in this place, foraſmuch as the Republick hath not ſpoiled any of the poſſeſſion of the Sea, but hath ſeized upon it, finding it abandoned & without Patron or Poſſeſſor : notwithſtanding in ſom ſort, it may bee called *Preſcription*, as if a Falcon were let flie and caſt off by its maſter, and thereupon growing wilde, ſhould after bee taken up by another, and by him mann'd, and for a long time fed; although not properly, yet not abſurdly it may bee ſaid, that this ſecond maſter hath it by *Preſcription*. Likewiſe, to ſpeak in terms of Law, the proprietie of ſpeech doth not admit the uſe of this word *Servitude*, unleſs to the proper Territorie of a State, there bee gotten ſom power over another State, and yet that State remain's Patron of its own notwithſtanding; in this ſenſ the Republick hath not brought the Sea in ſervitude to the Citie of *Venice*, becauſ it hath not gotten any ſpecial uſe or command over it, the Dominion for all that remaining to another Patron, but hath aſſumed the total and intire Dominion thereof, which was before abandoned, neither by any governed or protected: neverthelesſs it may in a certain proportion bee called *Servitude*, inaſmuch as the Republick hath been conſtrained to aſſume the total Dominion and Government thereof, for the ſervice of the Citie of *Venice*, whereof it had neceſſarie uſe.

Now as touching the *Privilege* of keeping this Sea, and who was the Donor, this neither can here have any place, foraſmuch as at the time of the aſſumption of it, there was not any who could make any grant thereof, the Emperor of the VVeſt never having any Power or Autoritie over it; and as little ſuperioritie or juriſdiction had any other weſtern Prince; and therefore could ſo much the leſs give it to another. The Emperor of the Eaſt, not having force ſufficient to keep it, had long ſince abandoned it, and beeing thereupon diveſted of all the Power hee had over it, and of the Poſſeſſion thereof, never made any grant thereof in the ſucceſsive Peace and Treaties which happened afterwards betwixt the ſaid Empire and the Republick. Notwithſtanding all which the *Italian* Lawyers, as Profeſſors of the Ceſarean Law, & ſworn to the

the very words of it, beeing besides most devoted to his Imperial Majestie, as if at this present day *Augustus* or *Antoninus* did reign, do force themselvs with all extortion, to verifie upon the western Emperor that saying, *Imperator est Dominus Mundi*, The Emperor is Lord of the world. VVhich at that very time when it was first pronounced, was not true in the hundred part of the world, and at this present not in any considerable proportion. And whilest they would honor the Emperor, and give him, with such words as these, that which hee neither hath nor can have, they consider not the absurditie of the speech, as if they should say, that no King possessed any estate lawfully, unless it were granted him by the Emperor, which is as true, as when they affirm that the *Venetians* possess the Adriatick Sea, by an Imperial privilege. But it appear's clear enough, in what sens this is spoken by them, becaus there is none of them do intend thereby, that there was ever any such Grant made thereof by the Emperor; but by that they do figuratively intend a privilege assumed by immemorable possession, which possession they interpret to bee with the knowledg and ſufferance of the Emperor, which is as much as if they ſhould ſay, that Chriſtian Kings poſſeſs their Kingdom, and the Republick poſſeſſeth the *Adriatick Sea*, as lawfully by their title of acquiring it, as if thoſe Kingdoms and that Sea had belonged to the Emperor, and from and by him to thoſe Princes, and to the Republick afterwards granted. So ſpaciouſly did *Chizzola* dilate in ſpeaking of the opinion of the Lawyers, it beeing the field of his profeſsion: hee concluded, that any one might reſt ſatisfied, as well in truth, as in reaſon, that by the Autoritie of the ſaid Doctors, there were ſure foundations laid to the cauſ, which hee did defend.

After the teſtimonie of the Lawyers, hee added that of the *Hiſtorians*, who do relate, that the Republick, for more then 300 years paſt, did receiv Cuſtom, of ſuch as ſailed that Sea, and kept armed veſſels in a readineſs, for to compel all ſuch Ships ſo ſailing, to go to *Venice*, teſtifying moreover, that even unto their preſent time the ſame Cuſtom was obſerved. But upon their atteſtations hee dwelled not much, ſaying, that

that though they were good Teſtimonies of preceding occurrences; yet when one goeth about to prove the intereſts of Princes, or of private perſons, hee ought to help himſelf by authentick writings, and to uſe the Hiſtorians with great diſcretion; ſom of them beeing moved by love, others with hatred, and others with hope of preferment; which conſtrain's them oftentimes to uſe flatterie, or Hyperboles, upon which cannot bee laid any ſure foundation.

Wherefore hee produced an act of the general Council of Lions, *anno* 1274, where the Abbot of *Nerveſa*, beeing delegated by the Pope (upon a pretenſion of thoſe of *Ancona* to have free Navigation upon the Adriatick Sea) ſentenced, that the demand ſhould bee rejected, and that the *Venetians* ſhould not bee moleſted in the defenſ and protection thereof, from the *Sarazens* and Pirates, neither ſhould bee diſturbed from exacting thereupon their Rights and Cuſtoms, which they had of victuals, merchandiſe and other portable Commodities.

Chizzola likewiſe added, that it is clean out of memorie, when firſt of all there was created

created in *Venice*, a *Captain of the Gulf*, becauſ in the year 1230, the Chancerie was burned, with the memorials of all ſuch elections; but from that time to this preſent, hee could ſhew out of the publick Regiſters, the continual ſucceſsion of the ſaid elected Captains without any interruption. Likewiſe hee added moreover, that there remain the Regiſters from that time to this, of the Licenſes granted to paſs the ſaid Sea, with armed veſſels or ſhips of war, and to the perſons and goods belonging to their uſe, at the requeſt of divers Princes, who had their Poſſeſsions upon the ſhore of the *Adriatick* Sea, and that as well by ſundrie Popes, Legates, Vicars, Governors, and Commonaltie of the Land of *Romania* and *Marca*, as by the Kings of *Naples* for *Puglia*, of which many were granted, ſom denied and others yielded to, but in part; But it beeing ſuperfluous to allege the Acts of thoſe, the Succeſſors of whom do not ſo much as queſtion this Title, hee deſcended to particularize onely the Predeceſſors of his Majeſtie, as Kings of *Hungarie*, and Arch-Dukes of *Auſtria*. Hee recited a Brief of Pope *Urbane* the ſixt, directed to *Antonio Veniero* the Duke of of *Venice*, bearing date *Luca* 14 Junii 1388. where hee give's him thanks, that with his Gallies deputed for the keeping of the Gulf, *Marie* Queen of *Hungarie* had been inlarged, who had been kept priſoner in *Caſtel-novo*; with two other congratulatorie Letters, the one to the ſaid Queen, the other to King *Sigiſmund*, who after was Emperor, beeing her Husband, rejoicing with them likewiſe of the ſaid enlargement made by means of the Captain of the *Venetian* Gallies, deputed to the cuſtodie of the *Gulf*. Afterwards hee cauſed to bee read a ſafe Conduct granted at the Petition of *Rodulph* Earl of *Sala*, in the name of *Ladiſlaus* King of *Naples*, and of *William* Arch-Duke of *Auſtria* anno 1399. 12 *Decembris*, that the ſiſter of the ſaid King (eſpouſed to the aforenamed Arch-Duke) might bee conducted by Sea from *Puglia*, to the Coaſts of her Husband, with Gallies and other Veſſels, in all to the number of about twelv; with condition that there ſhould not bee ſuffered to paſs upon them any *Bandito* or baniſhed perſon of *Venice*, who had don any thing againſt the Republick, which did merit death: which ſafe-conduct ſhould bee available to the *Auſtrians*, as well in going as in coming, ſo as by the ſame, they might alſo re-imbark at *Trieſte* and return unto *Puglia*. But yet this ſafe Conduct was not made uſe of, becauſ the King having deferred the departure of his ſiſter for a ſmall time, in the *interim* ſhee died.

Alſo hee produced two letters of the Emperor *Frederick*, unto Duke *Giovanni Mocenigo*, the firſt dated in *Gratz* 24 Sept. 1478 the other 2 Apr. 1479. from the ſame place, where hee tell's him that hee having taken order that there ſhould bee brought from *Puglia* and *Abruzzo*, to his caſtles of *Caſtro* and of *Iſtria*, a certain quantitie of corn, hee requeſt's that it may bee permitted him to do it freely, which beeing to him a great pleaſure, hee ſhall acknowledg it with many thanks.

This hee ſeconded with a letter of *Beatrice* Queen of *Hungarie*, to *Giovanni Mocenigo* Duke of *Venice*, dated the laſt of Jan. 1481. whereby deſiring for her proper uſe to have divers things from the parts of *Italie*, which ſhee could not bring from thence by Sea, without the permiſſion of the Republick, ſhee deſired that, for curteſie ſake and friendſhip, it might bee granted her, which ſhee ſhould take for a great favor, and correſpond upon the like occaſion.

And another of *Matthias* King of *Hungarie* to the ſaid Duke dated 26 *Febr.* 1482. where relating how the Republick was accuſtomed to give Licence every year to Count *Frangipani* Patron of *Segna* and other Maritim places, to bring from *Puglia* and *Marça* a certain quantitie of victuals, and that after the ſaid places, were paſſed over into his hands, hee had omitted to deſire it; wherefore hee now praied, that the ſame grace might bee ſhewed unto him, and that concerning this, hee would write his letters and give them to a perſon which hee had ſent expreſsly to receiv them; which hee ſhould acknowledg as a favor and correſpond accordingly.

And another of the ſame King to *Augustino Barbarigo* the Duke, dated 18 *Oct.* 1487. in the which relating, that hee having need of wood for the reparation of a fortreſs ſtanding in the mouth of *Narenta*, hee praied, that hee might have leav to carrie it unto *Segna* by Sea, and that there might bee Letters Patents made thereof, offering to gratifie him in a greater matter.

Hee added to this a Letter of *Anne* Queen

of *Hungarie* 30. *Aug*. 1502. in the which recounting the ſterilitie of the Countrie of *Segna*, ſhee deſire's leav to bring certain victuals from *Puglia* and *Marca*, and that hee would give to the bearer, who was ſent on purpoſe, Letters of Licenſ for the ſame, promiſing to acknowledg it as a great favor and courteſie.

Laſtly, hee produced a Letter dated 3 *Sept*. 1504 of *Giovanni de Dura* Captain of *Piſmo*, ſervant to the Emperor *Maximilian*, which hee writ unto the Duke *Leonardo Loredano*, importing, that *Giacomo Croato*, a ſubject of his Majeſties, parting from *Fianona*, entered into the Sea, which is under the Dominion of the Republick, for to go to *Segna*, and was there aſſailed by an armed Bark of Pirates in contempt of the Signorie or Republick, and ſupplicate's that ſom order might bee taken therein.

Upon all which particulars, hee weighed moſt that which ought beſt to bee conſidered, having reſpect to the times, perſons, and qualities of the ſeveral Princes, and for greater confirmation of their aſſent, hee remembred the yearly Cerimonie uſed at *Venice*; where the Duke, in preſence

ſence of the Ambaſſadors of other Princes, particularly of his Majeſties, did uſe to eſpouſ the Sea, by the caſting of a Ring into it, with theſe words: *Deſponſamus Te Mare in ſignum veri & perpetui Dominii*: Wee do marrie the Sea, in ſign of our true and perpetual Dominion over it. VVhich Cerimonie as the foreſaid writers do affirm, had beginning when Pope *Alexander* the Third was in *Venice*, notwithſtanding they add withal, that it was inſtituted in ſign of the Dominion which the Republick had formerly gotten, *jure belli*.

To the 400 complaints of the Emperors Subjects, and to the ſentence of *Lieſina*, hee anſwered, giving thanks for the remembring of them, as a thing brought in much to his favor, becauſ the complaints do preſuppoſe the prohibition, and the ſentences, either condemning or abſolving, do prove the juriſdiction.

And to the ſalt-barks, hee ſaid, that they were not ſuffered to go to *Venice*, as never any are ſuffered to go, all forrein ſalt beeing prohibited to enter into that Citie; and if it were not caſt into the Sea, it was a courteſie, which ought not to bee imputed to them to their prejudice.

Hee concluded, that hee had delivered the true ſenſ of the Capitulations, and proved the immemorable poſſeſsion of the *Adriatick* Sea; that hee could have ſaid much more, but it ſeemed to him ſuperfluous, and theſe two points were made moſt clear; *Firſt*, That this pretence of the *Auſtrians* was but new; And *ſecondly*, That their Petition at this Convention could have no place.

The Imperialiſts after they had conferred together, took a reſolution not to perſevere in the demand of Juſtice, and the Baron with *Suorz* ſaid openly, that the *Republick was Patron of the Gulf, and might impoſe what Cuſtoms they thought fitting; and that they thought ſo in their conſciences*: but therewithal they were of an opinion, that for honeſtie ſake, and for the friendſhip which the Republick had with the houſ of *Auſtria*, it ſhould bee don with the leaſt incommoditie of the ſubjects to that houſ, as could bee poſsible. The other three ſaid, that it was now no time, either to approve or to diſapprove the Dominion of the Sea, but rather

to

to finde by way of courtesie som kinde of temperature, whereby the Republick might receiv the Rights belonging thereunto from the *Austrian* subjects sailing those Seas, and on the other side, that such conditions annexed formerly thereunto, might bee taken away, which were incommodious to the *Austrians*, and no waies profitable to the *Venetians*. Whereupon divers waies to effect it were examined, and a conclusion taken to refer all to their several Princes, as it was necessarie to refer all things els; the Commission beeing to bee onely perfected by their ratification, and so this Convention ended.

FINIS.

---

www.ingramcontent.com/pod-product-compliance
Lightning Source LLC
Chambersburg PA
CBHW080753260426
43704CB00006B/44
9781584772729